THE CAMBRIDGE COMPANION TO
CRICKET

Few other team sports can equal the global reach of cricket. Rich in history and tradition, it is both quintessentially English and expansively international, a game that has evolved and changed dramatically in recent times. Cricket has a unique adaptability and a continuing ability to excite national passions. Demonstrating how the history of cricket and its international popularity is entwined with British imperial expansion, this book examines the social and political impact of the game in a variety of cultural sites: the West Indies, India, Pakistan, Sri Lanka, South Africa, Australia and New Zealand. An international team of contributors explores the enduring influence of cricket on English identity, examines why cricket has seized the imagination of so many literary figures and provides profiles of iconic players including Don Bradman, Brian Lara and Sachin Tendulkar. Presenting a global panoramic view of cricket's complicated development and its political and sporting controversies, the book provides a rich insight into a unique sporting and cultural heritage.

ANTHONY BATEMAN is a freelance writer and editor and an Honorary Visiting Research Fellow at the International Centre for Sports History and Culture at De Montfort University, Leicester, UK.

JEFFREY HILL is Emeritus Professor of Historical and Cultural Studies at De Montfort University, Leicester, UK.

D1333844

THE CAMBRIDGE
COMPANION TO
CRICKET

EDITED BY
ANTHONY BATEMAN AND JEFFREY HILL

CAMBRIDGE
UNIVERSITY PRESS

CAMBRIDGE UNIVERSITY PRESS
Cambridge, New York, Melbourne, Madrid, Cape Town,
Singapore, São Paulo, Delhi, Tokyo, Mexico City

Cambridge University Press
The Edinburgh Building, Cambridge CB2 8RU, UK

Published in the United States of America by Cambridge University Press, New York

www.cambridge.org
Information on this title: www.cambridge.org/9780521167871

First published 2011

Printed in the United Kingdom at the University Press, Cambridge

A catalogue record for this publication is available from the British Library

Library of Congress Cataloguing in Publication data
The Cambridge companion to cricket / [edited by] Anthony Bateman, Jeffrey Hill.
p. cm.
ISBN 978-0-521-76129-1 (hardback)
1. Cricket. 2. Cricket–Social aspects. I. Bateman, Anthony, 1966–
II. Hill, Jeffrey, 1943– III. Title.
GV917.C27 2011
796.358–dc22
2010052178

ISBN 978-0-521-76129-1 Hardback
ISBN 978-0-521-16787-1 Paperback

To the memory of David Underdown (1925–2009), who was to have been with us in this enterprise, and whose seminal work has inspired our labours

CONTENTS

CONTENTS

FIGURES AND TABLES

FIGURES

TABLE

ANTHONY BATEMAN is a freelance writer and editor and an Honorary Visiting Research Fellow at the International Centre for Sports History and Culture at De Montfort University, UK. He is the author of *Cricket, Literature and Culture: Symbolising the Nation, Destabilising Empire* and has contributed articles and chapters on cricket and its literature to a number of journals and books, as well as to the popular press. He is also co-editor of *Sporting Sounds: Relationships Between Sport and Music* (with John Bale). A former professional musician, he writes on music for *The Guardian* and other publications.

SIR HILARY MCD. BECKLES is Pro-Vice-Chancellor for Undergraduate Studies at the University of the West Indies and is currently Principal of the Campus at Cave Hill in Barbados. He is also the founder and Director of the C. L. R. James Centre for Cricket Research at Cave Hill Campus and a Director of the West Indies Cricket Board. He has published over ten academic books, including *Centring Woman: Gender Discourses in Caribbean Slave Society* and *The History of Barbados*. His two-volume *The Development of West Indies Cricket* was described by *Wisden Cricket Monthly* as 'the most important cricket book ever written'.

MIHIR BOSE is an award-winning journalist and author. He was the BBC's first Sports Editor, covering all BBC outlets including the Ten O'Clock News, the Today programme, Five Live and the website. Before joining the BBC he was the chief sports news correspondent for the *Daily Telegraph* for twelve years. He has written for nearly all the major UK newspapers, editing the Inside Track column of the *Sunday Times* and several business publications. He is the author of twenty-three books and has won several awards: business columnist of the year, the sports news reporter of the year, the sports story of the year and the Cricket Society's Silver Jubilee Literary award for his *History of Indian Cricket*. His book

Sporting Colours, a study of sport and apartheid, was runner-up for the William Hill Sports Book of the Year Award. He is currently working on a range of projects including a weekly 'Big Sports Interview' for the *Evening Standard*, a book on the power of modern sport and other projects for radio and television covering social and historical issues as well as sport.

RICHARD CASHMAN is an Adjunct Professor in the School of Leisure, Sport, Tourism at the University of Technology, Sydney. He twice received the Australian Cricket Society Literary Award for *''Ave a Go, Yer Mug!': Australian Cricket Crowds from Larrikin to Ocker* and *The 'Demon' Spofforth*. He has also published *Patrons, Players and the Crowd: The Phenomenon of Indian Cricket*; *Australian Cricket Crowds: The Attendance Cycle*; *Wicket Women: Cricket & Women in Australia* (with Amanda Weaver); and *The Red and Blue Wickies: Fifty Years of the Randwick CYM Cricket Club*. He was general editor of the *Oxford Companion to Australian Cricket* and edited *Early Cricket in Sydney 1803 to 1856* (with Stephen Gibbs). He was also a joint author of *Making the Grade: 100 Years of Grade Cricket in Sydney*.

DAVID DUNSTAN is Deputy Director of the National Centre for Australian Studies at Monash University, Australia. He is a co-editor of *Australians in Britain: The Twentieth Century Experience*. With his colleague Tom Heenan he is writing a history of Australia's cricketing relations with India.

DAVID FRITH, born in London in 1937 and resident in Australia intermittently for over twenty years, has written thirty books on cricket and cricketers since 1969, five of which earned awards. Editor of *The Cricketer* from 1972 to 1978, in 1979 he founded *Wisden Cricket Monthly*, editing the magazine until 1996. His major works have been biographies of John Edrich, A. E. Stoddart, Archie Jackson, Jeff Thomson and Ross Gregory; a history of Ashes Test cricket with over 1,000 illustrations; *Pageant of Cricket*, a history of the game with 2,000 illustrations; two books on cricket suicides; a history of the Australian Cricket Board; several accounts of the Ashes series, including a definitive book on the 1932–33 'Bodyline' furore, and a detailed chronicle of the first tours by England to Australia (1861–62); two books on the 'Golden Age of Cricket' (1890–1914); and an autobiography. He has also made video programmes on great batsmen and bowlers, and has presented archive cricket film shows in London since 1981. A player himself for half a century, he had several seasons of first-grade cricket in Sydney.

JON GEMMELL teaches History and Sociology at Kennet School, Thatcham. He is the author of *The Politics of South African Cricket*, and has written a number of articles exploring the links between race/ethnicity, politics and cricket in South Africa, Australia, Zimbabwe and Ireland. He is the co-editor of *Cricket, Race and the 2007 World Cup* and *The Changing Face of Cricket* and is currently working on a history of the ethos of cricket. He also writes a regular column on the politics of cricket for the *Morning Star*.

TOM HEENAN teaches Sport Studies and Australian Studies at Monash University's National Centre for Australian Studies. He is the author of the controversial *From Traveller to Traitor: The Life of Wilfred Burchett* and is writing a history of Australia's cricketing relations with India with David Dunstan.

JEFFREY HILL is Emeritus Professor of Historical and Cultural Studies at De Montfort University, Leicester, where from 2001 until 2007 he was Director of the International Centre for Sport History and Culture. Recent work has been largely focused on literary representations of sport, with a book on sport novels (*Sport and the Literary Imagination: Essays in History, Literature and Sport*), an article on Joseph O'Neill's *Netherland*, and book chapters on the place of the comic-book hero Alf Tupper in British post-war society. His *Sport in History: An Introduction* came out in 2010.

PRASHANT KIDAMBI is a Senior Lecturer in the School of Historical Studies, University of Leicester. His research explores the interface between British imperialism and the history of modern South Asia. Focusing in particular on the nineteenth and twentieth centuries, his work has addressed a range of major themes in colonial South Asian history: the nature of governance; the evolution of the public sphere and civil society; the formation of the Indian middle classes; and the social history of cricket. He is the author of a book, *The Making of an Indian Metropolis: Colonial Governance and Public Culture in Bombay, 1890–1920*. He is currently working on a research project funded by the Leverhulme Trust which explores the history of colonial cricket tours in the late nineteenth and early twentieth centuries.

ROB LIGHT is a member of the Cricket Research Centre at the University of Huddersfield, where he worked on the HLF-funded Calderdale and Kirklees Cricket Heritage Project between 2004 and 2005 and where he now lectures. He studied for his PhD at the International Centre for Sport History and Culture, De Montfort University, and successfully completed his thesis entitled 'Cricket's Forgotten Past: A Social and Cultural History of the Game in the West Riding of Yorkshire 1820–1870' in 2008. He has also published articles on professional cricketers in the nineteenth century and the relationship between the game in Yorkshire and regional identity during this period. His other main interest is in Rugby League, and between 2007 and 2008 he managed a major oral history project on the game in West Yorkshire at the University of Huddersfield. He plays cricket for his local club at Pateley Bridge in North Yorkshire.

BORIA MAJUMDAR, a Rhodes Scholar, is Executive Academic Editor of the journal *Sport in Society* and General Editor of the Series *Sport in the Global Society*. As consultant Editor of Times Now Television, India's number one television news channel, he has covered three editions of the Indian Premier League and has written extensively on the history and politics of cricket in India.

PATRICK F. MCDEVITT is an Associate Professor of History at the University at Buffalo, State University of New York. He teaches and writes about the British Empire, Ireland and the Atlantic World and is the author of *'May the Best Man Win': Sport, Masculinity and Nationalism in Great Britain and the Empire, 1880–1935*. He was educated at New York University, the University of Canterbury (NZ) and Rutgers University.

ANDRE ODENDAAL is an Honorary Professor in History and Heritage Studies at the University of the Western Cape. After graduating with a DPhil at Cambridge University, he taught at the University of South Africa and UWC before becoming founding Director of both the Mayibuye Centre for History and Culture in South Africa and, after democracy, the new Robben Island Museum (and UNESCO World Heritage Site). A former first-class cricketer and anti-apartheid activist, he is currently Chief Executive of the Western Province Cricket Association, responsible for the running of the famous Newlands Cricket Ground, the Cape Cobras professional team and around 20,000 amateur cricketers in Cape Town. His publications include *Cricket in Isolation*; *Vukani Bantu: The Beginnings of Black Protest Politics in South Africa to 1912*; *Beyond the Tryline: Rugby and South African Society* (with Albert Grundlingh and Burridge Spies); and *The Story of an African Game*.

GREG RYAN is a Senior Lecturer in History and Head of the Department of Social Science, Parks, Recreation, Tourism and Sport at Lincoln University, New Zealand. In addition to various articles and book chapters on sport in New Zealand he edited *Tackling Rugby Myths: Rugby and New Zealand Society 1854–2004* and *The Changing Face of Rugby: The Union*

Game and Professionalism since 1995, and has written three books: *The Contest for Rugby Supremacy: Accounting for the 1905 All Blacks; The Making of New Zealand Cricket 1832–1914*; and *Forerunners of the All Blacks: The 1888–89 New Zealand Native Football Team in Britain, Australia and New Zealand*. He is currently co-authoring a general history of New Zealand sport and completing a history of beer and brewing in New Zealand.

ROB STEEN is a Senior Lecturer on the BA Sport Journalism course at the University of Brighton. He has been writing about cricket since 1983 for publications ranging from *The Guardian, The Independent, The Sunday Times* and *The Financial Times* to the *Sydney Morning Herald*, the *Hindustan Times, India Today, Sport and Society, Observer Sports Monthly* and *The Wisden Cricketer/Wisden Cricket Monthly*. He has also written more than a dozen books on the game, including biographies of Desmond Haynes and David Gower – the latter won the 1995 Cricket Society Literary Award – and was the founder-editor of *The New Ball*, the cricketing *Granta*. In 2005 he won the UK section of the EU 'for diversity, against discrimination' Journalism Award for his investigation into the decline of Anglo-Caribbean cricketers for *The Wisden Cricketer*, which was also published in *The Observer* and the *London Evening Standard*. He currently writes a column for *Cricinfo*.

KENNETH SURIN is Professor of Literature at Duke University. In addition to books and articles in theology and the philosophy of religion, he has published articles on political economy, political philosophy, French and German philosophy, the philosophy of art, the philosophy of education, sports and philosophy, the philosophy of literature, and cultural anthropology. His latest book is *Freedom Not Yet: Liberation and the Next World Order*.

STEPHEN WAGG is Professor of Sport and Society at Leeds Metropolitan University in the United Kingdom. He previously taught in further education and at the universities of Leicester and Roehampton. He has written widely on the politics of sport, as well as on the politics of comedy and the politics of childhood. He has edited a number of books, including *Following On: Cricket and National Identity in the Post-Colonial Age*. He keeps wicket for Dunton Bassett CC Sunday XI.

CLAIRE WESTALL teaches in the Department of English and Comparative Literary Studies at Warwick University, where she also completed her doctoral research on cricket's place in English and Caribbean literatures. This comparative study emerged from C. L. R. James's postcolonial re-examination of Rudyard Kipling and an investigation of their respective but overlapping encounters with British imperialism. Alongside a sustained research interest in Caribbean and postcolonial literature, her work is concerned with literary and cultural negotiations with national identities, the intersection of postcolonialism and postcolonial theory with questions of Englishness and Britishness, and the economic, cultural and literary consequences of globalisation.

JACK WILLIAMS taught history at the Liverpool John Moores University, where he is now the Research Fellow in History. He is the author of *Cricket and England: A Cultural and Social History of the Inter-War Years*; *Cricket and Race*; and *Entertaining the Nation: A Social History of British Television*. He is the joint author of *Sport and the English, 1918–1939*, joint editor of *Sport and Identity in the North of England* and has published many articles on the social history of sport and broadcasting. His history of cricket's relationship with broadcasting is to be published shortly.

References to cricket are to be found in the period between the beginning of the fourteenth and the late-seventeenth centuries in England; cricket is referred to in Florio's Italian–English dictionary (1598); cricket is listed as a pastime of 'Inhabitants' in Edward Chamberlyne's *Anglia notitia* (1694); William Goldwin's Latin poem 'In Certamen Pilae; Anglice, A Cricket Match' (1706) describes a game recognisable to that which developed in the eighteenth century.

Early eighteenth century	Cricket matches being played by colonists in North America.
1720s	Cricket being played by the English in India (though native people not involved in organised cricket until the 1840s).
1744	Laws of cricket settled by the 'Cricket Club' of London's Artillery Ground.
1745	First recorded women's cricket match in England.
Mid eighteenth century	Organised cricket played in Kent and Sussex; prominence of Hambledon (Hampshire) club by 1770s.
1754	James Love's *Cricket: An Heroic Poem*.
1755	Samuel Johnson defines cricket as deriving from the Anglo-Saxon 'cryce' meaning 'stick' in his *Dictionary of the English Language*.
1774	Revision of the laws of cricket by the Star & Garter Club of London (further revised ten years later).

Late-eighteenth/early-nineteenth century	Main focus of cricket had shifted to London, where Marylebone Cricket Club (MCC – founded 1787) was based at Lord's cricket ground in St John's Wood from 1814; red leather cricket ball in use by mid eighteenth century in England; early curved bat gave way to straight-sided bat by 1770s.
1785	Additional third stump becomes 'law'.
1816	Publication of John Baxter and William Lambert's *Instructions And Rules For Playing The Noble Game of Cricket, As Practised By The Most Eminent Players*.
1830	First printed account of a match in Australia.
1832	Founding of Columbo Cricket Club, Ceylon (Sri Lanka).
1833	Publication in book form of John Nyren and Charles Cowden-Clarke's *The Young Cricketer's Tutor* and *The Cricketers of My Time*.
1835	Follow-on principle introduced, and official acceptance of round-arm bowling.
1840s	Cricket being played in South Africa and New Zealand.
1844	Match between USA and Canada, the first such international contest.
1845	Foundation of Melbourne Cricket Club; first match played at the Oval, London.
1846	Formation of All-England XI of touring cricketers by William Clarke of Nottingham; John Wisden's United England XI performed similar role of taking cricket to various parts of the British Isles.
1850s	Club cricket well established in Australia; first visit by a team from England was in 1861–62; cricket established in the Netherlands.
1851	Publication of James Pycroft's much reprinted *The Cricket-Field*.

1858	First recorded instance of a hat being awarded to a bowler taking three wickets with consecutive balls (a hat trick).
1859	First English team tour to North America.
1864	Official approval given to over-arm bowling, which became the generally accepted bowling method; *Wisden Cricketers' Almanack* first published.
1864–1908	Career of W. G. Grace, the most formative influence on the development of modern cricket.
1868	Team of Australian Aborigines toured England and Wales.
1873	Following the formation in the 1860s of an informal championship between county teams, an official county championship was created in 1873 with nine counties, gradually added to until, by the 1990s, there were eighteen counties (Durham being the most recent addition in 1991).
1877	First cricket Test match between Australia and England, Melbourne Cricket Ground, March 15, 16, 17, 19.
1880	First Test match in England; this period saw the emergence and dominance of one of the great fast bowlers – F. R. Spofforth, 'the Demon' – who took 14 for 90 to win the Test match at the Oval in 1882. This was the match that gave rise to the idea of 'the Ashes' after the *Sporting Times* printed an 'obituary' for English cricket: 'The body will be cremated and the ashes taken to Australia.'
c.1880–1914	Philadelphia the pre-eminent club in North America, with J. B. ('Bart') King a leading American cricketer of the pre-war era.
1883	Formation of the Netherlands Cricket Association.
1886, 1888	Visit to England by Parsee (Indian) cricket teams.

1887	Formation of the White Heather women's cricket club.
1888	A. G. Steel and the Hon. R. H. Lyttelton, *The Badminton Book of Cricket*.
1889	South Africa's first Test match (versus England).
1890	South African Cricket Association formed, following the first visit by an English team in the previous year; South African Coloured Cricket Board set up in 1897.
c.1890–1914	So-called 'golden age' of English cricket, with dominance of amateur batsmen.
1891	Inter-colonial tournament in the West Indies, and first visit by combined West Indies team to England in 1900.
1892–93	Sheffield Shield competition initiated in Australia.
1895	W. G. Grace scores 1,000 runs in May and reaches his 100th century.
1897	Publication of C. B. Fry and K. S. Ranjitsinhji's *The Jubilee Book of Cricket*.
1899–1912	Career of Victor Trumper, the outstanding Australian batsman of the pre-1914 period.
1900	Six-ball over introduced; cricket included as an event at the Olympic Games for the first and last time.
1903–34	Career of Jack Hobbs, pre-eminent English batsman of the twentieth century.
c.1903–10	Major innovation in bowling with development by B. J. T. Bosanquet of the 'googly' (or 'bosie'), used to great effect by South Africa in Test matches before the First World War.
1905	Establishment of the Australian Board of Control for International Cricket; publication of George Beldam and C. B. Fry's *Great Batsmen: Their Methods at a Glance* and *Great Bowlers: Their Methods at a Glance*.

1906–07	Plunkett Shield competition established in New Zealand.
1909	Formation of Imperial Cricket Conference comprising England, Australia and South Africa, as forum for the governing bodies of the Test-match playing countries.
1912	First (and only) triangular Test tournament organised by the ICC in England; publication of Pelham Warner's *Imperial Cricket*.
1915	Death of W. G. Grace (aged 67).
1922	MCC team visit Denmark, where cricket had been played since the 1860s.
1926	Following rise in popularity of women's cricket after the Great War, Women's Cricket Association formed; in 1934–35 an England women's team toured Australasia, and by 1939 there were seventeen county women's associations. An International Women's Cricket Association was formed in 1958; West Indies Cricket Board of Control established, and Test-match status accorded to the West Indies team in 1928. Tour of England that year brought L. N. (Learie) Constantine to fame; publication of H. S. Altham's *History of Cricket*.
1927	Board of Control for Cricket in India established; BBC radio begins to broadcast cricket.
1927–49	Career of Donald Bradman, leading batsman of the first half of the twentieth century, and Australian national hero.
1929–30	Test-match status accorded to New Zealand.
1930	Four-day Test matches introduced in England; publication of Neville Cardus's *Cricket*.
1932–33	Controversial 'Bodyline' Test series between Australia and England.
1933	Publication of Learie Constantine and C. L. R. James's *Cricket and I*, one of the first books by Caribbean authors to be published in Britain.

1933–34	First Test matches played in India by an English team; Ranji Trophy competition established in 1934.
1934	Publication of Marjorie Pollard's *Cricket for Women and Girls*.
1935	'Bodyline' bowling outlawed by MCC.
1937	Amendment of lbw law to include balls breaking from the off-side; first women's Test match in England.
1938	Test match cricket televised for the first time (England v. Australia at Lord's).
1939	'Timeless Test' between South Africa and England at Durban ends in a draw after ten days.
1944	Publication of Edmund Blunden's *Cricket Country*, one of several books celebrating cricket and Englishness published during the Second World War.
1945	Publication of Neville Cardus's *English Cricket*.
1948	Introduction of five-day Tests in England.
1950	West Indies win a Test series in England for the first time, beating England at Lord's in the process; publication of Donald Bradman's *Farewell to Cricket*.
1952	First Test match played by Pakistan; Len Hutton becomes England's first regular professional captain.
1953–74	Career of Garfield Sobers.
1956	Jim Laker, England, took 19 wickets for 90 v. Australia, Old Trafford.
1958	Publication of Donald Bradman's *The Art of Cricket*.
1960	After a public campaign, Frank Worrell becomes the first regular non-white captain of West Indies.

1963	Abolition of amateur–professional distinction in English cricket; introduction, following a decade of declining attendances in English county cricket, of the Gillette Cup, a sponsored one-day, limited-overs (originally sixty-five, later reduced to sixty) competition; death of Sir Jack Hobbs (aged 82); publication of C. L. R. James's *Beyond a Boundary*.
1966	Publication of E. W. Swanton *et al.*'s *World of Cricket: The Game from A to Z*.
1968	End of MCC's longstanding *de facto* control of English cricket with the creation of the Cricket Council and the Test and County Cricket Board.
1968–70	Controversy of the selection of Basil D'Oliveira to play for England on tour to South Africa 1968–69. The tour was cancelled and the repercussions of the 'D'Oliveira Affair' led to the cancellation of a planned tour by South Africa to England in 1970, and the exclusion in the same year of South Africa from international Test cricket in protest at the country's apartheid laws. The exclusion lasted until 1991.
1969	John Player Sunday League (forty overs per side) introduced in England.
1970	Publication of Rowland Bowen's *Cricket: A History of its Growth and Development Throughout the World*.
1971	First one-day international match played, Australia v. England, Melbourne.
1975	First cricket World Cup, at Lord's, won by West Indies.
1976	First women's match at Lord's, England v. Australia.
1977	Kerry Packer introduces World Series Cricket, signing fifty-one of the world's leading players to his organisation.
1978	First use of a full protective helmet in Test matches, by G. N. Yallop of Australia.

1979	Publication of Derek Birley's *The Willow Wand: Some Cricket Myths Explored*.
1980	Eight-ball over in Australia (used since 1922) abandoned.
1982	Sri Lanka achieved Test-match status.
1983	India win a historic victory at Lord's to win the third cricket World Cup.
1985	Publication of Mike Brearley's *The Art of Captaincy*.
1987	Publication of David Frith's *Pageant of Cricket*, a history of the game with over 2,000 illustrations.
1988 (and continuing)	Career of Sachin Tendulkar.
1990	Publication of Mihir Bose's *A History of Indian Cricket*.
1991	Durham became eighteenth English county, the first to be admitted to the county championship since Glamorgan in 1921.
1992	Test debuts of Shane Warne and Muttiah Muralitharan, the highest wicket-takers in Test cricket. Warne's Test career ended in 2007 when he had taken 708 wickets. Muralitharan retired in July 2010 with 800 wickets to his name; first Test match for Zimbabwe; Pakistan win World Cup with a victory over England in the final.
1993	ICC – previously administered by MCC – became an independent body with its own executive; publication of Gideon Haigh's *The Cricket War: The Inside Story of Kerry Packer's World Series Cricket*.
1994	Brian Lara (Warwickshire) became first player to score 500 runs in a first-class match (501 not out v. Durham); publication of Mike Marqusee's *Anyone But England: Cricket and the National Malaise*.
1995	Publication of Hilary Beckles and Brian Stoddart's *Liberation Cricket: West Indies Cricket Culture*.

1996	Sri Lanka win World Cup.
1999	Publication of Jack Williams's *Cricket and England: A Cultural and Social History of the Inter-War Years*.
2000	Bangladesh played its first Test match; W. J. (Hansie) Cronje, South African captain, was banned from cricket for life after being found guilty of match-fixing. Cronje died in an air crash in May 2002; Pakistan captain Salim Malik, and former Indian captain Mohammad Azharuddin, banned from cricket for life for match-fixing; New Zealand won the women's World Cup for the first time; publication of David Underdown's *Start of Play: Cricket and Culture in Eighteenth-Century England*.
2001	Death of Sir Donald Bradman (aged 92).
2002	Publication of David Frith's *Bodyline Autopsy*; publication of Ramachandra Guha's *A Corner of a Foreign Field: The Indian History of a British Sport*.
2003	Twenty20 cricket introduced in English first-class game; publication of Andre Odendaal's *The Story of an African Game*.
2004	Brian Lara becomes the first player to reclaim the world Test record score by overtaking Matthew Hayden's 380 on his way to 400 not out; publication of Greg Ryan's *The Making of New Zealand Cricket 1832–1914*; publication of Jon Gemmell's *The Politics of South African Cricket*.
2005	The ICC headquarters moved to Dubai after ninety-six years at Lord's.
2007	Inaugural Twenty20 World Cup.
2007–08	Establishment of Indian Cricket League and Indian Premier League for Twenty20 cricket.
2009	On 3 March, the Sri Lankan cricket team was attacked by gunmen on its way to the Gaddafi Stadium in Lahore for the third day of the

second Test against Pakistan. Six policemen and two civilians were killed and six Sri Lankan players, two staff and an assistant umpire were injured. Security fears led the ICC to strip Pakistan of its hosting rights and the Pakistan team was forced to play all its fixtures abroad; England win women's World Cup.

2010 Lalit Modi, chief executive of Indian Premier League, suspended by Board of Cricket Control in India over allegations of corruption; Pakistan players Salman Butt, Mohammad Amir and Mohammad Asif suspended by ICC under the provisions of the Anti-Corruption Code following allegations of their involvement in 'spot fixing' during the Lord's Test match against England.

FREQUENTLY USED ABBREVIATIONS

ABC	Australian Broadcasting Corporation
ACB	Australian Cricket Board
ACC	Asian Cricket Council
BCCI	Board of Control for Cricket in India
BCCP	Board of Control for Cricket in Pakistan (now PCB)
ECB	England and Wales Cricket Board
ICC	International Cricket Council (formerly Imperial Cricket Conference)
IPL	Indian Premier League
MCC	Marylebone Cricket Club
MCG	Melbourne Cricket Ground
NSW	New South Wales
NZCC	New Zealand Cricket Council
PCB	Pakistan Cricket Board (formerly Board of Control for Cricket in Pakistan)
SCG	Sydney Cricket Ground
TCCB	Test and County Cricket Board (now England and Wales Cricket Board)
WICB	West Indies Cricket Board
WSC	World Series Cricket

JEFFREY HILL AND ANTHONY BATEMAN

Introduction

> ... it was, after all – a little luck there, a stern battle there, in the sun or the foul light, going slow or flashing past – a glorious game.[1]

In an age of 'globalisation' – a concept made sense of for many people through sporting events – it is worth reminding ourselves that cricket is a world game. To be sure, its extent and impact is less than that of association football, but few other team sports can equal cricket's global reach. Over the course of the twentieth century cricket spread across the globe and in the process the locus of power in the game shifted. When the English cricket mandarin Pelham Warner published *Imperial Cricket* in 1912 he described a game that had developed beyond rudimentary levels in only a handful of countries.[2] The hub was very definitely to be found in England, even if pre-eminence in playing the game had already passed to Australia. A hundred years later 104 countries are members of its governing body, the ICC. This organisation bears the same initials as those it had at the time of its formation in 1909, when they denoted the Imperial Cricket Conference, a triumvirate of England, Australia and South Africa. Its influence was limited; power in the game rested largely with MCC at Lord's cricket ground, St John's Wood, London. But in the early twenty-first century there is no sense of the ICC being either a product of empire or a mere talking shop. Its headquarters are in Dubai in the United Arab Emirates (just next door to Abu Dhabi, where in 2010 the opening match of the English cricket season – for so long held at Lord's – was staged, with floodlights and pink ball), and its officers wield much clout in the world game. Such a geographical shift denotes, of course, the increased influence in the game's corridors of power of the countries of South Asia – India in particular. It signifies also a recognition of new economic potential. The passion for cricket in these parts presents commercial opportunities scarcely imagined in Pelham Warner's time, and further opens up the possibility of cricket's breaking out of its long-established colonial boundaries. We have seen in the very recent past that Afghanistan, notwithstanding its immensely troubled civil society, can put a very good international cricket team in the field. China, we are told, is on the brink of entering the cricket arena. And we might note that in one of the acclaimed literary works of 2008 – Joseph O'Neill's novel *Netherland* – a principal theme is the dream of making cricket in America a serious rival to baseball.[3] 'Think big' is the motto of the character Chuck Ramkissoon, who is building a stadium in New York to become a world stage for televised international matches. In one leap, therefore, a second-class sport played by immigrants will outshine America's traditional summer game. This, to be sure, is fiction but international cricket tournaments staged in Florida during 2010 suggest that the Ramkissoon dream is not entirely fanciful.

Such developments, which might suggest a form of 'reverse colonialism', are yet to be fully realised. The core of the game – the places where cricket has attained a state of organisation, support and playing proficiency that are deemed to represent its highest level – remains in that handful of former dominions and colonies of Great Britain where cricket was first implanted by 'missionaries' of various kinds through the agencies of colonial influence – the army, educational establishments, the civil administration, public works, commerce and religion.

It is within such a global and historical panorama that the *Cambridge Companion to Cricket* essays a scholarly discussion of the principal themes and issues that have emerged as the game has developed over the past two and a half centuries. A great deal of this development has been inscribed in literature. As the critic Benny Green once observed: 'it is almost as though the game itself would not exist at all until written about.'[4] Since at least the early 1830s, with the appearance of John Nyren's reminiscences of the champions of his Hambledon youth,[5] cricket and its players have been featured in writing. The game has generated a prodigious output, and thereby reached a wide audience in many forms: historical accounts (of which Nyren's classic text was one of the first examples); stories of the game and its play in a legion of press reports; technical analyses in publications such as *MCC Cricket Coaching Book*; autobiographies of players and administrators; a rich factual and fictional tradition of self-consciously literary representations of cricket in verse, short stories and serialisations in magazines; and, perhaps most famously, in *Wisden*, the annual 'almanack' (note the now-archaic spelling) that since its inception in 1864 has been almost the defining text of cricket. In whichever form, this literature stands as a memorial to the game, its people and its places.

Much of this material has (in contrast to other games) acquired a 'literary' status; that is to say, cricket prose and verse has received critical praise for its aesthetic style, whether the subject matter be the great players or simply cross-bat village greeners. Cricket writing's status owes something to its appearing to transcend mere sports reporting, a characteristic partly explained by the fact that the game has seized the imagination of those whose writing graces fields other than sport. The English poet and literary scholar Edmund Blunden (1896–1974) is a notable case in point. There is more than an authorial link between two of his most celebrated works: *Undertones of War* (1928), a contribution to that remarkable late-1920s upsurge of war literature, and *Cricket Country* (1944), a product of a different but still total conflict.[6] In spite of their very contrasting subjects and contexts both works express a love of nature and evoke the importance of human, especially male, comradeship. Blunden, whose academic career took him to Japan and China for long periods, retained a lasting feel for England. It is evinced poignantly in his memories of English soldiers in wartime, and of the English place-names they superimposed upon the French and Flemish originals as a way of re-creating pieces of England in a foreign land. The idea of a 'deep' England is there too in cricket. For Blunden the game is not one of great names, and only rarely of professional players. It is cricket played by ordinary folk in their own neighbourhoods – their 'country'; Blunden's use of that ancient term denoted lives and sport circumscribed by localities. How many athletic pursuits, we might wonder, have been appropriated by high literary culture in this way, to distil the essences that form a nation? Does cricket as a game possess some intrinsic quality that explains why writers are thus attracted to it? Or has cricket attained its special position as a consequence of having been appropriated by men of letters?

The answer is probably to be found in a combination of both: writing defines cricket as much as the game influences the writer. In one sense cricket writing's artistic distinction has worked to privilege the game socially and politically in relation to other sports. At the same time it has served to endow it with a special ethos. If cricket is perceived as having an 'essence' it is because of the qualities writers have ascribed to it. When the 'soul' of cricket is spoken of, as many traditionalists have done in reflecting on recent radical changes in the nature of the game, it is to a large extent the heritage of literary representations of the game that they are calling upon for this idea. What is more, when the 'soul' of the game appears to have been sold in a Mephistophelean pact with commerce, something more than just a game appears to be at stake.

Some might plausibly object that cricket writing, for all its literariness, has often been one-dimensional: that the class, gender and ethnic assumptions ingrained in its texts conspire to make much of it a repository of conservative myths, perpetuating the memory of people, places and relationships that have long since ceased to have relevance to either the game or the society in which it functions. A striking example of this is the tendency to marginalise women's cricket, in spite of the fact that it has been played at an international level since the 1930s. The televising in 2009 of the women's world cup, won by an excellent England team, might help to change perceptions of what constitutes 'cricket'. But old habits die hard, and there is little doubt that the act of writing about cricket has on many occasions been an opportunity to look back nostalgically at 'better days', to seek in a perceived past a relief from the economic and political pressures that bear down on us in the present. One feature of this mentality has been evident in the game's relationship with the 'outside' world; that is to say, the world outside cricket. In spite of cricket's own power structures and the political affiliations of many of its leading figures, the game has at crucial times been pressed into service to support the argument that 'sport and politics do not mix'. It was never more apparent than during the so-called 'D'Oliveira Affair' in the late 1960s.[7] Basil D'Oliveira, a non-white South African barred under apartheid laws from playing in the white cricket teams of that country, had been very successful in English county cricket after emigrating in 1960. The possibility that he might be chosen to tour South Africa as a member of the English team in 1968–69 provoked much backstairs manoeuvring by South African politicians seeking to prevent a selection that would embarrass the apartheid regime. MCC, the body responsible for the composition of the touring party, was caught between, on the one hand, choosing the players it deemed suitable for the tour and, on the other, not wishing to offend the South African cricket authorities, with whom it had had long and friendly relations. Its ambivalence on the matter made it seem that, in the words of the writer John Arlott, MCC was 'truckling to apartheid'.[8] The affair, partially resolved by the calling off of the tour, produced bitter controversy and led directly to the boycotting of sporting relations with South Africa during the 1970s and 1980s. Voices at the time were nonetheless raised in favour of the status quo; they proposed that relations with South Africa should be maintained, and in so saying they drew upon long-held notions of cricket as a 'pure' game insulated from the grubby world of politics. Such a notion was by no means new. It had been fostered in the earlier part of the twentieth century in the writings of one of cricket's most renowned authors, Neville Cardus.[9] Combining cricket reporting for the Manchester *Guardian* with his role as the paper's music correspondent, Cardus endowed both subjects with an 'apolitical' spirit. It was an attitude reflected in most British newspapers of the time, where, as if to emphasise the separateness of sport from all things political, it was detached from the rest of the news and confined to the back pages.

In more recent times attitudes have changed, to an extent at least. A new strand of writing and thinking has emerged that offers a serious academic analysis of cricket. It is connected with the growth over the past thirty or so years of a distinct 'sport history' with vigorous groups of practitioners in many countries, and it has given us many fine studies of cricket. If we were to choose one outstanding example it might well be the late David Underdown's *Start of Play*.[10] The book traces the origins and development of cricket in Kent, Sussex and Hampshire – the 'cradle' of the modern game – from the early-eighteenth century until the mid-nineteenth. It shows how a game of the people – a 'peasant' game in Underdown's term – was gradually appropriated by the upper classes and eventually developed into a commercial sport based in London. Underdown thus brings to bear on the game a social historian's sense of place, of class relations and of change impelled by the lure of money and markets, forces often overlooked or suppressed in many non-academic studies of cricket. David Underdown, in fact, performs a masterclass in how to write good sport history. When we read this wonderful book we would do well to have at our elbow a copy of William Cobbett's old classic *Rural Rides*.[11] Both writers, from different perspectives and separated by 150 years, are describing the passing of the same world.

Some forty years before Underdown's book appeared, the Trinidadian writer and political activist C. L. R. James had marked out a new path in cricket writing. His book was appropriately entitled *Beyond a Boundary*.[12] It was the first, and for some time the only, book to take cricket away from the field of play, or more precisely, to place the field of play in a broader arena of political, economic and social influences. Sport historians are now so accustomed to such a methodology that it comes as something of a surprise to remember that its provenance is relatively recent. The Jamesian influence has been immense, notably in regions where cricket from an early stage was politicised because of its colonial and racial setting, and where in the course of time the game came to play a part in the process of decolonisation. Alongside the West Indies, such a characteristic has been present in the Indian subcontinent and South Africa, with variations on the theme in Australia and New Zealand. Hilary Beckles and Brian Stoddart's study of cricket in the Caribbean[13] is a striking example of a work whose contributors carry strong traces of James's method and philosophy. There is plenty of cricket in the book, but there is much else besides. In England and Australia the same influence has been rather less noticeable. Derek Birley[14] and Mike Marqusee[15] have provided radical and stimulating correctives to many of cricket history's enduring myths, though in their work the influence of C. L. R. James, if present at all, is lightly worn. Where James's shadow has most obviously been cast in Britain is over those who have worked in postcolonial studies, some of whom have transported their concepts and theories into the realm of sport. Claire Westall's chapter in this volume offers a good example.

Academic sport history, however, is a small room in the very large mansion of cricket writing. The genre continues to be shaped, as it always was, by popular demands. It underscores very clearly a commonly held view that sport is too enjoyable a business to be entrusted to academics. The thrills of the cricket field must be reproduced, as nearly as possible, on page and screen. Traditional written and electronic forms still capture the public's imagination, and are now being augmented by various aspects of new technology. The England–Australia Ashes series of 2005, and its sequel in 2009, revealed cricket's capacity to generate astonishing amounts of written and visual record in rapid time, while the success of the Indian Premier League illustrates the game's ability to be, through the medium of television, a 'global brand'. Millions of people worldwide now find in the cricket of the early twenty-first century an excitement and quality rarely seen in any sustained form in the past. A global awareness has helped cricket to refashion itself with the injection of ideas and methods taken from other sports and from the world of business. Improvements in fielding, for example, have come from studying baseball techniques; improvisation in batting and new bowling methods have been devised to meet the challenges of the short game; television presentation, the staid forms of which were jolted into new life by the coloured clothing and floodlight initiatives of Kerry Packer's World Series Cricket in the 1970s, has been further developed in Twenty20 cricket with stagecraft that owes much to American football; a keener business sense, involving sponsors, advertising and official suppliers, has been adopted by all the national governing bodies of cricket drawing on models previously developed in sport by organisations such as FIFA (Fédération Internationale de Football Association) and the International Olympic Committee (IOC); and all of these have served to broaden the audience, not only geographically but in age and gender terms as well. Go to any Twenty20 fixture on a weekday evening in a big English city and, given fair weather, there will be evidence of the transformations wrought in recent years; lots of children, many more women than ever before, groups of men in business suits who have stepped in from the office after work; loud music accompanying a boundary or the fall of a wicket; big-screen coverage of the play; beer and burgers. Such an event bears a close resemblance to American sporting occasions. But it is undeniably fun, and it is all over in three hours. The contrast with Neville Cardus's descriptions of so-called 'Roses' matches between Lancashire and Yorkshire in the 1920s – where the male community of spectators rasped stentorian instructions to the players to 'get thi 'ead down' – could not be starker. The Twenty20 match is the apotheosis of commercialism in cricket.

The game, of course, has always possessed a commercial potential. The iconic Victorian cricketer himself, W. G. Grace, was never slow to exploit it, especially to his own advantage, and for a time in the mid-nineteenth century the possibility existed that cricket might follow a business-orientated path similar to that of American baseball.[16] That it did not had something to do with W. G. committing his own towering presence to the amateur-led 'county' game, and something also to do with the gradual reformation of manners in cricket, which cultivated a distaste for the perceived evils of commercial sport. One of these was gambling, a habit that had been prominent in cricket during the phase of aristocratic dominance and patronage in the eighteenth century, when matches were often the subject of wagers between rival patrons. Betting became endemic in the game (as it did in other sports – notably professional pedestrianism, which the Amateur Athletics Association later sought to combat). It provoked a number of incidents in cricket where professional players were thought to have profited by 'selling' matches, and by 1817 the problem had reached a point at which MCC took the lead in causing bookmakers and gambling to be banned from cricket grounds. Although gambling in cricket was not entirely eliminated as a result of these measures, it seems to have been less of a problem in the hundred years following the 1850s. But with the ending of amateur hegemony it started to make a comeback. In the 1970s, rules were relaxed to allow betting at grounds, and the intensified commercialism that the game was experiencing by the end of the twentieth century attracted a new betting craze. It was at its height among the millions of cricket followers in South Asia. Paradoxically, at a time when their remuneration from cricket was greater than it had ever been, some professional players seemed more susceptible than ever to the temptation to increase their earnings through dishonest practices. Several cases of match-fixing, of which that of the South African captain Hansie Cronje achieved the highest profile, did much to damage the credibility of the game in the eyes of its followers, though it did not necessarily stop malpractice. Apart from the deliberate fixing of match results, cricket's episodic structure provides further opportunities for corrupt behaviour through more subtle forms of 'micro' (or 'spot') fixing, in which players might conspire to affect certain passages of play (runs scored in a session, for example, or the number of no-balls delivered) in order to make money by betting in league with outside agents against the bookmakers' odds. During the 2010 series against England, allegations of such spot fixing were levelled against a group of leading Pakistan cricketers. Seen in the context of similar contemporaneous incidents – the suspension, for example, of the chief executive of the Indian Premier League, Lalit Modi, over allegations of financial misdemeanours – such developments no doubt caused many ordinary cricket followers to question the probity of what they were witnessing on the field of play. It is vital in any sport, as the ICC's chief executive has recently noted, that the public has confidence in the players;[17] and as David Frith's chapter in the present volume shows, cricket, its image as a game of fair play notwithstanding, has not been immune from charges of corrupt practice.

For much of its development, however, English cricket had succeeded in avoiding damaging irregularities of this kind. The game was fashioned in a form that might be described as 'semi-commercial'. Indeed, one aspect (perhaps the paramount one) of this amateur-led trajectory proved inimical to full-scale commercialism: the aesthetic of cricket. Cricket was regarded as more than a game; it was felt to express a set of values about correct human behaviour. Unacceptable conduct was simply 'not cricket'. Within this code was a notion of style. Cricket should be played according to an orthodox technique that involved among other things the 'straight bat' and the approved 'sideways on' method of bowling, with the ball aimed on a sportsmanlike length on or just outside off-stump. Expert practitioners of these skills became the great sporting heroes of the early twentieth century 'golden age', when in England cricket was still known as the 'national game': A. C. MacLaren – 'the noblest Roman of them all'[18] – Victor Trumper, Jack Hobbs and the versatile C. B. Fry, who excelled in all sports and whose classical physique seemed an embodiment of the Edwardian love of ancient Greece. To reach Twenty20 from this worldview required more than the mere application of business methods; it has needed a revolution of the intellect, which happened for the most part in the last quarter of the twentieth century. Nonetheless, there are continuities. The sheer pleasure that was had in the spectacle of Trumper batting is not absent from the modern game; indeed, much of cricket's commercial appeal lies in anticipating the arrival at the crease of a batsman like Sachin Tendulkar, or in simply observing the magisterial Andrew Flintoff bestriding a cricket field. These two modern champions are cast in the mould of the greats of the 'golden age'. To be sure, style has been valued in all sports and has inspired great sports writing: Alan Ross on Stanley Matthews, Hugh McIlvanney on George Best, Norman Mailer on Muhammad Ali. But cricket's style icons probably outnumber those of other sports, and the game even in its commercialised present still retains a place for the panache that the old masters brought to the game.

The long history of recording and analysing the game, from which there has arisen a myriad of texts, makes up what we might call the 'discourse' of cricket: in other words, the 'language', broadly speaking, through which people are able to think and argue about, commemorate and remember the game. In short, cricket discourse constitutes the mental map by which we 'know' cricket. Thus, this volume's specialist topics, whole and rounded in themselves, and which can be read in any order the reader might choose, nevertheless each relate to one or more of the big themes recurring throughout the volume:

- the heritage of cricket, articulated through its distinctive literary forms;
- newer representations of the game, especially through the medium of television;
- the increased commercialisation of cricket in the later twentieth century, and the various problems this has posed;
- the reactions that changed forms of play such as one-day and Twenty20 cricket have provoked;
- the worldwide development of the game, with particular emphasis on South Asia as well as the prospects for future growth in new areas such as China;
- the international politics of cricket and shifting balances of power within the game that make up the politics of international cricket;
- the place of cricket in the formation of regional, national, ethnic and other social identities.

The origins of cricket in southern England, together with the concentration of cricket publishing in much the same time and area, gave rise to an 'Anglocentric' vision of the game: the view from England, exemplified in Pelham Warner's survey of cricket on the eve of the First World War. It caused many to believe that what was most important in the game emanated from England, and from Lord's cricket ground in particular. Early on, however, a process of internationalisation began which created a challenge to the English hegemony, first on the field of play, then in the committee rooms and treasuries of cricket's administrative structure, and subsequently in its sources of communication. This book grapples with that long, sometimes harmonious but often troublesome, process of change.

NOTES

1 Edmund Blunden, *Cricket Country* (London: The Imprint Society, 1945 edn), p. 224.
2 Pelham Warner, *Imperial Cricket* (London: London and Counties Press Association, 1912).
3 Joseph O'Neill, *Netherland* (London: Fourth Estate, 2008).
4 Benny Green, *A History of Cricket* (London: Barrie and Jenkins, 1988), p. 14.

5 John Nyren, *The Young Cricketer's Tutor, Comprising Full Directions for Playing … Cricket (including 'The Cricketers of My Time, or recollections of the most famous old players')* (London: C. C. Clarke, 1833).

6 Edmund Blunden, *Undertones of War* (London: Richard Cobden-Sanderson, 1928); *Cricket Country*.

7 See, for example, Peter Oborne, *Basil D'Oliveira: Cricket and Conspiracy, the Untold Story* (London: Little, Brown, 2004).

8 Quoted in Tim Heald, *The Authorized Biography of the Incomparable Denis Compton* (London: Pavilion Books, 1996), p. 213.

9 See Anthony Bateman, *Cricket, Literature and Culture: Symbolising the Nation, Destabilising Empire* (Farnham: Ashgate, 2009), ch. 3.

10 David Underdown, *Start of Play: Cricket and Culture in Eighteenth-Century England* (London: Allen Lane, 2000).

11 William Cobbett, *Rural Rides* (London: Reeves and Turner, 1893 edn).

12 C. L. R. James, *Beyond a Boundary* (London: Hutchinson, 1963).

13 H. McD. Beckles and Brian Stoddart, *Liberation Cricket: West Indies Cricket Culture* (Manchester University Press, 1995).

14 Derek Birley, *Willow Wand: Some Cricket Myths Explored* (London: Queen Anne Press, 1979).

15 Mike Marqusee, *Anyone But England: Cricket and the National Malaise* (London: Verso, 1994).

16 Simon Rae, *W. G. Grace: A Life* (London: Faber and Faber, 1998).

17 See www.cricinfo.com/england-v-pakistan-2010/content/current/story/475673. html (accessed 3 September 2010).

18 Neville Cardus, *Good Days* (London: Rupert Hart-Davis, 1949), p. 80.

I

ANTHONY BATEMAN

Cricket pastoral and Englishness

English cricket has been portrayed in a substantial body of imaginative literature as quintessentially southern, rural and amateur. In this way English cricket pastoral has become an enduring cultural myth that obscures any sense of the game as a highly rationalised and commercialised national and international sport, as it has been for over two centuries.[1] Even when cricket had spread to the industrial centres of Victorian Britain and to the various parts of the British Empire, its literary image remained an overwhelmingly rural one. The rural cricket field, imaginatively at least, could be transported to the most alien urban and colonial environment to fulfil its cultural work. Not least among the reasons for this was the belief that the mythical notion of Anglo-Saxon racial purity resided in the English countryside. At the same time these representations consistently presented a nostalgic ideal based on both social hierarchy and social harmony. This mythical ideal of English cricket was thus profoundly conservative, a vision of Englishness in which 'organic' rural custom betokens 'organic' social order. Through a discussion of prose, poetry and fiction, this chapter traces the emergence and development of cricket pastoral between 1820 and the present day. In doing so it suggests that, though a consistent feature of the sport's literary tradition, cricket pastoral has tended to flourish during periods of accelerated social change or perceived national and imperial crisis, periods when collectivist concepts of Englishness were deployed within other forms of literary discourse as imaginary resolutions to such tensions.

Cricket literature and Englishness

Cricket's Englishness was as much an invention of its literary gatekeepers as it was due to the game's origins in rural southern England. Although in 1671 the philologist Stephen Skinner had calmly proposed French derivations for both the game and its name,[2] by 1755, in Samuel Johnson's *Dictionary of the English Language*, the sport was being Anglicised as deriving from the

Anglo-Saxon 'cryce', meaning a 'stick'.[3] Henceforth images of shepherd boys playing the game in a pastoral setting became commonplace. Yet by the mid eighteenth century cricket was already taking on the form of a recognisably modern sport, with clearly defined rules (or, more precisely, 'laws', codifying a seemingly pre-existing, 'natural' phenomenon) as well as financial support provided by aristocrats and entrepreneurs. Cricket was also attracting large crowds who frequently placed bets on the outcome of matches. However, its literary image somewhat concealed these commercial realities. In a poem called 'The Kentish Cricketers', for example, John Burnby located the Kent versus Surrey match of 1773 in an Arcadian landscape of ineffable beauty with 'matchless cricketers' in 'milk-white vestments' a seemingly organic part of the landscape.[4]

As cricket became increasingly commercial, as professionalism and gambling continued to accompany the sport, and as the economic and administrative power base of cricket moved to London, cricket pastoral continued to define the game's image. At the elite end of the literary spectrum particularly, cricket identified with its rural past at the very time that it was inaugurated as a product of modernity. William Blake's illustration of a boy cricketer in 'The Echoing Green' from *Songs of Innocence*, Leigh Hunt's essay on 'Cricket and other Pastimes', representations of cricket in the poetry of Wordsworth and Byron, and William Hazlitt's 'Merry England' all celebrate cricket as essentially rural. As it took on the form of a recognisably modern sport, cricket was being written into existence as a legacy of a near-extinct folk culture, as uncontaminated by modernity, and hence as authentically English.[5]

With the countryside and the rural communities under threat during the early Industrial Revolution, a form of popular literature emerged from the 1820s which both elegised the loss of this way of life and sought to reaffirm its ideals. Works such as William Cobbett's *Rural Rides* and Mary Mitford's *Our Village* thus contributed to a perception of the countryside and its inhabitants that was to remain deeply embedded in English literary culture. Significantly, Mitford's book, which was initially serialised in *The Lady's Magazine* between 1824 and 1832, contains the first comprehensive prose description of a cricket match. The account begins as follows:

> I doubt if there be any scene in the world more animating or delightful than a cricket-match: – I do not mean a set match at Lord's Ground for money, hard money, between a certain number of gentlemen and players, as they are called – people who make a trade of that noble sport, and degrade it into an affair of bettings, and hedgings, and cheatings ... nor do I mean a pretty *fete* in a gentlemen's park ... where they show off in graceful costumes to a gay marquee of admiring belles ...

No! the cricket that I mean is a real solid old-fashioned match between neighbouring parishes, where each attacks the other for honour and a supper, glory and half-a-crown a man.[6]

Mitford's often eroticised cricket episode is not simply a celebration of village cricket over and above urban, commercialised or more socially sophisticated versions of the sport. As Elizabeth Helsinger has noted, in describing aspects of village life Mitford's accounts frequently return to the idea of representation and draw attention to their own artifice by describing themselves as 'pictures' and 'scenes'.[7] As much as any feature of the village, Mitford's cricket field has no pretensions to be authentic; rather, it is a self-consciously rendered aesthetic artefact believed to possess significant symbolic capital at a time of unprecedented social and economic transformation.

The emergence of such cricket narratives should be understood in relation to this sense of traumatic change and not merely to the growing popularity and significance of the sport itself. This is particularly evident in John Nyren and Charles Cowden-Clarke's *The Cricketers of My Time*. Though published in serial form in 1832, the book is a deeply nostalgic account of the heyday of the Hambledon cricket club in rural Hampshire during the last quarter of the eighteenth century, a series of 'scenes, of fifty years bygone ... painted in [Nyren's] memory'.[8] Here, the rambunctious energies and apparent virility of late eighteenth-century rural cricket provide a point of contrast to the relatively temperate, effete and Europeanised present:

There was high feasting held on Broadhalfpenny during the solemnity of one of our grand matches. Oh! it was a heart-stirring sight to witness the multitude forming a complete and dense circle around that noble green. Half the county would be present, and all their hearts with us – Little Hambledon pitted against all England was a proud thought for the Hampshire men ... How those fine brawn-faced fellows of farmers would drink to our success! And then, what stuff they had to drink! – Punch! – not your new *Ponche à Romaine*; or *Ponche à la Groseille*; or your modern cat-lap milk-punch – punch be-devilled; but good, unsophisticated, John Bull stuff – stark! – that would stand on end – punch that would make a cat speak![9]

Despite its resolutely pre-Victorian attitude to the pleasures of strong liquor, the Victorian middle class loved Nyren's book, as they did texts such as James Pycroft's *The Cricket Field* (1851) and, with its valedictory cricket match, Thomas Hughes's novel *Tom Brown's Schooldays* (1857). In the wake of the Chartist agitations and the revolutionary fervour that had swept across Europe in the 1840s, Christian Socialists like Hughes and Charles Kingsley sought national symbols such as cricket that could pacify a potentially revolutionary working class. Throughout the period the middle class, concerned that their increasing prosperity was accompanied by a loss of spiritual values, were particularly drawn to forms of literary ruralism, including cricket writing. By the later nineteenth century cricket writing closely articulated with what Alun Howkins has called the 'discovery of rural England'.[10] In the context of fears about racial degeneration and the decline of England's pre-industrial structures, the popularity of cricket literature in the 1890s amongst middle-class readers echoed the broader revival of folk custom and culture typified by Cecil Sharpe's folk-dance movement.[11] Although pastoralism had been a consistent feature of the English literary tradition, there was a marked proliferation of such discourse in the late Victorian and Edwardian periods. For the urban middle class, literary visions of the countryside seemed to offer escape from the tyranny of industrialism and the ideological tensions of modernity.[12] Cricket literature formed part of this broader cultural context because it was a now well-established literary medium through which reassuring images of the rural could be disseminated. Indeed, influential and popular ruralist publishing houses, such as Country Life, published cricket books.[13]

That the late-Victorian literary construction of Englishness was a heady blend of patriotism, pastoralism and romanticism is evidenced by the willingness of both 'bardic' poets such as Henry Newbolt and Alfred Austin, and 'nature' poets such as G. K. Chesterton and A. E. Housman, to eulogise cricket. Related to this widespread escape into the English countryside were other emerging literary trends. In H. G. Wells's *The War of the Worlds* (1898) – an example of the new genre of 'invasion literature' that reflected contemporary fears of national defilement and miscegenation – a character suggests that through playing cricket 'we shall save the race'.[14]

Another version of this literary ruralism located the essence of Englishness in the country house. The late 1880s had been a period of considerable social unrest such as the Trafalgar Square Riots and widespread demonstrations against unemployment. Within this traumatic context the literary cult of the country house provided reassuring romantic images of the countryside for a middle-class urban readership. In this literature the country squire was invariably portrayed as the embodiment of Englishness and as the benevolent head of a harmonious quasi-feudal social order in which his elegant house functions as the architectural focus of this national imaginary.[15] A contemporary fashion for country-house cricket among the socially privileged neatly dovetailed with this prevailing literary conceit. Whole weeks could be dedicated to this leisurely form of cricket and, although it was primarily a social occasion for the elite, estate workers and local villagers often took part in the matches. When

L. P. Hartley nostalgically portrayed an Edwardian country-house game in his novel *The Go-Between* (1953), both Lord Hugh Trimingham ('a pretty bat') and his rival in love, the local farmer Ted Burgess, participate, necessarily on opposing sides.[16] For the cricketer Albert Knight and his likely co-writer E. V. Lucas, the ease and luxuriance provided by country-house cricket not only contrasted with the sordid commercial realities of elite cricket, it pointed to nothing less than a Morrisian rural utopia: 'Country-house cricket reminds one of days spent in eating apples under an old tree, reading the *Earthly Paradise* of William Morris. It is the cricket of an Eden future when we shall saunter through the fields, "without tomorrow, without yesterday", nor scent laziness in ease, nor distrust good-humoured chaff as incompatible with seriousness.'[17] In contrast to muscular Christian versions of the sport, Knight here magically projects cricket into a lost pre-industrial society, free from the earnest religious pieties and work ethic that underpinned the creation of modern industrial Britain, as well as its attendant social and political tensions.

Cricket pastoral in the inter-war years

The unprecedented trauma of the First World War, the spectre of the Bolshevik Revolution, the General Strike of 1926 and nationalist calls for independence in India and other parts of the British Empire meant that the England symbolised by the rural cricket field was seen as increasingly threatened. Furthermore, as the commercial and professional aspects of the game were consolidated, the sport called upon a loyal literary entourage to defend its integrity and to reinforce its anachronistically rural image. The intimate relationship between cricket and conservative literary figures was conspicuous in a number of literary cricket elevens such as J. C. Squire's 'The Invalids', famously portrayed in A. G. Macdonell's popular novel *England, Their England* (1933). Squire's team included noted writers such as Alec Waugh, Clifford Bax, Hugh de Selincourt and Edmund Blunden, who later, during the Second World War, wrote one of the most loving accounts of rural cricket, *Cricket Country*, one of many texts written during the conflict celebrating elements of the threatened national culture. The narrator of Somerset Maugham's *Cakes and Ale* wryly described the 1920s as 'the period when men of letters, to show their virility, drank beer and played cricket', and noted that the name 'Authors XI' frequently appeared in the fixture lists of a number of minor public schools and southern village sides.[18] This retreat to the village green in order to recapture a sense of stable pre-war social and gender relations suggests deeply conservative currents within the literary culture of the period.

The inter-war literary structuring of cricket's symbolic geography produced a generic place that was imaginatively transportable to wholly alien socio-economic and geographical locations. As the following short poem by George Rostrevor-Hamilton suggests, cricket was represented as a hegemonic component of the national culture with important cross-class appeal, and the ability to transform imaginatively the most irretrievably urban and socially deprived of environments:

> Where else, you ask, can England's game be seen
> Rooted so deep as on the village green?
> Here, in the slum, where doubtful sunlight falls
> To gild three stumps chalked on decaying walls.[19]

As 'A Country Vicar' put it, whether played at Lord's 'or on some rough corner of a patch of waste-land', cricket was always 'the same game'.[20] Despite its construction of distinct regional identities and senses of place, cricket discourse produced an image of temporal and spatial conformity in which the various manifestations of the sport were essentially the same.

This theme is given a distinctly imperial dimension in a speech written by J. M. Barrie. The speech was given at a dinner to mark the arrival in England of the Australian Test team in 1926 and was subsequently reprinted in *The Times*. It was conventional for major literary figures to speak at such events (as part of the elaborate ritualism of empire which surrounded colonial cricket tours) in order to validate cricket culturally and sanctify the bonds of empire it represented. As well as producing in *Peter Pan* (1902) the most famous narrative of perpetually arrested adolescence (a book that had profound resonance after the truncation of so many young lives in the war), Barrie frequently wrote on cricket and sought to enshrine the links between the sport and the literary field by organising a writers' cricket team known as the Allahakbarries which, before the war, had regularly included authors such as Arthur Conan Doyle and P. G. Wodehouse.[21] The Australian players may have been surprised to learn from Barrie that 'the great glory of cricket does not lie in Test Matches, nor county championships, nor Sheffield Shields, but rather on village greens, the cradle of cricket'. Like many interwar cricket writers, Barrie's speech positions the contemporary practice of Test cricket within a broader discourse of cultural decline and crisis by defining it as little more than a part of ephemeral modernity: 'As the years roll on they become of small account; something else soon takes its place, the very word may be forgotten.' Against this fallen image of impermanence, village cricket signifies sameness and continuity, not only through history, but across geographical space, a quality that endows this auratic English locale with an imperial dimension: 'but long, long afterwards, I think, your far-off progeny will still of summer afternoons hear the crack of the bat and the local champion calling for his ale on the same old bumpy wickets.' This generic location possesses not only an ability to transcend imperial space, but can enforce a diachronic conformity in which past and present seemingly merge into one. The aesthetic space of the rural cricket field can thus imaginatively obviate the violent separations of war: 'It has been said of the unseen army of the dead, on their everlasting march, that when they are passing a rural cricket ground the Englishman falls out of the ranks for a moment to look over the gate and smile. The Englishman, yes, and the Australian.'[22] Such synoptic imperial imagery had specific resonance at the time. In Australia, a series of economic and political factors, in conjunction with perceptions of the serious shortcomings of British leadership in the war (particularly at Gallipoli), were hastening and intensifying calls for the devolution of imperial power.[23] In its very denial, Barrie's speech relates to this context: although it eschews the blatant empire-binding rhetoric of many late nineteenth-century and early twentieth-century cricket books such as Pelham Warner's *Imperial Cricket*, Barrie's village green is nevertheless a symbol of an imperial culture whose past, present and future would be reassuringly the same.

The sheer weight of symbolic significance placed upon literary images of the rural cricket field meant that inter-war cricket writers became obsessed with certain prescribed formulas of representation. In a poem called 'The Season Opens', Edmund Blunden listed the necessary features of the cricket landscape:

> A tower we must have, and a clock in the tower,
> Looking over the tombs, the tithe barn, the bower;
> The inn and the mill, the forge and the hall,
> And the loamy sweet level that loves bat and ball.[24]

The individual features of the cricket landscape are then detailed in four stanzas until the scene is transfigured into a place in which past and present merge into one:

> Till the meadow is quick with the masters who were,
> And he hears his own shouts when he first trotted there;
> Long ago; all gone home now; but here they come all!
> Surely these are the same, who now bring bat and ball?

Likewise, at the beginning of A. G. Macdonell's fictional portrayal of a match played by J. C. Squire's Invalids XI, the scene is set so as to reveal it as a construction by ironically exaggerating the details of the cricket landscape; the scene is described as 'perfect to the last detail ... as if Mr Cochran had ... brought Ye Olde Englyshe Village straight down by special train from the London Pavilion':

> It was a hot summer's afternoon. There was no wind, and the smoke from the red-roofed cottages curled slowly up into the golden haze. The clock on the flint tower of the church struck the half-hour, and the vibrations spread slowly across the shimmering hedgerows ... Bees lazily drifted. White butterflies flapped their aimless way among the gardens. Delphiniums, larkspur, tiger-lilies, evening-primrose, monk's-hood, sweet-peas, swaggered brilliantly above the box hedges, the wooden palings, and the rickety gates. The cricket field itself was a mass of daisies and buttercups and dandelions, tall grasses and purple vetches and thistle-down, and great clumps of dark-red sorrel, except, of course, for the oblong patch in the centre – mown, rolled, watered – a smooth, shining emerald of grass, the pride of Fordenden, the Wicket.[25]

Macdonell's novel ends with a dream-like evocation of 'the muted voices of grazing sheep, and the merry click of bat upon ball, and the peaceful green fields of England, and the water-meads, and the bells of the Cathedral'. Intoxicated by the scene's sheer Englishness, the narrator, Donald, goes off 'to find some tea'.[26]

The mythical image of the rural cricket field was by now so closely associated with Englishness that it could unite figures of such disparate political persuasions as George Orwell and the twice Conservative (and once National Government) Prime Minister Stanley Baldwin. During the political traumas of the 1920s, Baldwin frequently used images of cricket to represent the ideals of his organic Conservatism: 'Lord's changes but Lord's remains the same,' he wrote, 'how unchanging is each phase of the everchanging game!'[27] As President of the English Association, Baldwin was a firm advocate of the healing and class-binding capacities of both literature and cricket. Also active in the English Studies movement was George Sampson, an 'immaterial communist', who likewise wrote of cricket as emblematic of a national culture in which social tensions could be resolved: 'You get real communism and "brotherhood of man" at a concert or a theatre or a cricket match. ... and that is the only kind of equality worth seeking for.'[28] By dint of its unimpeachable Englishness, cricket seems to have had a unique ability amongst sports to transcend party-political lines. J. C. Squire, who stood as a Labour candidate in the 1918 general election and as a Liberal in 1924, lauded cricket's rural essence, claiming that 'few men ... would not rather play on a field surrounded by ancient elms and rabbit-haunted bracken than on a better field with flat black lands or gasworks around'. He believed in the utopian idea of the cricket field as a space free of social tension because here 'the distinctions in life are temporarily forgotten: for the time being we live in an ideal republic where Jack is as good as his master, but may be a little better.'[29] Even the more rebellious Siegfried Sassoon recalled a dream in which Blunden and he scored centuries together, wrote a poem celebrating the unchanging and 'apolitical' quality of Lord's ('though the Government has gone vermillion ... Lord's will endure') and produced one of the most idealised of inter-war village cricket narratives, 'The Flower Show Match' (1928).[30] The left-wing ex-Etonian George Orwell – who was to famously dub international sporting competition as 'war minus the shooting'[31] – retained an affection for cricket in its pristine village green form. He chastised communists for jibing at 'Every English institution – tea, cricket, Wordsworth, Charlie Chaplin, kindness to animals'[32] and, in his review of Edmund Blunden's *Cricket Country*, defended the game against left-wing charges of snobbery in a traditional panegyric of amateur sporting values and village cricket's social inclusiveness.[33] J. B. Priestley later provided a variation on the political symbolism of the cricket field in his anti-statist manifesto for Britain, *Out of the People*, a work written during the Second World War. Priestley used the image of village cricket (in which there are 'more in the field than round it')[34] as a metaphor of a more participatory and less centralised politics, an image that reflected his aversion to centralised state socialism.[35]

Such political metaphors of village cricket had been elaborated in a deeply nostalgic form of cricket fiction that emerged in the aftermath of the First World War. Novels such as Hugh de Selincourt's *The Cricket Match* (1924) and its sequel, *The Game of the Season* (1931), apotheosised the literary conventions of the rural cricket field, rendering it a site in which the 'team' signified organic social order under the benevolent authority of the local gentry:

> And each man, as he came on to the ground, got slowly caught up in the spirit of the game, emerging, each in his own way, from the habits of worry and care; as each man was given the chance not too frequently offered in modern life of living for a time outside himself, with a common purpose, in which he took genuine interest; and nearly every man, each in his own way, availed himself of this great, good thing, unconsciously of course, for the most part, but none the less eagerly.[36]

The ending of the novel is equally synoptic: 'Night descended peacefully upon the village of Tillingfold. Rich and poor, old and young, were seeking sleep.'[37]

Neville Cardus and the garden of England

Neville Cardus holds a unique place in the canon of English cricket literature and, although his role as professional cricket writer necessarily distanced him from the cultural space occupied by J. C. Squire and his cricketo-literary cohorts, was a skilful and highly influential manipulator of the pastoral mythology of cricket. Like Mary Mitford in the 1820s, Cardus was conscious of the fictiveness of such imagery and, on a number of occasions, openly admitted that the formulaic village cricket green was an urban idealisation. At the same time he understood the salutary potential of such images and could rhapsodise about the aesthetic pleasures of the rural cricket scene as much as any author. Like so many of his inter-war literary contemporaries, Cardus's disaffection with modernity found imaginative resolution in a form of literary ruralism. For a commentator particularly despondent about the growth of professionalism in cricket and what he perceived as the mechanisation of first-class and Test cricket, such scenes provided a Platonic essence of the game against which the fallen present could be contrasted. In a passage from a piece called 'Cricket Fields and Cricketers' published in the early 1920s, Cardus described the style and ambience of cricket as played in different locations around the country. Though, like any organism, cricket responded to its environment, it was essentially rural:

> One, indeed, has heard folk ask for winter cricket, to be played in some glass-domed 'Olympia' brilliant with electric light. The cricketer with soul knows better than this. He knows that whoever would appreciate cricket rightly must have a sense, as he sits in the sun (there can be no real cricket without sunshine), that he is simply attending to one part, and just one part, of the pageant of summer as it slowly goes along, and yet a part as true to summer as villages in the Cotswolds, stretches of gleaming meadow-land, and pools in the hills. Cricket in high summer is played with the mind of the born lover of it conscious the whole time that all this happy English life is around him – that cricket is but a corner in the teeming garden of the year. Pycroft in *The Cricket Field* writes of 'those sunny hours ... "when the valleys laugh and sing,"' and plainly the memories of them as he wrote his book were as the memories of some sweet distillation of cricket itself.[38]

For Cardus, 'The real cricket that provides the continuity of English tradition is to be found on the village green where it can not be contaminated by professionalism and "imperialism".'[39]

Cardus's anti-imperialist line is seemingly at odds with the major contribution he made to the literary construction of a late Victorian and Edwardian golden age of cricket. The golden age was a cricketing idyll situated between about 1890 and 1914, a pristine point of contrast to the inter-war practice of cricket and, by implication, to the politics, industrial processes and aesthetics of the contemporary national culture. Cardus's construction of the golden age presented a naturally hierarchical social order in which the aristocracy display their inherent superiority through elegant and effortless bodily performance. The English countryside – or at least a highly cultivated version of it – was an important element of this temporal utopia:

> During the golden age of English cricket, the public school flavour could be felt as strongly as in any West End club. When Spooner or K. L. Hutching batted on a lovely summer day you could witness the fine flowerings of all the elegant cultural processes that had gone to the making of these cricketers; you could see their innings as though against a backdrop of distant playing fields, far away from the reach of industry, pleasant lawns stretching to the chaste countryside, lawns well trimmed and conscious of the things that are not done.[40]

Clearly Cardus was not only celebrating the bodily performance of pre-war batsmen such as Spooner and Hutching, but the economic conditions and social relations that apparently enabled such displays of aristocratic style to arise. This nostalgic social vision was also rendered by an aestheticisation of the amateur/professional divide that structured cricket's social relations until 1963. In creating a cast of pre-Great War professional cricketers, Cardus used the literary stereotype of the innocent countryman to endow them with a bucolic charm that highlights by antithesis the pedigree of the gentlemen amateurs. As well as providing humorous, homespun comments, they are presented as good honest rustics in the manner of the contemporary organicist writings of H. J. Massingham. In his deeply nostalgic essay 'Good Days' (1931), Cardus reveals himself as a shameless purveyor of a feudal vision of rural England. In this piece, Cardus introduced the figure of Old William (Bill Attewell), an ex-professional who was subsequently a cricket coach at Shrewsbury School where, for a time, Cardus worked as his assistant. Like Massingham's Samuel Rockall, Old William is organically embedded in a rural environment and thus beyond temporal change. Unlike Cardus's inter-war professionals, Old William's body does not disrupt the aesthetic ideals of cricket discourse, and can thus be seamlessly merged into the English rural landscape: 'he seemed as permanent at Shastbury as the ancient oak tree.' With this organic image connoting organic social order, his respectful comments, patronisingly rendered by Cardus, exemplify social deference and serve to underline the pedigree of Spooner and its relationship to the gentlemanly batting aesthetic: '"It were a pleasure to bowl to Maister Spooner ... his batting were as nice as he were hisself."' Compounded of the innocent swain with a home-spun, folkloric wisdom, and the salutary Wordsworthian archetype, Old William is resolutely pre-modern rather than upwardly mobile or acquisitive:

> He was one of the old school of professional cricketers; I cannot see him in a Morris-Cowley, as any day I can see many contemporary Test match players.

And I cannot see him in suede shoes, or any sort of shoes. William wore enormous boots which has some sort of metal protection built into the edge of the heel. You could hear him coming up the street miles away.

Here Cardus displays a Kenneth Grahame-like hostility to the motor car as a symbol of modernity and conspicuous consumption, whilst Old William's footwear loudly announces his unambiguous class status and unimpeachable masculinity at a safe distance. Old William represents an ideal of a mythical economically and socially immobile social formation that in its political deference merely consented to, and complemented, the cultural authority of the public-school-educated elite: 'I am glad that he loved Shastbury and knew it was a beautiful place.'[41] In these nostalgic evocations of cricket, Cardus was presenting a more desirable picture of an Englishness based upon both social cohesiveness and clearly demarcated inequality under aristocratic benevolence, a seductive vision for many of his contemporaries.

The Englishness of English cricket?

Cardus's highly influential construction of Englishness has continued to exert a cultural hold, as the many reprints and editions of his work testify. Other writers continue to evoke rural cricket as a symbol of the national culture. In a 2000 study of Englishness, *England: An Elegy*, by the philosopher Roger Scruton, cricket represents the expression of various supposedly natural English characteristics. His use of the past tense suggests the loss of the Englishness once symbolised by cricket on the village green:

> The game of cricket was an eloquent symbol of this experience of membership: originally a village institution, which recruited villagers to a common loyalty, it displayed the reticent and understated character of the English ideal: white flannels too clean and pure to suggest physical exertion, long moments of silence and stillness, stifled murmurs of emotion should anything out of the ordinary occur and the occasional burst of subdued applause.[42]

As Scruton himself acknowledges in a footnote, however, this portrayal of village cricket is based on descriptions taken from two literary texts written over one hundred years apart – Mitford's *Our Village* and Francis Brett Young's *Portrait of a Village* (1937), another text that emerged from a period of perceived traumatic social change during which the English rural way of life was seen as further threatened. Clearly Scruton's view of cricket is an intensely literary one. To remark upon this is not to deny the social importance of cricket clubs in village communities then or now, it is only to point out that the notion of village cricket as a symbol of Englishness relies on the existence of a convention of literary and artistic representation, one that is often ideologically inflected. Though it is not surprising to find such a portrayal of cricket in the work of a writer such as Scruton, preoccupied with the need to elegise a mythical construction of Englishness in the face of perceived challenges to it such as multi-racialism and European integration and expansion, such symbolic uses of cricket have been, and continue to be, widespread across the political spectrum. The former Conservative Prime minister, cricket author and former President of Surrey County Cricket Club, John Major, evoked images of shadowy village greens, warm beer and cricket as a desirable image of English society, even though he was shamelessly borrowing his imagery from George Orwell, one of the most influential literary figures on the political left during the middle decades of the twentieth century.[43] In the words of Mike Marqusee, 'This is the myth at cricket's heart, the myth of an enduring and natural social hierarchy, the myth of the village green.'[44]

Such representations of the cricket field were always anachronistic, even in the 1820s, but they continue to have popular resonance and appeal. The England and Wales team currently enters the field at start of play during home Test matches to the strains of William Blake and Hubert Parry's 'Jerusalem', nostalgically associating the game at its highest level with 'England's green and pleasant land'. At the same time, as other chapters in this volume show, cricket is now no more English than it is Australian, Pakistani or West Indian and is now fully implicated within the patterns of global economics. Anglocentric views of cricket seem hopelessly outdated, particularly given the plurality of voices that now surround the game as expressed through the new media in particular. Yet cricket will continue to perform cultural work in England and to yield meanings and invite interpretation. Because of its important role within the former British Empire, it is perhaps ideally placed to symbolise a more inclusive and less backward-looking sense of Englishness. The written word will play a major part in such a process.

NOTES

1 John Bale, *Landscapes of Modern Sport* (Leicester University Press, 1994), pp. 153–65.
2 Thomas Henshaw, ed., *Etymologican lingua anglicanae, seu explication vocum anglicarum etymologica ex propriis fontibus* (London: T. Roycroft, 1671).
3 H. S. Altham and E. W. Swanton, *A History of Cricket* (London: George Allen and Unwin, 1946), p. 19.
4 John Burnby, 'The Kentish Cricketers (in 1773)' in Leslie Frewin (ed.), *The Poetry of Cricket – An Anthology* (London: Macdonald, 1964), pp. 439–41.
5 See Robin Simon and Alistair Smart, *The Art of Cricket* (London: Secker & Warburg, 1983), pp. 16–17; Leigh Hunt, 'Cricket and Exercise in General' in *The Seer; or, Common-Places Refreshed* (London: Edward Moxon, 1840), pp. 34–36;

William Hazlitt, 'Merry England' in A. R. Waller and A. Glover (eds.), *The Collected Works of William Hazlitt, Volume XII: Fugitive Writings* (London: J. M. Dent, 1904); Lord Byron, 'Childish Recollections' in Jerome J. McGann (ed.), *Lord Byron: The Complete Poetical Works* (Oxford: Clarendon, 1980), vol. I, p. 166; William Wordsworth, 'Composed in the Valley Near Dover, on the Day of Landing' in *The Poetical Works of Wordsworth* (London: Frederick Warne, 1885), p. 171.

6 Mary Russell Mitford, *Our Village* (London: Bracken Books, 1992), p. 131.

7 Elizabeth Helsinger, *Rural Scenes and National Representation: Britain, 1815–1850* (Princeton University Press, 1997), pp. 119–24.

8 John Nyren, *The Cricketers of My Time: The Original Version*, Ashley Mote (ed.) (London: Robson Books, 1999), p. 73.

9 Ibid., pp. 71–72.

10 Alun Howkins, 'The Discovery of Rural England' in Robert Colls and Philip Dodds (eds.), *Englishness: Politics and Culture 1880–1920* (London: Croom Helm, 1986), pp. 63–88.

11 Georgina Boyes, *The Imagined Village: Culture, Ideology and the English Folk Revival* (Manchester University Press, 1993), ch. 4; David Matless, *Landscape and Englishness* (London: Reaktion Books, 1998), ch. 4.

12 Martin Wiener, *English Culture and the Decline of the Industrial Spirit 1850–1980* (Harmondsworth: Penguin, 1992), p. 51.

13 Thomas Hutchinson, *Cricket* (London: Country Life, 1905).

14 H. G. Wells, *The War of the Worlds* (London: Heinemann, 1951), p. 158.

15 Wiener, *English Culture*, p. 50.

16 L. P. Hartley, *The Go-Between* (Harmondsworth: Penguin, 1977), pp. 177–89.

17 A. E. Knight, *The Complete Cricketer* (London: Methuen, 1906), pp. 284–85.

18 W. Somerset Maugham, *Cakes and Ale or the Skeleton in the Cupboard* (Harmondsworth: Penguin, 1948), p. 15.

19 George Rostrevor-Hamilton, 'Cricket' in Frewin, *The Poetry of Cricket*, p. 103.

20 'A Country Vicar', *Cricket Memories by a Country Vicar* (London: Methuen, 1930), p. 242.

21 See J. M. Barrie, *The Greenwood Hat* (London: P. Davis, 1927); David Rayvern-Allen, *Peter Pan and Cricket* (London: Constable, 1988).

22 J. M. Barrie, *Cricket* (London: by the author, 1926).

23 Patrick F. McDevitt, *'May the Best Man Win': Sport, Masculinity and Nationalism in Great Britain and the Empire, 1880–1935* (Basingstoke: Palgrave Macmillan, 2004), pp. 83–88.

24 Edmund Blunden, 'The Season Opens' in Frewin, *The Poetry of Cricket*, p. 378.

25 A. G. Macdonell, *England, Their England* (London: Picador, 1983), p. 74.

26 Ibid., p. 207.

27 Stanley Baldwin, *Our Inheritance: Speeches and Addresses* (London: Hodder & Stoughton, 1928), p. 303.

28 George Sampson, 'Preface' to *England for the English: A Chapter on National Education* (Cambridge University Press, 1926), p. x.

29 Quoted in Eric Midwinter, *Quill on Willow* (Chichester: Aeneas Press, 2001), p. 135.

30 Siegfried Sassoon, *Diaries 1923–1925*, Rupert Hart-Davis (ed.) (London: Faber & Faber, 1985), p. 92; Sassoon, 'The Blues at Lord's', *The Nation*, 27 December

1924, pp. 42–43; Sassoon, 'The Flower Show Match' in Andrew Pinnell (ed.), *A Celebration of a Cricketing Man* (Bristol: Makingspace, 1996), pp. 19–38.

31 George Orwell, 'The Sporting Spirit' in *George Orwell: Essays* (Harmondsworth: Penguin, 1994), pp. 321–24.

32 Sonia Orwell and Ian Angus (eds.), *The Collected Essays, Journalism and Letters of George Orwell, Volume 1: An Age Like This 1920–1940* (London: Secker & Warburg, 1968), p. 357.

33 George Orwell 'Review of Edmund Blunden's Cricket Country' in *The Collected Essays, Journalism and Letters of George Orwell, Volume 2: My Country Right or Left 1940–1943*, Sonia Orwell and Ian Angus (eds.) (London: Secker & Warburg, 1968), pp. 47–50.

34 J. B. Priestley, *Out of the People* (London: Collins, 1941), p. 101.

35 Kevin Davey, *English Imaginaries: Six Studies in Anglo-British Modernity* (London: Lawrence & Wishart, 1999), p. 4.

36 Hugh de Selincourt, *The Cricket Match* (Oxford University Press, 1987), p. 68.

37 Ibid., p. 194.

38 Neville Cardus, *Days in the Sun* (London: Grant Richards, 1924), p. 27.

39 Neville Cardus, *A Cricketer's Book* (London: Grant Richards, 1922), p. 13.

40 Neville Cardus, *English Cricket* (London: Prion, 1945), p. 106.

41 Neville Cardus, *Good Days* (London: Jonathan Cape, 1934), pp. 100–104.

42 Roger Scruton, *England: An Elegy* (London: Chatto & Windus, 2001), p. 14.

43 *Independent on Sunday*, 25 April 1993.

44 Mike Marqusee, *Anyone But England: Cricket and the National Malaise* (London: Verso, 1994), p. 29.

2

ROB LIGHT

Cricket in the eighteenth century

Revolutionary events that were taking place across the English Channel during that summer may have had a far wider historical significance, but on 26 June 1789 one of the most symbolic matches in the history of cricket took place in what was to become Dorset Square, London. It was on this day that an eleven representing the Hambledon club took the field on the first of only two recorded occasions at Thomas Lord's ground, the home of the recently formed Marylebone Cricket Club.[1]

This brief association between what had been the game's most influential institution until this point and the organisation which was soon to take its place clearly marks a watershed in the history of cricket. But although the game's formative period of development was drawing to a close, this match offers a profound illustration of cricket's accelerated growth during the eighteenth century and the distinctive dynamics that shaped it. Whilst the significance it later assumed was clearly not yet apparent, the match was still a major event. Cricket had been at the forefront of a thriving commercial leisure culture in London for the previous forty or so years and any major contest such as this one received a considerable level of publicity.[2] Both teams were also assembled by members of the aristocracy, which reflected how far the predominance of the social elite at cricket's highest level had influenced the game's development. Their growing involvement resulted in a version of its laws first being codified in 1744 and published in 1752. The impetus for this set of regulations came from a group of cricket clubs, and Hambledon's position at the forefront of the game demonstrated the way in which such organisations had thrived as they became an important nexus for the Georgian gentry's pervading culture of sociability and idiosyncratic leisure habits.

Hambledon's victory in the match also reflected the origins and continued popular strength of cricket in the south-eastern counties of England where it had been played as a folk game since at least the fifteenth century. It was inspired by an innings of 94 from William Beldham, a twenty-three-year-old farmer who learned to play in his home village of Farnham and was soon to become the leading batsman of the era. His grounding in the game demonstrated how cricket first became a strong focal point of communal identity in these vibrant rural parishes, and through its success over the previous four decades Hambledon had also come to embody the sense of local and regional pride that marked cricket in this context.

The Hambledon club also marked the convergence of these various strands in the development of the eighteenth-century game and consequently has often provided the focus for writing on cricket during this period.[3] In the most important of these works David Underdown expertly set the development of both the club and the game within the broader contemporary social, economic and cultural context of eighteenth-century Britain.[4]

The aim here, however, is to offer a different perspective by concentrating on the context which shaped Hambledon cricket, and the one pivotal feature of the eighteenth-century game that bound its key themes together was highlighted in an advertisement which was published by the *Morning Star* prior to the 1789 match. It explained that 'Eleven of the Hambledon club are to play thirteen of *All England* … the odds on the side of the Hambledon club are now six to five. The sum played for is considerable, the bets very great.'[5] The stake was in fact 1,000 guineas, a figure way beyond the means of the farmers and tradesmen who were paid to play in the match. But they were representing members of the aristocracy and gentry whose resources and immense appetite for gambling enabled them to make such wagers on a regular basis.

'To pursue that wholesome Exercise': cricket and the eighteenth-century aristocracy

The appropriation of cricket by the gentry around the start of the eighteenth century shaped a new era in the game's development. Their growing involvement initiated a fundamental shift in cricket's social and cultural dynamics which altered general perceptions of the game. Before the start of the eighteenth century most references to cricket relate to prosecutions for Sabbath-breaking or associate it with the perceived immorality of other recreations that were popular amongst the lower classes. Indeed, as late as 1712 a Puritan pamphlet which was written as a deterrent against Sabbath-breaking gave:

> … a very dismal Account of four Young-Men, who made a Match to Play at Cricket, on Sunday the 6th of this Instant July 1712, in a meadow near Maiden Head Thicket; and as they were at Play, there arose out of the Ground

a Man in Black with a Cloven-Foot, which put them in a great Consternation; but as they stood in the Frighted Condition, the Devil flew up in the Air, in a Dark Cloud with Flashes of fire, and in his Room he left a very Beautiful Woman, and Robert Yates and Richard Moors hastily stepping up to her, being Charm'd with her Beauty went to kiss her, but in the Attempt they instantly fell down Dead. The other two, Simon Jackson and George Grantham, seeing this Tragical Sight, ran home to Maiden-Head, where they now lye in a Distracted Condition.[6]

However, notices of matches between groups of gentlemen who endowed the game with a far more virtuous image began to appear at around this time. For example, in 1730 the *British Journal* explained that 'His Grace the Duke of Richmond, and several other young Noblemen and Gentlemen, have begun to divert themselves each Morning, at the Play of Cricket in Hyde Park and design to pursue that wholesome Exercise every fair Morning during Spring' [sic].[7]

But there was far more behind the increasing aristocratic interest in cricket than its value as a healthy form of recreation. The patronage of popular sport and entertainment played an important role in reinforcing relationships that underscored the eighteenth-century social structure of Britain. Members of the aristocracy often staged lavish events which aimed to attract a wide audience in order to court popularity and emphasise the importance of a common English culture that crossed class divisions. Such displays of wealth and power were also a means of demonstrating economic and social standing through which the position of the aristocracy at the head of society could be reinforced. Consequently, matches like the one in 1725 'between a set of Gamesters headed by his Grace the D. of Richmond on one side and a set headed by Sir William Gage, Bart and Knight of the Bath' at Berry Hill near Arundel in Sussex began to take place. It was watched by a 'vast concourse of people', before 'his Grace the Duke of Norfolk gave a splendid Ball and Entertainment that Night at the Castle' [sic].[8]

As well as offering suitable opportunities for their social and economic status to be expressed, cricket was clearly a form of recreation which could also accommodate the distinctive leisure habits of the Georgian aristocracy. The game provided a convivial environment in which other sociable activities could take place and offered a natural focal point for the pervading contemporary associational culture. So as formal matches involving groups of gentlemen in places such as Dartford in Kent and Chertsey in Surrey became increasingly common, a wave of cricket clubs was established. In the earliest reference to such an organisation 'the Gentlemen known by the name of the London Club, who are composed of several parishes in London, Southwark &c' attended 'a meeting at the Three Tons and Rummer in Grace

Church Street' in 1722.[9] It was held to make a match against a team from the 'Parish of Dartford' where a club was formed in 1756, and by the 1770s similar organisations were also active at Bridge Hill, Bishopsbourne and Coxheath in Kent, Coulsdon in Surrey, the Star and Garter Inn in Pall Mall and, of course, Hambledon.[10]

It was this growing structure of formal clubs that initiated the wider regulation of the game. The adoption of a leadership role in cricket by a select number of clubs in the south-east of England mirrored that of elite societies in other areas of British life, such as medicine and the law. These organisations recognised the need to set out and maintain uniform standards and began to regulate their respective professions during the eighteenth century. As we shall see, the growing popularity of cricket began to demand a degree of rationalisation for much less respectable reasons. But the 1744 laws of the game were agreed upon at a meeting of clubs initiated by the Star and Garter Club in London, and it was this organisation which led subsequent revisions before Hambledon, briefly, and then Marylebone Cricket Club took on the responsibility.

The membership of these organisations provides a clear reason why they were looked upon to provide leadership for the sport: all three included high-ranking aristocrats. Those representatives of the Star and Garter Club, who presided over the laws of the game, were described as a 'Committee of Noblemen and Gentlemen' in publications of their regulations and it was also members of this august organisation who eventually formed the Marylebone Cricket Club.[11] They included the Earl of Winchelsea and Col. the Hon. Charles Lennox who both provided Thomas Lord with financial backing to open his new ground in 1787.[12] By this time both men were raising teams to play the Hambledon club which, in its heyday, included aristocrats such as Lord Dunkellin and Viscount Palmerston, father of the Victorian statesman, as well as the renowned patrons of eighteenth-century cricket the Earl of Tankerville and the Duke of Dorset.[13]

Participation in cricket clubs, however, was not confined to members of the aristocracy. Although specific information relating to clubs in London's surrounding market towns is scarce, it is likely that the expanding urban gentry rather than members of the nobility formed such organisations in places like Dartford and Bromley in Kent and Croydon in Surrey. The membership pattern of some more prestigious clubs also developed on a relatively broad social basis, which suggests they began to serve as a locus of social formation for an expanding middle class during this period. Even in an organisation with the stature of Hambledon, recent arrivals in Hampshire society, professional men and those whose status was built upon new wealth, such as Edward Hale, the son of a local surgeon, and Captain Erasmus Gower, were able to mix both with each other and with members of the traditional landed elite.[14]

These organisations were primarily aimed at providing recreational activities for their members, and participation in the sport often took place on a social footing in the form of 'pick up' matches between teams of members. During the 1780s, clubs at Coxheath, Bridge Hill and the Sudbury 'cricket society' in Suffolk all staged such matches on a regular basis. Dining and drinking were usually incorporated into proceedings and at Coxheath the day's play was concluded with a dinner which cost 2 shillings for members and 3 shillings for non-members. Professionals were also employed to raise the standard of play. They received expenses for horse hire, 1 shilling and 6 pence for food and drink, and a payment of 5 shillings if on the winning side, 2 shillings and 6 pence if they lost.[15] Matches between teams representing different clubs also became common and again these could be primarily social events. But they nearly always carried a competitive edge in the form of a wager and this was clearly the case in a match at Shacklewell near Stoke Newington in 1743 between 'eleven Gentlemen belonging to a cricket club there and eleven Gentlemen of the Westminster club, for a considerable Sum of Money'.[16]

Indeed it is unlikely that any of these developments could have taken place had cricket not been ideally suited to gambling, which was arguably the most popular leisure activity in Georgian society. Before the start of the nineteenth century it was uncommon for matches not to carry a wager between the participants, whoever they were. But at the pinnacle of the sport stood the 'Great Matches', in which teams assembled by cricket's aristocratic rivals played for high stakes. Many of these contests took place between two sides that represented individual patrons, and as early as 1735 it was announced that a match between 'his Royal Highness the Prince of Wales and the Earl of Middlesex for 1,000 L [£1,000], is to be played on Bromley common by Eleven of a side'.[17] However, individuals or groups of backers also put together teams that played in the guise of counties, such as Kent and Sussex, or as All England, or sometimes bearing the names of leading aristocratic clubs. So, for example, in 1776 Hambledon played matches against England in June for £525 and Surrey in August for £1,050.[18]

''Tis lawful for the Duke': the structure and culture of eighteenth-century cricket

Significant sums of money were wagered upon cricket matches by members of the eighteenth-century social elite and this created a heightened sense of competition that shaped the game in its pre-modern context. But the key concept in understanding the distinctive culture and structure that drove cricket forward during this period is the 'challenge'.

Although on a fundamental level the challenge was a necessary means of organising matches at a time of irregular work patterns, it also introduced the use of written regulations for cricket, and this process reveals much about the cultural dynamic which prevailed in the pre-modern period. Despite its accelerated early development, cricket, like other sports, was a localised and informal game in the first half of the eighteenth century, not far removed from its folk origins. This meant that, alongside the basic parameters of the game, variant elements also existed, and it was necessary to clarify which of these would be used in any single contest.

As in other sports, the large amounts of money wagered on matches by the aristocratic patrons of cricket meant that disputes were relatively common, and court cases held to settle them were not unknown. These could prove expensive and inconclusive and on 16 May 1719 the *Saturday Post* explained how:

> Last week a Tryal was brought at Guildhall before Lord Chief Justice Pratt, between two Companies of Cricket Players, the Men of Kent Plaintiffs and the Men of London Defendants, for Sixty Pounds played for at Cricket, and after a long hearing and near 200 l. expended in the cause, my Lord not understanding the Game, ordered them to play it over again.[19]

So it became common for contests to be governed by written contractual agreements. A set of regulations was consequently made during the process of issuing and accepting the challenge, which aimed to prevent disputes by both clarifying various aspects of play and setting out the terms of the wager. The historian Adrian Harvey has identified the distinction between these twin purposes as a 'crucial difference between codes and contracts' [sic].[20] He defines the sporting 'code' as a means by which the specifics of general play were usually governed, and it was from these agreements that the generally accepted laws of the game evolved. The 'contract', however, related to separate arrangements for individual matches that usually referred to the wager, such as the means of arbitration, the composition of the teams and the size of the stake.

The distinction between the 'code' and the 'contract' is clearly demonstrated in an early set of 'Articles of Agreement', which presided over two matches between the Duke of Richmond and Mr Alan Broderick in 1727. Of the sixteen points that were set out in the document, the following six relate to the code by which the match was played, and state:

> 2nd. That the wickets shall be pitched in a fair and even place, at 23 yards from each other.

3rd. A ball caught, cloathed or not cloathed the Striker is out.

4th. When a Ball is caught out, the Stroke counts nothing.

5th. Catching out behind the Wicket allowed.

7th. That 12 Gamesters shall play on each side.

14th. The Batt Men for every One they count are to touch the Umpires Stick.[21]

Each of these points relates to a familiar aspect of cricket that is covered by its present laws and this set of 'Articles' is generally seen as the first written codification of the game. It is likely that, along with similar agreements, it provided a model which was adhered to in other contests before attempts to establish a single more generally accepted code began with the publication of the laws in 1752. Consequently, the precedent of written regulations was established for a game that had been built on informal oral folk traditions, which became a key feature of modern sport.

But the purpose of this and other similar documents bears little relation to the concept of fair play that underscored the widespread development of codified rules in sport around 150 years later. The central function of the 1727 'Articles of Agreement' are dealt with by the 'Articles' which relate to the 'contract' and attend to the conditions that presided over the wager. Most importantly, the tenth 'Article' stated 'that each Match shall be for twelve guineas of each Side'. Although this was a relatively small sum, the contests were still keenly competitive and the sixth 'Article' stated:

> That 'tis lawful for the Duke of Richmond to choose the Gamesters, who have played in either of his Grace's two last matches with Sir William Gage; and that 'tis lawful for Mr Broderick to choose the Gamesters within three miles of Pepperharowe, provided they actually lived there last Lady day.[22]

By the 1720s, wealthy patrons had already begun to employ leading players on their estates in order for them to play cricket. So, as Lady Day was traditionally the day for hiring servants, this regulation was clearly aimed at ensuring that both the Duke and Mr Broderick were aware of the players they would encounter by preventing new men from being engaged after the agreement had been made.

Competition was clearly fundamental to eighteenth-century cricket and the challenge provided the key means through which it was articulated. But the versatility of the concept meant that these competitive dynamics were not confined to expressing the rivalries of aristocratic patrons. In the rural parishes that surrounded London, those lower down the social order played in less formal challenge matches and despite the lack of written references to cricket in this context some details have survived. They suggest that the popular game served as an important expression of local identity as early as 1708, when a Kentish farmer declared in his diary 'Wee beat Ash Street at Cricketts'.[23]

By the second half of the eighteenth century the sense of local identity that was invested in cricket amongst these rural communities had been transposed into the elite context of the sport. Leading players from Sussex, Hampshire and Kent began to gain wider recognition and find engagements to play in the 'Great Matches'. Consequently, William Beldham could later speak of how these men became 'the pride and honour in the parishes' when describing the way local people, in the villages where most early professionals learned to play the game, followed their performances in London.[24]

The synthesis of aristocratic patronage and local identity was most profound at Hambledon and played a key role in the club's success. Between 1770 and 1790 it has been estimated that the predominantly professional teams which represented the club played for £32,527 in stake money and won £22,497.[25] But the roots of both the club and most of its players in rural Hampshire meant that on occasions such as when Hambledon played England for £1,050 in 1777, the importance of the contest went far beyond the stake money that had been wagered. The compelling sense of local identity that was invested in these matches was vividly expressed in John Nyren's famous reminiscence that:

> There was high feasting on Broadhalfpenny during the solemnity of one of our grand matches. Oh it was a heart-stirring sight to witness the multitude forming a complete and dense circle round that noble green. Half the county would be present, and all their hearts with us – Little Hambledon, pitted against all England was a proud thought for the Hampshire men. Defeat was glory in a struggle – victory, indeed, made us 'a little lower than angels'.[26]

'The pride and honour of the parishes': professionalism and eighteenth-century cricket

The growing prevalence of professional players in the 'Great Matches' offers a further insight into the wider social, economic and cultural relations that shaped the game during this period. Initially these men were employed through a form of 'retained' or 'indentured' professionalism, by which they were given token jobs on the estates of aristocratic cricket patrons and spent the greater part of the summer months playing in challenge matches. Thomas Waymark, who was a groom on the Duke of Richmond's estate at Goodwood in the 1720s, is the earliest known example of a professional cricketer. According to the Goodwood accounts he was paid seven shillings a week plus board from Christmas 1729 until the following summer. Waymark also has the distinction of producing the first recorded match-winning performance by a professional player. On 6 September 1728, the *London Journal* described how, whilst playing for 'Sussex, Surrey and Hants' against Kent, a groom of the Duke of Richmond's, who is widely accepted to have been Waymark, 'signalized himself by such extraordinary agility and dexterity to the surprise of the spectators which were some thousands and 'tis reckoned he turned the tide of victory which for some years has been generally on the Kentish side'.[27] Leading players continued to be engaged in this way throughout the eighteenth century, and in the 1770s John Minshull, the man who scored the first recorded century, worked as a gardener on the Duke of Dorset's estate.[28]

But although the finance and opportunities that enabled professionalism to first develop were provided by aristocratic patrons, the origin of the players offers a further illustration of cricket's origins as a folk game and its continued vitality as a popular recreation. The matches which took place between local parishes in the rural south-east of England clearly developed a vibrant competitive culture in which talented local players could come to the attention of aristocratic patrons. Although the exact social backgrounds of the earliest recorded indentured professionals are largely unknown, it is likely that these players worked at the lower end of the rural economy, as they were willing to accept fairly menial positions on the aristocratic estates in order to play in major cricket matches. So the cultural association between professionalism and the lower classes, which later came to mean much more in cricket, existed from the outset and already offered a way into a life of greater possibilities for men of humble backgrounds.

By the second half of the eighteenth century, however, employment opportunities for professional cricketers had begun to expand. The game's growing popularity led to an increase in demand for major matches, and a form of independent professionalism was developed that saw players receive payment for the individual contests in which they took part. The introduction of match payments saw a subtle but significant shift in the economic background of professional players, which became even more prevalent during the next century. Although they were still members of the lower classes, the players who were engaged to play cricket through this system commonly enjoyed a relatively independent economic status. Many were tradesmen or farmers who were clearly not willing to give up their occupation for more menial work on the aristocratic estates. So, for example, when Lord John Sackville's Kent XI faced an All England XI at the Artillery Ground in 1744, his team included Mills of Bromley, who was a bookmaker, and Hodswell of Dartford, a tanner.[29]

The Hambledon team became a model for this type of independent professionalism. Travelling expenses and a system of fees for both practices and 'Great Matches' were paid to the farmers, publicans and tradesmen who made up the club's match-play team. They received 'four shillings if winners and three shillings if losers' on practice days and, according to William Beldham, five guineas for a win and three guineas if they lost in the 'Great Matches' during the 1780s.[30]

In view of subsequent attitudes towards gambling in cricket, it comes as little surprise that these players have been widely recognised for achievements other than the phenomenal amount of stake money they won. Regular practice and competitive matches between the era's leading players saw advancements in playing technique and equipment manufacture take place at Hambledon that resulted in significant changes to the way the game was played. First Richard Nyren and then David Harris developed the practice of length bowling, which exploited the irregular bounce of uneven pitches in a way that the old style skimming delivery did not. Then, in response, batsmen like John Small and 'Silver' Billy Beldham pioneered the straight bat approach, through which they used forward and back play and brought the bat down in a vertical position. Indeed, Small, a master bat maker, turned his playing innovation into a literal one by first changing the shape of the bat from its original curved form to one similar to that which is used today. John Nyren later described the benefits of Small's technique in his book *The Young Cricketer's Tutor*, which included instructions on 'How to play at a ball dropped rather short of a length on the off side of the wicket'. In it Nyren explained how 'Old Small, one of the finest batsmen of his own day and perhaps of any other, always played such balls with an upright bat; he would pass his left foot across the wicket and this action gave him power and command over the ball'.[31]

But the importance of professionals within the context of eighteenth-century cricket was perhaps most clearly demonstrated through the position they were afforded by the game's aristocratic patrons. It was marked by a level of respect which differed significantly from the inferior status that was later ascribed to them in first-class cricket and could result in a blurring of the social hierarchy that was remarkable even for this period. Indeed, professionals sometimes captained sides that included members of the aristocracy, and in 1744 Valentine Romney, who was employed as a gardener on the Duke of Dorset's estate at Knole, led a Kent Eleven which included his employer and the Duke of Richmond in a match against All England.[32]

'The greatest Match that ever was play'd': cricket and commercialism in the eighteenth century

The game's growth also meant that professional players could gain considerable popular recognition during the eighteenth century and some became star attractions in the increasingly commercialised context of cricket in London. Along with events such as foot races and prizefights, cricket was staged at commercial venues and promoted to attract a popular audience in the capital throughout most of the eighteenth century. Publicans were often at the centre of these events, and the Ram at Smithfield was rated for a cricket field as early as 1668.[33]

However, the first important venue for cricket was the Artillery Ground in Finsbury, which grew in prominence whilst George Smith was the proprietor in the 1730s. Smith clearly recognised the growing commercial potential of cricket and was able to attract large crowds to watch the game by developing a relatively sophisticated business strategy. As well as hosting the 'Great Matches', he staged more explicitly commercial events such as single-wicket contests in which leading professionals played against each other in teams of less than eleven or as individuals. These events were also publicised regularly in the press, and the growing celebrity of leading players was used to promote them. For example, in 1743 an estimated 10,000 people attended a contest which was publicised in the *Daily Advertiser* as a:

> Match at Cricket in the Artillery Ground, London, for Five Hundred Guineas viz, Hodswell of Dartford, Romley of Sevenoaks, and Cutbush of Maidstone, against Sawyer of Richmond, Newland of Slindon in Sussex, and Bryant of London; as this is the greatest Match that ever was play'd three on a side, all persons are desired to be particular in keeping the full bounds of the line. [sic][34]

The large crowds that watched cricket during this period also offer an insight into the way the game became embedded in the popular culture of London and parts of the south-east of England during the eighteenth century. Gambling was equally popular amongst the lower classes and considerable amounts of betting often took place at matches. Furthermore, crowd disturbances were not unknown. In 1731, the Duke of Richmond's Eleven was 'greatly insulted by the mob some of the men having their shirts tore off their backs' following a match with Mr Chambers' Eleven' [sic].[35] There had been much betting on the result but the contest ended in a draw with Chambers's side needing just '8 or 10 Notches with 4 or 5 more to have come in' [sic].[36] Direct popular action against perceived injustice was a customary practice in contemporary society and was clearly not confined to redressing breaches of the 'moral economy'.[37] George Smith used a ring of benches to keep spectators away from the playing area.[38] But in 1744 'there was great disorder' during a contest between 'the county of Kent and All England' at the Artillery Ground and 'it was with difficulty the match was played out'.[39]

The incident resulted in a temporary rise in admission charge from 2d to 6d, which proved unpopular and costly to Smith's business. However, the crowd continued to exert its own form of moral justice and after a pickpocket was caught stealing during a match at the Artillery Ground in 1746 'he was most severely duck'd by the populace'.[40]

Nevertheless, the model pioneered by George Smith was followed by other entrepreneurs well into the next century. Thomas Lord's ground staged commercial events throughout the first fifty years of its existence and in June 1800, for example, a contest between All England and Surrey for 1,000 guineas was advertised in the *Morning Herald*.[41] Indeed, during the 1820s this form of commercial cricket played a pivotal role as the game first spread across the expanding urban industrial regions of the north and midlands. An estimated crowd of 20,000 watched Sheffield play Nottingham for 200 sovereigns at Darnall, Sheffield in 1824.[42] The Nottingham team for this contest was assembled by William Clarke, who later opened a commercial venue at Trent Bridge, Nottingham in 1843. It was also Clarke who took the model of professional-centred commercial cricket a step further in 1846 when he began touring the British Isles with a team that included the leading professionals of the day. Clarke's All England Eleven is widely recognised to have played a pivotal role as cricket became a sport of truly national dimensions, and his successors later looked to exploit the potential of new commercial markets by undertaking international tours which stimulated the game's growth overseas.

The legacy of eighteenth-century cricket

Cricket's growth during the eighteenth century was clearly remarkable. Yet, as the Hambledon Eleven's first appearance at Lord's illustrates, for all its progress the game continued to revolve around the distinctive social, economic and cultural relations of pre-modern society throughout this period. Consequently, cricket's development was also constrained by the inherent limitations of contemporary Britain. As commercial and demographic growth was heavily concentrated in and around London before the start of the nineteenth century, the high level of aristocratic influence, popular interest and commercial investment that stimulated cricket's growth in the region did not exist elsewhere. So although the increasing spread of British influence overseas meant the game was played as far afield as North America from 1710 and India from 1721, and whilst even ill-timed plans for a team to tour Paris were made in 1789, little sustained development took place away from the south-east of England before the nineteenth century.

When economic conditions which could support the game's development spread elsewhere in the country, however, they were built around a new set of social economic and cultural relations which began to transform the face of cricket. The changing structure of agriculture in rural south-eastern England resulted in a significant reduction in work and wages which began to undermine many of the region's communities. Their decline was met by an increase in social unrest that exacerbated the general withdrawal from public life of the aristocracy following the French Revolution. The fusion of aristocratic enthusiasm and popular vitality, which characterised the eighteenth-century game, largely disappeared. Aristocratic involvement became centred on London, and especially MCC, at the expense of the game's rural heartland. At its highest level, cricket was increasingly dominated by social relations that were shaped by class divisions which prevailed until the end of the next century.

Yet, as David Underdown noted, there was a 'shift in the game's regional vitality to the industrial Midlands and the North, to Yorkshire, Lancashire, and Nottinghamshire, where by the later 1820s the game was spreading rapidly and attracting great crowds'.[43] Here, cricket's growth continued to be driven by the competitive pre-modern culture and structure of sport. Initially, through challenge matches and the professional-centred commercial model pioneered by George Smith, then developed by William Clarke, cricket's popular cultural traditions were transposed into the new urban industrial setting where they later found expression through the development of league cricket. Indeed, it could be argued that commercialism and the kind of popular professional-centred spectacle that marked the eighteenth-century game have re-emerged in the twenty-first century as cricket enters a new phase of development.

NOTES

1. Ashley Mote, *The Glory Days of Cricket: The Extraordinary Story of Broadhalfppeny Down* (London: Robson Books, 1997), pp. 222–29.
2. *St. James's Chronicle or the British Evening Post*, 2 July 1789; *Whitehall Evening Post*, 2 July 1789; *Morning Star*, 3 July 1789; *World*, 3 July 1789.
3. See David Underdown, *The Start of Play: Cricket and Culture in Eighteenth-Century England* (Harmondsworth: Penguin, 2000) and Mote, *The Glory Days of Cricket*.
4. Underdown, *Start of Play*.
5. *Morning Star*, 18 August 1789.
6. In Michael Davie and Simon Davie, *The Faber Book of Cricket* (London: Faber and Faber, 1987), p. 260.
7. *British Journal*, 11 April 1730.
8. *Daily Journal*, 26 July 1725.

9   *Weekly Journal or British Gazetteer*, 21 July 1722.

10 Underdown, *Start of Play*, pp. 67–158.

11 Christopher Brookes, *English Cricket: The Game and its Players Through the Ages* (Exeter: Weidenfeld and Nicolson, 1978), illustration 5.

12 Underdown, *Start of Play*, p. 160.

13 Ibid., pp. 126–51.

14 Ibid., pp. 130–34.

15 Ibid., pp. 126–27.

16 *Daily Advertiser*, 3 June 1743.

17 *Old Whig or The Constant Protestant*, 24 July 1735.

18 Mote, *The Glory Days of Cricket*, pp. 182, 188.

19 *Saturday Post*, 16 May 1719.

20 Adrian Harvey, *The Beginnings of a Commercial Sporting Culture in Britain, 1793–1850* (Farnham: Ashgate, 2004), p. 116.

21 www.peperharow.info/cricket.htm (accessed 15 March 2010).

22 Ibid.

23 Brookes, *English Cricket*, p. 24.

24 Underdown, *Start of Play*, p. 170.

25 Keith A. P. Sandiford, *Cricket and the Victorians* (Aldershot: Scolar Press, 1994), p. 26.

26 Ashley Mote (ed.), *John Nyren's The Cricketers of my Time: The Original Version* (London: Robson Books, 1998), p. 71.

27 Derek Birley, *A Social History of English Cricket* (London: Aurum Press, 1999), p. 20.

28 Brookes, *English Cricket*, p. 61.

29 Ibid., p. 62.

30 Ibid., p. 58; Underdown, *Start of Play*, p. 119.

31 Mote, *John Nyren's The Cricketers of my Time*, p. 133.

32 Underdown, *Start of Play*, p. 66.

33 Rowland Bowen, *Cricket: A History of its Growth and Development Throughout the World* (London: Eyre and Spottiswoode, 1970), p. 262.

34 *Daily Advertiser*, 7 July 1743, 8 July 1743, 11 July 1743; *Westminster Journal or New Weekly Miscellany*, 16 July 1743.

35 *Daily Post*, 25 August 1731.

36 *Daily Journal*, 25 August 1731.

37 E. P. Thompson, 'The Moral Economy of the English Crowd in the 18th Century', *Past & Present*, 50, 1971, pp. 76–136.

38 *London Evening Post*, 24 July 1744.

39 *Daily Advertiser*, 29 June 1744.

40 *Westminster Journal or New Weekly Miscellany*, 14 June 1746.

41 *Morning Chronicle*, 10 June 1800.

42 *Sheffield Independent*, 11 September 1824.

43 Underdown, *Start of Play*, p. 209.

3

DAVID FRITH

Corruption in cricket

For 100 years or more, since the mid-Victorians elevated it to something approaching a holy devotion, the game of cricket stood principally for gentlemanly, and preferably heroic, conduct. So pure was cricket's image that it sometimes resembled a branch of Christianity. Any man or boy who behaved in a disapproved fashion on the field was branded a 'bounder'. Englishmen took the game with them as a symbol of fair play wherever they advanced the causes of the British Empire.

In stark contrast, in recent decades cricket at the highest level has been dragged into the realms of brash show business, financial profit almost the sole driving force among those who aspired to the responsibility of preserving and steering the game. Cricketers at this level usually seek to justify excesses by pointing to the fact that this is their means of livelihood in a competitive world where the millions – even billions – of pounds, dollars and rupees blind almost everybody to the ethical values of old. By the twenty-first century, so remote a vision has the earlier benevolent concept of sport become that even in minor club matches instances of cheating and abuse, physical as well as verbal, are not rare.

Corruption in cricket embraces a multitude of sins, including biased umpiring, fraudulent promotions, deliberate preparation of pitches to suit home teams, thefts from dressing-rooms and of memorabilia, or – a rare occurrence this, but witnessed at international level – deliberate scuffing of the pitch by a fieldsman. All these offences have soiled the virtuous façade of cricket's traditional image.

In the 1990s, frantic headlines flashed as accusations of ball-tampering emerged, a widespread and complex problem. Pakistan's Wasim Akram and Waqar Younis were at the eye of the storm for their unexplained late swing at high speed. The conclusion of many opponents was that these bowlers must have been gouging the ball. Then came the realisation that a ball may be made to deviate late in its flight path not solely through the aerodynamic principle that the less shiny side drags it down, but now also by a method known as 'reverse swing' (caused by applying a copious amount of natural moisture to one side while letting the other become rough). This had the theorists chattering, speculating and demonstrating. Widespread suspicion of tampering receded, the sense of relief aided by the new procedure of regular examination of the ball by the umpires.

To a degree it remains true that there is nothing new in cricket. Ted Peate, a Yorkshire slow left-armer of the 1880s, was one bowler who slyly tampered with the ball, in his case by surreptitiously applying mud to one side of it to create bias. There is no scarcity of early recorded instances of cheating, bribery and match-fixing. Wider society, however, had no cause to recoil on a grand scale until the dark deeds which hung depressingly over the last few years of the twentieth century and the early years of the twenty-first.

Even so, modern cricket has yet to throw up anything quite of a magnitude to match the dishonourable deed of which William Lambert was adjudged guilty in 1818.[1] It was not that he was the only cricketer deemed to have 'thrown' a match, because he wasn't. Such a sin was anything but a rarity. What shocked the comparatively small cricket world of the time, when pitches were usually rough but bowling was still underhand, was the revelation that the crime had been committed by a cricketer who by general consent was the pre-eminent batsman in the land – and therefore in the whole world at a time when no cricket of consequence was played outside England.

A strongly built Surrey man with all-round cricket skill, Lambert had astounded everyone by scoring two hundreds in a match at the semi-rural Lord's ground only the summer before. But as a member of the so-called England side which played against Twenty-two of Nottingham in Nottingham, Lambert was stumped for 7 and caught for 9; and although he caught, stumped or bowled thirteen of his opponents he was deemed, through his batting failures, to have engineered his team's unexpected downfall by 30 runs. The noblemen at Lord's banned him from playing at their select ground thereafter. Today, Lambert would have been hunted by television crews and reporters. Almost 200 years ago, he quietly faded from view, although it is thought that it could have been none other than Lambert who unburdened himself to the Reverend James Pycroft, who devoted pages of his 1851 classic *The Cricket-Field* to an interview with an old cricketer: 'But for that Nottingham match I could have said with a clear conscience to a gentleman like you that all which was said was false, and I never sold a match in my life; but now I can't.'[2]

Pycroft also recorded a precious interview with the celebrated Surrey batsman 'Silver Billy' Beldham, who, like the previous witness, declared that betting and match-fixing were rife early in the nineteenth century. It seems

that only after it had touched excessive levels did it undergo a natural evap-
oration. This was probably expedited by the sense of shame stemming from
its exposure.

The Green Man and Still, a tavern in London's Oxford Street, was where
cricket's 'underworld' used to congregate, mixing with the players, planning
and rigging matches as well as individual performances for the benefit of
the few. There was no International Cricket Council Anti-Corruption and
Security Unit (ACSU) to shadow them and monitor them and move in to press
charges; nor did the shady dealers and gamblers, the 'legs', and their cricketer
targets and accomplices have mobile telephones to facilitate contact.

As for the gentlemen who proudly developed Lord's in north-west London
as the premier venue, all they could do was ban bookmakers from entry.
There had been widespread distaste for the gambling and manipulation
associated with prizefighting, foot racing, and principally horse racing, a
'sport' which in England was eventually brought under limited control in
1740 by an Act of Parliament which prohibited stakes of less than a very
substantial £50. So, although horse racing remained a major social attraction for the wealthy, cricket now became a ready substitute for those who
made their livings not only from gambling but also from illicit manipulation. While a number of noblemen underwrote cricket matches around the
country for sumptuous wagers, some of them were at the same time known
to have been rigging those matches. In doing so, they usually won appre-
ciably more than they lost in stake money. A rare insight was afforded by
another of cricket's outstanding players of the 1840s, Alfred Mynn from
Kent, who recalled being approached by a baronet who wished to discuss
the possible fixing of a match – a 'foul proposal' – only to be told by the
heavyweight Mynn: 'Get out of my sight, or, Baronet as you are, I am sure I
shall be knocking you down.'[3]

While the wretched Lambert was the top cricketer of his era, his lasting
fame was as nothing beside that of the rough-hewn Gloucestershire giant
W. G. Grace, doctor of medicine, record-breaker extraordinaire and – not
least because of his imposing stature and great beard – as famous, then
and now, as any cricketer. Drawing upon the popular anecdotes about him,
modern readers might easily conclude that W. G. owed his extraordinary
record as batsman and bowler to his inclination to cheat. That record might
indeed have owed a little to his domineering manner towards opponents and
umpires, but the stronger ones, such as Bob Thoms, ignored his attempts to
overrule them. Wilfred Rhodes, the young Yorkshire slow left-arm bowler,
once hit W. G. on the pads, appealed and saw Thoms's finger raised; but the
batsman refused to budge – until Thoms said adamantly, 'You're out! You're
out! You've got to go!' And Grace went.[4]

If the world-famous doctor – an amateur who demanded and was paid fees and 'expenses' well above those granted to professionals – was ever party to undisguised corruption it might have been during the 1873–74 tour of Australia, when he agreed terms to take his team to the South Australian mining town of Kadina while shunning any fixture in Adelaide, the state capital. After the farcical Kadina game, it became clear that Grace and his players were hurrying away to play in a lucrative fixture in Adelaide after all, thus devaluing Kadina's proud promotional claim that theirs was the only match the Englishmen would be playing in South Australia. W. G.'s duplicity and money hunger gave rise to some imaginative terms of insult in Kadina's *Wallaroo Times*, one opinion concluding that 'his name will become a synonym for mean cunning and systematic fraud'.[5]

It was not the only taint on W. G. Grace's name, or on his wider family, since his cousin Walter Gilbert, a fellow tourist on that 1873–74 venture, left England in shame in 1886 after having been caught stealing in the dressing-room. This was only one of many instances of pavilion theft across the decades, almost all of them hushed up.

Throughout most of the twentieth century, suspicions of match-fixing were rare, mostly fanciful as English county captains sought outright results in four-innings matches confined to three days. Challenges were regularly and necessarily struck through impromptu declarations, and risks were calculated, often conjointly, in the quest for precious points. At the highest level – Test match cricket – came a story from the imaginative pen of the Australian spin bowler Arthur Mailey. At the team hotel in Adelaide during the 1924–25 series, his captain Herby Collins, playing cards as usual in the early hours, was approached by a cigar-smoking stranger who made a proposition: tomorrow, on the sixth day, England needed 27 runs to win with two wickets in hand. Allow them to win, suggested the stranger, and it would be worth £100 to the Australian captain. 'Let's throw him downstairs', said Collins.[6]

In the later years of the century and into the next, a time when litigation became a somewhat more accessible and popular pursuit, many a writ or 'stop writ' was the consequence as fiercely competitive newspapers strove ever harder to increase circulation. Media excess proliferated in close parallel with the show-business façade created by the rebel World Series Cricket, a cash-oriented form of loud and colourful cricket entertainment bankrolled by media magnate Kerry Packer in Australia towards the end of 1977.

The feverish excitement generated by the 'new' brand of cricket brought with it the occasional conjecture about possible corruption, an instance of which occurred when, under the headline 'Come on Dollar, Come on' in an edition of the Melbourne *Age* newspaper in January 1982, an article was perceived by some as having implied that West Indies had deliberately lost a limited-overs match to Australia in Sydney a few days earlier in order to ensure that the home side qualified for the finals at the expense of Pakistan. (It was calmly pointed out later in *Wisden* that an Australia v. West Indies final – rather than a match between West Indies and Pakistan – would generate much extra money at the turnstiles.) West Indies captain Clive Lloyd, who had not played in the match in question, decided to sue the newspaper publishers, David Syme & Company, claiming that the report in the *Age* 'imputed that he had committed a fraud on the public for financial gain by pre-arranging a match, or was suspected of or prepared to commit such a fraud'.[7] In September 1984 the New South Wales Supreme Court found in favour of Lloyd and awarded him damages of $A100,000; but later that year the Court of Appeal decided by a majority that Lloyd had not been defamed. The damages award was set aside and Lloyd had to pay costs. He then appealed to the Privy Council in London, where the decision was reversed a second time, restoring Lloyd's damages award – and causing uproar in Australia's parliamentary corridors, where the majority wish had long been to cut the traditional legal legislative links with the United Kingdom.

For over 100 years cricket's clean image remained largely unbesmirched, even after betting tents returned to England's major cricket grounds in the 1960s. A Northamptonshire CCC employee was arrested after £247,000 went missing in 2004; there were scandals in Canada when $100,000 was secreted from the Maple Leaf Club; and Zimbabwe's accounts were found by auditors to have serious irregularities in 2008 (though the ICC did nothing about it). Kenya's chief executive Tom Tikolo resigned in 2009 after $10,000 went missing.

Although serious conjecture over conspiracy to rig matches remained practically non-existent, a risible occurrence during the famous 1981 Headingley Test match would not have been allowed to pass some years later after cricket had been exposed as a hotbed for match-fixing. England were in such deep bother against Australia that Ladbroke's betting tent at the ground offered a wild 500–1 against them. Australia's fast bowler Dennis Lillee and wicketkeeper Rod Marsh grasped the opportunity and placed bets against their own side, rather as a joke. They were red-faced a day later when Ian Botham's hellcat batting and Bob Willis's ferocious spell of fast bowling brought England the unlikeliest of victories by 18 runs.

In the early 1990s emerged a variety of rumours which were not followed up, as much because of scepticism about the sensationalist nature and excesses of a competitive media industry as for fear of a legal backlash. Australians Dean Jones and Greg Matthews spoke of approaches to them to help fix a match in Colombo, Sri Lanka in 1992, while in England, Essex player Don Topley claimed in a tabloid newspaper article that in a match in 1991 between his county and Lancashire, both teams had been paid to fix the result. Cricket-lovers cringed at the thought and few wished to believe it. Meanwhile, another Australian, Allan Border, spoke of attempts to bribe the team on the subcontinent; and soon afterwards Tim May, Shane Warne and Mark Waugh revealed that Pakistan's Salim Malik had tried to tempt them into match-fixing. Malik was exonerated through insufficient evidence after the Ibrahim Inquiry.

Meanwhile, Aamir Sohail, the Pakistan batsman, and Rashid Latif, a team-mate, had spoken of approaches by certain Indian players, by bookies and also by their captain Salim Malik during one-day tournaments and Test matches. Many more names were bandied about, some as accusers, others as the accused. Sohail, despite his endeavours to shed light on the developing murkiness, was to receive a six-month ban from the Pakistan Cricket Board. It was now fairly obvious that the game was in a turbulent state.

An official inquiry was set up in Pakistan upon the initiative of Pakistan Cricket Board chief Majid Khan, the former Test captain. Opened in 1998 before Judge Malik Mohammad Qayyum, a High Court judge in Lahore who had earlier sentenced former Pakistan Prime Minister Benazir Bhutto to five years' gaol for corruption, the inquiry dragged on for many months, with dozens of current and former Test cricketers and bookmakers testifying, and a special court in Melbourne hearing evidence from Shane Warne and Mark Waugh. Pakistan's defeats in the 1999 World Cup by Bangladesh and by Australia in the final were high on the list of matters to be investigated.

The outcome indicated that Judge Qayyum had not been supported as he might have wished, and that perhaps he had even been under pressure not to damage his country's national and cricket reputation. Examination of some of the players' telephone records would have been revealing, but no such process was pursued. The judge also had to cope with evidence which some of the players later insisted on altering. Nor, apparently, was there sufficient probing into Pakistan matches under Salim Malik's captaincy in the 1990s, fixtures which had been subject to considerable suspicion, particularly in South Africa and Zimbabwe in 1995. It was there, immediately after lowly Zimbabwe's unexpected victory by an innings in the Harare Test match, that one journalist heard angry shouting coming from the Pakistan dressing-room. Soon afterwards wicketkeeper Rashid Latif, then at the peak of his career, abruptly announced his retirement. Basit Ali soon followed him. Latif was to return to the game, and courageously wrote to the ICC warning the world body that corruption was rife in international cricket. His adventurous career found him captaining Pakistan, then suspended for five matches for wrongly claiming a catch in a match against Bangladesh, before being appointed as his country's wicketkeeping coach.

The inquiry's meandering course concluded at last in 2000, with Judge Qayyum ruling that certain punishment should be handed out, including life bans for captain/batsman Salim Malik and pace bowler Ata-ur-Rehman, and a fine for world-ranked all-rounder Wasim Akram, who was barred from captaining Pakistan, the judge having felt that the player's integrity had been compromised; Waqar Younis and Saeed Anwar were also fined, as was heavyweight batsman Inzamam-ul-Haq for not co-operating with the inquiry: but little else transpired immediately.

At least a viable legalese definition of match-fixing emerged from the Qayyum Inquiry, should anyone have been wondering: it was declared to be 'deciding the outcome of a match before it is played and then playing oneself or having others play below one's/their ability to influence the outcome to be in accordance with the pre-decided outcome'.

Sri Lanka's cricket authority decided to look into its own team's collapse to lose the Singer Cup final after they had been in a quite formidable position against Pakistan. But again no conclusive condemnatory evidence could be found. Elsewhere, Ms Fareshteh Gati-Aslam alleged that the world-class fast bowlers Wasim Akram and Waqar Younis had deliberately bowled badly against England in a one-day international at Trent Bridge in 1992, when the home side smashed 363 runs off their 55 overs, Pakistan eventually losing by 198 runs. Whether corruption was a factor or not, nervous suspicion was in the air, and people were burdened by it whenever anything untoward occurred in a cricket match. Given that the game of cricket has long been renowned for its unpredictable nature, the advent of apparently commonplace illegal and immoral practices had a depressing effect on the once-glorious summer game. Almost the only compassion to be aired, feeble though it seemed, concerned the comparatively low remuneration received by most Asian international cricketers, which fact underlined their vulnerability to corrupt 'bonuses' to their incomes.

When Dave Richardson, South Africa's wicketkeeper, revealed a few years after the event that an Indian bookie had offered his captain $250,000 to throw Mohinder Amarnath's benefit match (played in December 1996 at the end of an exhausting tour, and which caused resentment among the touring cricketers when their Board agreed to elevate it to an official one-day international), the odour of a game rotting perhaps mortally was being picked up by even the most resistant cricket-lover. To this despair was added anger that the body which was supposed to be doing all it could to protect and advance the game of cricket – the ICC – was apparently still doing little or nothing to investigate and attempt to flush out the miscreants.

If the danger of failing to protect cricket from the gambling fraternity was still not obvious to everyone, the implication of statistics given in a *Times of India* editorial in April 2000 caused fresh shudders: each one-day international was thought to attract an estimated $US227 million in bets across India, and the total sum gambled in a year on India's matches was estimated as being between six to nine billion US dollars. 'Since betting is illegal in India, the whole of it is generated in black [illicit] money', wrote Indian investigative journalist Pradeep Magazine.[8] Tales of underworld killings bewildered and frightened innocent cricket spectators and viewers – and without doubt some cricketers as well. Where was it all leading?

The spotlight had suddenly swung glaringly over Australia when it was revealed in December 1998 that Shane Warne and Mark Waugh, two of the nation's most popular players, had accepted $5,000 from a friendly stranger calling himself 'John' (later identified as Delhi bookmaker Mukesh Gupta) in a nightclub in Sri Lanka in 1994. The money was in return for a few superficially innocent items of information concerning team selection and pitch conditions in the forthcoming match, responses to casual enquiries such as a genuine cricket journalist might make – except that this was part of a clever grooming process.

Once exposed, the young cricketers pleaded that their acceptance of the inexplicably disproportionate gift had simply been a case of naivety on their part. Their personal popularity plummeted, if only temporarily. Many cricket-lovers felt that the punishment should have been much harsher. Warne was compelled to forfeit a couple of lucrative newspaper contracts, but soon picked up another. What further horrified the cricket fraternity was the subsequent revelation that the executives of the Australian Cricket Board, in a desperate attempt to avoid destabilising their team at the start of a tour of the Caribbean, decided to keep private the matter of Warne's and Waugh's indiscretions. ICC chairman Clyde Walcott and chief executive David Richards were informed but were also asked to keep the matter to themselves. It later became clear that a kind of paralysis induced by panic and fear was affecting administrators whenever murmurs and evidence of corruption stirred, even in the offices of cricket's world governing body, to which the game justifiably looked for prompt positive action in such alarming circumstances.

Insinuations had been rumbling for several years. Pakistan batsman Salim Malik – banned and fined £12,500 by the Pakistan Cricket Board (which itself had a history of financial unaccountability) – had been implicated early, as had Ijaz Ahmed and Wasim Akram. One of the most ominous and chilling quotes following the exposure and expulsion of Malik after the Qayyum Inquiry was the player's statement that 'when you've got the main players in your hand you'll have to be really unlucky to lose [i.e. money]. You pay and they will be out. He'll run himself out, whatever, but he will be out. You'll have four or five players in hand and they will be playing just for you. No matter what the rest of the team do, they will do what they've agreed to do.'[9]

Australia set up an inquiry of its own, conducted by Rob O'Regan QC, who set about interviewing six dozen people behind closed doors. His conclusions came after two months of questions and statements: the bookmaker who had approached and paid Mark Waugh had, it seemed, a large network of cricketers around the globe who regularly fed him information, presumably for substantial 'fees'. O'Regan strongly condemned not only the behaviour of Warne and Waugh in this matter but was critical of the moderate weight of the fines dished out by the Australian Cricket Board, which 'did not reflect the seriousness of what they [the implicated players] had done'. In his opinion they should have been suspended. He rejected the players' excuses based on the claim that they were 'naïve and stupid'.

Retrospectively, incidents which had seemed merely dubious and slightly puzzling in this complex game of cricket were now recalled and reconsidered. India had refused to play matches against Pakistan in Sharjah because of suspicions that some behaviour at that venue sometimes seemed irregular. India's captain in 1979–80, Gundappa Viswanath, later wrote that he went to toss the coin with Pakistan's Asif Iqbal, who did not even check how the coin had fallen before saying, 'Congratulations. You've won the toss.'

Sarfraz Nawaz, a former team-mate of Asif Iqbal, believed that betting on cricket became big business around that time when Pakistan were led by Iqbal, with matches against India, as always, generating widespread frenzy. Sarfraz said that the betting grew to a 'big scale' when matches were staged in Sharjah. It was remarked that Asif Iqbal never did come forward to clear his name after these and other allegations, though there was no actual legal requirement for him to defend himself. Some time later he did protest his innocence.

Elsewhere, New Zealand's respected captain Stephen Fleming decided to air a claim that he had known of match-fixing, while England manager Ray Illingworth declared that in 1996 he had been approached by a Pakistani bookmaker who wanted him to engineer an England defeat in a World Cup match. South African umpires Cyril Mitchley and Rudi Koertzen stated that they had been offered bribes to influence play in matches involving Pakistan and Australia in Lahore in 1994 and West Indies and India in Singapore in 1999. Further, England all-rounder Chris Lewis (who was to be sent to gaol for thirteen years in 2009 for smuggling cocaine worth £140,000 into Britain when returning from St Lucia) claimed in 1999 that two Indians had offered him £300,000 to persuade some England cricketers to throw the 1998 Old Trafford Test match against New Zealand. He further asserted that three England players had actually accepted bribes recently. One England one-day player who had something to add was Adam Hollioake, who referred to approaches he had received during the 1997 Sharjah tournament. Allegations by an Indian bookmaker that England batsman–wicketkeeper Alec Stewart had been given £5,000 'for information' after India's Manoj Prabhakar had introduced them to each other were disposed of when the bookie declined to testify and the England and Wales Cricket Board exonerated Stewart. Prabhakar had also named the greatly admired Indian all-rounder Kapil Dev as one who had tried to bribe him, a charge strongly denied, with the counter-accusation that Prabhakar had never forgiven his former captain for omitting him from Tests in England in 1986. Kapil was cleared, but the investigation did reveal that he had over 25 million rupees of undeclared income. The unsavoury theme inflated further in 2000 when Indian bookmaker Rajesh Kalra told *India Today* that he offered players $4/500,000 to fix a recent one-day series between India and South Africa.

It was the Cronje Affair which truly rocked the world of cricket to its foundations. Hansie Cronje was South Africa's forceful captain, a top player, a brooding, serious man ever eager to parade his devotion to Christianity, a cricketer who hotly denied the first suggestions that he might be involved in rigging individual performances or the outcome of big matches. In April 2000, with cricket-lovers divided, some desperately unwilling to believe the rumours, others suspicious, the shocking truth suddenly emerged. Delhi police claimed to have twelve tapes of incriminating telephone calls which involved Cronje. The police said that Cronje and four of his team, via an intermediary known as 'Sanjay' (later revealed to be Sanjiv Chawla, with Hamid 'Banjo' Cassim as the go-between), had 'fixed' the recent series of five one-day internationals in India in exchange for a huge sum of money. It came as no surprise when Cronje denied any involvement in corruption.

When the full text of the police statement emerged, it brought shock and disgust to practically everyone who cherished the game of cricket: 'Those involved in such fixing', the statement read, 'have illegally amassed huge sums of money both in Indian and foreign currencies and made huge gains by wrongful means and by clearly deceiving the cricket fans and general public.'[10]

The recordings revealed details of a deal wherein South African players Herschelle Gibbs, Henry Williams and Pieter Strydom, in return for bribes, were to underperform to suit the bookmakers' needs. Spin bowler Nicky Boje was also implicated. The only morsel of humour came when it was later revealed that Gibbs, having agreed to get out before his score had reached 20 in a one-day international at Nagpur, seemingly forgot his lucrative pledge and raced on to score 74. He was still fined 60,000 rand; Williams was fined R10,000.

Cronje's adamant denial of the Indian authorities' accusation sent waves of indignation and incredulity across South Africa. This man was a national hero, and surely always spoke the truth? India's Cricket Board, similarly horrified, jumped to support the wave of denial and disbelief.

However, Cronje soon found he could carry the burden of guilt no longer, and a nocturnal call to Dr Ali Bacher, managing director of the United Cricket Board of South Africa, triggered a sensational passage in cricket history. Cronje was instantly stripped of the captaincy.

As people were now giving or selling their stories to the media, most of them requesting anonymity, a frightening reality emerged. Claims from years earlier, by the likes of Pakistan captain Imran Khan (himself a confessed ball-tamperer[11]), were now being re-evaluated. He had said that India was the centre of a gambling underworld worth probably two billion US dollars annually. From the betting network's Mumbai centre, agents worked at making tempting deals with cricketers. These deals were not so disingenuous as to concern the deliberate losing of matches, although any notable upset, such as Pakistan's losses to Zimbabwe and Bangladesh, and Kenya's extraordinary victory over West Indies in the 1996 World Cup, now aroused suspicion. The means of deceit were almost imperceptible to onlookers. A batsman would be well rewarded simply to get out before a nominated score; a bowler would be bribed to bowl loosely or deliver a certain number of no-balls or wides; a wicketkeeper would be set up to allow deliberate byes; a captain would be paid for making orchestrated moves on cue. The impenetrable nature of these murky schemes and their implications had a depressing effect. Certain players would not risk going to India. To the fear of arrest and interrogation was added the perceived threat of a faceless underworld and its violent reach.

Cronje was called before a full-scale inquiry chaired by Judge Edwin King, who had been appointed by President Thabo Mbeki. The King Commission hearings began on 7 June 2000 at the Centre for the Book, in Cape Town, with the cricketer guaranteed immunity from criminal prosecution in return for full disclosure of wrong-doing. Cronje's biographer Garth King described the cricketer's appearances at the ten-day inquiry as 'misery itself for the Cronje clan, a kind of sadistic, legalistic farce, watched live by millions. One can hardly imagine a more shameful and tragic end to a top international cricketing captain's career.'[12]

The trail of widespread deceit and subterfuge was exposed at last. One stunning revelation came when Mark Boucher, Jacques Kallis and Lance

Klusener told of how Cronje had approached them in the team hotel in Bangalore and suggested possibly throwing the upcoming Test match; Ali Bacher startled the hearing with an allegation that the umpire Javed Akhtar, from Pakistan, was 'on the payroll' of a bookmaker when he umpired the England v. South Africa Test at Headingley in 1998, giving some questionable decisions in England's favour; but the most extraordinary narrative concerned Cronje's involvement with Marlon Aronstam, a gambler and racehorse owner, who persuaded him to make a deal with England's captain on the final morning of the severely rain-shortened Test match at Centurion early in 2000. With no prospect of a result, if England forfeited their first innings and South Africa their second (an unprecedented arrangement in Test history) a run-chase on agreed terms would restore purpose and excitement to a dying match. The captains finally agreed a target, England won the match by two wickets, and Cronje was rewarded by Aronstam with £800 and a leather jacket.

The deposed and disgraced South Africa captain read out a 70-clause statement to the King Commission, his voice and manner vacillating between near-flippancy to dark introversion. At times he wept. He told of how he had 'turned from Jesus' and 'allowed Satan and the world to dictate terms to me'. He disclosed that between 1996 and 2000 he had accepted at least $US130,000 from illegal bookmakers and others. A cascade of detail stunned those present and radiated across a cricket world now aghast.

The inquiry did not reconvene, and in due course it was announced that Cronje was banned from any involvement in cricket for life. Some months later his life ended when a cargo aircraft in which he had hitched a lift crashed on a frozen mountainside on a flight to his home in George. Notwithstanding inevitable rumours, foul play was ruled out, and to general astonishment around the world, Hansie Cronje was now hailed as a martyr not only by those close to him but by a wider circle in his South African homeland. Among calmer assessments, former coach and friend Bob Woolmer, whose own mysterious death during the 2007 World Cup was to inspire theories about corruption, conspiracy and murder, said of Cronje that 'he dabbled too much and got caught. I would perceive that he got too much power and felt invulnerable.'[13]

The ICC's Anti-Corruption and Security Unit was set up in 2000 as a matter of some urgency following the Cronje case. It was designed to be the operating division of the ICC Code of Conduct Commission (chairman Lord Griffiths), with former London Metropolitan Police Commissioner Lord (Paul) Condon as its head, and Jeff Rees as general manager and chief investigator until 2007, succeeded by Navindra Nath Sawani, a former police officer who led the inquiry in 2000 into match-fixing in India. Five regional security managers were also appointed, one for every international series, to ensure that anti-corruption protocols were enforced, not least in the vicinity of the dressing-rooms, where mobile phones were banned.

The spotlight fell brightly on India, whose Central Bureau of Investigation (CBI) launched a powerful and thorough inquiry, focusing principally on Manoj Prabhakar, who had been liberal with his accusations, and on Mohammad Azharuddin, whose charming batsmanship during his 99 Test matches had drawn comparisons with Ranjitsinhji's, and whose involvement in match-fixing had first been exposed during the Cronje hearing. The homes of several Indian players were raided and their tax records seized. While bookie Mukesh Gupta spoke freely, naming several non-Indians, including Brian Lara, Aravinda de Silva, Arjuna Ranatunga and Sanath Jayasuriya (all exonerated in due course), suspensions were imposed upon Prabhakar, Ajay Jadeja, Ajay Sharma and a physiotherapist following the CBI report of November 2000. It so happened that the ICC president at the time, India's Jagmohan Dalmiya, had been the subject of allegations that he had abused his position as sole negotiator for the ICC in a television rights deal for a tournament in Bangladesh in October 1998. His predecessor as BCCI president, I. S. Bindra, told a press conference that Dalmiya was 'in the grip of the mafia and sharks'.[14] In May 2000, the ICC cleared Dalmiya of malpractice.

Azharuddin, however, was headline news, and for his misdemeanours the BCCI banned him for life. The CBI investigation discovered that he had once made sixty calls to a bookie in one day, and after the discovery of one of his bank accounts (in Dubai) and over 200 expensive watches, his personal wealth was estimated at $50 million.

Within six years of its ban on Azharuddin, the Indian Board – to expressions of disapproval and astonishment from the ICC and elsewhere – had lifted it, and 'Azha' not only took his place among the honoured former captains in a parade during the Champions Trophy but in 2009 became an MP for the Indian National Congress Party.

Thenceforth, even though the game was on full alert, instances of suspicion and proven misbehaviour in top-class cricket were not uncommon. West Indies batsman Marlon Samuels was banned for two years for links with an Indian gambler, having pleaded that he had merely borrowed some money to settle his hotel bill. For several weeks in 2008 the cricket administrators in the Caribbean and in England were taken in by the lurid proposals of Texan Allen Stanford, operating out of Antigua. The millions of dollars he dangled before them in return for staging clamorous Twenty/20 matches proved to be of dubious pedigree, and by 2010 Stanford was in gaol pending weighty charges relating to the legitimacy of his money-making.

The phenomenon of the IPL, masterminded by Lalit Modi, inevitably generated fears of corruption, not only because of the unprecedented amounts of money attached to this globally televised circus, but through the reality that there would be no ICC security in attendance. (Sir Ronnie Flanagan, former Royal Ulster Constabulary Chief Constable, succeeded Lord Condon in June 2010.) It was now accepted that anything was possible. Writs were served around the IPL enterprise, while the crowds went on cheering wildly as the sixes fell into their midst. During the ICC's own World Twenty/20 tournament in England in 2009, approaches by bookmakers to players were reported to the ACSU, while at the start of the Under-19 World Cup, staged in New Zealand, it was thought necessary to brief the young players about the risk of corruption and to warn them about drugs, imprecations that their Victorian-era counterparts would little have understood.

So deeply had suspicion bitten into the game that when Pakistan, having been in an almost impregnable position in the Sydney Test of January 2010, somehow managed to lose to Australia, suspicions circulated. Their captain in 2009, Younis Khan, had already stood down in October, 'disgusted' by allegations that Pakistan had deliberately underperformed in the Champions Trophy. But dropped catch, missed stumping or loose stroke could now readily arouse public suspicion. Wicketkeeper Kamran Akmal's possibly unique 'achievement' of *four* missed stumpings and a fluffed run-out in one day's play became a major talking point. Team coach Intikhab Alam and manager Aaqib Javed told the PCB inquiry that they thought that bookies may have been involved in this match, while captain Mohammad Yousuf also aired suspicions about some of his players' performances. Kamran, meanwhile, protested that people were now hooting him in the field, and that he was 'mentally disturbed'. There were several fines and sackings when the touring players returned home, and Pakistan Board chairman Ijaz Butt announced that two (unnamed) players were under investigation for match-fixing. Younis Khan and Mohammad Yousuf were banned from any form of international cricket; a one-year ban was imposed on Shoaib Malik and Rana Naved-ul-Hasan; a six-month probation came the way of Shahid Afridi (who had been shown on television biting pieces out of the ball), and also Kamran Akmal and his brother Umar. These last three were all fined: three million rupees each for the first two and two million for Umar Akmal. Ijaz Butt then announced that the inquiry was closed, no evidence of match-fixing having been uncovered.

Tim May, chief executive of FICA, the professional players' world body, reminded everyone after these announcements that the ACSU had recently stated that 'this cancer' (match-fixing) should never be regarded as beaten. Furthermore, the boom form of the game, Twenty/20 cricket, not least the phenomenal multi-million-dollar Indian Premier League, which was not monitored by the ICC, was 'just ripe for corruption – the shorter the game the more influence each incident can have'. Cricket, said May, 'needs to be very, very careful'. To which England spin bowler Graeme Swann added: 'You would be an absolute idiot if you did it. It is lunacy and anyone who tries it gets what they [sic] deserve.'[15] And in spring 2010, two Essex players, Mervyn Westfield and Danish Kaneira, the Pakistan spin bowler, were arrested and bailed following allegations of match-fixing and/or spot-fixing (fixing a minor element of a match such as deliberately bowling a wide delivery or dropping a catch at the behest of a corrupt party). Meanwhile, Bangladesh captain Shakib al-Hasan claimed to have been approached by a bookmaker in 2008. Cricket's fragile hope was that sharp vigilance and advanced technology would somehow keep corruption at bay.

NOTES

1 Fred Lillywhite, *Scores and Biographies of Celebrated Cricketers from 1746 [1744] to 1826: Volume I* (London: Lillywhite, 1862), p. 289.
2 James Pycroft, *The Cricket-Field* (London: St James's Press, 1922), pp. 133–40.
3 Ibid., p. 134.
4 Rhodes in conversation with David Frith, 1968.
5 Bernard Whimpress, *W.G. Grace at Kadina: Champion Cricketer or Scoundrel?* (Adelaide: the author, 1994), pp. 9–11.
6 Arthur Mailey, *10 for 66 and All That* (London: Phoenix, 1958), p. 67.
7 *Sydney Morning Herald*, 13 November 1985.
8 Pradeep Magazine, *Not Quite Cricket: The Explosive Story of How Bookmakers Influence the Game Today* (Harmondsworth: Penguin, 2000), p. xxiv.
9 *News of the World*, 21 May 2000.
10 Ibid.
11 Ivo Tennant, *Imran Khan* (London: H.E. and G. Witherby, 1994), pp. 134–35.
12 Garth King, *The Hansie Cronje Story: An Authorised Biography* (Oxford: Monarch, 2007), p. 195.
13 Ibid., p. 196.
14 Scyld Berry, *Sunday Telegraph*, 30 April 2000.
15 *Daily Telegraph*, 17 February 2010.

4

JACK WILLIAMS

Broadcasting and cricket in England

No survey of cricket in England since the Second World War would be complete without a discussion of its relationship with broadcasting. Radio and television have provided instantaneous reporting of top-level cricket. The leading commentators have been among the game's star personalities and, while most have specialised in one medium, they have usually worked in both radio and television. The BBC has always dominated radio coverage of cricket and had a near monopoly of televised cricket until the 1990s. But radio and television have presented differing images of cricket and have had different impacts on its organisation and finances. Radio has done more to reflect the traditional atmosphere of cricket while television has done more to stimulate change in cricket.

The scale of cricket broadcasting

The scale of cricket broadcasting has reinforced cricket's standing as one of England's leading sports. Given the relatively small numbers who attend matches, one can argue that broadcasting has exaggerated the significance of cricket. BBC radio match coverage started in 1927 and by the end of the 1930s it broadcast cricket for more hours than any other sport. Since the start of *Test Match Special* (TMS) in 1957, which has provided live commentary on every ball of Test matches played in England, cricket has probably been the sport broadcast for most hours on national radio, while local radio also has extensive coverage. The BBC coverage of the England–Australia Test at Lord's in 1938 was the first cricket match broadcast by television anywhere in the world. In most years from the mid-1950s to the end of the 1980s, cricket was televised for more hours than any other ball sport. The expansion of BSkyB in the 1990s led to a massive increase in televised cricket. In 2004, Channel 4 broadcast almost 300 hours of cricket and BSkyB had more than 2,400 hours, but cricket had become the fourth most frequently televised sport, accounting for a little over 5 per cent of sport televised by the terrestrial channels and BSkyB. Coverage of football, the sport televised most often, had become nearly five times greater than that of cricket.[1]

As with other sports, cricket broadcasting has consisted overwhelmingly of reports and commentaries on matches. Investigative journalism into the administration and financing of cricket is rare. Magazine programmes have formed only a tiny proportion of cricket broadcasts. Only occasionally has cricket been the subject of fictional programmes, though village cricket grounds are often used to evoke a sense of rural England in television drama. Almost all coverage on national radio and television has been of men's international or county cricket, although local radio reports some club cricket. Between 2001 and 2009, BSkyB showed only twenty-four broadcasts of women's cricket and all of these were concerned with international cricket.[2]

Broadcast cricket has rarely attracted very large audiences. The seven million who listened at some time to the final day of the fourth England–Australia Test in 1948 may have been the highest number listening to cricket on radio.[3] Unconfirmed reports suggest that the *TMS* audience averaged around five million for the Ashes Tests in 2009.[4] Other England–Australia Test series had smaller audiences. In July 1961, the *TMS* average audience was usually higher than that for Wimbledon or horse racing but the July average in 1981 was only a third of that of 1961. By the 1960s televised cricket usually had bigger audiences than radio, though modest compared with other televised sports. On weekdays the final session of play in Tests in 1961 and 1965 often had over five million viewers but by 1969 barely exceeded one million, possibly because it was then on BBC2 and not all sets could receive this channel. Viewing numbers were not vastly different in the 1980s and 1990s. In 1987, fifteen other sports exceeded the average of 1.7 million viewers for BBC cricket transmissions[5] and in 1997 the fourth day of the first England–Australia Test was the only cricket programme in a list of the hundred largest audiences for sport on terrestrial television. Cricket did not figure in a similar list of satellite television sport programmes.[6] Channel 4 had very high viewing figures for the especially dramatic 2005 England–Australia series. For the last four Tests the average audience was always above a quarter of the total television audience.[7] On the Saturday of the fourth Test, 8.4 million, almost half of all those viewing television at that time, were watching.[8] Since 2006 only BSkyB has shown cricket played live in Britain but its audiences, no doubt because it is a subscription service, have generally been lower than when live cricket was on free-to-air channels. In 2009, the average number of 4–15-year-olds watching the Ashes series on BSkyB was only a fifth of those who saw the 2005 series on Channel 4.[9]

Limited audiences for broadcast cricket, and for televised cricket in particular, prompt the question of why so much cricket has been broadcast. One explanation is that cricket's authorities never banned live cricket broadcasting. BBC radio was allowed to choose its broadcasting hours from 1948 and BBC television from 1959. Cricket had attractions for broadcasters. Although rained-off matches and matches finishing early inconvenienced television broadcasters, cricket had higher viewing figures than most other programmes on midweek mornings and afternoons. The introduction of *Test Match Special* helped the BBC to fill the under-used Third Programme wavelength. Cricket also filled BBC2 airtime. By 1974, BBC1 and BBC2 showed equal amounts of cricket, but in the 1980s BBC2 showed more. Until the 1990s, fees for broadcasting cricket, and other sports, were not especially high. In the 1980s cricket administrators often complained that the ITV network's lack of interest in televising cricket depressed television fees, but because its sponsorship agreements often depended on television exposure, the TCCB could not risk losing BBC coverage. Fiercer competition among broadcasters in the 1990s for televised cricket drove up broadcasting fees. In 1998, Channel 4 outbid the BBC for the rights to the terrestrial coverage of cricket. BSkyB's establishment of four sport channels by 1999 indicates that its management saw sport as a means of selling subscriptions and the length of cricket matches may have helped to fill its sport channels. The decision in 1998 of Chris Smith, Secretary of State for Culture, Media and Sport, to delist live Test cricket from those sporting events for which cable or satellite could not have a monopoly encouraged BSkyB to outbid Channel 4 in 2004 for the rights to live cricket in the United Kingdom. No doubt because BSkyB competition had driven up the costs of all television sport rights, no terrestrial broadcaster bid for live cricket rights in 2009. Many suspected that because of its determination to keep the Grand National, Wimbledon and Formula One, the BBC could not afford to bid for cricket.

The cultural ramifications of cricket may have been a major reason why the BBC broadcast so much cricket for so long. The BBC and cricket were seen as establishment organisations. 'Misgivings abounded' alongside worries over the 'seemliness' of selling the rights to the 1968 Gillette Cup Final to the ITV network.[10] Among those with social and economic power, cricket had been regarded as expressing conceptions of Englishness which cohered with pastoralism, perceptions of imperialism as a civilising mission and respect for tradition. Cricket's supposed traditions of fair play and of putting the interests of one's side before oneself were thought to reflect Christian teachings and to encourage moral qualities including selflessness, honesty, physical courage, respect for others, courtesy, camaraderie and cheerfulness in the face of adversity. Such beliefs about cricket harmonised with assumptions about the BBC being a public service broadcaster and with Reith's claim that its mission was to 'inform, educate and entertain', a view which persisted at the BBC after Reith's departure in 1938. Cricket could be regarded as morally uplifting entertainment. Failure to bid for television rights in 2004 and 2009 provoked complaints about the BBC ignoring its public service broadcasting remit.

The nature of broadcast cricket

Technological developments have had greater impacts on televised than on radio cricket coverage although the quality of the sound, especially of matches played abroad, is now far superior on radio to that of the 1950s and e-mail has made it easier for listeners to make instant contact with radio producers and commentators. The visual quality of televised cricket improved in the 1960s with video-recording systems permitting instant playbacks of key incidents in matches, the coming of 625-line pictures in 1964 and colour in 1968. In 2006, BSkyB's high-definition facility enhanced picture clarity although only a minority of viewers have HD receivers. Over the past quarter of a century pitch microphones, cameras in stumps, a greater array of graphics and facilities to track the course of the ball have extended the range of visual material which is presented to viewers. With over twenty cameras at matches, virtually every run is now shown from at least three perspectives.

The essence of cricket commentary has remained the description of each ball and the batsman's reaction to it. As radio commentary has to be continuous, the natural breaks of play have permitted more analysis of play and descriptive material not directly related to play than occurs with other team sports. John Arlott described Howard Marshall, who emerged as the BBC's leading cricket commentator in the 1930s, as 'eminently suited to cricket: he had a deep, warm, unhurried voice; a respect for the hard news ... and a friendly feeling towards the men who played the game.'[11] John Arlott, who was also a poet, was widely praised for his descriptive powers and wit. The Australian commentator Alan McGilvray wrote that Arlott could make a rainy day sound interesting: 'His colourful turn of phrase, his creative word pictures, could not be matched by any other commentator. You could close your eyes and listen to Arlott's commentaries and see everything as if you were sitting on the mid-on boundary.'[12] Henry Blofeld, a commentator since 1974, is famed for his references to buses, butterflies and birds. A tone of self-conscious levity was introduced to TMS in the 1970s following Brian Johnston's move from television and this has been continued by Jonathan Agnew's verbal practical jokes played on other commentators.

Brian Johnston's failure to commentate because of a fit of the giggles after Agnew said that Ian Botham had collided with the stumps because he 'didn't quite get his leg over' has become one of the most memorable moments in radio sport commentary. Don Mosey, a radio producer and commentator, recalled that when rain stopped play, Johnston could 'sustain and unobtrusively direct a conversation (ideally with two others involved) far better than anyone else and he never failed to come up with a new topic when one seemed to be fading'. His interviews were 'enduringly and unfailingly brilliant' because of his ability to follow up what was said and to make an interview more like a conversation. Mosey believed that chatting with Johnston about *Neighbours* on *TMS* was carrying on a conversation that '*involves* the listening public as part of it'.[13]

Since the Second World War radio Test match coverage has always included commentators, who describe play as it happens, and summarisers, usually retired Test cricketers, who comment on the play. Initially, summarisers were invited to speak between overs or when wickets fell but over the past twenty years the talk between commentators and summarisers has become more like a conversation, with summarisers speaking when they wish. The summariser Mike Selvey welcomed this more conversational approach because 'I don't like to think of it as two separate people working apart from each other', but added that 'It's a little less formal and it's a lot harder than it used to be.'[14]

Television commentary was long governed by the dictum that commentators should speak only when they could add to the picture. In a recording of the last day of the final England–Australia Test in 1968, a highly exciting day's play, commentators said nothing if no run was scored from a ball or if a wicket did not fall. Richie Benaud, a successful captain of the Australian Test team, was a BBC television commentator from 1964 to 1998 and then for Channel 4 and for Five's cricket highlights. Widely regarded as the best television commentator, Benaud has often been praised for saying so little. Over the past decade the amount of talk on television coverage has increased, although commentators still tend to remain quiet while the bowler is running in and the batsman plays the ball. The greater range of technical aids has perhaps provided more opportunities for comment. For Test matches, BSkyB has more or less abandoned having a distinction between commentators and summarisers, although commentators take it in turn to act as the 'third man' who uses action replays to analyse technical matters for viewers. Richie Benaud and Jim Laker in the 1960s were the first former Test players to be television commentators but now almost all BSkyB commentators have played Test cricket.

The esteem of *Test Match Special*

By the 1970s, *Test Match Special* had become a major feature of the English cricket scene. Its critical acclaim perhaps explains why the BBC has continued to broadcast it. George Scott of the *Listener* wrote in 1974 that the 'glory of the English summer is cricket, and one of the glories of British broadcasting is the ball-by-ball commentary on Radio 3'.[15] In 1988, Simon Barnes of *The Times* defined it as 'more than a programme: a tradition, a heritage, a responsibility. It is part of the fabric of the English summer.'[16] John Perara, the ECB commercial director, said in 2008 that *TMS* was 'an iconic programme which has become a part of the very tapestry of British life' and had set the standard for cricket broadcasting on radio across the world.[17] The Queen's meeting with the *TMS* team at Lord's in 2001 registered the esteem of the programme with 'the great and the good'. The radio critic Gillian Reynolds wrote on the fiftieth anniversary of *TMS* that 'If cricket is more than a game, *Test Match Special* is more than a programme.'[18]

The launch of *TMS* with its ball-by-ball coverage was simply an expansion of how BBC radio had been covering cricket. Arlott wrote in 1981 that *Test Match Special* 'was already itself before it was recognised and titled' in 1957. Unlike other acclaimed radio programmes of the 1950s, *TMS* has survived. It has outlasted the BBC's *Grandstand*, which was the world's longest-running television sport programme. No other radio sport programme in Britain has stimulated such affection or prestige. In the last third of the twentieth century many claimed to turn off the sound when watching BBC televised cricket so that they could listen to *TMS*.

Although some cricket enthusiasts complained about the levity of *TMS* and discussion of matters not directly concerned with play, others have argued that these features appealed to those with little knowledge of cricket. Not concentrating exclusively on play encouraged forms of audience participation before they became more common in radio sport broadcasting. Soon after the start of *TMS* listeners began forwarding gifts to the commentary team, and by the 1970s sending cakes had become one of the programme's rituals. The Queen has presented the *TMS* team with a cake made in the royal kitchens. Interviews with those from other walks of life, telephone and e-mail enquiries from listeners and discussion among commentators and summarisers about cricket matters when rain stops play – one often meets those who say that they enjoy the programme most during interruptions for rain – are related to the nature of cricket. Highly articulate commentators and summarisers have resonated with, and helped to foster, the notion that cricket is more cerebral than other sports and dovetails with assumptions about much cricket writing being a branch of high literature. Arlott thought that cricket had a contemplative dimension which was expressed in writing and painting and that commentary was 'only a step down from this'.[19]

Praise for the BBC's televised cricket rarely matched that for *TMS*. Until the 1970s, adverse comment was unusual, possibly because so little was seen of coverage overseas, but in the last quarter of the twentieth century its visual quality was often criticised as inferior to that of Australian television. The BBC began showing every ball from behind the bowler's arm only in 1989, but this was adopted by Australian television in the 1970s. Some inside the BBC felt that its cricket presentation was too slow to change. Tony Lewis, the former England captain who had been a commentator and presenter for BBC televised cricket, wrote that the BBC 'never pushed to take a lead in the televising of the game. It was tugged along by the popular experiments of others' and was 'not in the van of technical experiment and improvement'. When part of *Grandstand*, cricket coverage was interrupted by increasingly frequent visits to horse racing and other sports. Australia's Channel Nine, Lewis argued, 'advanced miles ahead of the BBC in production and pictures'.[20]

The ECB decision to sell the rights for showing cricket on terrestrial television from 1999 to Channel 4 was not based entirely on the money offered by Channel 4. The ECB was impressed by a Channel 4 presentation which promised to do more to reach women, the young and ethnic minorities. Will Wyatt, Deputy Director-General of the BBC, conceded later that 'the lack of new ideas in our coverage was a factor in our losing the contract'.[21] For its coverage of cricket for Channel 4 between 1999 and 2005, the production company Sunset+Vine won around thirty awards, including four BAFTAS and the Royal Television Society prize for the best live outside television broadcast.[22] The House of Commons Culture, Media and Sport Select Committee concurred 'wholeheartedly' with 'the critically acclaimed coverage' of Channel 4 cricket.[23] Channel 4 innovations had included more use of a split-screen facility to provide technical analysis of play, longer previews of play, discussion during the lunch interval and women presenters. Praise for Channel 4 cricket reinforced beliefs about BBC televised cricket having been behind the times. Although BSkyB has provided more extensive coverage of cricket than other broadcasters, has employed a wider range of technological devices to explain the course of play and gives the impression that cricket has a high level of action, it has not obtained a standing and affection within cricket equal to that of *TMS*.

Broadcasting and the image of cricket

Radio and television have projected different images of cricket. Class privilege has long been associated with cricket. In 2009, three members of the

England team, including the captain, were educated at public schools, usually a signifier of a wealthy background. Until the 1963 season first-class cricketers were divided into amateurs, who mostly had upper- or middle-class backgrounds, and professionals, who usually had working-class origins. County captains were normally amateurs. In the twentieth century England did not have a professional captain until 1952. At many grounds amateurs and professionals had separate changing rooms. Broadcasting did not defend the class relationships of cricket or campaign for the amateur–professional distinction to be scrapped, but radio in particular reflected cricket's power relationships and tended to accept them as normal. Peter Baxter, producer of *TMS* from 1973 to 2007, agreed in 2009 that *TMS* had a 'public schooly world' but explained that this was not by design.[24] Brian Johnston and Henry Blofeld attended Eton and most of the other long-serving commentators were educated at public schools. John Arlott and Don Mosey, educated at grammar schools, at times resented the public-school presence on the programme. Between 1958 and 1973 the English summarisers had all played cricket as amateurs, but Fred Trueman, a miner's son, was a summariser from 1974 to 1999. Adding 'ers' to the names of commentators, a practice encouraged by Brian Johnston, can be seen as a public-school habit, though even Fred Trueman took this up. Some listeners were irritated by the public-school tone. In 1989, Val Arnold-Foster of the *Guardian* thought that not everybody enjoyed the 'silly-billy bits … the nicknames and the giggles, the jolly bottles and the chocolate cakes, the whole public-school lark'.[25]

With television, the presence of those not from public schools expanded earlier than with radio. By 1987, none of the BBC television commentary team had been educated at a public school. Few from public schools have been employed as anchormen, commentators or summarisers by BSkyB or Channel 4. BSkyB sacked Henry Blofeld as a commentator in 1996. Mark Nicholas, educated at Bradfield College, was the main presenter and a commentator for Channel 4 and now presents Five's recorded highlights. David Gower, who attended King's School, Canterbury, presented the BBC cricket magazine programme *Gower's Cricket Monthly* and is a BSkyB anchorman and commentator. But one can also argue that having summarisers and television commentators who were former Test cricketers, whether from public schools or not, recognises meritocratic expertise rather than class privilege.

Cricket has often been considered a symbol of England, as expressing an Englishness which emphasises pastoralism, decorum and restraint. Claims that *TMS* is different from cricket broadcasts overseas reinforces the assumption about cricket reflecting an English identity. The broadcasting critic Bernard Davies pointed out in 1980 that Arlott's accent was 'rustic' and that his commentaries showed that cricket was less of a game than a

Figure 4.1. John Arlott making his final Test match commentary at the England–Australia Centenary Test in September 1980. (Press Association)

'pageantry of Englishry' and underlined England's 'deep moral sense and feelings for pastoral beauty',[26] though this could not be said of most other commentators. Radio and television commentary in England has always exuded restraint, although summarisers could be withering in their criticisms of players. Broadcast commentary has rarely sounded so frenzied as football commentary, possibly because football has fewer natural pauses than cricket. Australian television cricket commentators in particular have often been criticised for sounding more excitable and for shouting more than their English counterparts. In 1990, Paul Fitzpatrick of the *Guardian* found Sky's cricket commentary 'the height of good taste' and contrasted it with the 'near-hysterical commentating and the superficiality and vulgarity' of Australia's World Series cricket coverage.[27] Although English commentators and summarisers clearly want England to win international matches, their commentary is rarely so stridently nationalistic in support of England as occurs with other broadcast sports, possibly because commentary teams have usually included broadcasters and retired players from England's opponents. Radio commentary has reflected the pauses of cricket, whereas BSkyB's visual presentation, with its replays of each run and graphics, gives an impression of cricket being faster and more action-packed. The light-hearted tone and gentle humour of commentary have rarely descended to belly laughs and can be regarded as an expression of English reserve and restraint.

Even today beliefs that cricket has higher standards of sportsmanship than other sports, though less widespread than before the Second World War, are not dead. In the 1950s and 1960s commentators were reluctant to suggest that players deliberately flouted the laws of cricket. Little attention was drawn to the doubtful action of the England bowler Tony Lock. Radio did not condemn England's slowing the over rate to save the Leeds Test in 1953. In the 1970s and 1980s broadcasters were more reticent than the press in criticising the tactics of the four-man West Indian pace attack, and in the 1990s the press, not radio or television, revealed the suspicions of England players that Pakistan fast bowlers were obtaining reverse swing by illicitly gouging the ball. In 1994, BBC television showed Michael Atherton, the England captain, rubbing what was thought to be dirt from his pocket on the ball. A BBC employee said that the shots of Atherton 'fiddling' with the ball had been recorded during a quiet period of play. The producer used them 'so the commentators had something to talk about', not realising 'what a row' they would cause. 'If the BBC had known,' he added, 'I'm sure they would have kept the pictures off the air.'[28] Jonathan Agnew, the BBC cricket correspondent, felt that Atherton should have resigned the England captaincy.

By exposing cheating, the increasing numbers of television cameras may have discouraged unfair play. Broadcasters have been prepared to co-operate with cricket authorities' attempts to ensure that broadcasting does not sully cricket's reputation for sportsmanship. The prohibition on pitch microphones eavesdropping on conversations between players may be intended to mask the extent of sledging – players making disparaging comments about opponents in order to disrupt their concentration – which is usually regarded as sharp practice in England though not in Australia. Attitudes among broadcasters to sportsmanship have changed with time. Although sledging is not broadcast, commentators now praise players for 'getting in the faces' of opponents. Commentators do not usually urge fast bowlers to use short-pitched bowling to intimidate batsmen, although in 2009 Shane Warne argued that a fast bowler should have tried to 'knock the head off' a new batsman, but they do call on bowlers to direct their attack around a batsman's chest. Some former England players were uncomfortable when England managed to draw the first Test of the 2009 Ashes series by time wasting, but Jonathan Agnew on radio defended this as gamesmanship which all of today's Test sides would have used.

With its growing technological sophistication, television is being employed to help umpires make decisions. Since 1993 a third umpire in the stands with access to television replays to advise on all line decisions has been used at all Tests in England. From 1996 the third umpire was able to initiate contact with the umpires on the field about boundary decisions and in 1997 the ICC decided that the third umpire could be consulted over catches. In 2008 the ICC recommended that in Test matches a side could refer up to three unsuccessful decisions to the third umpire, but for LBW appeals technology would be used only to establish where the ball struck the batsman and not its possible further path. Broadcasters have often called for greater use of technology in decision-making. Ian Botham argued in 2007 that the next step had to be for 'TV umpires' to rule on more decisions and allow on-field umpires to 'get on with their main job of making sure the game runs smoothly without the intolerable pressure of being proved wrong by the cameras'. Because umpiring errors could affect adversely a cricketer's livelihood, he thought it 'perverse' not to use television.[29] Some umpires feared that television technology was undermining their status. In the 2008 issue of *Wisden* David Frith wrote of umpires who 'jealously prize their power' and saw television replays as threatening their authority.[30]

Television has always shown shots of spectators but in recent decades it has been accused of undermining the dignity of cricket by encouraging noisier and more flamboyant spectator behaviour. In the 1970s, commentators criticised spectators who ran onto the square to congratulate players when a wicket fell or centuries were scored and the subsequent refusal to show streakers and pitch invasions reflects an assumption that television coverage influences crowd behaviour. Possibly, television coverage of other sports provoked rowdier behaviour at cricket. Television seems to have encouraged groups of spectators to wear fancy dress, although in the 1990s some Test match grounds disapproved of this. A man who was the back half of a pantomime cow needed hospital treatment after being crash-tackled by stewards at Headingley. In 1997, the cricket journalist Michael Henderson wrote that 'a Test match offers an unrivalled opportunity to show off, particularly as television cameras love to focus on people dressed as vegetables'. He also thought that on radio Agnew 'likes to tell his listeners what the cavorters in the bleachers are wearing'.[31]

Matthew Parry and Dominic Malcolm have drawn parallels between the so-called 'Barmy Army', who give England vociferous support at home and overseas, and broader cultural changes including New Laddism and a legitimation of consumption expressed through foreign travel, but they also link its rise with BSkyB's cricket coverage. They argue that to sell subscriptions, BSkyB tried to appeal to 'a larger "football-type" audience and the "New Lad" culture more generally' and made fans at matches integral to its cricket coverage. The Barmy Army provided 'easily identifiable scenery for broadcasters' becoming 'the prime target of television cameras seeking animated sections of the crowd ... The Barmy Army feeds on this attention; it contributes to their fun, encourages their exhibitionist pre-occupations and bolsters their notion that they can exert an influence on playing events.'[32]

Broadcasting and the financing of cricket

Broadcasting fees are now the financial life-blood of cricket. Initially, cricket received little money from broadcasting. In the 1930s the BBC claimed that it was not paying for the right to broadcast a match but providing a facility fee as compensation for gate receipts lost through its equipment occupying seats. After the War it became accepted in effect that facility fees were paid for the right to broadcast matches. Radio fees, never a vast contribution to cricket finance, were overtaken in the 1950s by those from television. For the Tests against Australia in 1953, BBC radio payments of seventy-five guineas for each day's play were tiny compared with total gate receipts of more than £200,000.[33] If rumours that the BBC agreed in 2000 to pay the ECB £17.5 million over five years for the radio rights to cricket in England are correct, radio payments would have been about only a seventh of those from television. In 1965, BBC payments to televise cricket played in England exceeded £50,000 and by 1981 payments from the BBC and the Australian Broadcasting Commission were almost one million. Television fees from broadcasters for cricket played in the UK totalled £3 million in 1990, £25 million in 1999 and £63 million in 2009. Much of cricket's income from sponsorship and advertising has also been dependent on television. In the early 1990s the TCCB's sponsorship and advertising revenues exceeded broadcasting fees.

For much of the twentieth century most county clubs could not support themselves but were subsidised by what are called the central distribution of profits arising from international cricket, overseas tours, centrally nego-tiated sponsorship and advertising agreements and broadcasting fees. In 1995, the central distribution accounted for 40 per cent of the income of the first-class counties and samples of county balance sheets since then sug-gest that it has remained over a third. The contribution of broadcasting fees to the central distribution was proportional to what it constituted to the income of cricket's central authority. By the late 1970s broadcasting fees were providing a quarter of the central distribution, 40 per cent in 2000 and 80 per cent in 2009, and these figures do not include the impact of television on sponsorship and advertising.[34] Without the central distributions some counties could have been forced to abandon their first-class status.

During the past two decades it has been argued that the central distributions, by propping up eighteen first-class counties, have discouraged thoroughgoing reform of the highest level of domestic cricket and so been inimical to the best interests of cricket in England. Yet a strong case can be made for arguing that the need for television income brought massive changes to county cricket. Television has been at the heart of the expansion in limited-overs cricket, an enormous change in cricket. The BBC did not campaign for the launch of the Gillette Cup, the counties' first limited-overs competition in 1963, but the Sunday League in 1969 and the Benson and Hedges Cup in 1972 almost certainly would not have started without sponsorship and sponsors wanting guaranteed television coverage. The first three cricket world cups, all limited-overs competitions, held in England in 1975, 1979 and 1983, were planned on the basis that television coverage would attract the necessary sponsorship. Yet not all cricket sponsorship has been dependent on television exposure. In the early 1980s the sponsorship for the County Championship, which was rarely televised, was greater than that for the limited-over county competitions. Twenty20 cricket has grown in recent years partly because the length of matches suits television schedules.

The significance of television income and its effects on sponsorship and advertising have led to an expansion of England cricket. England played forty-eight Test matches at home in the 1950s but seventy-one between 2000 and 2009. In the 2008 season England played seven Tests, eleven 50-overs internationals and two Twenty20 matches. Higher gate receipts for England games did much to stimulate this growth of international cricket but broadcasters paid more for England matches. During the 1990s England's failure to win a Test series at home against Australia, West Indies, Pakistan and Sri Lanka provoked fears that television viewing figures could fall and that broadcasters would pay less to televise cricket. County cricket was transformed to make it a more effective preparation for Test cricket. In 1993 all County Championship matches were scheduled for four days. The Championship was split into two divisions with promotion and relegation in 2000, a reform originally discussed before the First World War. In 2000, central contracts were introduced for players likely to play for England. These were paid by the ECB and the England team management was permitted to specify when players with central contracts could play county cricket. The big names of England cricket now play very little county cricket.

The welfare of cricket in England is now very much dependent on broadcasting, and television in particular. Through television fees cricket has more financial security than it has ever known but economic reliance on broadcasting may have dangers. The long-term health of cricket will be decided by the level of interest in the sport and by the vigour of cricket as a participant sport. The ECB has argued that television fees have allowed more to be spent on promoting recreational cricket. In 2008, the ECB gave £14 million to 2,000 community cricket clubs, £5 million to schools cricket and £10 million in interest-free loans to community cricket clubs and to subsidise half the cost of 10,000 coaches.[35] It maintained that in 2006–07 participation in club and school cricket increased by 27 per cent, but the Department of Culture, Media and Sport reported a slight drop in participation among those aged over sixteen.[36] Although the televising of women's cricket has increased over the past two decades, it still forms only a tiny fraction of all televised cricket, but the merger of the Women's Cricket Association with the ECB has given the women's game a bigger share of broadcasting income and stimulated playing by women and girls. In 2006–07 the number of women and girls participating in cricket increased by 45 per cent. In 2007, 43,000 girls took part in more than 7,000 Kwik Cricket matches played at primary schools.[37] In 2009, a major part of the ECB case against Ashes Test series becoming listed events once more was that subscription broadcasters would pay far less for non-exclusive rights and so reduce what could be spent on supporting participation. Others have maintained that limiting the viewing of live cricket to those who can afford a subscription will be disastrous. The editor of *Wisden* wrote in 2005 that 'the overwhelming majority of the British population will never come across a game of cricket in their daily lives. Never, never, never, never … the longer term consequences will take a generation to unfold. Some believe these could be serious. I think we're looking at a potential catastrophe.'[38] Negotiating its relationship with broadcasting looks likely to remain the key issue for the ECB.

NOTES

1 Mintel Cricket and Rugby: The Consumer, p. 7, Market Factors, p. 6, www.academic.mintel.com/sinatra (accessed 9 July 2008).
2 Women's Cricket, www.bufvc.ac.uk/tvandradio/trilt (accessed 14 April 2010).
3 John Arlott, 'The Origins of "Test Match Special"' in P. Baxter (ed.), *Test Match Special* (London: Queen Anne, 1981), p. 16.
4 'Review of Free-to-air Listed Events: Report by the Independent Advisory Panel to the Secretary of State for Culture, Media and Sport', November 2009, paragraph 83, www.culture.gov.uk (accessed 1 December 2009).
5 R9/992/1 Audience Research Continuous Services Reports CS/88/04: Sport on TV 1988, BBC Written Archives.
6 *TV Sports Markets*, 16 January 1997, pp. III–IV.
7 *Broadcast*, 2 September 2005.
8 Ibid.
9 'Review of Free-to-air Listed Events', paragraph 82.
10 Jack Bailey, *Conflicts in Cricket* (London: Kingswood, 1989), p. 35.

11 Arlott, 'Origins of "Test Match Special"', p. 11.

12 Alan McGilvray and N. Tasker, *The Game Is Not The Same …* (Newton Abbot: David & Charles, 1986), pp. 78–79.

13 Don Mosey, *The Alderman's Tale* (London: Weidenfeld and Nicolson, 1991), pp. 129–30.

14 Douglas Booth, *Talking of Sport: The Story of Radio Commentary* (Cheltenham: SportBooks, 2008), p. 289.

15 *Listener*, 20 June 1974.

16 *The Times*, 12 October 1988.

17 'BBC secures radio rights', www.ecb.co.uk/news/england/npower-tests (accessed 19 January 2009).

18 *Wisden Cricketers' Almanack 2007* (Alton: John Wisden, 2007), p. 53.

19 *John Arlott: The Voice of Cricket* (BBC Enterprises, 1990), National Sound Archive ICA 0005500.

20 Tony Lewis, *Taking Fresh Guard: A Memoir* (London: Headline, 2003), pp. 135–36, 191.

21 Will Wyatt, *The Fun Factory: A Life in the BBC* (London: Aurum, 2003), p. 267.

22 *Broadcast*, 21 January 2000, 20 October 2006.

23 'Broadcasting Rights for Cricket: Ashes to Ashes: The Death Knell for Live Test Cricket on Free-to-air TV?', House of Commons Culture, Media and Sport Select Committee Report, 1 February 2006, HC720, paragraph 20, www.culture.gov.uk (accessed 14 September 2009).

24 Radio 4 'Midweek', 13 May 2009.

25 *Guardian*, 1 July 1989.

26 *Broadcast*, 8 September 1980.

27 *Guardian*, 15 February 1990.

28 *Sunday Mirror*, 14 August 1994.

29 Ian Botham, *Head On: The Autobiography* (n.p.: Ebury, 2007), p. 345.

30 *Wisden Cricketers' Almanack 2008* (London: John Wisden, 2008), pp. 92–93.

31 *Cricketer International*, November 1997.

32 Matthew Parry and Dominic Malcolm, 'England's Barmy Army: Commercialization, Masculinity and Nationalism', *International Review for the Sociology of Sport*, 39, 1 (2004), pp. 86–89.

33 R. Aird to Test Match Ground Secretaries, 1 April 1955, B10F2, MCC archives.

34 TCCB balance sheets; ECB accounts, ECB website (accessed 12 December 2009).

35 www.ecb.co.uk/ecb/about-ecb/media-releases/ecb-record-funding (accessed 29 May 2008).

36 www.static.ecb.co.uk (accessed 12 December 2009); 'Taking Part: England's Survey of Culture, Leisure and Sport: Annual Data 2006/07', www.culture.gov.uk (accessed 12 December 2009).

37 www.ecb.co.uk/news/womens/international/extra-money (accessed 29 May 2008).

38 *Wisden Cricketers' Almanack 2005* (Alton: John Wisden, 2005), p. 50.

5

PATRICK F. MCDEVITT

Bodyline, Jardine and masculinity

Douglas Robert Jardine was born to Scottish parents in the exclusive Malabar Hill section of Bombay in October 1900. In retrospect, his birth came arguably at the absolute apex of the British Empire. Bloemfontein, Johannesburg and Pretoria had all recently been captured, and the war in South Africa was (erroneously) thought to be won. The aged Queen still sat comfortably on her throne and oversaw an empire upon which the sun famously never set. The viceregality of Lord Curzon was less than a year old and gave no sign of diminishing prospects for the Raj. Even far off in the Antipodes, the upcoming federation of the six colonies into the Commonwealth of Australia on the first day of the new century seemed to be more a culmination of the promise of empire than a harbinger of its dissolution. In short, Malcolm and Allison Jardine welcomed their only son into a predictable, stable world in which any person in their position could feel confident about the future, secure in the knowledge that British values had shown themselves to be the basis for civilisation as proven by a great empire. In keeping with the tradition of the time, young Douglas was sent back to Britain at the age of nine to be educated. He attended Horris Hill Preparatory School and Winchester before going up to Oxford in 1919, where his cricketing prowess outshone his academic performance. Although he quickly earned his blue as a freshman, he finished with only a fourth-class degree in modern history. Upon graduation, Jardine supported himself as a bank clerk while playing as an amateur for Surrey and later England. He topped the first-class batting averages table in 1927 and 1928. Jardine was named 'Cricketer of the Year' in 1928 by *Wisden*, which declared: 'Nobody plays with a straighter bat; few hit harder in defence whether in a forward or a backward stroke, and not often does he lift the ball. As with all really sound batsmen, fast bowling possesses no terrors for him.'[1]

In a biography entitled *Douglas Jardine: Spartan Cricketer*, Christopher Douglas described him as 'the epitome of the old-fashioned amateur'.[2] This, I believe, is the crux of the matter when it comes to explaining and understanding Jardine and his role in Bodyline. In 1932/33, Jardine's vision of cricket and sportsmanship was firmly rooted in the past. He learned his cricket from his father, a distinguished university and county cricketer, and from H. S. Altham, who was renowned as a cricketer, schoolmaster and cricket historian. High Victorians approached cricket as a deadly serious affair, success at which depended on both mental and physical endurance. Indeed, *Wisden*'s praise of Jardine's 'mental gifts for cricket', which Jardine 'possesse[d] in abundance', rivalled its praise of his actual batting.[3] For Jardine, leg-theory bowling was simply an adaptation of previous tactics for the purpose of exploiting Don Bradman's admittedly limited weaknesses. He expected that this would present a supreme test of a batsman's physical courage and skill and mental fortitude, as Test bowling rightfully should. What he clearly did not expect was the vehemence of Australian opposition which, as it transpired, only caused him to stand his ground ever more firmly. The British Empire was not built by Britons who backed down when challenged but, to paraphrase Kipling, by men who kept their heads while others lost theirs.

Of course, the Australians also saw themselves as defending the long tradition of cricket by demanding fair play and by not abandoning the match even though Bodyline bowling put them at risk of serious injury. Australian bowler Bill O'Reilly described Australian captain Bill Woodfull as 'heroic' for containing the anger of the Australians and thought that his continued batting after being struck in the chest was 'the stuff that Empires were made of'.[4] The imperial crisis which was Bodyline resulted in part from a confluence of circumstances beyond anyone's control – Harold Larwood's incredible pace, Australian summertime wickets, tensions frayed by the Depression, the growth of Australian nationalism, the emergence of the singular Bradman, etc. – but it also was a product of the certainty possessed by all the actors that their position was the morally sound and manly one. Jardine honestly believed that Bodyline was indeed cricket and the Australians believed the opposite. That, coupled with the heat of the moment, meant that compromise was not easily forthcoming.

The 1932/33 Ashes tour was not Jardine's first. After a Test debut against West Indies in 1928, Jardine toured Australia in 1928/29. His later troubles there were clearly foreshadowed during this first antipodean campaign. Fielding on the boundary for much of the time, Jardine was exposed at close range to Australian crowds for whose boisterous nature he was unprepared and ill-suited. With his aristocratic Harlequin cap and his intense single-mindedness, he found favour with the Australian crowds only as an object of their scorn. With the obvious exception of Bradman – who was a national hero despite his less than outgoing personality – Australians preferred their cricketers to be jovial, gregarious and democratic. These were three words that would not leap to mind when describing the dour Scotsman. By the time his Harlequin cap had become an iconic emblem of mutual hostility during Jardine's second visit to Australia on the infamous Bodyline Tour of 1932/33, Australian contempt for Jardine had reached unprecedented levels. English bowler G. O. 'Gubby' Allen wrote in a letter home to his parents from Australia, 'Jardine is loathed and, between you and me, rightly, more than any German who fought in any war'.[5] Writing half a decade after the tour, H. S. Altham and E. W. Swanton's verdict on the tour in their *History of Cricket* was that 'the price paid for victory was terribly heavy. Future generations may find it hard to imagine the resentment evoked in Australia.'[6] That Jardine reciprocated the crowds' feelings is undoubted.

The Australian summer of 1932/33 marked both the summit and nadir of Jardine's career. He accomplished the greatest goal of any English cricket captain when he led his side to a 4–1 Ashes victory. But the uproar over the tactics that brought about that victory left an indelibly dark mark on his name ever after. It is fair to ask how this could come to pass. How did the captain of the MCC team – an Oxford blue and county captain, leading a distinguished group of English cricketers – reach the point that he endangered relations with Britain's closest dominion over the results of a game? These were men for whom 'cricket' was a watchword for all that was right and noble in their civilisation, and Jardine was as exemplary a specimen of gentlemanly manhood as one could imagine. It was, after all, axiomatic that it did not matter whether one won or lost, but how one played the game. Even now, nearly eight decades later, it is still difficult to accept that an English captain in his position would pursue a course of action that he knowingly believed to be unsportsmanlike. The answer lies, I would argue, in the fact that Jardine truly believed that his behaviour was sportsmanlike and in the finest traditions of the game. The problem lay in the fact that the game of cricket relied on both the laws of the game and the spirit of the game to organise itself. As times changed, disputes over what constituted sportsmanship arose. No incident illustrates this more than Bodyline, as the scandal that convulsed the world of international cricket during the 1932/33 Ashes campaign came to be known.

The controversy began when the Jardine-led tourists adopted new bowling tactics against a formidable Australian team, particularly young Bradman. O'Reilly argued that it was Bradman, like a 'modern Napoleon ... laying waste their cricket grounds as he waged his brilliant 1930 batting campaign', that made Bodyline possible, even necessary from the perspective of the English. He writes: 'This had to be met with true British fighting spirit.'[7]

These new tactics, called 'fast leg-theory' by the English and 'Bodyline bowling' by journalists hoping to limit expensive international telegraph charges, entailed short, fast balls bowled on the leg-side and often bouncing to chest and head height, while surrounding the batsman with a ring of close fielders. This was not just the attack used by Fred Root in the mid-1920s in England, which employed inswingers on a good-ish length at fast-medium pace to a packed leg-side field. With Larwood and Voce's fantastic pace, bowling short on the hard, dry Australian wickets with fielders encircling the batsman, this attack gave the batsman, in essence, no sporting chance, while at the same time imperilling his health. In the third Test at Adelaide, which was described by *The Times* as 'the most disagreeable match that has been played since the game began',[8] Australian wicketkeeper Bert Oldfield suffered a broken skull when he was struck in the head with a ball while facing the English fast bowlers, albeit not against Bodyline. To add insult to injury, Jardine switched to a Bodyline field placement immediately after Woodfull was 'struck over the heart', which infuriated the Australian spectators. Trying to placate an enraged public, the Australian cricket authorities cabled their English counterparts and decried the tactics as unsportsmanlike – the gravest charge one could level in the world of imperial sport – and threatening to the heretofore good relations between dominion and mother country. The English, seeing little choice but to defend their captain and team, refused to accept the charge of unsportsmanlike behaviour and, in return, levelled perhaps the second gravest charge possible at the Australians: they compared the Australians to women.[9] Larwood, the English bowler at the centre of the controversy, argued, 'If certain critics had not made such an effeminate outcry about it during and after the third Test the whole bother would be too childishly ludicrous to merit further consideration by grown-up men.'[10] In a line of argument that was typical of the general English tone of reporting, one columnist asked: 'Would they have us believe that the manly game of cricket must, to suit their taste, be mutilated to be fit for eunuchs, not men?'[11]

While the English tour of the southern dominion would conclude under an uneasy truce, English commentators continued to insist that the tactics were fair and sporting. A change of heart would come about only when a West Indian cricket team came to the British Isles in the northern summer of 1933 and employed these same tactics against the English at home, where they could witness them for themselves. Even the watered-down West Indian version of Bodyline, rendered much less intimidating by the heavier atmosphere and damper wickets of England, which lessened the danger posed by fast bowlers Learie Constantine and E. A. Martindale, was enough to lead to the banning of the practice, although not an apology, by the English.[12]

The controversy is important for historians because it produced volumin-
ous commentary that strayed from the technicalities and clichés of everyday
cricket reporting and instead revealed why the game was important to the
societies that played it. In this commentary, we see that the game was a vital
way in which hierarchies of gender, race and nationality were maintained
and/or challenged and national visions of true manhood could be promul-
gated. Race, gender and class all contributed to the importance attached to
this contest and for men in the empire – West Indian, Briton and Australian
alike – defending their definition of cricket became equated with defending
their very manhood, especially as the hold of the Great Depression seemed
to squeeze ever tighter and national morale was low.[13]

For imperial Britain, cricket was more than just a game; it was a code
of conduct and the expression of a British and imperial sense of right and
wrong. The common usage of the phrase that something was 'not cricket'
meant simply and succinctly that it was not morally right. It was a game in
which how one played mattered more than the outcome. In a letter to *The
Times* about the kerfuffle, the author A. A. Milne called for calm heads to
consider the English tactics since the 'bitter feeling already aroused by the
colour of Mr. Jardine's cap has been so intensified by the direction of Mr.
Larwood's bowling as to impair friendly relations between England and
Australia'.[14] A letter to the editor of the *Morning Post* stated that regardless
of whether the English are right or wrong about the appropriateness of the
tactics, 'If one side or another thinks that the tactics of its opponents are
"not cricket" in any sense of the word, that should be quite sufficient for
those tactics to be dropped. After all, cricket is a game, and while it remains
a game it does not matter who wins.'[15] Even at the time, in the midst of the
matches, the speedy unravelling of so much cricket tradition seemed unintel-
ligible to observers and participants alike. Bradman bemoaned how, by the
middle of the tour, 'players of both sides got to passing each other without
a word of greeting'; he lamented, 'Oh, that cricket should ever have got to
that.'[16]

So it was doubly shocking when the bad blood emerged on a cricket tour
between England and her closest dominion, Australia. Cricket tours were
meant to celebrate common values and cement imperial fellowship, but in
1933 the game revealed very deep divisions instead. At the root of the issue
was whether it was unmanly to employ this tactic (the Australian position)
or whether it was unmanly to complain about it rather than simply facing
it and taking whatever lumps might come one's way (the English and West
Indian position). Larwood wrote that any attempt to curtail Bodyline bowling would 'make of cricket a less manly game. That would be an Imperial
disaster.'[17] However, from the perspective of history, it is clear that the true

imperial disaster from the point of view of the English was not that the game would become less manly, but that the English claim to be the arbiters of both civilisation and manliness would be challenged. An article in the *Australian Cricketer* that was reprinted in the *Barbados Advocate* makes this argument explicit by stating: 'Australia, by practically claiming the right to make laws, automatically ranked herself as equal first in cricketing nations.'[18]

The ruling ethos of cricket, and indeed all imperial sport, was that games provided an arena for a fair contest under pre-set rules to determine which side was better at that moment, at that game. Essential to this vision of sport was that the game was fairly and honestly played. The English language is littered with expressions that use sport as a metaphor for justness: 'level playing fields' imply an equality of opportunity for everyone, 'to play with a straight bat' is to be honest and trustworthy, etc. However, being better in a particular moment in a particular contest quickly became a synecdoche for being the better man overall. This, however, became more complicated as colonies and dominions challenged British superiority. Two quotations from C. L. R. James's autobiographical cricket book *Beyond a Boundary* sum up the basic tensions between English sporting ideology and conceptions of race and gender in the empire. The first highlights the disparity between the ideals of sports and the realities; he wrote: 'The British tradition soaked deep into me was that when you entered the sporting arena you left behind you the sordid compromises of everyday existence. Yet for us to do that we would have had to divest ourselves of our skins.'[19] Likewise, he demonstrated the intimate connection between games, conceptions of masculinity and power when he stated: 'I knew we were man for man as good as anybody. I had known that since my schooldays. But if that were the truth it was not the whole truth.'[20] It is important to remember that the basic ideals of the game and its relationship to masculinity were shared by all three groups in this controversy; what differed was the interpretation of how those ideals would be played out in real life. For the British in general, and Jardine in particular, by the time the fateful Ashes tour commenced, 'may the best man win' became not an invocation of good luck to a competitor, but something which needed to be confirmed by an English victory.

Although sportsmanship is often defined as a list of attributes and behaviours, Australian Test player Alan Kippax provided a more nuanced definition when he wrote: 'Sportsmanship is not a strictly defined and absolute code … It is, in fact, a convention, established by public opinion as a result of experience.'[21] Bodyline, while strictly within the laws of the game, seemed to most Australians to be outside the spirit of the game. To the English, the practice was well within the traditional bounds of acceptable play; people had set close fielders before; people had bowled fast bumpers before; and people had consistently attacked the leg-side before. For English commentators, there was nothing new in the attack except a sensationalist name created by journalists hungry for increased circulation. The fact of the matter is that both positions are valid. Intimidation by fast bowlers had long been part of the tactical arsenal of every first-class cricketing team since overarm bowling was first legalised. However, the bowling attack devised and employed by Jardine and implemented by Larwood and Bill Voce on the hard wickets of Australia endangered the batsmen to an unprecedented level. The resulting conundrum sent international cricket into a major crisis. The fact that two prominent amateurs on the English side objected to the tactics as unsporting illustrates that the tactic was far from universally accepted, even among Jardine's own men. Gubby Allen refused to bowl Bodyline and was subsequently estranged from Jardine. Similarly, Muhammad Ibrahim Ali Khan, the Nawab of Pataudi, refused to move from the off- to the leg-side and take up a Bodyline fielding position, a refusal which prompted Jardine to acidly observe: 'I see His Highness is a conscientious objector today.'[22] Pataudi was dropped despite having hit a century in the first Test at Sydney, which England won by ten wickets.

The Australians, on the other hand, were nearly unanimous in their disapproval. As the tour progressed, the rhetoric surrounding the tactics grew more and more heated. *The Australian Worker*, a Sydney newspaper with the motto 'An Australian Paper for Australian People', declared that the 'MCC will either have to denounce the basher gang methods which its team has employed or forfeit the esteem in which it is held wherever the game of cricket is played'.[23] When E. T. Crutchley, the British government's representative in Australia, met members of the Australian Board of Control to get the charge of unsportsmanlike behaviour withdrawn, *The Australian Worker* wondered: 'Perhaps they are uneasily wondering if there is any possibility of an incident resembling the historical tea raid in Boston Harbor prior to the American War of Independence arising out of this cricket imbroglio.'[24] Indeed, O'Reilly asserted in his memoirs: 'I am as certain of it as of the cosmic fact that night follows day ... that violence would have erupted mid-field during that disgraceful season had it not been for the magnificent character of the heroic William Maldon Woodfull ... Woodfull knew, and through him we knew, that we were being called upon to make a colossal sacrifice for the good of the game.'[25]

The English defenders of the tactic claimed that the Australians had departed (in a particularly unmanly way) from the traditions of the game by complaining about an opponent's tactic. It was largely unspoken, but the implication was certainly that this was especially bad form if that opponent was the

MCC. Many English critics based their arguments on the premise that it is inconceivable for the tactics to be unsportsmanlike simply because they have been used by an English captain, which, in the minds of many English, by definition made them fair. Larwood argued that if he were not a fair bowler then MCC would not have selected him and his captain would not have continued to play him.[26] This, it would seem, brings us back to the central actor in the Bodyline drama – Jardine. In the end, it was his decision to employ the tactics. While well-off amateurs like Allen and the Nawab of Pataudi might have the freedom to object, for the sons of Nottinghamshire coalminers like Larwood and Voce, there was little choice but to implement the captain's game plan as instructed to the best of their abilities. Jardine's worldview was that of the high Victorian period, when the British ruled the waves and waived the rules. Jardine's expectations of behaviour fit squarely in a world in which colonial subjects of the Crown deferred to Englishmen in matters of taste and culture, including in cricket. The English way was, by definition, the proper and civilised way, contradictions and hypocrisy be damned. Yet the world in which the Bodyline tour occurred was a very different one. Three decades after federation, Australians saw their country as a full-grown man, not a child. And, like a man who still loves his nagging mother, Australians held England in great regard, but she was no longer an unquestioned authority. This was an Australia that had come of age at Gallipoli, shortly before Britain was shaken to its core at the Somme. Times had changed and neither Australian nor West Indian acquiescence was forthcoming.

In a chapter with the perhaps overly dramatic title 'Decline of the West', James contended that Bodyline was much more than simply a response to Bradman's batting or a moment of lost composure or poor judgement. Rather, he argued:

> Bodyline was not an incident, it was not an accident, it was not a temporary aberration. It was the violence and ferocity of our age expressing itself in cricket. The time was the early thirties, the period in which the contemporary rejection of tradition, the contemporary disregard of means, the contemporary callousness, were taking shape. The totalitarian dictatorships cultivated brutality of set purpose ... It began in World War I. Exhaustion and a fictitious prosperity in the late twenties delayed its maturity. It came into its own in 1929. Cricket could no more resist than the other organizations and values of the nineteenth century were able to resist. That big cricket survived the initial shock at all is a testimony to its inherent decency and the deep roots it had sunk.[27]

Although, generally speaking, one disagrees at one's own peril and usually to one's detriment with James's position on the cultural significance of cricket, I think that James is mostly mistaken here. James was arguing that

Bodyline was part and parcel of the age of nascent fascism and Stalinism on the one hand, and of industrialised, mechanical, Taylorist efficiency, on the other. And perhaps it was in part those things. However, I believe it would be more accurate to see Bodyline less as the modern world asserting itself, than as a clash of Jardine's insistent Victorian masculinism with a modern world for which it was no longer suited. James believed that 'modern society took a turn downwards in 1929 and "It isn't cricket" is one of the causalities'.[28] However, it is not James's view of the 1930s that is too harsh, but his view of Victorian culture that is too rosy. W. G. Grace may have been the most emblematic and popular figure of the age, but the Victorian period is not best understood in terms of good sportsmanship, white flannel and afternoon tea. Rather, I would argue that the response to the Indian Rebellion of 1857 is the truer face of England and the British Empire in the age of Victoria. Decorum, noble values and attention to good form ruled the day until they were insufficient to maintain British hegemony, and then they were replaced by a willing brutality that could be set alongside any act of barbarism in the history of man.

Jardine's actions make sense when considering them through the lens of the high Victorian British masculinity that combined the ideals of sportsmanship with the concrete reality of British material superiority. This is not dissimilar to the way that the Victorian belief in free trade remained dominant as long as Britain's industrial and imperial power made that ideology profitable. This is not to suggest that these ideologies were insincerely held; the fact that an ideology works in the self-interest of its proponents does not necessarily render that belief insincere. It is not that Jardine did not believe that the best man should win; it was simply that he could not believe that the English side were not the best men.

To that end, it is worth exploring the nature of Jardine's conception of manliness, which would have encompassed his understanding of sportsmanship as well as imperial relations. There are two often-repeated stories about Jardine that are used to explain his insistence on employing a dangerous and unsportsmanlike bowling attack against the Australians. The first is a remark made by the West Indian-born manager of the 1932/33 English team, Pelham Warner, who stated that 'when [Jardine] sees a cricket field with an Australian on it, he goes mad'.[29] Although pithy, this is certainly an inadequate explanation of Jardine's steadfast refusal to abandon the controversial tactics. Whatever Jardine was, he was neither crazed nor out of control due to an over-exuberance of emotion. His whole personality was methodical and calculating, and so was this decision. Cold-blooded and ruthless he may well have been, but mad he was not. To be sure, Jardine hated the behaviour of the Australian crowds as much as they detested him. He wrote: 'It is often suggested in Australia that ... every free-born Australian has an absolute and inalienable right to self-expression. Whether one subscribes to this Article of Faith is not of much importance. My objection is limited to the hostility and lack of taste to which this self-assumed licence gives rise.'[30] 'Taste' is of course decided by its relative proximity to middle-class English mores. Similarly, in what seems like a pure case of the pot calling the kettle black, Jardine wrote: 'Australians, however, would do well to remember sometimes that there are other standards of behaviour besides their own, and that it is possible that there is much to be said in favour of those other standards.'[31] Nonetheless, playing the game the best way he knew how was more important to Jardine than smoothing over the ruffled feathers of his colonial opponents, much less the Australian masses and press. In fact, according to Larwood, Jardine donned this multi-hued hat just to annoy the Australian crowds.[32]

The second popular anecdote relates that, upon learning that MCC had selected Jardine captain of England, an old schoolmaster of his at Winchester is said to have remarked: 'Well, we shall win the Ashes – but we may lose a Dominion.'[33] This is, I believe, a more accurate assessment of Jardine's motives. Over the course of the Victorian and Edwardian period, sport had obviously come to be more than a pastime, especially for public school and Oxbridge old boys. For many who excelled at games, athletic achievement came to be an all-encompassing worldview, from which one could divine an individual's values and place in society. Modern sports were born in the British public schools where male administrators sought to control the energies (sexual and otherwise) of unruly boys; from that highly gendered beginning, sports came to be bound up with the development and policing of gender norms.[34] Games not only displayed the proper attributes of manhood, but they actively instilled those traits that were deemed essential for true manhood: physical strength, moral fortitude, discipline, co-operation and subordination to a group at the expense of individualism. Being born in an era of imperial expansion and dominance ensured that sport and its attendant gendering would be incorporated into a nexus of colonial power relations, both as a means to train and develop a ruling caste and in attempts to 'civilise' the 'uncivilised' colonial subjects.[35] In some cases – for example, cricket in Australia – sport normally worked to unite imperial elites with colonial subjects.[36] In others, such as Gaelic football and hurling in Ireland or baseball in the United States, sport worked to draw sharper distinctions between groups.[37] What is certain is the fact that, once modern sports were introduced into a new context, the intentions of the original proponents became nearly irrelevant, as the games and the meanings attached to them took on lives of their own. Jardine's stubborn insistence on his own correctness reflects his fundamentally Victorian attitude towards imperial sport, including the superiority of English manhood.

Connections between sport, gender and colonialism should be seen as fundamentally hegemonic, but also fluid. Not only were some men 'more manly' than other men, but manliness could be developed within an individual or group. For the purposes of historians, this also implies that what it meant to be a man – i.e. the attributes that would be seen as ideal and definitional – changed from time to time, place to place, class to class and race to race. Consequently, ideal manhood for an aristocratic amateur English cricketer, for example, was not necessarily the same as ideal manhood for a middle-class Australian playing against him. It is still nonetheless true that both would have seen the game as an integral way to instil, develop and perform manliness in line with their societies' values. Yet the reception of games by colonial subalterns was influenced as much by the preference and dictates of colonial culture as it was by British attempts at cultural imperialism or social control. The Australians had learned cricket from the English, but how they played the game and the values they attached to various aspects were products of their own culture, not English culture. One example of this is when O'Reilly wrote that by the end of the campaign 'Test cricket had lost all appeal. Indeed I felt that I could not care less whether I ever turned out again for Australia against England, and the thought occurred to me that it was a matter of some serious discussion whether there were any Englishmen worth playing against.'[38] Clearly, the English were not the only ones using the frame of masculinity to judge their opponents.

In his book *Anti Body-Line*, Australian Alan Kippax diplomatically wrote: 'I don't think any reasonable person, however partisan, has in cold blood accused either bowler, or Jardine, of wishing to injure a batsman. Such a suggestion is unthinkable; but I state without reservation that I believe that the campaign was from the first one of intimidation, aimed in the first place at Bradman and Woodfull, and, secondly, when it began to prove successful, at all the recognized Australian batsmen.'[39] Kippax took a long-sighted view of the affair and argued that it is possible for two sportsmanlike parties to disagree on whether a tactic is sportsmanlike or not. If, after a debate, it is deemed unsportsmanlike, the original practitioners should not necessarily be condemned. He wrote: 'Occasionally there crops up in the arena of sport something new, something which public opinion has not yet been able to label.'[40] In general, Australians saw themselves as the true guardians of the shared imperial culture of sportsmanship, which had deteriorated in England. For example, the president of the Victoria Cricket Association, Cannon Hughes, stated: 'Cricket is a game worth fighting for, and it is in peril now. All of us should see that the grand old traditions are not broken down.'[41] Likewise, in discussing British defences of Bodyline, *The Australian Worker* dryly noted: 'Most comments contend that the ends justified the means, a new code of ethics in regard to cricket.'[42]

Jardine and the English would have none of this. They steadfastly held that the Australians were cowards and poor cricketers. Larwood explicitly stated so: 'You ask why Woodfull could not stand up to my fast leg-theory bowling? These are the true reasons: Woodfull was too slow and Bradman was too frightened. Yes frightened is the word. Bradman would just not have it. He was scared of my bowling. I knew it as everybody did.'[43] This is a view that was shared, coincidentally, by Australian great Warwick 'The Big Ship' Armstrong, who covered the series for the London *Evening News*, and was very critical of Bradman for using batting tactics against Bodyline which he (Armstrong) thought were bred of fear.[44] Jardine believed that 'upon good wickets if a good batsman is hit playing leg-theory he has no one to blame but himself'.[45] When one Australian writer pondered what Jardine would have done if he had been hit in the head when such a leg-side attack had been levelled against him, Jardine replied: 'I should have said that it was a case of poor batsmanship on my part and that the time had come when I should very seriously consider the desirability of ceasing to play first-class cricket owing to my obvious lack of skill.'[46] While it may be easy to dismiss this as pure bravado, it is not inconceivable that that indeed would have been Jardine's response. His belief in the stiff upper lip in that situation was undoubtedly quite deeply and sincerely held. Nonetheless, Jardine's ability for self-criticism was limited.

Shortly after the conclusion of the Bodyline tour, Jardine published *In Quest of the Ashes* as a defence of his behaviour. For Jardine, the blame for the fiasco lay solely with the behaviour of the crowds, the press and the Australian cricketing authorities. One suspects that Jardine would have preferred a world without cricketing spectators, in which cricketers-cum-knights could engage in chivalrous combat as they supposedly had in the days of yore. For Jardine, it was the crowd – full of people made irrational because of the bets they had placed on the matches – which transformed a game into warfare, not the violent tactics ruthlessly employed by his team and at his instruction. In the foreword to the 2005 edition of Jardine's book, former England captain and president of MCC Mike Brearley argued that Jardine was completely unrepentant about his use of Bodyline. He wrote:

> If the crowd had been demure, chivalry would never have been in question. It looks rather as if the highwayman blames the darkness of the roads, or the reactions of the public, for hold-ups. Perhaps part of Jardine's extreme loathing of the Australian public was down to their forcing him to examine (and doubt) the truth of his own supposed 'chivalry'.[47]

Jardine's worldview could easily encompass accepting responsibility for a weakness in his batsmanship while refusing responsibility for the reactions of others to his captaincy. His sureness in his own propriety was absolute. Brearley writes: 'one imagines that, like Socrates, if he were found guilty and invited to propose a penalty, he might well suggest being fed at the city's expense of the rest of his life.'[48] Jardine knew that he had acted with the highest sense of honour and the fact that most Australians and some of his own countrymen disagreed with him was reflective of their inadequacies, not his own. In fact, this disagreement was to be expected since it was one of the main objects of international cricket to teach the subjects of the empire how to behave. As MCC captain, Jardine was no more likely to feel obligated to listen to the complaints of the Australian masses than a public schoolmaster was obligated to listen to his pupils complain about their workload.

While this posture had worked well enough (for the English) in earlier decades, by the 1930s it was outdated. After the West Indies tour to England in 1933 concluded, Bodyline was effectively banned by MCC. Larwood never bowled in another Test match and Jardine's captaincy ended after leading MCC to India in 1934. In a way, then, Jardine was a tragic figure out of time. If his captaincy had come earlier when England was more self-assured and Australia less and before the modern telegraph provided the illusion of instantaneous coverage, or later in a more aggressive and well-padded age, perhaps Bodyline as we know it would not exist at all. Jardine would simply be remembered as a hard-nosed and insightful captain. However, to borrow from Marx, men make their own history even if not in circumstances of their own choosing. Jardine may have been unfortunate to play in the same era as Bradman at the height of his batting powers and in an unsettled age as the empire was evolving into a commonwealth. But play then he did, and the choices he made have left a legacy which still fascinates decades later and extends far beyond the boundaries of the cricket field.

NOTES

1 'Douglas Jardine – Cricketer of the Year 1928', *Wisden Cricketers' Almanack 1928* (London: John Wisden, 1928), www.cricinfo.com/wisdenalmanack/content/story/154704.html (accessed 22 April 2010).
2 Christopher Douglas, *Douglas Jardine: Spartan Cricketer* (London: Methuen, 2002), p. 58.
3 'Douglas Jardine – Cricketer of the Year 1928'.
4 Bill O'Reilly, *Tiger* (Sydney: William Collins Pty Ltd, 1985), pp. 194–95.
5 Quoted in Mike Brearley's foreword to D. R. Jardine, *In Quest of the Ashes* (London: Methuen Publishing, 2005), p. xvi.

6 H. S. Altham and E. W. Swanton, *A History of Cricket* (London: George Allen and Unwin Ltd, 1938), p. 337.

7 O'Reilly, *Tiger*, p. 74.

8 *The Times*, 24 January 1933.

9 See David Frith, *Bodyline Autopsy: The Full Story of the Most Sensational Test Cricket Series: England v Australia 1932–33* (London: Aurum, 2002); Ric Sissons and Brian Stoddart, *Cricket and Empire: The 1932–33 Bodyline Tour of Australia* (London: George Allen & Unwin, 1984); Laurence Le Quesne, *The Bodyline Controversy* (London: Secker & Warburg, 1983); R. Mason, *Ashes in the Mouth: The Story of the Bodyline Tour 1932–1933* (London: Penguin, 1984); Brian Stoddart, 'Cricket's Imperial Crisis: The 1932–33 MCC Tour of Australia' in Richard Cashman and Michael McKernan (eds.), *Sport in History: The Making of Modern Sporting History* (St Lucia: University of Queensland Press, 1979); Edward Wyburgh Docker, *Bradman and the Bodyline Series* (London: Angus & Robertson, 1983).

10 Harold Larwood, *Body-line?* (London: Elkin Matthews and Marrot, 1933), p. 33.

11 'Is Cricket This?', *The Saturday Review*, 21 January 1933.

12 Altham and Swanton, *A History of Cricket*, p. 363.

13 See Patrick F. McDevitt, *May the Best Man Win: Sport, Masculinity and Nationalism in Great Britain and the Empire, 1880–1935* (Basingstoke: Palgrave Macmillan, 2004), pp. 81–137.

14 *The Times*, 20 January 1933.

15 *Morning Post*, 24 January 1933.

16 Donald Bradman, *My Cricketing Life* (London: Stanley Paul, 1938), p. 96.

17 Larwood, *Body-line?*, pp. 44–45.

18 *Barbados Advocate*, 2 August 1933.

19 C. L. R. James, *Beyond a Boundary* (Durham: Duke University Press, 1993), p. 66.

20 Ibid., p. 112.

21 Alan Kippax, *Anti Body-Line* (London: Hurst & Blackett Ltd, 1933), pp. 82–83, 86–87.

22 Gilbert Mant, *A Cuckoo in the Bodyline Nest* (Kenthurst, New South Wales: Kangaroo Press, 1992), pp. 81, 111.

23 *The Australian Worker*, 18 January 1933.

24 *The Australian Worker*, 8 February 1933.

25 O'Reilly, *Tiger*, pp. 194–95.

26 Larwood, *Body-line?*, p. 20.

27 James, *Beyond a Boundary*, pp. 187–88.

28 Ibid., p. 192.

29 Le Quesne, *The Bodyline Controversy*, p. 34.

30 Jardine, *In Quest of the Ashes*, pp. 209–10.

31 Ibid., p. 198.

32 R. S. Whitington, *Time of the Tiger: The Bill O'Reilly Story* (London: Stanley Paul, 1970), p. 187.

33 Stoddart, 'Cricket's Imperial Crisis', p. 132.

34 Richard Holt, *Sport and the British: A Modern History* (Oxford: Clarendon Press, 1989); J. A. Mangan, *Athleticism in the Victorian and Edwardian*

Public School: The Emergence and Consolidation of an Educational Ideology (Cambridge University Press, 1981).

35 J. A. Mangan, *The Games Ethic and Imperialism: Aspects of the Diffusion of an Ideal* (Cambridge University Press, 1981); Mangan, *Pleasure, Profit, Proselytism: British Culture and Sport at Home and Abroad 1700–1914* (London: Frank Cass & Co. Ltd, 1988); Hilary McD. Beckles and Brian Stoddart (eds.), *Liberation Cricket: West Indies Cricket Culture* (Manchester University Press, 1995).

36 Wray Vamplew and Brian Stoddart (eds.), *Sport in Australia: A Social History* (Cambridge University Press, 1994).

37 Mike Cronin, William Murphy and Paul Rouse, *The Gaelic Athletic Association, 1884–2009* (Dublin: Irish Academic Press, 2009).

38 O'Reilly, *Tiger*, p. 99.

39 Kippax, *Anti Body-Line*, pp. 19–20.

40 Ibid., pp. 82–83, 86–87.

41 *Sydney Morning Herald*, 23 May 1933.

42 *The Australian Worker*, 5 July 1933.

43 *Sydney Morning Herald*, 8 May 1933.

44 Gideon Haigh, *The Big Ship: Warwick Armstrong and the Making of Modern Cricket* (London: Aurum Press, 2003), pp. 395–98.

45 Jardine, *In Quest of the Ashes*, p. 73.

46 Ibid.

47 Ibid., p. xi.

48 Ibid., p. x.

6

TOM HEENAN AND DAVID DUNSTAN

Don Bradman: just a boy from Bowral

On 27 February 2001, Australia's greatest cricketer, Sir Donald Bradman, died in Adelaide aged ninety-two. Tributes flooded in from around Australia and the world, including one from the Australian Prime Minister, John Howard, who lamented the passing of 'the quintessential Australian hero'. Howard considered Bradman an Australian 'battler' who had risen above his humble origins by hard work and exceptional talent to inspire the nation by his cricketing deeds. Howard often compared Bradman's inspirational qualities to those of the Australian and New Zealand Army Corps (ANZAC) during the Great War. Like them, Bradman's batting feats during the Depression 'reinforced the national spirit … and helped to display the independence and self-reliance of a young nation barely decades old'. His record-breaking efforts proved 'that Australians were capable of being a talented and resourceful people'.[1] In muddling his ANZAC and sporting myths, Howard neglected to mention that Bradman's own military service during the Second World War was brief and plagued by ill-health. But Howard deliberately politicised Bradman's life, elevating him to the status of national hero. Curiously, little is known of Bradman's private life, and whether he was worthy of such elevation. Perhaps he was just a boy from Bowral who was blessed with rare cricketing ability and little else.

With the opening in 1989 of a museum at Bowral dedicated to Bradman, the place and the man became linked again. They had been linked in the early 1930s, when Bradman was at the height of his run-getting powers and popularly known as 'the boy from Bowral'. His small stature and impish grin reinforced this perception, which Bradman did little to dispel. As Brett Hutchins notes, the link situated Bradman in Australian bush mythology. Drawing on Russel Ward's *The Australian Legend*, Hutchins contends the bush supposedly moulded a new type of Australian who was resourceful and an improviser.[2] Like the bushman, Bradman's skills were honed supposedly with whatever implements were on hand. He did not have the English amateur's refined, classical batting technique, but was a natural product of concrete and matting bush wickets. But the Ward analogy is flawed. Ward held that the bushman was a collectivist and putative unionist who valued his mates.[3] Bradman was no collectivist or unionist and appeared to have few mates, though he was resourceful. Bradman's first bat was rudimentary and his technique owed more to improvisation than the textbook. His precocious talent confounded 'the Poms' and pricked all claims about their superiority. But if Bradman was proof of the Australian bush type's superiority, it was only as a cricketer.

According to the sports journalist Philip Derriman, Bradman's accomplishments were 'a product of his Bowral upbringing'. Derriman suggested that by the time Bradman left Bowral for Sydney aged twenty he was a grown man with a fully formed sense of personal responsibility. Like his brother and sisters, Bradman led a 'notably happy and productive li[fe] in which security was at the forefront'.[4] Derriman did not mention Bradman's rift with his older brother, Victor, nor delve into Bradman's failure to attend family funerals. The image of the poor but contented bush family does not quite fit either. Another Bradman and Bowral lie beyond the idyll painted by the Bradman mythmakers.

The Bowral of Bradman's youth was not a bush town. It was white, Protestant and very Anglo-Saxon, well-to-do and oriented towards small business. It had straight-laced notions about keeping up appearances and advancing one's social standing. Perched in the New South Wales highlands, Bowral was totally unlike the dustier Riverina town of Cootamundra, where Bradman was born in 1908. Bowral was where Sydney's wealthier citizens escaped in summer to avoid the heat and humidity. Sydney was but a short train ride away. Indeed, it was so close that when Bradman commenced playing for the Sydney grade club, St George, he commuted by train. Bradman was steeped in the town's lower-middle-class provincial culture that valued the Protestant work ethic and thrift. He sang in the church choir, was a diligent student and socially responsible. He was good with figures and quickly developed a sound – though cautious – business brain. But he had a precocious side. At the age of twelve he was moving motions at the Bowral Cricket Club's annual meetings. At sixteen Bradman was the Club's secretary and running the office in Percy Westbrook's Bowral real-estate agency. He wanted to move beyond his current station in life. The Bradmans were comfortable but not wealthy. They lived in a three-bedroom house overlooking the oval that now bears Bradman's name. Bradman's father, George, was a carpenter and fencing contractor, who secured regular work through the local timber merchant, builder and later mayor, Alf Stephens, who was also president of the Bowral Cricket Club. The paternalistic Stephens became

Don Bradman's sporting mentor as well. Don Bradman soon realised that cricket offered career and social advancement.

If the Bradman myth is to be believed, he spent hours with a cricket stump and golf ball in front of a corrugated iron tank stand. Apparently, he would hit the ball repeatedly with the stump against the stand, sharpening his skills to an extraordinary degree. The story is etched into Australian and cricketing folklore, and couched as essential to explaining Bradman's success. It also bolsters the myth that the inventive bush type, with his roughly hewn skills, is superior to the elite public-school-trained and cultured English archetype. But other aspects of the Bradman character have been ignored. To begin with, there is the fact that Bradman was not a sociable child, as his only childhood friend of note was his future wife, Jessie. Bradman suggested he was forced to play by himself because none of his schoolmates lived nearby.[5] But Bowral was a sizeable but compact town, and genuinely sociable children will go to great lengths to mix with their peers. Bradman, however, preferred his own or the company of his elders. His loner tendencies explain his later reticence to socialise with team-mates and his pursuit of individual rather than collective goals. By the time Bradman left Bowral, the loner and the careerist in him had merged to form a peculiarly driven individual.

This individualism brought him into conflict with his more collectively minded team-mates, in particular the Irish Catholics. Some Catholic players – most notably Jack Fingleton and Bill O'Reilly – disliked Bradman and suspected he was a religious bigot. But Bradman was from a far different Australia to them and their differences stemmed from the sectarian politics of their day. With justification, Catholics had felt they were not offered the same opportunities in the largely Protestant controlled colonies. By Bradman's time, however, many Australian Catholics of predominantly Irish background had found their political voice in the newly formed Labor Party. Its opponents feared Labor as much for its sectarian composition and appeal, as for its claims to represent the unionised working classes.

Another sticking point was the opposition of Catholicism and Freemasonry. With networks in business, the public service and especially in country towns, Freemasonry provided social and career opportunities for its adherents. Like his father, George, and mentor, Alf Stephens, Bradman was a Mason. When he went to Sydney he stayed with the Australian Board of Control member Frank Cush, who was also a Freemason. Indeed, the majority of the Board and many Australian cricketers were Freemasons. For Bradman, Freemasonry was part of his early life. Though he claimed he rarely attended Lodge meetings, Freemasonry provided a network through which he could advance his career. But for Catholics it was a 'closed shop'. Being a 'Mason' was enough to tar one as a religious bigot.

Bradman could not comprehend Irish Catholicism's clannish political culture. Like many conservatively minded Australian businessmen, he gave the appearance of being apolitical. Given his Protestant upbringing, his business grounding with Westbrook and his individualistic predisposition, Bradman's allegiances lay with the non-Labor parties. This placed him in opposition to Irish Catholics who sided predominantly with Labor. Fingleton was raised in clannish inner Sydney Paddington amidst the collectivist traditions of the union movement and Labor Party. His father was a trade unionist and Labor member of the New South Wales Legislative Assembly. As with O'Reilly, Fingleton was more likely to join his cricketing mates at the bar for a beer than Bradman, who preferred to retire to his room, sip tea and listen to music. After a taxing day in the field, Bradman considered seclusion 'my most important need'. The bar-room antics of some of his fellow players offended him. They 'engage[d] in ... beer drinking contest[s]' and were often late for meals.[6] For Fingleton and O'Reilly, such attitudes set Bradman apart from the team. But Bradman was a loner whose upbringing was far removed from the clannishness that shaped their outlooks. In both politics and religion, Bradman batted for the other side.

In cricket, individual feats often can transcend the collective efforts of the team, and this was the case and problem with Bradman. His batting feats made him the dominant individual in the game. By 1930 he had broken the highest first-class and Test scores by an individual batsman. But Bradman's on-field success masked deep-seated insecurities about his lack of education and financial position. His rise to cricketing prominence and courting of his wife-to-be, Jessie, coincided with the Great Depression. Coming from an aspirational lower-middle-class household, in which the man was the breadwinner, Bradman was concerned about his capacity to fulfil this role. Jessie's family was a social cut above the Bradmans. Her uncle was a governor of the Commonwealth Bank. Bradman's insecurities were exacerbated in 1929. Seeking to exploit the rising Sydney property market, Westbrook had opened a Sydney office and dispatched Bradman to run it. But the office closed after a slump in the market. Like most of his contemporaries, Bradman had left school aged fourteen. With the sharp rise in unemployment, all that distinguished him from his contemporaries was his cricket ability. He later remarked in *Farewell to Cricket* that his lack of education had held him back throughout his life.[7] From this point his sport and his career was cricket. Hence, Bradman used cricket to secure employment from local sports store magnates and advance his interest in journalism. He quickly realised that the more runs he accumulated, the greater his market value and bargaining position.

In numerous Bradman biographies and in Bradman's own writings, his constant use of cricket as a bargaining tool has been neglected. With his individualistic streak and a mountain of runs behind him, the young Bradman was well aware of his value to Australian cricket, which he sought to exploit in his periodic disputes with the Australian Board during the early 1930s. Bradman portrayed himself as a victim of administrative intransigence rather than as a bargainer seeking to extract top price and fair conditions for his services.[8] This scenario is too crude to fit the Bradman myth. But it is very much part of the Bradman reality, and understandably so. As the game's greatest draw card, Bradman considered himself entitled to the trappings of success. During his record-breaking 1930 tour of England, Bradman wrote for the London *Star* and was endowed with endorsements and gifts. After his record-breaking 334 during the Leeds Test, he received £1,000 from the Australian-born English soap manufacturer A. E. Whitelaw. To his team-mates' dismay not a penny was laid on the bar. On his return to Australia, Bradman was presented with a Chevrolet Roadster motorcar, again to the ire of his team-mates. He later remarked that this was unfortunate. As with the Whitelaw cheque, Bradman kept the car.

After the 1931–32 series against West Indies, the Lancashire League club Accrington made Bradman a substantial offer. For a young and insecure man contemplating marriage, who had few discernible talents or qualifications other than cricket, the offer was tempting. Bradman wanted to continue his career in Australia, but as an individual considered he had the right to 'play or go wherever he wish[ed]'.[9] Eventually, Bradman stayed and continued his career in Australia. Rather than placing his duty to team and country ahead of his pocket, Bradman sought to maximise his income and advance his career. The Accrington offer gave Bradman unprecedented bargaining power. He had wearied of his promotional job with the Sydney sporting goods firm of Mick Simmons Ltd. The autobiographical *Don Bradman's Book* and popular song music, including Jack O'Hagan's 'Our Don Bradman' and Bradman's own 'Every Day Is A Rainbow Day For Me', had seeded ambitions of a media career. Although details are sketchy, Bradman got his wish. To keep him in Australia, he was contracted to write and comment on the game for the Sydney *Sun* and Radio 2UE, and to do promotional work for the sportswear manufacturers F. J. Palmer & Sons. As Bradman later related, the contract allowed him to continue playing 'big cricket'.[10] Without it, he would have been lured to Accrington. In this deliberation it appears the Australian Board of Control was sidelined completely.

When, in 1932, the Board challenged Bradman's right to combine his writing and cricket commitments, he threatened to stand down as a player. Fingleton was also a journalist, but he was allowed to continue to write as, unlike Bradman, journalism was his sole source of income. Bradman considered it a matter of principle. He was contracted to do a job and intended to complete it. But he was also determined to protect his right to earn a living in his chosen profession. Eventually, Associated Newspapers' Clyde Packer released Bradman from his contract with the *Sun*, allowing him to play in the Bodyline series. But the affair revealed Bradman's willingness to use his position to extract concessions. He and the Board knew he was cricket's major draw card, which placed him in a very powerful bargaining position.

Bradman biographers often claim his critics were jealous of his success. On the contrary, many were simply irritated by his tendency to place his interests above those of the team. Contemporaries like Fingleton, O'Reilly and Victor Richardson acknowledged Bradman's batting ability, but never warmed to him as a person. He was too aloof and a self-promoter, evident on the team's triumphal return to Australia after the 1930 tour. While his team-mates clunked across the Nullabor Plain by rail, Bradman was whisked over it in a light plane and fêted wherever it landed. Some players complained it detracted from the overall team effort of winning back the Ashes. Bradman declared he was entitled to leave the team and travel independently once in Australia. Furthermore, as his then employer Mick Simmons Ltd. had organised the flight, he was obliged to undertake it. Both were capitalising on his successes in England. Focusing on the team effort would detract attention from Bradman's run-scoring feats, thereby lessening his marketability and earning potential. Bradman often failed to see the impact of such individualistic pursuits on those around him.

In 1932, Bradman faced his most serious challenge in Bodyline. Then known as the leg-theory, the tactic involved the bowling of bouncers at the batsman's body to packed leg-side fields, and was designed to stop Bradman's dominance. The English captain, Douglas Jardine, and his key fast bowler, Harold Larwood, had noticed during the 1930 Oval Test that Bradman flinched at lifting balls aimed at his body. Larwood suggested that Bradman had shown fear. His contention was reinforced during the 1932–33 series by Bradman's efforts to counter leg-theory by backing away to the leg-side in attempts to hit bowlers through the unprotected off-side field. Larwood thought the tactic hinted at panic. Bradman considered Larwood's remark a slight on his character and was keen to counter it. In *Farewell to Cricket* he reminded both Larwood and Jardine that he had scored a double hundred during the 1930 Oval test. Bradman also stated that Bodyline was unsporting and later declared illegal by MCC. In so doing, Bradman shifted the emphasis from questions concerning his courage to Bodyline's legality. Bradman claimed Larwood was a lesser bowler under normal circumstances, and that Bodyline had inflated his Test record and reputation.[11] It might equally be claimed, however, that Larwood was a great fast bowler and Jardine a masterful tactician who both turned the formerly staid and dull tactic of leg-theory into a series-winning stratagem on the faster and bouncier Australian wickets.

Bodyline enabled Bradman to reinvent himself – accidentally – as the wronged and noble hero, while Jardine and Larwood were demonised. But Bradman's reinvention owes much to outside events. The Great Depression was a difficult time in Anglo–Australian relations. The Bank of England's Otto Niemeyer was in Australia demanding governments meet their financial obligations to British creditors. The New South Wales Premier, Jack Lang, threatened to withhold repayments, and in May 1932 was dismissed by the King's representative, Sir Philip Game. Meanwhile, in Ottawa, Australian politicians were reinforcing their allegiance to Britain through bolstering the imperial trade preference scheme, while in Australia successive governments decided not to ratify the 1931 Statute of Westminster that ceded legislative authority to the self-governing Dominions of the British Empire overseas. Australians did not want greater autonomy. Yet cricketing folklore has it that Jardine's tactic threatened Anglo–Australian relations. In reality, Bodyline was a storm in a teacup, although Bradman did become an accidental symbol of Australian discontent with 'the mother country'. As an Empire loyalist and Anglophile, he was a most unlikely candidate for the part.

Bradman's unstated grievance about Bodyline was that it threatened his livelihood. Bradman was still Australia's most successful batsman in the series, but in weighting the game in the bowlers' favour Bodyline halved his effectiveness. This adds an extra twist to one of cricket's most enduring 'whodunnits': the leaking to the press of the Woodfull–Warner exchange. When, after the Australian captain and opening batsman Bill Woodfull's torrid experience batting on the second day of the Adelaide Test match, the English manager, Pelham Warner, sought to express his sympathy, Woodfull reputedly replied: 'I don't want to see you, Mr Warner. There are two teams out there. One is trying to play cricket and the other is not.'[12] Bradman and Warner blamed Fingleton, because he was close by and a journalist. Fingleton denied this, claiming the Sydney journalist Claude Corbett later disclosed that Bradman had leaked the story. The mystery has remained unresolved. Like Fingleton, Bradman also worked with newspapers, although to be disclosed as the story's leaker would have tarnished his image. Bradman fought all challenges to his good name and security. He had opposed the Board's attempts to stop his journalism, and complained to uninterested Board members about leg-theory. He worked clandestinely to stop the tactic, because it threatened his cricketing dominance, and hence his livelihood.

Bradman's cricketing stocks soared again after another English run-spree in 1934. By the 1938 tour he was captain, team selector, the game's main attraction and a famous face around the Empire. Captaincy gave him the scope to further reinvent his public persona from the driven individualist to the Empire's cricket-playing statesman. After the acrimony of the Bodyline series Bradman felt the 1934 and 1938 English tours, and the 1936–37 English tour of Australia, were bridge-builders. On gaining the captaincy in 1936, the statesman-like Bradman emerged, emphasising the game's role in bolstering Empire loyalty and its finer values. Privately, however, cricket remained a means of securing his economic ends.

Bradman thought the 1938 English tour would be his last, but the War intervened. His run-sprees and the anxiety of captaincy had extracted physical and psychological tolls. So, the lull in the game and a restful war – despite being plagued apparently by ill health – prolonged his career. Once cricket resumed, Bradman saw it as his 'No. 1 duty' to help in its post-war reconstruction by continuing to play.[13] During the war years he had added some extra strings to his cricketing bow. In 1945 he was appointed as the South Australian Cricket Association (SACA) representative to the national Board. When the English team arrived in 1946, Bradman held unprecedented sway as team captain, selector and Board member. His dominance was extending into the game's administration.

After a rusty start, runs again flowed. Bradman was also proving an unrelenting though successful captain. By 1948 – on his own admission – he had moulded a team that was second to none. There were no recalcitrants like Fingleton and O'Reilly, and so Bradman felt he had the team's full support. This was not the case before the war. During the 1936–37 series, O'Reilly and four other Catholic team members were summoned before the Board for showing disloyalty to Bradman. Though Bradman denied prior knowledge of the Board's action, O'Reilly remained unconvinced. Bradman later claimed the Board's action jeopardised his authority. Undoubtedly, it brought sectarian prejudices into the dressing-room. For O'Reilly and Fingleton, it reinforced the sense that the game's leadership was overwhelmingly Protestant and Masonic, and that Bradman was an important part of it.

With their retirement, Bradman could mould a side in his own image – relentless and driven by a strong work ethic. Before the war, Bradman had been considered too individualistic to forge a unified team. But this view altered with the 1948 Ashes series in England. With the team remaining undefeated, Bradman silenced his detractors. But as Fingleton pertinently argued, a Bradman-captained side was merely an extension of himself.[14] The team's success was important but secondary to Bradman's reinvention of himself as a captain with few peers and the game's elder statesman.

Figure 6.1. Donald Bradman (second from right) with King George VI in 1948. (Image courtesy of the State Library of South Australia.)

Captaincy was the final facet of the game that Bradman needed to dominate before retirement. By going through the tour undefeated, Bradman achieved his goal.

With no more playing fields to conquer, he retired. During the tour he had paraded as the game's grand old man and Empire loyalist. He was now as comfortable in Britain as he was in Australia. But Bradman's Britain was an exclusive place. Cricket had provided him with uncommon access into British society. He was famously photographed walking, hands in pockets, with the King. He dined with lesser-titled aristocrats and was fêted at exclusive English institutions. On returning to Australia, he was knighted for his services to cricket. For the aspirational Bradman, knighthood acknowledged his acceptance in Britain and enhanced standing in Australia. It symbolised the virtues of 'true' democracy in that a boy from Bowral could rise above his humble origins.[15] Bradman was writing not as a putative bush collectivist or *naif*, but as an individual whose talents had brought him fame and social acceptance at the Empire's heart. But the knighthood had not quelled his insecurities or emptied the skeletons from his closet.

One of those skeletons was Harry Hodgetts. A minor presence in the Bradman myth, Hodgetts is an important though neglected figure in the cricketer's life. A more prominent Hodgetts in the myth would pose dis-comforting questions about Bradman's professional life. The relationship stemmed from Bradman's anxiety and youthful desire for a reassuring and powerful older patron. Hodgetts was a Board member, a SACA power bro-ker and a leading South Australian stockbroker whose clients included the Governor, Lord Gowrie. In the mid-1930s, Hodgetts had lured Bradman from New South Wales to South Australia to boost the Adelaide Oval's gate-takings. For Bradman, Hodgetts's invitation reinforced the business oppor-tunities provided by cricket. Bradman claimed that the Hodgetts offer meant he was no longer financially dependent on the game, and had the chance at a new career in stockbroking. But Bradman was being economical with the truth, as the SACA historian Chris Harte discovered. Of Bradman's annual income of £700, Hodgetts contributed only £200. The remainder was paid by the SACA.[16] Prior to the war Bradman was a professional cricketer and part-time stockbroker's office worker. Cricket in those days prided itself on upholding the amateur tradition with its spirit of fair play. As the game's elder statesman Bradman espoused these values. Behind the scenes, his motives were more self-serving and pecuniary. Paradoxically, he wanted the status that went with being an amateur, but the financial security accorded to the professional. Like his great English counterpart of the previous cen-tury, Dr W. G. Grace, he was a 'shamateur'.[17] This view, however, has no place in the Bradman myth.

Bradman's association with Hodgetts ended in 1945, when the latter was declared bankrupt. In an attempt to trade out of difficulties, Hodgetts stole funds from his clients' trust accounts. Found guilty of fraud, he was imprisoned for five years. The case shook the Adelaide establishment and Bradman. Bradman was always reluctant to discuss the bankruptcy, or his knowledge of whether the company had traded illegally while insolvent. Bradman claimed he was only an employee and not a partner in the firm, and so his knowledge and responsibility were limited. But Bradman was concerned about the bankruptcy's effect on his financial security and social standing. He told the journalist Frank Devine that Hodgetts's downfall threatened all that he had worked for, including his Adelaide house.[18]

Bradman not only survived but prospered from Hodgetts's fall. For some time, Bradman had wanted to establish his own business. In 1943 he secured a seat on the Adelaide stock exchange at a wartime bargain price, and Hodgetts's bankruptcy offered him an opportunity. In a highly irregu-lar move, the receivers handed the former employee, Bradman, Hodgetts's client list. The list was the property of Hodgetts's debtors. Auctioning it by tender would have enabled all of Adelaide's stockbrokers the opportunity to bid and a chance to clear some of Hodgetts's debts. Instead, Bradman was quickly trading out of Hodgetts's office under the banner, 'Don Bradman & Associates'. Other stockbrokers had concerns about Bradman attracting clients by trading under his cricketing name, as the advertising of broking services was frowned upon. The more conventionally formal 'D. G. Bradman' or 'Donald G. Bradman' would have lessened their concerns. But Bradman had a history of exploiting his cricketing name for commercial gain.

Although Bradman and Jessie worked to build the business, the perception prevailed that he had profited from Hodgetts's misfortune. Consequently, Bradman was ostracised from certain circles of the cliquish Adelaide business establishment. The Bradman myth glosses over the scandal, failing to address important questions about Bradman and Hodgetts's relationship. Hodgetts's demise perhaps enabled Bradman to finally become his own man. He took control of his affairs and overcame the illnesses and anxieties that had plagued him in the early war years. With this controlling authority figure gone, Bradman was free to pursue a career outside the game, yet he chose not to.

The Hodgetts affair meant that Bradman's return to cricket was not simply a matter of 'duty'.[19] His return to the game enabled him to gloss over the affair and enhance his business prospects. According to the myth, Bradman was in no fit condition to consider a cricket comeback in 1945. Apparently, he suffered from chronic fibrositis and had hardly picked up a bat during the war years. Furthermore, with the pressure of establishing his business in a hostile environment, a cricket comeback would have seemed remote. On the contrary, it was essential to re-establishing his reputation. Potentially embarrassing questions about the Hodgetts affair and the irregular means by which Bradman acquired the business were swept aside in the publicity surrounding his comeback. Cricket enabled Bradman to step above small-town scandal and promote his good name in the business and broader community and throughout the Empire.

Although a committed Anglophile, Bradman lived in a small and notoriously conservative Australian city and shared the ordinary but narrow attitudes and values of his times. He had scant regard for what he considered the Empire's peripheral parts. The players of non-white cricket-playing countries he numbered amongst the Empire's second-class citizenry. This was apparent when Lala Amarnath's 1947–48 Indian side toured Australia. India had played against the English in the 1930s and 1940s, but had not yet met the Australians. With Bradman in merciless form, supported by a powerful Australian combination, the Indians proved no match. Bradman later related that the series was among his most enjoyable. But the Board – of which he was a member – ruled against encouraging further cricketing contact between the two countries until the Indians were of a sufficient standard to compete on near equal terms, thus increasing the odds of a good financial take at the gate. Bradman's disregard of the Indians surfaced en route to England in 1948. When the Australian team docked at Bombay, they found the BCCI had arranged a function for them at the recently completed Brabourne Stadium. Senior Indian officials had travelled long distances to meet the team and Bradman, but he stayed on board ship. A high-level Indian contingent finally boarded the ship to meet Bradman. Bradman related in *Farewell to Cricket* that the Indians had to be hurried off so the ship could depart. Bradman would not have written so dismissively of a delegation from Lord's.[20]

Bradman was more partial to the white South Africans. By the late 1960s South Africa had the strongest cricket team in the world, but the Vorster government's apartheid policy and refusal to allow Basil D'Oliveira to tour as part of the 1968–69 English team had cast doubts over the Springboks' cricketing future. These doubts intensified with the violent protests the Springboks met with on their 1970 rugby tour of Britain. Bradman was the Board's chairman and Bill Lawry's Australian team was due to jointly tour India and South Africa. Though the BCCI was loath to criticise the Australian Board's decision to continue sporting contact with South Africa, the Indian government did so in United Nations and Commonwealth forums. The Australian Board's scheduling of a combined India–South Africa tour revealed that it and Bradman resided in an apolitical vacuum. With world opinion shifting on sporting contacts with South Africa, their position was growing increasingly untenable.

As Chairman, Bradman shaped the Board's position. The South Africans were the game's champions at a time when Test and first-class cricket's appeal was diminishing and were due to tour Australia in 1971–72. Bradman flew privately to South Africa to discuss the matter with Vorster, while asserting publicly that sport and politics did not mix. He maintained the tour should proceed, while politicians dealt with the apartheid matter separately. Violent demonstrations during the 1971 Springbok rugby tour of Australia finally convinced him that the cricket tour was not possible. In cancelling the tour, moral questions about apartheid were secondary to pragmatic concerns about costs and law and order. Bradman wanted the South Africans in the game, despite increasing international condemnation. He held secret discussions with the McMahon Liberal Coalition government on the possibility of a 1975–76 South African tour of Australia, but the incoming Whitlam Labor government in 1972 banned all sporting contact. In *The Art of Cricket*, Bradman wrote of the game uniting the disparate countries of the old British Empire.[21] As an administrator, he was not governed by such ideals, but by the financial bottom line and the conviction that cricketing power was the preserve of a white, Anglo–Australian elite. Bradman never understood cricket's postcolonial age. If his views had prevailed, cricket may have split on racial lines.

Bradman's Board also saw the rise in player discontent. As an administrator, his strength was mastering the game's rules. He was less effective in dealing with player demands for increased match payments and a greater voice in the game's administration. Bradman held that the Australian game could not afford the increase, or the professionalisation of Test or first-class cricket. Seizing on this, the media tycoon Kerry Packer was able to hire the game's best players for his own ends and in the process revolutionised the game. For all his business acumen, Bradman and the Board failed to see the Packer revolution coming. The seeds of player discontent were sown on his watch. The Board's suppression of match payments to less than the players' real market value, and its reluctance to negotiate with Packer on television rights, created the conditions for his raid on the Australian game. Bradman and the Board were slow to recognise the emerging synergy between sport and the entertainment industry, and that sponsorship and advertising would supplant gate revenue as the game's major income stream. As a player, Bradman had challenged the Board's authority to secure his future. Once in administration he was not prepared to grant the same entitlements to players, and so was perceived by them to be a hypocrite.

As a batsman, Bradman had dominated all bowlers. As a captain, his crowning achievement was leading the unbeaten 1948 team. As the writer of *Farewell to Cricket*, he sought the last word on the Bodyline story and to stand above fellow player-writers Fingleton and O'Reilly as the game's elder sage, while in *The Art of Cricket* he ruled on technique and etiquette. As an administrator he scrutinised rules, mastered agendas and insisted on the primacy of the bottom line. Consistent in all facets of Bradman's career was the need to dominate. For a man of undoubted intelligence and drive – but a limited education and a narrow and inflexible worldview – cricket fulfilled this need. It determined his response to the players' demands and blinded him to the dangers posed by Packer. His retirement from cricket administration in the early 1980s coincided with the settlement of the Board's dispute with the tycoon. With Packer securing the television and marketing rights, the Board's semi-feudal hold ended. Bradman's domineering style was anachronistic in the game's new corporatised structure.

But circumstances provided a final opportunity for Bradman mythologisers with the fiftieth anniversary of the Bodyline series. The Australian television mini-series *Bodyline* was based on Paul Wheeler's fictionalised account.[22] The mini-series ran the well-trodden lines: the sinister Jardine and his Englishmen employing unsporting tactics to defeat the brave and plucky Australians. With 'pommy-bashing' spin and Bradman rejuvenated as a symbol of plucky Australian bush nationalism thwarted by nasty English upper-crust types, it proved a ratings success and rekindled public interest in Bradman and Bodyline. As Brett Hutchins has indicated, Bradman was reinvented as a populist nationalist hero and additional commercial possibilities were created with the growing fetishistic market for cricket memorabilia. Bradman items fetched far more than those from other players of the same era.[23] His aura was bolstered by the republication of *Farewell to Cricket* and *The Art of Cricket*, but the Bradman apotheosis came with the Bradman Museum's establishment in Bowral. Despite having lived most of his life in Adelaide, Bradman and Bowral were again linked. With the 1988 Bicentennial celebrations approaching, Australians looked for reassuring mythologies. Bradman and ANZAC were swept along on a wave of populist nostalgia. The heroic Bradman was deemed essential to the Bradman Museum's success. Hence, his life became bound in a heroic straitjacket with the game's scribes and ever-compliant publicists happy to oblige. Critical depictions of Bradman were shunned or kept from the public domain.

The Howard government joined the gatekeepers in 2002 when it legislated to protect Bradman's name from commercial exploitation under the Copyright Act. With the Museum's opening and the establishment of the Bradman Trust, an industry had emerged which sought to protect its brand for its commercial ends and to limit discussion on Bradman's life to his on-field heroics. Bowral did make Bradman. As a white, conservative, Protestant town, with loyalties to King and country, it forged the young Don Bradman's values and beliefs. There he learned about thrift and business caution, and also to realise that cricket could help provide career and social advancement. The town also reared his insecurities: anxiety, individualism and a need for dominance. But this side of Bradman is rarely found among the many hundreds of thousands of words written on his life. Instead, the focus has been on Bradman's uncommon cricket ability, his folksy Bowral background and his deceptively unassuming public persona. Unlike other Australian sporting champions of the Depression era, such as the billiards ace Walter Lindrum, the cyclist Hubert Opperman and the legendary racehorse Phar Lap, Bradman's reputation was forged playing Australia's national game against the 'mother country'. Like Australia's other demigods, the ANZACs, Bradman's life has become encrusted in myth and obscuration to assert the superiority of the national type. In returning Bradman to Bowral, the Museum and Trust continue this obscuration of his life. While the real Bradman with all his remarkable exploits on and off the cricket field was a product of Bowral, the mythical Don is a Bowral product wrapped in myth and nostalgia.

NOTES

1 *The Australian*, 27 February 2001; *Courier Mail*, 18 August 2000; Paul Kelly, *The March of Patriots: The Struggle for Modern Australia* (Melbourne University Press, 2009), p. 328.

2 Brett Hutchins, *Don Bradman: Challenging the Myth* (Cambridge University Press, 2002), pp. 37–42.

3 Russel Ward, *The Australian Legend* (Melbourne: Oxford University Press, 1966), pp. 1–2, 170, 213.

4 Philip Derriman, 'Bowral Boy at the Heart of a Noble Man', *Sydney Morning Herald*, 19 August 2000.

5 Don Bradman, *Farewell to Cricket* (Watsons Bay, Sydney: Editions Tom Thompson, 1994), pp. 2–3.

6 Ibid., p. 257.

7 Ibid.

8 Ibid., p. 53.

9 Ibid., pp. 38–39.

10 *Don Bradman's Book: The Story of My Cricketing Life, with Hints on Batting, Bowling and Fielding* (London: Hutchinson, 1931); *Farewell to Cricket*, p. 38.

11 *Farewell to Cricket*, pp. 60–61, 289.

12 David Frith, *Bodyline Autopsy: The Full Story of the Most Sensational Test Cricket Series; Australia v England 1932–33* (Sydney: ABC Books, 2002), pp. 185–92.

13 Ibid., p. 119.

14 V. Y. Richardson with R. S. Whitington, *The Vic Richardson Story: The Autobiography of a Versatile Sportsman* (Adelaide: Rigby, 1967), p. 205.

15 Bradman, *Farewell to Cricket*, p. 237.

16 Chris Harte, *SACA: The History of the South Australian Cricket Association* (Adelaide, Sports Marketing (Australia), 1990), pp. 270–72, 286, 288; Hutchins, *Don Bradman*, p. 81.

17 Keith A. P. Sandiford, *Cricket and the Victorians* (Aldershot: Scolar Press, 1994), pp. 83–84.

18 Frank Devine, 'Bradman Insecure Battler but No Crook', *The Australian*, 22 November 2001.

19 Bradman, *Farewell to Cricket*, p. 119.

20 Ibid., pp. 150–51.

21 Sir Donald Bradman, *The Art of Cricket* (Watsons Bay: Imprint Book, 1998), p. 235–36.

22 *Bodyline* (Kennedy Miller Productions, Australia, 1984); Paul Wheeler, *Bodyline: The Novel* (London: Faber and Faber, 1983).

23 Hutchins, *Don Bradman*, pp. 100–106.

7

RICHARD CASHMAN

The Packer cricket war

There is no doubt that the dramatic intervention of Australian media magnate Kerry Packer in Australian and world cricket in 1977 represented a great upheaval that appeared cataclysmic and confusing at the time. Supporters of WSC variously labelled it as a 'great cricket hijack' (Christopher Forsyth), a 'staggering coup' (Trevor Kennedy) and even a 'democratic revolution' (Andrew Caro). Others contended that WSC contributed to the 'Americanisation of cricket' (Chris Harte), the 'proletarianisation of cricket' (Adrian McGregor) and the promotion of hyper-masculine values (Bill Bonney).

Because World Series Cricket had been such a well-kept secret for more than six months, the cricket world was stunned after Australian journalists Peter McFarline and Alan Shiell reported the news on 9 May 1977. The cricket establishment reacted with a great sense of outrage and betrayal at what it regarded as an underhand attack on world cricket traditions and authority.

The world cricket media, with relatively few exceptions, condemned and denigrated WSC. The upheaval in world cricket was described variously as a 'circus', 'Packerball' and 'Packer cricket' rather than by its name, World Series Cricket, which had been registered on 16 August 1976. After night cricket and coloured clothing were introduced another pejorative term, pyjama cricket, was added to the list. Players who signed up with Packer were described as 'a bunch of money-hungry mercenaries' (Eric Beecher). Such descriptions questioned the legitimacy of WSC and Kerry Packer was demonised in the press as an ogre with a 'meat-mangler smile'.[1]

Surprisingly, after just two years of a bitterly fought war, a rapprochement was announced on 30 May 1979 and the World Series Cricket war was over. The war had damaged establishment cricket to such an extent that it readily agreed to Packer's terms: exclusive television rights for international cricket in Australia and some additional promotional rights.

Since 1977, assessments of WSC have varied remarkably. During the war and its immediate aftermath some regarded WSC as a revolution, changing the landscape of world cricket. In more recent times researchers have tended to see World Series Cricket as a catalyst rather than a change agent in world cricket. There has also been disagreement as to whether World Series Cricket enhanced the game or whether it was detrimental to its culture and traditions.

The roots of the war

Gideon Haigh believed that 'a volatile combination of factors made the Packer named World Series Cricket almost inevitable'.[2] Cricket had boomed in Australia during the 1970s, when a youthful and marketable Australian team, full of buoyant personalities, swept England aside in 1974–75 and did likewise to West Indies in 1975–76. The crowds at the Ashes series were the largest since 1946–47. The staging of a memorable Centenary Test, played at Melbourne in March 1977, may have lulled cricket officials into a false sense of security (with a number of players signing WSC contracts during this Test).

The boom in Australian cricket was linked to the improved quantity and quality of television coverage. The potential of television to transform the cricket world was evident during the 1970–71 series against England in Australia, when there was a national hook-up for the first time enabling viewers to watch an entire series. While the series drew a respectable 616,196 live spectators (a daily average of 20,279), the television audience by the later Tests was one million a day – approximately fifty times that of the live audience. Cricket was enhanced by the introduction of colour television during the 1974–75 series and the introduction of slow-motion replays, which allowed each stroke, catch and wicket to be analysed and admired.

The increasing popularity of limited-overs (one-day) cricket was another important factor. One-day cricket had been introduced to English domestic cricket in 1963, where it proved successful and helped to revitalise the game. The first international one-day cricket match had been played in Melbourne, when an astonishing 46,006 turned up to a hastily arranged match at the MCG on 5 January 1971 on what would have been the fifth day of a Test between Australia and England. (The Test had been abandoned after three days of rain.) The popularity of this new form of cricket was further demonstrated at the time of the first World Cup, held in England in 1975. A fluctuating and exciting nine-hour final between Australia and West Indies represented the first occasion when an overseas cricket match was broadcast in its entirety in Australia. Although the coverage began at 8 p.m. on the east coast and did not finish until 5.30 a.m., the ABC broadcast secured an astonishing rating of 21 at midnight (far more than the average time rating of 14 of Packer's Channel 9).[3] The advertising potential of cricket was clearly evident.

The ACB either failed to recognise the commercial potential of one-day cricket or was reluctant to promote this new format of the game. Between 1971 and 1977 Australia participated in fourteen limited-overs internationals but only three were staged in Australia. Following the initial game in 1971, one limited-overs match was scheduled against England during the 1974–75 series and another one was staged against West Indies during the 1975–76 series. When India toured Australia in 1977–78, the first year of the cricket war, no one-day internationals were played between Australia and India. Limited-overs cricket was an untapped market awaiting an entrepreneur to exploit.

World Series Cricket was built on significant player disenchantment even though there was a sharp increase in payments to players in the immediate seasons preceding WSC.[4] However, Braham Dabscheck identified several continuing player grievances. The first was a lack of adequate financial support given that an expanding cricket programme required players to devote as much as eight to nine months of the year to the game. This made it difficult for cricketers to maintain regular employment or to prepare for alternative careers. Players lacked the certainty of an annual salary based on a contract and were paid in a piecemeal fashion after each Test and tour. A second grievance was that officials did not sufficiently consider player needs and interests in making decisions about travel arrangements, hotel accommodation, food and rest days. During the 1969 tour of India, players had to put up with substandard accommodation and arduous travel conditions. Tacking on a tough South Africa tour immediately afterwards 'was arranged with little thought for the welfare of players'.[5]

When Kerry Packer provided cricketers with a more attractive salary package, including a fixed annual contract, the leading cricketers deserted the Board en masse. Jack Pollard noted that 'the fact that so many signed at a point when match fees were rising and no organisation existed to stage WSC games, demonstrated how unanimous was the players' discontent and how badly key ACB officials misjudged the players' mood'.[6]

The trigger for the war

Kerry Packer, the owner of Channel 9, recognised by the mid-1970s that television sport was an attractive, high-rating and cheap option to counter the problems of dwindling audiences and to meet local content requirements.

An added advantage of cricket was that it was a 'sure way of attracting advertising revenue' during the slack Christmas–New Year period.[7] Packer actively pursued the television rights for major golf and tennis tournaments as well as cricket. However, his quest for Australian cricket television rights was rebuffed by the ACB, which had a longstanding relationship with the national broadcaster, the Australian Broadcasting Corporation, which had traditionally acquired non-exclusive rights for radio and television broadcasting. The ACB awarded non-exclusive broadcast rights to the ABC for three years until 1979 for $210,000, even though Kerry Packer was prepared to pay $1.5 million, seven times the amount for the three years from 1979.

When Packer met Board members Bob Parish and Ray Steele on 22 June 1977, they were astonished by the amount he offered and his quest for exclusive rights, an option that the Board had never previously considered. Conservative Board officials were nonplussed by the blunt and even crude stance of this media tycoon.

While Packer was outraged by the Board's non-acceptance of his offer, he did not immediately proceed to set up World Series Cricket. The idea took form after a chance conversation with associate John Cornell, who suggested that Packer enlist the world's best players and organise his own competition.

However, World Series cricket was not a fait accompli until June 1977. When Packer arrived in England in early May he stated that he was prepared to co-operate with cricket authorities and added that 'there is no reason why Test cricket as it is now will be affected'.[8] However, the response of English cricket officialdom was hardly encouraging. The Cricket Council issued a statement on 13 May that Tony Greig, who had been a recruiting agent for Packer, would not captain England in the forthcoming series because 'his action has inevitably impaired the trust which existed between cricket authorities and the Captain of the England side'.[9] When Packer met the ICC on 23 June 1977, he explained that 'he did not see himself as being a permanent fixture in cricket. He did not want to replace Boards of Control. He wanted to work with them but this had not been possible in Australia and that was why he had taken the action that he had.'[10] However, negotiations collapsed when Packer's demand for exclusive rights to international cricket was flatly rejected. With compromise out of the question Packer issued his famous defiant comment: 'It's now every man for himself and the devil take the hindmost.'

After the ICC banned WSC-contracted players from Test cricket, Kerry Packer instituted action against the English TCCB and the ICC in the High Court. The hearing began on 26 September and lasted thirty-one days.

Justice Slade ruled in favour of the three WSC-contracted litigants, Tony Greig, Mike Proctor and John Snow, stating that the ICC ban from Test cricket amounted to an unreasonable restraint of trade.[11]

WSC was less successful in Sydney's Federal Court in September 1977, when the ACB contended that the WSC use of phrases such as 'Super Tests' and references to 'The Australian Team', 'Australia', 'the West Indies' and 'the World' flouted section 52 of the Trade Practices Act. While the Federal Court ruled in favour of the ACB, it permitted the word 'Supertest' and the phrase 'WSC Australians'.[12]

By the time that the news of WSC became public in May 1977, thirty-five of the leading international players had signed contracts. Australia had the largest contingent with eighteen players, including thirteen out of the seventeen that toured England in 1977. WSC recruits included four prominent West Indians (captain Clive Lloyd, Viv Richards, Andy Roberts and Michael Holding) as well as four of the leading Pakistanis (captain Mushtaq Mohammad, Majid Khan, Asif Iqbal and Imran Khan). While a majority of the English team remained loyal to establishment cricket, four signed with WSC: Tony Greig, Derek Underwood, Alan Knott and John Snow.

Kerry Packer also recruited five South Africans to his WSC troupe, but such inclusions were controversial because an apartheid sports boycott had operated since 1971 and continued until the early 1990s. Australian Prime Minister Malcolm Fraser was a passionate supporter of the apartheid sports boycott.

Packer's specific problem was that the WSC West Indies were unlikely to agree to play against South Africans. Packer gave influential Jamaican Prime Minister Michael Manley an assurance that the South Africans recruited to WSC would not come directly from South Africa but via English county cricket. This was the case with Barry Richards, Mike Proctor and Eddie Barlow.

Packer attempted to stretch the rules further when he enlisted Denys Hobson and Graeme Pollock, who were South African-based cricketers. The Australian Department of Immigration and Ethnic Affairs received two visa applications for these players and granted the visas when Packer informed the Minister that he had another agreement with Manley that the two players, if granted visas, would not play in Supertests and only appear in country and one-day matches. When the Australian High Commissioner conveyed this situation to Manley, he dismissed Packer's second assurance as a 'breach of their original undertaking'.[13]

Hobson and his wife arrived in Australia on 24 November, and Pollock a week later, and were VIP guests at the first Supertest. After the two South

African-based players were blacklisted by the West Indians, they were excused from their WSC contracts and returned to South Africa.

India and New Zealand were the only countries with no defections to WSC cricket in its first season. Mihir Bose commented that 'Indians did not see [this non-recruitment to WSC] as a snub but as a chance to reaffirm the values of traditional cricket'. He added that the Indian Board was keen to show that its cricketers were 'untainted by Packer'. As a result a full-strength Indian team toured Australia in 1977–78, as a rival attraction to WSC.[14]

By the time WSC began in December 1977, over fifty players had been recruited, with sufficient numbers and reserves to form three teams: the WSC Australian, the WSC West Indian and the World XI. Twenty-two Australians and seventeen West Indians had joined WSC by that time and the World XI was made up primarily of Englishmen, Pakistanis and South Africans.

Recruiting WSC players

In December 1976 Packer authorised John Cornell and Austin Robertson, Dennis Lillee's agents, to recruit a troupe of internationals. Australia's leading fast bowler, Lillee was the first to sign up for $105,000 over three seasons. In addition to current Australian players, three retired Australian players, Ian Chappell, Ian Redpath and Ross Edwards, were enlisted. Most of the player contracts covered a period of three years and ranged from $16,500 to $35,000 per season (the average being $25,000) plus incentive payments.[15]

After Packer contracted South African-born English captain Tony Greig, he volunteered to recruit additional international players. Greig and Robertson travelled to Trinidad in January 1978, when West Indies were playing Pakistan, and signed up some of the leading West Indian and Pakistani players.

Given that the legitimacy of WSC was widely challenged, the appointment of well-respected ambassadors and consultants added to its credibility. Former players such as Richie Benaud, Bill Lawry, Keith Stackpole, Fred Trueman, Gary Sobers, Bob Cowper and John Gleeson 'were used extensively as consultants, commentators and ambassadors'. Other sportsmen, such as legendary Australian footballer Ron Barassi and tennis great John Newcombe, 'were sought out to express solidarity for the cricketers in their push for better conditions'.[16] The recruitment of respected commentator and former Australian cricket captain Richie Benaud was pivotal, as his wholehearted support of WSC added gravitas to television broadcasts and modified perceptions that WSC was a 'bread and circus' event.

The battle for the spectator in 1977–1978

Although WSC staged matches in the West Indies and New Zealand, the primary battlefield was in Australia, because this was the market that Packer most wanted to win. From May 1977 the battle was waged for players, grounds and, above all, for spectators, the ultimate arbiters of who would control cricket.

World Series Cricket was handicapped by a failure to gain access to major cricket grounds in 1977–78, having been rebuffed by cricket authorities in their applications to use them. WSC staged its major matches at two football grounds (in Melbourne and Adelaide), an agricultural showground in Sydney and a trotting ground in Perth. No matches were staged in Brisbane in the first season. Matches were only possible at these venues because Gabba groundsman John Maley performed the miracle of creating hot-house pitches, which were dropped in when necessary, thereby creating a tradition of drop-in pitches.

WSC launched an ambitious programme to challenge the official ACB international programming by organising a concurrent rival series of six Supertests, staged between Australia, West Indies and a World XI. A second strategy was to stage fifteen one-day matches between the same three teams. A travelling troupe of cricketers took part in the Country Cup, playing thirty days of cricket in various regional centres.

WSC made an inauspicious start in the battle for the spectator. Although the first Supertest between Australia and West Indies featured some of the leading cricketers in the world, its first day drew only 2,847 spectators (far less than Packer's prediction of 15,000) on 2 December 1977 in the 80,000-capacity VFL Park. The ground was located at Glen Waverley, a relatively inaccessible venue in an outer suburb, twenty-five kilometres from the city. The match began at 11 a.m. and at twelve noon television viewers could switch to the broadcast of the rival establishment Test between Australia and India at the Gabba, with a crowd of 6,015 patrons. Although the establishment Australian team included six debutants, the recall of the experienced forty-one-year-old Bob Simpson, who had retired from Test cricket almost a decade ago, proved fortuitous. Simpson scored 539 runs, including two centuries, during the series, at an average of 53.90, and proved an able leader of a young side. The team also had the benefit of world-class bowler Jeff Thomson, who had signed a WSC contract initially but withdrew because it jeopardised his ten-year contract with a Queensland radio station.

It was only in Sydney that the Supertests gained greater spectator traction, possibly because the Showground was more conveniently located, adjacent to the Sydney Cricket Ground, than VFL Park. Sydney cricket fans may possibly have been more open to cricket innovation than their Melbourne counterparts: 23,762 watched the second Supertest and 36,424 attended the fourth Supertest. The Sydney total of 60,186 spectators represented almost half the aggregate of six Supertests (124,532). By contrast, the closely fought five-Test series between Australia and India, which was decided only in the final Test with Australia winning 3–2, attracted 256,954.

WSC achieved much greater success in the one-day International Cup. The potential of night cricket, played with a white ball, was evident when Australia met the World XI in a hurriedly arranged day–night practice match at VFL Park on 14 December, when 6,449 spectators attended.[17] It proved the harbinger of a brighter future for WSC, and three back-to-back night matches at VFL Park from 23 to 25 January 1978 attracted 52,831 patrons, including 24,636 who watched Australia play West Indies – the second largest crowd of the summer. (The first day of the establishment third Test at Melbourne on 30 December attracted 26,110.) One-day cricket subsequently attracted good crowds at Perth, Adelaide and Sydney.[18]

Summing up the achievements of WSC in its first year, *Cricket Close-up* stated that the total WSC attendance at all levels of cricket of 354,933 was 'well below expectations' and was 'far from a great success but not a failure', with the numbers at one-day matches providing some hope for the future.[19] Packer himself admitted that the first season of WSC was a 'disappointment', but he believed that it had occurred because 'people had been so heavily indoctrinated against the idea [of WSC]'.[20]

Tony Cozier, West Indian and WSC commentator, contended that WSC had realised many of its aims: player salaries had increased, cricket had been promoted more aggressively, there was the innovation of night cricket and the white ball, and television coverage, with ingenious camera-work, had captured 'every stroke, every wicket, every catch and every emotional reaction with such precision'. However, he admitted that a lack of public response to the Supertests was disappointing and it may have been a blunder to stage the Supertests in opposition to the establishment Tests. He added that WSC was seen too much as 'Packer cricket', as it appeared that many people did not like the idea of one man controlling cricket simply because he was wealthy.[21]

The financial losses incurred by both sets of protagonists were substantial by the end of the 1977–78 season. Estimates of WSC losses varied from $3 to 4.5 million. The ACB didn't fare much better: its tour profits were slashed by more than half ($400,000 for five Tests in 1977–78 compared to $1.13 million for six Tests in 1975–76). The ACB, like other Boards, was also expected to contribute to the ICC's unsuccessful High Court case.[22]

A matter of even greater concern was the level of damage done to the sport by a surfeit of televised cricket. During the 1977–78 season, Channel 9 broadcast 306 hours of cricket and ABC 234 hours, 540 hours in total. This was three times the 170 hours broadcast during the 1975–76 series.

1978–1979

Some believed that an Australia–England (Ashes) series might pose a sterner test for WSC in its second season of 1978–79, but it proved to be a triumph for Kerry Packer. Bob Simpson had retired again and Jeff Thomson was forced to sit on the sidelines for most of the season. The Sydney Equity Court ruled on 3 November 1978 that Thomson was bound by his ACB contract and could not play for WSC until April 1979.[23] Inexperienced Australian captain Graham Yallop proved no match for the shrewd English captain Mike Brearley, whose side had suffered relatively few WSC defections. Despite some good individual performances, notably Rodney Hogg's 41 wickets in six Ashes Tests, it soon became apparent that the series was a mismatch: England comfortably won by five Tests to one.

While the crowds for the six Ashes Tests (370,574) were larger than for the five Tests against India in 1977–78 (256,594) and more than double the five Supertests in 1978–79 (156,859), they were much smaller than the numbers attracted to the two previous Ashes series: 616,196 (in 1970–71) and 777,333 (in 1974–75).

The disastrous Ashes series was only one reason why the balance swung in favour of WSC in the second season of the war. While cricket officials had denied WSC access to the major cricket grounds of the country, a number of prominent politicians were more sympathetic to the WSC cause. Packer gained the ear in particular of Neville Wran, Labor Premier of New South Wales, who intervened to allow WSC games at the SCG in 1978–79. Wran decided that a good turn for Packer served his and the public's interests and he may also have relished dismissing the establishment-minded SCG Trustees. Packer returned the favour: his media was fulsome in its support for Wran during the 1978 state elections.[24] The support of the New South Wales government not only enabled WSC to gain access to the ground during the 1978–79 season but also facilitated the erection of six giant light towers.

When the newly installed floodlights were turned on for the first time at the SCG on 28 November 1978, during the one-day match between Australia and West Indies, there was a bumper crowd of over 50,000. The gates were thrown open after 44,377 patrons had passed through the turnstiles because there were still long queues outside. Tony Adams commented

Table 7.1. Attendances at World Series Cricket matches in 1977–78 and 1978–79

	1977–78	1978–79
Supertests	124,532 (6 matches)	156,859 (5 matches)
International Cup	136,954 (15 games)	360,912 (21 games)
Country matches (Country Cup, 1977; Cavaliers, 1978)	60,983 (30 days)	58,575 (31 days)
TOTAL	322,469	576,346

NOTE: This table is reproduced from Cashman, *"Ave a Go, Yer Mug!"*, p. 164. WSC crowd figures have to be treated with some caution as there was considerable variation from source to source. WSC critics also claimed that many tickets were given away free. However, a surge in one-day figures in the second season seems undeniable.

that there was a 'buzz of excitement' around the ground when the lights came on and the arrival of night cricket 'had swept Sydney off its feet'.[25] Bill O'Reilly, no admirer of WSC, admitted that night cricket was an 'incredible performance' and that the enthusiastic crowd was similar to those at football finals. He added that Kerry Packer had won this first Sydney round of the 1978–79 season 'by the proverbial mile'.[26]

That night was a triumph for WSC and a turning-point in the cricket war. WSC had successfully stormed one of the citadels of cricket power (the SCG being second only to the MCG as the most important cricket site in the country) and proved that one of its core products was popular and marketable. One-day matches and night cricket were primarily responsible for the expansion of WSC audiences in its second season.

Towards the end of the disastrous second year of the war, the ACB had no option but to capitulate and sought a compromise with Kerry Packer. The tour profits from the 1978–79 Ashes series of $126,634 were approximately one-quarter the return of $501,652 from the previous 1974–75 Ashes series.[27] It has been estimated that two years of WSC resulted in a loss of $6 million for the Packer organisation. However, Packer did secure a significant return for his cricket investment, as he was able to meet much of the government-required quota of Australian content at a cheap price.

An agreement was signed between the Australian Cricket Board and PBL Sports Pty Ltd by 30 May 1979 and lodged with the Trade Practices Commissioner. Under the agreement PBL Sports was given 'the exclusive right, for a period of ten years, to promote the programme of cricket organised by the Board and to arrange the televising and merchandising in respect of that programme'.[28] Packer thus secured his core objective of securing exclusive Australian television rights. Although the agreement represented an abject surrender by the ACB, it enabled the Board to claw back a monopoly of Australian cricket.

Having achieved his major objective from the war, Packer shrewdly recognised that it was to his advantage not to further impoverish official cricket. Shayne Quick noted that 'Packer's foray into cricket, and televised sport, could only grow and prosper with a healthy and solvent ACB ... The downfall of the ACB would result in the demise of WSC and Australian cricket in general.'[29]

Interpretations of the cricket war

Interpretations of the Packer cricket war have changed markedly over time. Initially, academics sided with the cricket establishment, the majority of the world media and the public in condemning Packer and World Series Cricket. At the first conference of the Australian Society for Sports History, for example, held in June 1977, there was not a good word said in favour of Packer and his new cricket troupe. Packer was regarded as a selfish corporate raider who had little interest in the culture and traditions of cricket.

During the next decade a number of academics were critical of the WSC-inspired changes in cricket. Sociologists Geoffrey Lawrence and David Rowe described the Packer involvement in cricket as a striking example of a 'corporate pitch': commercial cricket telecasts helped to 'socialise viewers to accept the values of capitalism'. Lawrence and Rowe contended that the public were the 'losers' since they were 'exposed to an increasingly aggressive spectacle, manipulated by commercial television for the benefit of advertisers'.[30]

Ian Harriss extended this criticism of WSC when he argued that it had reduced cricket to a form of soap-opera entertainment. Packer cricket offered 'the consumer instant gratification which is so much a part of the consumer culture of late capitalism'. Harriss explained the shift to limited overs as:

> The emergence of an era in which the game is no longer based on the rational, calculating bourgeois individual. Indeed, the essence or 'depth' of Test cricket has given way to the glittering surface and spectacle of the highly commercialised commodity that is One-Day cricket ... The one-day spectacle is packaged in much the same way as a one-hour television melodrama. There is some variation in each individual episode, but the conclusion is inevitably a hectic chase sequence.[31]

Brian Stoddart challenged this view, contending that 'far from degrading cricket, Packer gave it new dimensions by challenging outmoded visions of the game's social position'. Stoddart believed that Packer needed the game 'to establish his channel as the leading sportscaster' in the country, to meet his 'legislatively required Australian content levels at an economically viable level' and to attract more high-level sponsorship. The game, however, also needed the media tycoon to 'deliver it a new audience share, boost its fragile economic base, and stimulate a new social popularity'.[32] In Stoddart's view, the Packer upheaval in cricket occurred in part because the ACB was unable to deal adequately with structural changes in the world of cricket during the increasingly televisual years of the 1970s. The payment for elite players was inadequate and there was no recognition of the commercial potential of the limited-overs game.

More recent researchers have regarded Packer as the catalyst rather than the instigator of change that became evident in cricket from the 1960s. Shayne Quick concluded that 'it is clear that the era [of WSC] was one of progression rather than a radical revolution with television the vehicle for change rather than its cause'.[33] Bob Stewart considered that World Series Cricket was a product of the hyper-commercialisation of leisure, recreation and sport because of changes that had occurred in the economic structure and cultural mood of advanced capitalist societies, which he referred to as postmodernism during the 1960s and 1970s.[34] Gideon Haigh concluded that 'WSC was less an initiator of change – reliance on fast bowling, one-day cricket, and even frequency of international competition – than an expediter'. WSC's changes were 'stylistic rather than substantive'. Haigh added that Packer 'proved less a cricket revolutionary than a remarkable resurfacer'.[35]

WSC did lead to an increase in player payments and improved conditions of employment. The WSC practice of placing the leading players on an annual contract was continued by the ACB after 1979. The emergence of a Professional Cricketers Association in September 1977, which was supported by Kerry Packer (who provided the association with a loan of $10,000), contributed to greater player representation. While the Association was sustained only for a few years beyond WSC, it encouraged the ACB to take greater notice of player issues. Dabscheck concluded that during the 1970s cricket 'was transformed from a semi-amateur sport where Test and leading players were paid relatively small amounts of money, to a fully-fledged professional operation with leading players employed on well-remunerated contracts'.[36] However, Haigh questioned the degree to which cricket had been professionalised. He noted that, while there were radical short-term improvements in cricket salaries, Australian players after 1979 still largely depended on the generosity of an unchanged administration.[37]

Reflections

Undoubtedly WSC helped to transform Australian and world cricket; it helped strip away many of the Anglicist, clubby, gentlemanly vestiges of the game. Cricket was promoted to a wider market than before and WSC attracted new audiences to the game: youth, women and Australians from non-British backgrounds. While Packer helped to market the game more effectively than the ACB, Haigh and Frith contended that it was a myth that 'Kerry Packer made cricket popular; on the contrary, Packer coveted cricket because it *was* popular, and had seldom been more so'.[38] However, Packer did add value to Australian cricket, as before him 'the idea of Australian cricket having a "market value" would have been unthinkable'.[39]

The promotion of World Series Cricket combined American rhetoric and Australian populism. The phrases World Series Cricket and Supertests drew on American sports hyperbole. World Series Cricket at the same time was also more unashamedly and chauvinistically Australian. While the ABC commentators attempted to be measured, fair and objective in their commentary, some Channel 9 commentators were far more excitable and stridently Australian. Bill Bonney contended that WSC also promoted a patriarchal and 'ocker' (an archetypal unconventional Australian) masculine ideology with the camera focusing on 'Lillee's vigorous rubbing of the ball on his crutch' as he walked back to bowl or 'on Chappell and Lillee in their most loutish and convention-flouting acts'.[40]

Gordon Ross referred to the WSC brand as 'jet-age cricket'.[41] The innovations were numerous: night cricket, a white ball, coloured clothing, fielding restrictions, hot-house pitches, as well as a host of other giveaways and gimmicks. The popular WSC anthem, 'C'mon Aussie, c'mon', which had been written by the advertising company Mojo and was introduced in the second season of WSC, became a hit in its own right, and was symptomatic of the changed culture of cricket, which embraced pop music and youth culture.

However, the greatest contribution of WSC was the enhancement of cricket television broadcasts. In traditional sports coverage the idea was to locate the viewer like a spectator at the ground with the camera swivelling, like the head, to capture the action at various parts of the ground. The viewer was no longer 'anchored to one spot like the ground spectator' in WSC coverage but was provided with a range of angles and perspectives. With eight cameras rather than four, every ball was filmed from behind the bowler's arm. Interviews, computerised statistics, the grunts and expletives of players via stumpcam, all provided viewers with privileged access to play and removed that reverential distance between players and spectators that had been part of traditional cricket coverage.[42]

WSC also contributed to a rash of head injuries, as there were no limits on short-pitched bowling. The worst occasion was when a bare-headed David Hookes received a sickening blow on the head from an Andy Roberts bumper on the first day of the second Supertest at the Sydney Showground, resulting in a double fracture of the jaw and the cheekbone. The event had two consequences. It demonstrated, first of all, that WSC was not a sham and mere exhibition cricket. It also encouraged cricketers to don protective headgear and stimulated the development of appropriate cricket helmets.

Postscript

Wisden, the official Bible of establishment cricket, virtually ignored World Series Cricket. It included just five pages in the 1978 annual and slightly longer articles in the 1979 and 1980 annuals. Written by Gordon Ross under the heading 'The Packer Case', the articles covered court action, financial issues and negotiations, with only limited discussion of the cricket played. Gideon Haigh noted that *Wisden* provided little more than a skeleton of WSC scores in the 1979 and 1980 annuals, occupying less space than what was devoted to county second XI averages.[43] The runs scored, wickets taken and catches caught by many of the leading international players between 1977 and 1979 are still not counted because WSC matches are still not considered first-class cricket.

The cricket war poisoned relationships between players before and after WSC, particularly in Australia. The Australian team which toured England in 1977 was split between the WSC-aligned majority of thirteen and four who remained loyal to establishment cricket. Enmities generated by the cricket lasted for years after the rapprochement of 1979. Kim Hughes had the problem of captaining (during occasional Greg Chappell absences) WSC players, which included Lillee and Marsh, who never forgave Hughes for his loyalty to the Board during the cricket war.

When interviewed about World Series Cricket by Alan Lee in February 1979, Packer stated that 'I spent a disproportionate amount of time on cricket at first – it's only three to five per cent of my business'. Packer's personal attention to cricket was 'staggering' given his wide business interests.[44] When asked by Lee whether he would 'do it all over again', Packer stated that his answer was probably 'No'.[45]

Gideon Haigh has reflected on whether the establishment 'should have seen Packer coming' and whether the Packer cricket war was inevitable. Minutes of the ACB's annual meeting of 6–7 September 1977 suggest that members of the Board were not 'steadfastly resistant to an exclusive agreement with a commercial broadcaster' beyond 1979. However, the dispute proved intractable because of clashes of personalities and philosophies: 'Packer's idea of compromise was the other side giving up.'[46] The longstanding custodians of the game in Australia and England misread the intentions of Kerry Packer (who did not want to run cricket) and consequently overreacted to the threat posed by Packer. 'The reaction was strongest in Britain, where it was coloured by sentimentality, indignation, anti-colonial arrogance and a not unjustified feeling that the team had been betrayed by the South African-born Greig.'[47] (Conservative middle-class men also had an inadequate understanding of a rapidly changing society and the appetite of many fans for new forms of the game.)

At the outset of the cricket war, Kerry Packer was regarded as the devil incarnate by cricket authorities and many cricket supporters. After he died on 26 December 2005, during the Melbourne Test there was a minute's silence, and black armbands were worn.[48]

NOTES

1 Richard Cashman, *"Ave a Go, Yer Mug!' Australian Cricket Crowds from Larrikin to Ocker* (Sydney: William Collins, 1984), p. 154.

2 Gideon Haigh, 'World Series Cricket' in *The Oxford Companion to Australian Cricket* (Melbourne: Oxford University Press, 1996), p. 605.

3 Bill Bonney, *Packer and Televised Cricket* (Sydney: NSW Institute of Technology, Media Papers, 1980), p. 4.

4 Gideon Haigh and David Frith, *Inside Story: Unlocking Australian Cricket's Archives* (Australia: News Custom Publishing, 2007), p. 183.

5 Braham Dabscheck, 'The Professional Cricketers Association', *Sporting Traditions*, 8 (1991), pp. 10–11.

6 Jack Pollard, *Australian Cricket: The Game and the Players* (Sydney: Hodder and Stoughton, 1982), p. 1138.

7 Bonney, *Packer and Televised Cricket*, p. 5.

8 Gideon Haigh, *The Cricket War: The Inside Story of Kerry Packer's World Series Cricket* (Melbourne: Text Publishing Company, 1993), p. 64.

9 *Wisden Cricketers' Almanack 1978* (London: John Wisden, 1978), p. 123.

10 Haigh and Frith, *Inside Story*, p. 187.

11 John Scott, *Caught in Court: A Selection of Cases with Cricketing Connections* (London: Andre Deutsch, 1989), pp. 101–111.

12 Haigh, *The Cricket War*, pp. 100, 115.

13 Richard Cashman, *Australia's Role in the Apartheid Sports Boycott* (Canberra: NAA and DFAT, 2008), pp. 25–28.

14 Mihir Bose, *A History of Indian Cricket* (London: Andre Deutsch, 1980), pp. 291, 301.

15 Dabscheck, 'The Professional Cricketers Association', p. 10.

16 Haigh, 'World Series Cricket', p. 607.
17 Haigh, *The Cricket War*, pp. 126–27.
18 Ibid., pp. 153–54; Cashman, *"Ave a Go, Yer Mug!'*, p. 159.
19 Cashman, *"Ave a Go, Yer Mug!'*, p. 161.
20 *Wisden Cricketers' Almanack 1980* (London: John Wisden, 1980), p. 123.
21 *Sun-Herald*, 5 February 1978.
22 Haigh, *The Cricket War*, pp. 17, 174, 175.
23 Scott, *Caught in Court*, pp. 110–11.
24 Mike Steketee and Milton Cockburn, *Wran: An Unauthorised Biography* (Sydney: Allen & Unwin, 1986), p. 165.
25 *World of Cricket*, quoted in Cashman, *"Ave a Go, Yer Mug!'*, p. 163.
26 *Sydney Morning Herald*, 29 November 1978.
27 Haigh, *The Cricket War*, p. 279.
28 *Wisden Cricketers' Almanack 1980*, p. 127.
29 Shayne Quick, 'World Series Cricket, Television and Australian Culture', unpublished PhD thesis, Ohio State University (1990), quoted in Haigh, *The Cricket War*, p. 280.
30 Geoffrey Lawrence and David Rowe, *Power Play: The Commercialisation of Australian Sport* (Sydney: Hale & Iremonger, 1986), pp. 164, 177.
31 Ian Harriss, 'Packer, Cricket and Post Modernism' in D. Rowe and G. Lawrence (eds.), *Sport and Leisure: Trends in Australian Popular Culture* (Sydney: Harcourt Brace Jovanovich, 1990), pp. 117–18.
32 Brian Stoddart, 'Sport and Television: Reflections upon a Cultural Phenomenon' (unpublished paper), pp. 13–14.
33 Quick, 'World Series Cricket', p. 196.
34 R. K. Stewart, 'A Theoretical Framework for Analysing the Commercial Development of Australian First Class Cricket', unpublished ASSH Conference paper, Launceston, 1993.
35 Haigh, *The Cricket War*, pp. 316, 322.
36 Dabscheck, 'The Professional Cricketers Association', pp. 2, 22–23.
37 Haigh, *The Cricket War*, pp. 317, 318.
38 Haigh and Frith, *Inside Story*, p. 182.
39 Haigh, *The Cricket War*, p. 328.
40 Bonney, *Packer and Televised Cricket*, p. 27.
41 *Wisden Cricketers' Almanack 1980*, p. 121.
42 Bonney, *Packer and Televised Cricket*, p. 17.
43 Haigh, *The Cricket War*, p. 326.
44 Ibid., p. 323.
45 *Wisden Cricketers' Almanack 1980*, p. 123.
46 Haigh, *The Cricket War* (Melbourne University Press, 2007), p. x; Haigh and Frith, *Inside Story*, p. 188.
47 *Wisden Cricketers' Almanack 2006* (London: John Wisden, 2006), p. 1517.
48 Ibid., p. 1519.

8

GREG RYAN

New Zealand cricket
and the colonial relationship

Cricket as 'cultural baggage', 1840–1870

Cricket was an integral part of the 'cultural baggage' which accompanied the European settlement of New Zealand during the nineteenth century. Missionaries encouraged Maori interest in the game from as early as 1832, but substantive growth came only with the distinct patterns of provincial settlement from the 1840s. The so-called 'systematic colonisation' schemes promoted by Edward Gibbon Wakefield ensured that cricket, as an essential institution of England in general and its leisured class in particular, emerged early and naturally, when one might normally expect other amenities and necessities of colonial life to have taken priority. As the tensions of industrial transformation and rapid post-Napoleonic social change came to a head during the early 1830s, Wakefield sought to create a safety valve for British society through colonisation. In addition to a migrant population carefully selected with regard to gender balance and personal morality, his prime mechanism was a 'sufficient price' on land – set at such a level as to both limit the number of colonial landowners, and regulate class relationships by creating a subservient workforce among those without means to purchase. With population distribution confined in this way, the perceived chaos and dislocation of 'frontier' settlements in Australia and North America would be avoided.[1] Wakefield envisioned an essentially conservative pre-industrial rural idyll described by Keith Sinclair as 'a vertical section of English society excluding the lowest stratum. It would form not a "new people", but an "extension" of an old, retaining its virtues, but eliminating its poverty and overcrowding.'[2] In reality, the scheme foundered on problems of both conception and application, and although responsible for the creation of five settlements ultimately contributed only a fraction of overall European migration to New Zealand during the nineteenth century. Sluggish investment left insufficient funds to develop settlement infrastructure and illegal land purchases created antagonism with both Maori and the British Crown.

Nevertheless, the guiding principle has important implications for New Zealand cricket in that the game was deliberately fostered as a means for elites to consolidate their position at the head of the new society. Moreover, Wakefield was conscious of the moral usefulness of the game in a new colonial setting. As he wrote in 1850: 'I tell the boys in summer time to play at cricket and play well, that those who are the best cricketers most likely will be the best readers and writers.'[3]

It is no coincidence that Canterbury, where the Wakefield ideal was applied with greatest success, was early recognised as the 'home' of New Zealand cricket. The first cricket club, formed in June 1851, epitomised Wakefield's emphasis on social delineation and a cultivated leisured class. It contained the local political, mercantile and landed elite, the subscription was preclusive and membership was by nomination. Because of the club's status, Canterbury cricketers had little difficulty overcoming the perennial colonial problem of limited funds to establish suitable facilities and playing space. As the local *Lyttelton Times* remarked, 'English liberality in support of an English game' ensured the club had a ground, groundsman and pavilion by 1854.[4] Long after the Wakefield ideal collapsed, the cricketing elite was reinforced by Canterbury's appeal to a disproportionate number of the public school and Oxbridge graduates reaching New Zealand in the last third of the nineteenth century. Up to 1914, the burgeoning Christchurch club competition contained a much higher proportion of middle-class players than were to be found anywhere else. While artisans and labourers were certainly present in this cricketing fraternity, they were drawn together in distinct clubs very much at odds with prevailing myths of colonial egalitarianism.[5]

No other New Zealand province attained the sophistication of Canterbury cricket. During the early 1840s, the Wellington game certainly displayed the class divisions born of initially strict adherence to systematic colonisation. The first cricket club in 1841–42 included several future politicians of note, leading merchants and landholders. A separate Albion Cricket Club was established for tradesmen and labourers. But the collapse of Wakefieldian ideals in favour of random, unselected migration and a 'levelling' social attitude implicit in the opportunities open to independent colonists prompted many of Wellington's original settlers to depart. Its cricket altered accordingly, with clubs functioning only sporadically during the late 1840s and almost extinct during the 1850s. Only when New Zealand's capital shifted from Auckland to Wellington in 1865 did the administration of the local game begin to attract influential politicians and public figures. Yet the playing strength of Wellington teams remained largely in the hands of minor clerical staff and skilled tradesmen.[6] Auckland followed a similar pattern, but for different reasons. Without the strictures of systematic settlement, it grew from commercial and trading interests during the 1830s, there was no deliberately transplanted leisured class and its earliest cricket clubs struggled under the patronage of a small group of government servants and staff. In addition, vulnerability to Maori attack during the mid-1840s and again during the early 1860s necessitated a strong military presence which determined that cricket thrived among the garrison but was moribund in the years when they were stationed elsewhere. Relative peace after 1865 brought expansion and patronage from the business and legal community of Auckland, but the lack of an elite civilian tradition produced a game more democratic than in other provinces and with significantly less social stratification among its clubs.[7] Otago, although colonised on 'systematic' principles, was initially shaped by a conservative Scottish Presbyterian theocracy which disparaged English diversions. Such cricket as there was during the 1850s revolved around a small English faction, or 'Little Enemy' as the Scots termed them. Only with the discovery of gold during the early 1860s and an influx of miners from Australia did the game take root. Although gold prosperity financed a visit by George Parr's All England XI in January 1864, once the bulk of the mining population departed during the 1870s there was no intrinsically English cricketing tradition to foster players of an appropriate standard. Otago remained the least active and least successful of the main cricketing provinces into the twentieth century.[8]

Impediments to participation, 1870–1914

Even as New Zealand's population and infrastructure expanded in the wake of the gold rushes and renewed immigration schemes during the 1870s, cricket, perhaps more than most sports in that it was relatively expensive, time-consuming and reliant on a reasonable quality of playing surface, moved only slowly beyond its urban middle-class bulwark. Indeed, the distribution of the growing population denied many access to cricket. The dominance of the agricultural economy determined that well into the twentieth century the population remained largely rural and engaged in primary occupations with barely a third living in the four main cities by 1914.[9] Many small towns and country areas simply lacked the population and resources to sustain regular fixtures or develop cricket grounds. The mobility of rural workers also militated against organised cricket. The 1891 census reveals that seasonal workers, who were largely rural, constituted perhaps a third of the adult male European labour force, and that more than half were itinerant for some part of the year. This pattern did not alter during the early twentieth century and was especially true of the young, single males who made up most of the sporting fraternity.[10] Although rural

areas generally possessed a stable core of permanent residents, the departure or ageing of a portion of the local population could signal the end of a
cricket club in that membership was not likely to be replenished as quickly
as in the cities. Rural working hours also presented a barrier to cricket in
that the Saturday half-holiday, or any half-holiday for that matter, was still
not standard for rural labourers into the twentieth century and it seems that
many of those who did have a half-holiday viewed it as a time for doing
washing and other chores in order to keep Sunday free for rest and recreation. However, prevailing Sabbatarianism ensured that organised cricket
or any other sport was seldom played on Sunday before the 1960s. Nor did
most of New Zealand's hinterland possess transport and communication
networks favourable to cricket. While the main towns on the East Coast
of the South Island were well connected by rail from the late 1870s, coverage in the eastern and central North Island was limited until the easing of
tensions between Europeans and Maori during the 1890s. The main trunk
railway linking Wellington and Auckland was not completed until 1908. Only
after the turn of the century did rail networks progress substantially beyond
the main coastal centres. Roads, aside from those in dairying areas such as
the Taranaki plains and Southland and amid the generally drier climate and
greater wealth of Canterbury and Otago, were frequently marginal until at
least the late 1920s.[11] The difficulty in arranging fixtures under these conditions is typified by the Arrowtown cricket team's journey to Lumsden to play
Invercargill at the end of 1895. Despite the match being played at a mid-point
between the two towns, the itinerary for the Arrowtown team involved seven
hours of coach, steamer and train travel in each direction for barely six hours
of cricket in between. For their efforts they lost by eighty runs.[12]

The main cities presented their own problems for cricketers. There is
ample evidence of transience among the urban population, long working
hours and limited access to a weekly half-holiday. Low wages and periods of
economic depression, especially during the 1880s, also reduced disposable
income and severely restricted opportunities for leisure. Significant change
occurred only after 1890, when a wave of reform legislation extended the
weekly half-holiday. Yet many workers remained outside the scope of the
legislation, and others were denied easy access to cricket in that their half-
holiday was during the week rather than on a Saturday. Consequently working-class players were significantly under-represented in the upper echelons
of cricket. While those variously described as manual or blue-collar workers
comprised a fairly static 60 per cent of the New Zealand adult male workforce during the period 1896 to 1926, it is doubtful whether they constituted more than a third of senior cricketers in the main cities. Further, a
large majority of this group belonged to the skilled, and to a lesser extent

semi-skilled, working class. Unskilled workers are entirely absent.[13] With work leave required for days or weeks at a time to play and tour, inter-provincial cricket became the domain of those with independent means or the most flexible working arrangements. Numerous provincial and national teams suffered from the unavailability of original selections. Undoubtedly, the most extreme case was Otago's Alec Downes, the best spin bowler in New Zealand before 1914, who missed numerous matches and played only twice in the North Island during a twenty-six-year first-class career, as he was unable to obtain leave from employment as a brass-finisher.[14]

Given these obstacles to potential European players, it is unsurprising that Maori involvement in cricket was minimal until the later twentieth century. The Maori population was almost entirely rural and isolated. Only 19 per cent were urbanised by 1945 and they did not become a predominantly urban people until the late 1960s. Of those who did play inter-provincial cricket before 1914, almost all spent time at elite New Zealand schools and experienced greater integration with the mainstream of European society than was the norm for most Maori. One, J. G. Taiaroa, was a solicitor. Another, J. H. W. Uru, became a Member of Parliament.[15]

The 'peculiar' economics of New Zealand cricket

Certainly this range of impediments to cricket was common to most if not all settler societies. Yet New Zealand's small population gave it a particular disadvantage when it came to removing impediments for cricketers of talent. Above all, there was not a substantial spectator base from which to derive revenue to develop facilities, cover basic operating costs and pay the touring expenses of players such as Downes, who could not otherwise afford to participate. By contrast, the dramatic population expansion of Victoria and New South Wales following the gold rushes of the 1850s saw Sydney grow from 54,000 in 1851 to 400,000 in 1891 and 648,000 in 1911. Melbourne increased from 29,000 in 1851 to 493,000 in 1891 and 593,000 in 1911. The largest New Zealand city by 1911 was Auckland, with 102,676. Inevitably, although it seems that similar *proportions* of population attended important cricket matches in Australia and New Zealand, Australian crowds were much larger and more lucrative. H. H. Stephenson's England XI attracted at least 25–30,000 for its match against a Melbourne XVIII in 1861 and another 30,000 in Sydney. Attendance for Test matches in Australia increased from a daily average of 4,750 in 1877 to in excess of 12,000 by the mid-1890s. Attendances at inter-colonial fixtures and those against touring teams were also frequently in excess of 10,000 per day.[16] While similarly comprehensive details are scarce for New Zealand, the 'tolerably numerous' crowd on the second day of Canterbury's match against Parr's All England XI in February 1864 amounted to only 1,500. The same fixture against James Lillywhite's England XI in 1877 attracted 15,000 for the whole match. The best attendances for the most popular and profitable touring team in New Zealand, Lord Hawke's England XI of 1902–03, barely exceeded 5,000 on the best days while the record single-day attendance before 1914 appears to have been 10,000 for the New Zealand capitulation against Australia at Wellington in 1905. Yet this tour as a whole made a loss.[17]

Until the mid-1880s there were also significant constraints on how much could be charged of those who did attend. The 1877 and 1881 Public Reserves Acts restricted both the enclosure of public grounds and the ability to charge admission. This reflects a colonial reaction against the sort of privilege and patronage in Britain which prevented access to playing spaces and recreational amenities. There is a similar pattern in New Zealand hunting and fishing laws that were always far more liberal than their British antecedents.[18] The 1881 Act stated that local bodies could not lease any reserve set aside for public health or recreation and could only charge admission for a maximum of ten days in each year.[19] Unable to cover costs from gate money, the provincial cricket associations in particular were at the mercy of public subscriptions and donations. The visit of the 1881 Australian XI highlighted a familiar problem when a large attendance at Hagley Park, Christchurch, yielded a gate of only £150. As the *Lyttelton Times* explained: 'The generosity of people who are not compelled to pay for their pleasure, is always a precarious thing to depend on.'[20] The solution was to establish private grounds that were exempt from the legislation. But the development of major venues such as the Basin Reserve in Wellington, Lancaster Park in Christchurch and Carisbrook in Dunedin entailed considerable costs. By the end of 1882 the annual interest on the £4,000 loan to develop Lancaster Park was £260 with another £150 required to pay a groundsman and maintenance. It was twenty years before the one and only cash dividend was paid to original investors in the project. In the meantime, all Canterbury sporting bodies, and the Canterbury Cricket Association especially, operated under the shadow of huge liabilities.[21]

The escape from debt was frequently through avenues totally unrelated to sport. Typical is the Wellington Cricket Association, which from its formation in 1875 to the announcement of its first profit in 1887 estimated that it spent £2,590 5 shillings and 7 pence on the Basin Reserve. Association finances were so precarious in 1879 that a concert committee was formed to help clear debts. They raised £44. The Wellington Amateur Dramatic Club repeated the gesture in 1883 after the failure of a call for all cricketers to give 5s. By 1910, the Association had an overdraft of £227.3s.11d after the failure of a lottery organised to clear debts.[22]

New Zealand was little different from the English game, where the vast majority of clubs were economically fragile. Indeed, the editor of the *Athletic News* observed in 1886 that 'It would be difficult ... to point to a cricket club which did not get into debt. It is one of their brightest privileges.' What income they had was derived from membership subscriptions and gate money, with a select few able to augment this by renting their grounds to other sports such as athletics and football. The majority of county clubs were sustained only by the generosity of patrons, and members such as Lord Sheffield spent a vast sum supporting Sussex during the 1880s and 1890s. The esteem in which Victorians held cricket ensured that 'on many occasions emotion superseded economics'.[23] New Zealand cricket possessed none of these saviours and, given that its administrators were frequently drawn from the English public school system or its local equivalent, there was never any inclination to tamper with the structure of cricket to make it more appealing to spectators and hence more commercially viable. Further, while there is ample evidence of the colonial wealthy involving themselves in the administration of cricket and making the largest contributions to the public subscription lists that were frequently used to raise funds, these contributions were minute in comparison to some of the benevolence displayed in English cricket. As Jim McAloon argues, the New Zealand wealthy of the nineteenth century were little disposed to philanthropy and saw little need of it as a key to establishing their identity. There was a feeling that the making of money, rather than the giving away of it, was a greater indicator of worth in both senses of the term. Moreover, such charity as was dispensed tended to be directed towards 'serious' and 'deserving' objectives – churches, benevolent societies and the like.[24] The attitude of prominent Dunedin merchants Ross and Glendinning is instructive. In 1892, the firm's Christchurch office was rebuked for having given £2 for a cricket match and making similar donations previously. Christchurch was ordered to 'in future, please give no subscriptions at all without reference to us, and only refer to us such applications as we are likely to approve of for what seem to be necessitous cases calling for legitimate help. All amusements can be declined right off.'[25]

To these constraints a more speculative explanation can be added – that New Zealand cricket was hampered by an unfavourable climate. The game was too firmly entrenched in English tradition ever to submit to the weather, but the elements may have been a determinant on the sporting choices made in new societies. The hotter climate of India and the West Indies was naturally conducive to cricket, but a more vigorous contact sport such as rugby gained almost no following. In Australia and South Africa, with a somewhat more temperate climate in the main areas of settlement, both winter and summer sports flourished. In New Zealand, where the climate is generally mild, winter sport held a distinct advantage over summer. A statistical comparison with Australia leaves no doubt that a combination of temperature and rainfall contributing to damp, inferior pitch and ground quality had a dramatic impact on performance. By 1914, 25.7 per cent of all completed team innings in Australian first-class matches produced totals in excess of 300, compared to 33.3 per cent for the period 1900–14. For New Zealand the figures are 7.2 per cent and 11.9 per cent. By so greatly restricting opportunities for batsmen and placing bowlers at a deceptive advantage, New Zealand pitch conditions did nothing to assist local players in developing the technique necessary to counter the superior skills of touring teams. Australian players, and Warwick Armstrong especially, frequently observed that New Zealand cricket would only improve when the quality of its pitches improved. Daniel Reese, New Zealand captain 1907–14, was in no doubt that the failure of New Zealand batsmen on tours of Australia in 1899 and 1914 was directly attributable to a lack of experience of hard, fast wickets or of playing long innings. Without being able to cultivate a proper match temperament, a pronounced inferiority complex developed among local players.[26]

Educational opportunities embody perhaps the most complex of the forces shaping New Zealand cricket. Into the twentieth century, primary schools were slow to shift from quasi-military physical drill to organised sport. The majority of the population therefore went without the benefits of easy access to formal instruction. By 1900, less than 3 per cent of the European population attended public secondary schools. Despite the availability of free secondary education from 1902, and the increasing educational emphasis demanded by a changing occupational structure, the overall attendance had risen to perhaps 20 per cent by 1939.[27] Yet the secondary schools, and especially the elite institutions such as Christ's College, Wellington College and Wanganui Collegiate which cloned the English public school model, were crucial training grounds for cricket. By 1914, Christ's College had produced at least fifty-seven first-class cricketers – for Canterbury, Hawke's Bay, Otago and the universities of Oxford and Cambridge. Other elite schools were not far behind.[28] Although relatively more egalitarian than their English counterparts, the New Zealand institutions nevertheless conveyed a message to their pupils that the school was both a symbolic link with 'home' and an important step towards the acquisition of a sense of culture and tradition in a recently formed colonial community. As Gary McCulloch observes of Auckland Grammar School, 'Imperial ideals and the trappings of tradition helped to conceal the fact that the school's character and role had in reality adapted quickly to its colonial setting'.[29] The influence of a succession of headmasters who embodied the tenets of public school and Oxbridge athleticism and amateur idealism, and in several cases were talented sportsmen in their own right, soon began to produce a core of young men committed to the pursuit of sport for its own sake and as training for the greater challenges of life. This idealistic coterie dominated the playing and administrative strength of the New Zealand game.[30]

Imperial ideals and Australian neglect

The relative difficulties facing New Zealand cricket were crystallised as it made tentative steps in the international arena. New Zealand representative teams won four, lost thirteen and drew one of their first-class matches prior to 1914. Against first-class opposition, touring teams in New Zealand won forty-three, lost ten and drew fifteen. Of the losses, three were sustained by Tasmania, two by Fiji and two by a weak MCC side in 1907. Most of the draws were caused by bad weather. Of the 175 matches played by all touring teams, 114 were won, twelve lost and forty-nine drawn.[31] In short, and especially compared to the regular successes enjoyed by Australian teams against English visitors, let alone the achievements of New Zealand rugby teams at home and abroad, there was simply nothing for New Zealand cricket to be confident about. Whilst Australian cricketers were combative and their supporters sometimes bellicose, the New Zealand game was passive, deferential and preoccupied with the best English amateur 'form' of the game. This is most apparent in the response of E. C. J. Stevens, Chairman of the NZCC, to the impending visit of Lord Hawke's team in 1902: '[He] thought that nothing could be better for New Zealand cricket than the visit of a team such as that now proposed, and … he would rather see a team of English amateurs than a professional team or one from Australia.' Moreover, when Hawke announced that the team would contain two professional bowlers, the Auckland Cricket Association threatened to withdraw its financial guarantee for the tour.[32] It is similarly revealing that the provincial cricket associations taxed their already strained finances with the extra expense of engaging professional coaches from England rather than Australia. There were three in Auckland during 1911, and another influx during the 1920s.[33]

From the 1860s to at least the 1930s, New Zealand reactions to contact with English teams scarcely varied in their tone of awe and deference. The address of welcome presented to George Parr in January 1864 by the 'Cricketers in Otago' stressed that they were 'humble imitators at these distant antipodes … [who] gladly hail the opportunity of witnessing the excellence to which your prowess has brought the manliest of English pastimes ... To look for anything like success in the forthcoming struggle, when pitted against the Champions of the world, would be presumptuous on our part.' In April 1927, on the arrival of the first New Zealand team to England, the captain Tom Lowry declared that his players 'felt like a lot of schoolboys who had got into long trousers for the first time' and that they 'were Britishers anxious to appear on the cricket map, [and] came "home" not to beat the best sportsmen, but to learn the rules as England taught them'.[34]

While successive generations of historians have wrestled with the extent of New Zealand's enduring imperial ties or emergent nationalism in a debate that is too complex for the space available here, the relationship is best seen in terms of a middle path as outlined by W. D. McIntyre: 'Sentiments of imperialism became mingled with a growing nationalism. There was much overlapping, parallel development and sometimes regression from growing autonomy to greater dependency. Things would sometimes seem to be moving in opposite directions at the same time.'[35] New Zealand cricket represents one of the strongest 'sentiments of imperialism', and one that gained added strength precisely because it simultaneously represented one of the less engaged strands in New Zealand's relationship with Australia. Although links between the two have always been dynamic, with a multitude of cultural, economic and political exchanges, waves of trans-Tasman migration and some coalescing and co-operation as 'Australasia', various nineteenth-century propagandists and politicians nevertheless strove to draw a clear distinction between 'wholesome' New Zealand, with an emphasis on selected 'stock' and systematic colonisation, and apparently 'convict' Australia. Consequently, the official relationship between the two remained somewhat detached until late in the twentieth century. Disinterest also emerged in sport as the geographical isolation and scarcity of funds that had drawn New Zealand to be part of Australasian teams in the 1908 and 1912 Olympic Games and in Davis Cup tennis in particular was replaced by a quest for separate sporting identity after the Great War. While trans-Tasman exchanges abounded in a range of sports, it is clear that both player and spectator alike viewed encounters with Britain as being of greater significance.[36]

Common cricketing interests also receded over time. Of the twenty-two international sides to tour New Zealand from 1864 to 1914, fourteen were Australian, seven English and one Fijian. It was also accepted that any sufficiently talented New Zealander could be included in an Australian team to play England. Between 1921 and 1928 another five Australian sides toured New Zealand. Yet at precisely the point when New Zealand cricket began to move forward with tours to England in 1927 and 1931 and admission to Test cricket from 1930, Australia withdrew its patronage. New Zealand's apparently negligible standard, as evidenced in a number of lop-sided encounters during the 1920s, had little to offer at a time when Australian international commitments were expanding to include South Africa and West Indies. A low point was reached in December 1930, when the Australian Board of Control stated that while it was willing to assist New Zealand cricket by sending young players on development tours after the completion of the Sheffield Shield programme, sending more experienced men to New Zealand would unfairly deprive local clubs during important end of season grade games. In January 1934, the NZCC acrimoniously cancelled a proposed Australian second XI tour after most of its leading players withdrew citing personal or business reasons, although more likely was a general dissatisfaction with the low rate of tour pay offered by the Board. Throughout the inter-war years, Australia was willing enough to assist by staging state fixtures that defrayed some of the costs for second-string English teams bound for New Zealand, such as the eight played by A. C. MacLaren's team in 1922–23, but the Board strengthened its longstanding resistance to full-strength English teams compromising any part of a lucrative Ashes tour itinerary in order to visit New Zealand.[37] As NZCC Treasurer D. E. Wanklyn remarked in January 1932: 'It appeared that we must assert our independence of Australian assistance, much as we might deplore it.'[38] After 1928 there was no Australian tour of New Zealand until an ill-conceived Test match in March 1946. With first-class cricket hardly recovered from the abeyance of the war years, and a number of its best players still overseas on active service, New Zealand scored 42 and 54 to lose by an innings within two days. Thereafter New Zealand was accommodated only insofar as it provided a useful trial for emerging players. Five Australian 'B' teams visited New Zealand from 1949 to 1969. From their first visit in 1898–99, New Zealand teams played only twenty-nine first-class games in Australia until 1973–74, when the two countries finally began regular Test match competition.[39]

Administrators and the cricket public did not resent their enforced reliance on England. The NZCC Chairman Daniel Reese claimed in June 1928 that the Australians had taken their recent New Zealand tour too seriously, seeing it more as good preparation for future Test matches against England, and had not played the type of cricket that the public had come to expect.[40] The New Zealand press reinforced these sentiments with extensive coverage of the English County Championship and English touring teams in all parts of the world, and frequently editorialised on performances and developments within the English game, but paid scant attention to the Australian domestic game. New Zealand reactions to the 1932–33 Bodyline controversy also reveal a very pro-English sentiment, with many accusing the Australian media of sensationalism, recalling the damage inflicted on England by the Australian fast bowlers Jack Gregory and Ted McDonald in 1921, and praising MCC for its strong condemnation of 'sweeping charges' made by the Australian Board. Others suggested that Bodyline was neither dangerous nor unplayable, and that the real fault lay in the techniques of Australian players.[41]

Tentative modernisation since 1945

New Zealand's population increased from 1.7 million in 1945 to 4.1 million in 2006, yet it is still significantly smaller than any other major cricket-playing country – including the combined nations of the West Indies. Certainly as a developed country it is better able to draw revenue and potential players to the game, but this is mitigated by the wider variety of recreational, cultural and sporting opportunities offered in such countries. Moreover, cricket faces many of the same, and sometimes greater, basic running costs as its international counterparts. Consequently, cricket finances remained precarious throughout the twentieth century with little scope for rapid growth, the retention of professional players or compensation to amateurs for expenses, let alone lost earnings. The NZCC was accordingly reluctant to make demands on its players. The first-class fixture list did not extend beyond five matches a season for each province until 1975–76. Moreover, the staging of this first-class programme around the Christmas holiday period to minimise the need for work leave, and the timing of most visits from touring teams in late February or early March, usually after a series in Australia, meant that players were frequently expected to make the transition to Test cricket without adequate preparation. For good reason New Zealand teams were often given the sobriquet 'Saturday afternoon cricketers'.[42] New Zealand struggled for twenty-six years before its initial Test victory, against West Indies in March 1956, but there was no display of nationalist triumphalism. As the *New Zealand Herald* remarked, 'One swallow does not make a summer, and one Test match victory … does not make New Zealand a top-class cricket country.'[43] The position was confirmed later the same year when the All Blacks defeated South Africa to secure the unofficial title of world rugby champions. New Zealand did not win another cricket Test until 1962 in South Africa, and not at home until 1968. It did not win a series until 1969–70, and has won only sixty-seven of 356 Test matches to the end of 2009. Its losing percentage is only exceeded by Bangladesh and Zimbabwe.[44]

As British cultural and economic influences decreased in significance during the 1970s, cricket, and the emerging one-day version especially, certainly had a role to play in New Zealand's resurgent relationship with Australia. The controversial underarm bowling incident in early 1981 galvanised public interest in trans-Tasman sporting rivalries, and increased television coverage of one-day cricket triggered an unprecedented growth in player numbers, especially at school level. Consistent international success during the early 1980s, spearheaded by the performances of Richard Hadlee, New Zealand's premier fast bowler and the first player to take 400 Test wickets, and at important events such as the 1992 World Cup, also boosted the profile of the game. In turn, its administration became fully professional and better able to 'package' cricket for corporate sponsorship and marketing opportunities. Women's cricket, which struggled for respect and visibility from its first appearance in the late nineteenth century, has also enjoyed significant popularity and success following the merging of its administration with the men's game in 1992. New Zealand won the Women's World Cup in 2000.

Notwithstanding a range of enduring socio-economic and cultural impediments that produced only the slightest non-white involvement in the game for much of its history, perhaps the most significant transformation of the early twenty-first century is the growing Maori, Pasifika and migrant presence as the NZCC has consciously attempted to broaden its player base. Community-focused Pasifika derivations such as Kilikiti are also growing in popularity and several international tournaments have been staged.[45]

Yet progress for New Zealand cricket is somewhat relative – particularly in relation to rugby, which became openly professional in 1995 and maintains a dominant hold within New Zealand sporting consciousness. The decidedly negative public reaction to industrial action by New Zealand representative cricketers at the end of 2002 was a clear indication of attitudes to a game that has experienced more troughs than peaks and is only occasionally able to hold centre stage in the sporting imagination of the country.[46] Perhaps, as lucrative opportunities become available through the popularity and international financing of Twenty20, there is scope for cricket to again become consistently dominant in the sporting culture of New Zealand.

NOTES

1 Keith Sinclair, *A History of New Zealand* (Auckland: Penguin, 1991), pp. 57–61.
2 Ibid., pp. 60–61.
3 Quoted in C. Lansbury, 'A Straight Bat and a Modest Mind', *Victorian Newsletter*, 49, Spring 1976, p. 13.
4 *Lyttelton Times*, 7 January 1854; Greg Ryan, *The Making of New Zealand Cricket 1832–1914* (London: Frank Cass, 2004), pp. 12–13, 37–40.

5   Ryan, *New Zealand Cricket*, pp. 66–71.

6   Ibid., pp. 27–30.

7   Ibid., pp. 32–37.

8   G. Griffiths, 'Sale, Bradshaw, Wills, Manning and the "Little Enemy": Notes on Some Early Arrivals in Otago, No. 4' (Dunedin: the author, 1971).

9   Erik Olssen, 'Towards a New Society' in Geoffrey W. Rice (ed.), *The Oxford History of New Zealand* (Auckland: Oxford University Press, 1992), p. 256.

10 Ibid., p. 275; John E. Martin, *The Forgotten Worker: The Rural Wage Earner in Nineteenth-century New Zealand* (Wellington: Allen & Unwin, 1990), pp. 14–15.

11 Greg Ryan, 'Rural Myth and Urban Actuality: The Anatomy of All Black and New Zealand Rugby 1884–1938', *New Zealand Journal of History*, 35, 1, April 2001, pp. 45–69.

12 T. W. Reese, *New Zealand Cricket 1841–1914* (Christchurch: Simpson & Williams, 1927), p. 110.

13 Ryan, 'Rural Myth', passim; Nigel Beckford, 'Working Class Participation in Wellington Club Cricket 1878–1940', BA Hons research essay, Victoria University of Wellington, 1981.

14 Ryan, *New Zealand Cricket*, p. 74.

15 Greg Ryan, 'Few and Far Between: Māori and Pacific Contributions to New Zealand Cricket', *Sport in Society*, 10, 1, 2007, pp. 85–90.

16 Richard Cashman, *Australian Cricket Crowds: The Attendance Cycle – Daily Figures, 1877–1984* (Kensington, New South Wales: History Project Incorporated, 1984), pp. 26–35, 72–80, 134–56.

17 Reese, *New Zealand Cricket*, pp. 186, 194, 211, 414–23, 439–40.

18 R. M. McDowall, *Gamekeepers for the Nation: The Story of New Zealand's Acclimatisation Societies, 1861–1990* (Christchurch: Canterbury University Press, 1994), pp. 1–10.

19 Ryan, *New Zealand Cricket*, pp. 135–36, 140–41.

20 *Lyttelton Times*, 24 February 1881.

21 T. W. Reese, *History of Lancaster Park* (Christchurch: the author, c.1935), pp. 7–10.

22 Ryan, *New Zealand Cricket*, p. 143; D. O. Neely, *100 Summers: The History of Wellington Cricket* (Auckland: Moa Publications, 1975), pp. 28, 78–79.

23 Keith Sandiford and Wray Vamplew, 'The Peculiar Economics of English Cricket Before 1914', *British Journal of Sports History*, 3, 3, 1986, p. 311.

24 Jim McAloon, *No Idle Rich: The Wealthy in Canterbury and Otago 1840–1914* (Dunedin: Otago University Press, 2002), pp. 143–70.

25 Quoted in ibid., p. 158.

26 Ryan, *New Zealand Cricket*, pp. 162–65; Daniel Reese, *Was it all Cricket?* (London: Allen & Unwin, 1948), pp. 390, 395.

27 Olssen, 'Towards a New Society', pp. 276–77.

28 Ryan, *New Zealand Cricket*, pp. 104–125.

29 Gary McCulloch, 'Imperial and Colonial Designs: The Case of Auckland Grammar School', *History of Education*, 17, 4, 1988, p. 262.

30 Greg Ryan, 'Cricket and the Moral Curriculum of the New Zealand Elite Secondary Schools c1860–1920', *The Sports Historian*, 19, 2, 1999, pp. 61–79.

31 Ryan, *New Zealand Cricket*, pp. 167–69, 206–207.

32 NZCC Committee Minutes, 26 April 1902; Special Committee Minutes, 30 August 1902.

33 *100 Not Out: A Centennial History of the Auckland Cricket Association* (Auckland: The Association, 1983), pp. 115–19.

34 Quoted in D. O. Neely, R. P. King and F. K. Payne, *Men in White: The History of New Zealand International Cricket 1894–1985* (Auckland: Moa Publications, 1985), p. 74; *The Times*, 7 May 1927.

35 W. D. McIntyre, 'Imperialism and Nationalism' in Rice, *Oxford History*, p. 337.

36 James Belich, *Paradise Reforged: A History of the New Zealanders from the 1880s to the Year 2000* (Auckland: Allen Lane, 2001), pp. 46–52; A. and R. Burnett, *The Australia and New Zealand Nexus* (Canberra: Australian Institute of International Affairs, 1978), pp. 58, 112; Charles Little, 'Trans-Tasman Federations in Sport: The Changing Relationships Between Australia and New Zealand' in Richard Cashman, John O'Hara and Andrew Honey (eds.), *Sport, Federation, Nation* (Sydney: Walla Walla Press, 2001), pp. 63–80.

37 Ryan, *New Zealand Cricket*, pp. 199–217.

38 NZCC Management Committee Minutes, 14 January 1932.

39 Greg Ryan, 'New Zealand' in Richard Cashman, Warwick Franks, Jim Maxwell, Brian Stoddart, Amanda Weaver and Ray Webster (eds.), *The Oxford Companion to Australian Cricket* (Melbourne: Oxford University Press, 1996), pp. 382–87.

40 NZCC General Meeting Minutes, 28 June 1928.

41 Ryan, *New Zealand Cricket*, esp. chs. 7–10; 'Extravagance of Thought and Feeling: New Zealand Reactions to the 1932–33 Bodyline Controversy', *Sporting Traditions*, 13, 2, June 1997, pp. 41–58.

42 Ryan, 'Trials and Tribulations: The Story of New Zealand Cricket' in J. A. Mangan and B. Majumdar (eds.), *Cricketing Cultures in Conflict: World Cup 2003* (London: Routledge, 2004), pp. 51–66.

43 *New Zealand Herald*, 14 March 1956.

44 cricinfo.com (accessed 3 March 2010).

45 Ryan, 'Few and Far Between', pp. 91–100.

46 Ryan, 'Amateurs in a Professional Game: Player Payments in New Zealand Cricket c1977–2002', *Sport in History*, 25, 1, 2005, pp. 114–35.

9

KENNETH SURIN

C. L. R. James and cricket

Cyril Lionel Robert James (1901–1989), known universally as 'CLR', or 'Nello' to those who were closer to him, was born in Tunapuna, Trinidad (at that time a British colony), though he spent most of his adult life in Britain and the United States. James is probably cricket's greatest writer, but was also a renowned historian, Marxist scholar and interpreter of literary texts (Melville most notably); as well as being (more often than not several of these at the same time) a deeply engaged socialist organiser and militant, newspaper editor, cricket correspondent for the *Manchester Guardian*, writer of novels and children's stories, and a polemicist and essayist who used his pen indefatigably on behalf of a wide range of causes (West Indian independence from Britain, the Pan-African movement, the plight of black sharecroppers in the American South, decolonisation and struggles against racism, the social and economic predicament of workers in the Lancashire cotton mills of the 1930s, to mention but a few).

Cricket, along with mountaineering, has been notable amongst sports for the quality of its associated literary productivity, and well-known authors who have written on the former include, to mention but a few, William Hazlitt, Siegfried Sassoon, Dorothy Sayers, P. G. Wodehouse and Hugh de Selincourt.[1] These fictional depictions deal overwhelmingly with a form of the game known in England as 'village cricket', very far removed in terms of expertise and competitive rigour from the international, and the county (England), state (Australia) or island (the West Indies) forms of the game described and analysed by James. James is laudatory about club cricket in the West Indies, but the level of skill required for the West Indian club cricket of his time – the top West Indian international players would play for local clubs on a weekly basis when not doing duty elsewhere – in nearly every instance far exceeds that of English village cricket, where, as some readers will confirm, the cricket sometimes yields primacy to the consumption of mountainous quantities of food and ale during prescribed breaks in the game. Cricket, after all, prides itself on being a game of a day (or days) with designated lunch and tea intervals, and the almost mythical figure of the village butcher or blacksmith with a Falstaffian belly, barely able to run, but with a good 'eye' when it came to swinging his bat, and thus able on the right kind of day to smite opposing bowlers out of sight (with the invariable assistance of a lucky break or two from the beer-soaked umpires), is a commonplace in the lore of English village cricket.

Most of the renditions of the game provided by these authors have, of course, been fictional, and while Hazlitt was revered by James and stated by him to be a model for his own style of writing, James, as a writer on the game itself and those who played it, really had no precursors, and certainly no equals, amongst the mostly run-of-the-mill journalists who plied their trade as cricket correspondents for the English newspapers of his time. The one possible exception was the somewhat older Sir Neville Cardus (1888– 1975), who was for many years the cricket correspondent and music critic for the *Manchester Guardian*.[2]

It is widely acknowledged by cricket historians that Neville Cardus transformed cricket writing in a way that had no precedent. In place of the often dreary reportage that passed for newspaper coverage of cricket at that time – as in 'an hour after the tea interval on a rain-affected second day, Surrey declared its innings closed at 229 for 7, with Hobbs scoring 81 not out' (this typical 'account' being, of course, a rhetorical invention on the part of this author) – Cardus, who professed to love music more than cricket, preferred instead to register and convey the force of the impressions involved in *seeing* a particularly notable passage of play or a crucial turn of events in the course of a game. Here is a typical sample of his writing:

> Many a great match has been lost by a missed catch; terrible are the emotions of long-on when the ball is driven high towards him and when he waits for it – alone in the world – and the crowd roars and somebody cries out, 'He'll miss it – He'll miss it!' Years ago, in a match for the rubber [Test match series] in Australia, Clem Hill and Victor Trumper were making a mighty stand, turning the wheel of the game against England. Here were two of the greatest batsmen of all time thoroughly set, scourging the English attack with unsparing weapons. Hour after hour they cut and drove right and left. Wilfred Rhodes, who seems always to have been playing cricket, tossed up over after over, angling for the catch in the deep. At the very moment when the fortunes of the battle were on the turn, moving definitely Australia's way – at this moment of fate, Clem Hill let his bat swing at a ball for all he [was] worth in valour and strength. Up into the sky the ball went, and it began to drop where A. E. Knight was standing. All eyes were resting on Knight; the vast Sydney multitude were dead still as the ball fell like a stone. Knight held his catch, but as he did so, he was seen to go down on one knee, and bow his head. Some of the English players, thinking Knight was ill, moved towards him. But as they

approached, Knight raised himself, made an explanatory gesture, swallowed emotion in a gulp, and said to his anxious colleagues, 'It's all right, it's all right; I was only thanking my maker.' Cricket can mean much to a man: responsibility can weigh down the strongest.[3]

Cardus was a cricketing romantic, a disposition which fuelled his unconcealed love of the game and contributed at the same time to the impressionistic tenor of his writing, but he tended always to view the game as a self-contained aesthetic entity: the outside world, with its economic and political mainsprings, did break through occasionally in the writings of Cardus, but it was precisely this, an aberration on his part rather than the manifestation of a powerful conviction about cricket and its relation to any underlying historical and social conditions. With James, as we shall see, it was quite otherwise. James combined detailed and sometimes recondite descriptions of the technical aspects of the game with constant references to its place in a wider historical and social setting, invariably in the same essay on a cricketer he considered noteworthy. As an example of the former, this description of Garfield Sobers (1936–), widely regarded as the greatest all-round cricketer in the history of the game, is representative of James's love of the technical aspects of the game:

> He [Sobers] can, and usually does, play back to anything about which he has the slightest doubt. More rarely he uses a forward defensive stroke. But he never just plays forward to put the bat on the ball and kill it. He watches the ball off the pitch and, even in the most careful forward defensive, plays the ball away … His type of mastery of the forward defensive gives us the secret of the capacity of Sobers to punish good length bowling on anything like a reasonable wicket. He does not need the half-volley of a fast or fast-medium bowler to be able to drive. From a very high backlift he watches a ball that is barely over the good length, takes it on the rise and sends it shooting between mid-on and mid-off. That is a later acquisition to a stroke he has always had: to move back and time the good length through the covers.[4]

The ability evinced by James in this passage to analyse meticulously the ins and outs of a player's technique is complemented by his stress on the need to provide a historical context for all forms of the game. This passage from the same essay on Sobers is a case in point:

> I cannot think seriously of Garfield Sobers without thinking of Clifford Goodman, Percy Goodman, H.B.G. Austin (always H.B.G. Austin), Bertie Harragin, and others 'too numerous to mention' (though not very numerous). They systematically built up the game, played inter-island matches, invited English teams to the West Indies year after year, went to England twice before World War I … The mercantile planter class led this unmercantile social activity and very rapidly they themselves produced the originator of West Indian

batting, George Challenor. In 1906 he was a boy of eighteen and made the trip to England. He saw and played with the greatest cricketers England has ever known, the men of the Golden Age. Challenor returned to set a standard and pattern for West Indian batting from which at times it may have deviated, but which it has never lost. That history is a history of its own, going deep, too deep for the present area of discourse.[5]

The 'deep history' referred to here is dealt with by James in his masterpiece *Beyond a Boundary*, as well as in numerous other texts. This complex and 'deep' history concerns the slow and uneven transition from a West Indian cricketing team drawn predominantly from the white plantation class (apart from Sobers, all the players of an earlier generation named by James in the above passage were white) to a world-beating team, including, of course, the incomparable Sobers, that consisted entirely of Afro-Caribbean and Asian-Caribbean players belonging to the hitherto subaltern (i.e. non-white) West Indian classes. For example, the 1900 and 1906 West Indies teams that toured England (the latter being the first West Indies team to play first-class matches in England) each contained five black players out of a squad of fifteen. For one of these black players in 1906, William Burton, the tour ended prematurely and 'in acrimony' when he was sent home after refusing to carry out menial duties for white members of the side. That ended his cricketing career and also made him virtually unemployable, and he was forced to emigrate again, this time to Panama. He returned to Barbados shortly before his death so that he could 'die where I was born'.[6] One can safely assume that all black members of the 1906 team were expected 'to carry out menial duties for white members of the side'. Moreover, blacks were not allowed to play in the inter-island cricket competition, so the 1900 tour of England evinced the absurdity of black players representing the West Indies internationally without being able to play for their islands at home.[7] Or, in the phrase which is perhaps the most widely recognised of any uttered by James: 'What do they know of cricket who only cricket know?'[8]

For James this twofold development – the emergence in the 1960s of a now superior West Indian team and the fact that non-whites were able for the first time in West Indian history to form the entire team – was not merely coincidental. As James saw it, cricket, and indeed any sporting or aesthetic phenomenon, is what it is by virtue of its capacity to express underlying historical conditions. Hence the rise of the West Indian team to an undeniable primacy amongst cricketing nations (at any rate from the 1960s to the 1990s, after which time Australia came to possess a similar cricketing predominance which lasts to the time of writing) is linked by James to the successful outcome of the West Indian islands' quest for independence from Britain in the 1960s. The casting-off of a colonial tutelage by the soon to be independent West Indian islands had for James an inextricable connection with the coterminous discarding of a cricketing tutelage, this being a veritable inferiority complex that was overcome against the odds by the most brilliant and obdurate of the early generation of West Indian cricketers. A major part of this colonial legacy was the compartmentalisation of West Indian cricket on terms dictated by the administrative exigencies of the British colonial government. These administrative imperatives were premised on an artificial separation between the West Indian islands, resulting in a governmental form which placed British directorial expediency above everything else. The West Indian cricket team, which by its very nature is formed by players from several independent states, has been bedevilled for most of its history by inter-island rivalries – many of which go back to pre-independence days – that encompass not just team selection but also the choice of cricket administrators and the apportioning of match revenues. The presence of a great team captain, such as Sir Frank Worrell (from Barbados) and Clive Lloyd (from Guyana), able to transcend these rivalries by the sheer quality of their leadership, is thus a seeming prerequisite for West Indian cricketing success. Other international teams have sometimes to deal with regional rivalries (where India is concerned there is an undeniable 'edge' to the competition between Mumbai and Kolkata), but these problems are much more pressing and deep-seated in the case of the West Indies. This critique of the artificial separation between the West Indian islands imposed by the British does not imply that there is an original and 'natural' configuration of their relationship to each other – only that the primary rationale for this separation imposed by the British was mere administrative convenience. James provided several multi-angled narratives of this development, narratives which intertwine an array of literary and philosophical references ('ideas') with 'facts' drawn from history and politics.

James had received a literary education, and *Beyond a Boundary* is itself replete with references to Matthew Arnold, Edmund Burke, Carlyle, Hazlitt, Milton, Shakespeare, Shelley, Thackeray, Tolstoy and Wordsworth, amongst others – the literary references are multiplied exponentially if we include James's hundreds of references to other texts dealing with cricket. But James's allusions to numerous other texts are never merely ornamental, because they are inserted in a theoretical edifice that includes a rigorous analysis of history, politics and philosophy (James, of course, wrote books which had nothing to do with cricket in all of these disciplines). To appreciate what James says about cricket therefore necessitates some kind of acknowledgement of his ability to create endlessly productive oscillations between the aesthetic and the political and the historical (here, his acknowledged inspiration was Hegel, as mediated by Marx where James was concerned) – any treatment of culture and its attendant forms undertaken by James was always and irreducibly a political analysis. James achieves this movement between the aesthetic/literary and the political and historical by adverting in his writings on cricket to the following three logics of description and analysis.[9]

James's first logic

The first of these logics can perhaps best be described as the politico-analytic 'algebra' he derives from Hegel's *Logic*, and which he expressly uses as a tool of historical and social investigation. In *Notes on Dialectics*, James asserts that this 'algebra' – which he believes could be 'used in any analysis of constitution and development in nature or in society'[10] – makes possible a powerful delineation of the (for him) always dialectical relationship between the two movements which are determinative for a Hegelian (and thus for a Jamesian) philosophy of history: to wit, the movement of *thought* and the movement of *history* (which the Marxist James unequivocally identifies with the history of labour 'from 1789 to the present day'). These two movements are reciprocally permeating, and James, in using this 'algebra', invokes, on the one hand, the history of the labour movement to examine and verify the movement of thought, and, on the other, the movement of thought 'to understand and develop for contemporary and future needs the history of the labour movement'.[11] In *Beyond a Boundary*, James's proposition ('a movement of thought') is used by him to understand the productive relationships of capital as these enable and also constrain the constitution of cricket as a game, and, in turn, the movement of thought that is *Beyond a Boundary* is interrogated by the productive relationships ('the movement of labour') which enter into the construction of the game that is cricket in its different manifestations. Only through this mutual interrogation can social and historical 'truth' be expressed. James clearly identifies such 'truth' with 'the total emancipation of labour', a liberation which 'can only be achieved when it contains and overcomes its complete penetration by its inherent antagonism, the capital relation'.[12]

In his use of this Hegelian 'algebra', James may seem at times close to espousing something akin to a problematically 'deterministic' philosophy of history, whether Marxist or Hegelian. This superficial notion must, however, be resisted. For while James believes that socialism is inevitable, this is not because a secularised fate or destiny is functioning as part of a surreptitious 'cunning of history' to bring about socialism's ultimate success. Where James is concerned, Marxists are justified in their conviction that there will be an ultimately unvanquishable liberation of labour only because of the practical endeavours of the working classes to change their world. It is not some inexorable historical force which gives the oppressed of the world grounds for this belief in an ultimate victory, contends James, but precisely the concrete *experiences* of these classes in their everyday lives, quotidian experiences which give the oppressed resources to see and know the world in a way that 'posits' the final abolition of the source of their oppression, namely capitalism. The political logic underlying this Hegelian 'algebra' is world-historical in its reach, but the Jamesian insists that this 'algebra' delivers to those exploited by capitalism the basis of an absolutely tangible 'knowledge' grounded in the specificities of the *places* of those who are subjugated in this way. This oppositional and potentially emancipatory knowledge, serving as a 'counterlogic' to the 'logic' of capitalism, therefore connects the world-historical realities of capitalism with its concrete–particular manifestations in the lives of those myriad human beings who are not its beneficiaries.

Where cricket is concerned, James uses this 'algebra' to provide the following historical scheme for the trajectory taken by the game from its inauguration as England's national game up to the 1980s. James viewed cricket's epoch of inauguration as England's national game (an age associated above all with the charismatic W. G. Grace (1848–1915), an overlooked 'eminent Victorian', according to James) in terms of the historical conjuncture in which the British bourgeoisie achieves a decisive primacy over other social classes. This time of inauguration was succeeded by cricket's 'Golden Age' of technical virtuosity, a 'Golden Age' associated by James with such supremely stylish batsmen as C. B. Fry (1872–1956), Gilbert Jessop (1874–1955), Victor Trumper (1877–1915) and K. S. Ranjitsinhji (1872–1933); this age is correlated historically by James with the phase in which the British imperial order reaches the point of its fullest extension (i.e. from around the 1890s to the onset of the First World War) – for James it is no 'accident' therefore that while Fry and Jessop are Englishmen, Trumper is an Australian and Ranjitsinhji an Indian maharaja, albeit playing for England. Cricket's inter-war phase of stasis and machine-like remorselessness came next (and is identified by James with the unrelenting and riskless batting proficiency of the Australians Donald Bradman (1908–2001) and Bill Ponsford (1900–1991), and the Englishmen Walter Hammond (1903–1965) and Len Hutton (1916–1990), as well as the fast-bowling strategy of physical intimidation used in 1933 against Australia by the Indian-born English captain Douglas Jardine (1900–1958), who devised it for his fast bowler Harold Larwood (1904–1995), a Nottinghamshire coal miner); this phase is associated by James with what he calls 'the age of J. M. Keynes', that is, the epoch marked by the bureaucratic management of the unruly economic cycle that had led to the Great Depression. The post-war period of cricket's 'postcolonial' revitalisation came after this (and is associated by James with Frank Worrell's great West Indies team of the 1960s – Worrell (1924–1967) being the first Afro-Caribbean to regularly captain a West Indies team); this age is mapped by James onto the phase of anti-colonial and nationalist struggle in the so-called Third World. This was also the time when India and Pakistan became cricketing powers (though strangely enough, James did not have much to say about the emergence of these nations).

James's second logic

The second 'logic' deployed by James in *Beyond a Boundary* is that of what could be called an 'imaginative structure'.[13] James can persuasively be said to refer to something like an 'imaginative structure' when he claims, in *Notes on Dialectics*, that an analysis of society requires understanding of 'certain mass impulses, instinctive actions, spontaneous movements, the emergence of personalities, the incalculable activities of which constitute a society'.[14] It is the function of an 'imaginative structure' to generate these elements of 'impulse', 'instinct', 'spontaneity', 'personality' and 'incalculable activity', and to give them their special and active characters. An 'imaginative structure' characterised in this way would have several affinities with Raymond Williams's 'structure of feeling'. It is obvious that James sets out in *Beyond a Boundary* to chart the effects and outcomes of the elements of specific 'imaginative structures': those belonging to the Trinidad of his youth, the Lancashire of his first stay in Britain, the Trinidad of the time of its independence from Britain and so on. James's 'imaginative structures' enable him to register in profound and suggestive ways the multi-levelled connections between historical and social knowledge and place, the premise here being that the places in which we are formed are thus the loci of deep currents of thought and feeling, currents which, in the words of *Beyond a Boundary*, generate the 'unstated assumptions' we are 'often not aware of' and which are 'usually the mainsprings of our thought'.[15] These unspoken assumptions, which mediate between place and knowledge, belong to imaginative structures that enable agents to reproduce their social and cultural positions in their practical activities. (Hence James is able to say of George John (c.1883–1944) and Wilton St Hill (1893–c.1957), who belonged to the first generation of great black West Indian cricketers, that '[everything] they were came into cricket with them'.[16]) The locus classicus of James's use (as imputed by me) of this notion of an 'imaginative structure' has to be – due in large part to Sylvia Wynter's wonderful and evocative treatment of it[17] – his compelling description of the ne'er-do-well of his boyhood days, Matthew Bondman.

Bondman is a cricketing genius, but a self-destructive streak undermines his career as a cricketer. James shows how Bondman displays in his batting, and alas only in his batting, the independence and ability that could not be displayed in a wider public domain regimented by the British colonial order. Bondman is thus placed in an imaginative structure in which he can testify with his bat (but sadly only with his bat) to the absence, in the prevailing social and political colonial nexus, of a more open and generous world which could come into being only with the elimination of colonial rule. Through the operation of imaginative structures, all cultural phenomena (and this includes bat and ball, implements of the game of cricket) have a political significance. The reader of *Beyond a Boundary* cannot avoid noticing how James 'reads' a batsman's stance or a bowler's action for its cultural and social resonances. Through the mediation of the always particular imaginative structure, the paramountcy of the colonial order comes, with whatever degree of effectiveness, to be challenged in the domain of culture. Indeed, on the cricket field this colonial hegemony is already being undone by the first generation of great Afro-Caribbean (as opposed to white West Indian) batsmen. The rhythms and forms of the game are thus inseparable from its political–cultural spaces (as these are constituted by particular imaginative structures). James's complementary juxtaposition in *Beyond a Boundary* of the above-mentioned 'logics' – that of the Hegelian 'algebra' with its world-historical range and that of the 'imaginative structure' with its almost micrological emphasis on place and localisation – is augmented by at least one other Jamesian 'logic'. (I overlook here the possibility that these 'logics' with their somewhat differing scopes and emphases may not sit entirely comfortably with each other.)

James's third logic

This third Jamesian 'logic' is elaborated via an invocation of the categories of 'microcosm' and 'macrocosm'. Using this 'logic', James is able to insist that West Indian (or indeed any so-called Third World) culture is a 'microcosm' (among other such microcosms) of a larger matrix or network which for him amounts to something on the scale of a world civilisation. The outcome for James here is a productive way of making historical and cultural connections that anticipate the emancipatory and popular–democratic politics that was the primary focus of his long life. For James can now overturn, at a stroke, any kind of 'metropolitan/core–colonial/periphery' distinction. He is also able to unearth radical traditions and historical figures that have been submerged or obscured by dominant, often metropolitan, cultural and political forms. James's attachment to the ordinary men and women of many cultures and ages comes through especially in this aspect of his work; Edward Thompson's wonderful phrase (though used in another context) – 'to rescue … from the enormous condescension of posterity' – aptly characterises this segment of James's output. James's loving anamnesis of the *lumpen* (and therefore diminished and overlooked) Matthew Bondman has already been mentioned, but we can also refer in this connection to the entire chapter in *Beyond a Boundary* which James devotes to George Headley (1909–1983). In this chapter, James makes a case for regarding the Jamaican Headley as a greater batsman than the Australian Sir Donald Bradman, who still holds most of the batting records in Test-match cricket even though he retired over sixty years ago. James's advocacy of Headley is quite persuasive: he shows how Headley played for a much weaker team which gave him considerably less support than Bradman received from his highly accomplished team-mates, and how Headley's best batting was often done in far from ideal playing conditions (rain-affected pitches and so on) – Bradman was not so adept at dealing with adverse playing conditions. Bradman only played in Australia and England, where for mainly economic reasons better-prepared pitches were the rule rather than the exception. It has become somewhat customary for cricket historians to refer to Headley as 'the black Bradman', but James argues that there is in principle just as good a case for deeming Bradman 'the white Headley'. In this way the diminishing of Headley and his achievements (the successful Headley who prevailed against overwhelming odds was for James the counterpart of Matthew Bondman the tragic failure, though the colonial conditions underlying the failure of the latter pave the way, dialectically, for the success of the former) is overcome decisively; the propensity, always 'political', to marginalise a colonial figure, whether it be the flawed Bondman or the batting colossus Headley, is reversed. The Jamaican and the Australian, both acknowledged by James to be cricketing geniuses, are positioned within the same cultural/cricketing plexus, so that the cultural–historical and cricketing worlds of Jamaica (Headley) and Australia (Bradman) are effectively 'microcosms' of a single, unified socio-political and cricketing cosmos. (In the same way, in the *Black Jacobins*, James shows how Toussaint L'Ouverture – the leader of the Haitian revolution between 1791 and 1804 – is in every way a personage comparable in significance to Napoleon.)

Conclusion

The C. L. R. James depicted here is very much someone possessing a remarkable eye for the technicalities of the game along with a considerable philosophical and historiographical competence. A narrative of this kind, focusing on the intricacies of both philosophy and cricket, cannot really do justice to the vitality and beauty of an unadorned English prose that was perhaps matched only by Bertrand Russell amongst James's contemporaries. *Beyond a Boundary* is replete with descriptions of how a particular bowler flicks his wrist to spin a ball, how someone's forearms are used to punch the ball in a batting stroke, the alignment and extension of the arm in this bowler's delivery, the movement of a batsman's feet as he faces a particular bowler, the direction of a bowler's leading shoulder when he makes his final stride, a fielder's pick up and throw of the ball in the same movement, and so forth. If Headley clipped a ball in this way, or Sobers spun the ball in that way, James described it with an unfailing combination of elegance and sparseness of expression. Derek Walcott has rightly noted 'that every one of its sentences ... is like a lesson in that game, whose criterion is elegance'.[18]

Today cricket has become a worldwide circus where commercial interests trump the emphasis placed in a bygone age on style and elegance. But cricketers who marry classiness of style with deftness and power and a relentless determination are still in evidence – Brian Lara (1969–) the peerless West Indian batsman, Sachin Tendulkar (1974–) the record-breaking Indian batsman renowned for his sportsmanship, Jonty Rhodes (1969–) the electrifying South African fielder who also represented his country at hockey, Waqar Younis (1971–) the great Pakistani fast bowler, and so on. James, in his fundamental dispositions as a cricket writer, was a unique and at times puzzling combination of the Victorian or Edwardian and the post-imperial, someone who could find a way in an article to place (say) W. G. Grace and the Guyanese experimental novelist Wilson Harris in virtually the same frame of reference. Would James have a descriptive and analytical frame capable of doing justice to the undeniably great cricketers of today, or would he regard the contemporary *mores* of the game – as evidenced by the shorter forms of the game where players wear pyjama uniforms festooned with corporate logos in the manner of Formula One racing drivers, where millionaire players refuse to play for their country in a quest for even more money, where players routinely swear at opponents in order to distract them (the practice known as 'sledging'), and where celebrity cricketers, living in gated mansions, hob-nob with rock stars and supermodels, etc. – as an abomination with no redeeming features? What would James make of the precipitous decline of West Indian cricket since the 1990s?

The decline of West Indian cricket cannot be attributed to a mere one or two indigenous factors (such as the growing popularity of basketball and football among West Indian youth). Rather, the main contributing factor has been the momentous change in the structure of the international game itself, where all the leading teams have a coaching and support staff that is sometimes bigger than the team itself (masseurs, physiotherapists, dieticians, strength trainers, video analysts, sports psychologists); where a South

African and Sri Lankan, say, will sometimes play for the same regional or club team in India, England or Australia, so that the best players in every country are usually completely familiar with their rivals and with playing conditions in several countries; where there are coaching academies throughout the world that serve as 'centres of excellence' for promising teenagers, etc. Cricket is therefore much more standardised than it was in James's day, a development that enables New Zealand (smaller than Jamaica) to beat West Indies these days, a state of affairs that would have been unthinkable in the 1960s and 1970s.

This points to a problem with a key premise underlying James's analysis of cricket, perhaps seen most clearly in his inability to anticipate a time when cricket would transcend the boundaries of the nation-state, so that a cricketer's allegiance nowadays to a country has in principle become as flexible and maybe even as optional as the choice of citizenship itself is in many countries today. South African cricketers generally find it easier these days to get into the English team once they have qualified on the basis of residence, an Australian-born cricketer (Brendan Nash) who would not even be a reserve for that country currently plays for West Indies (his father was born in Jamaica), a Trinidadian of Asian descent (Robin Singh) played for India a few years ago, and so on. This phenomenon did exist in cricket's 'Golden Age', when Test-match cricket was confined to two countries (England and Australia), thereby creating a situation in which (white) South Africans, Indian princes and (white) West Indians represented England, and New Zealanders would play for Australia. Cricket is not alone in this respect – football and rugby have been similarly transformed, perhaps to an even greater degree than cricket. But unlike during the 'Golden Age', cricket, like football and rugby, has today become a circus (in the non-pejorative sense of the term) to ensure its economic and cultural survival. James's cricketing 'logics', based as they are on the primacy of the nation-state where cricket is concerned, have clearly become less applicable in this situation. However, despite the dyed hair, body piercings, tattoos and face paint sported by today's international cricketers, one suspects that James, while resolutely Edwardian in his deepest impulses, would nonetheless have found a way to account for the absolute genius of a Shane Warne or a Brian Lara.

NOTES

1 William Hazlitt, 'Merry England' in *The Collected Works of William Hazlitt, Volume XII, Fugitive Writings*, A. R. Waller and A. Glover (eds.) (London: J. M. Dent, 1904); Siegfried Sassoon, *Memoirs of a Fox-Hunting Man* (London: Faber, 1928); Dorothy Sayers, *Murder Must Advertise* (London: Gollancz, 1933); Murray Hedgcock (ed.), *Wodehouse at the Wicket: A Cricketing Anthology*

(London: Hutchinson, 1997); Hugh de Selincourt, *The Cricket Match* (Oxford University Press, 1981).

2   Christopher Brookes, *His Own Man: The Life of Neville Cardus* (London: Methuen, 1985).

3   'Cardus on Cricket – Neville Cardus', in *Gentleman's Game No More*, at http://ninthslip.blogspot.com/2007/03/cardus-on-cricket-neville-cardus.html (accessed 1 February 2010).

4   C. L. R. James, 'Garfield Sobers' in Anna Grimshaw (ed.), *The C. L. R. James Reader* (Oxford: Blackwell, 1992), pp. 380–81.

5   Ibid., p. 384.

6   See Martin Williamson, 'Tommie Burton', on the Cricinfo website at www.cricinfo.com/ci/content/player/51417.html (accessed 13 April 2010).

7   Hilary McD. Beckles, *The Development of West Indies Cricket: Volume 1, The Age of Nationalism* (London: Pluto Press, 1998).

8   C. L. R. James, *Beyond a Boundary* (New York: Pantheon Books, 1983), p. xvix.

9   Kenneth Surin, '"The Future Anterior": C. L. R. James and Going Beyond and Boundary' in Grant Farred (ed.), *Rethinking C. L. R. James* (Oxford: Blackwell, 1996), pp. 187–204; Anna Grimshaw (ed.), *C. L. R. James: Cricket* (London: Allison and Busby, 1986).

10 C. L. R. James, *Notes on Dialectics: Hegel, Marx, Lenin* (Westport, CT: Lawrence Hill, 1980), p. 8.

11 Ibid.

12 Ibid., p. 10.

13 Michael Sprinker, *Imaginary Relations: Aesthetics and Ideology in the Theory of Historical Materialism* (London: Verso, 1987), p. 33.

14 James, *Notes on Dialectics*, p. 9.

15 James, *Beyond a Boundary*, p. 63.

16 Ibid., p. 83.

17 Sylvia Wynter, 'In Quest of Matthew Bondman: Some Cultural Notes on the Jamesian Journey' in Paul Buhle (ed.), *C. L. R. James: His Life and Work* (London: Allison & Busby, 1986), pp. 131–45.

18 Derek Walcott, review of *Beyond a Boundary*, *The New York Times Book Review*, 25 March 1984.

10

CLAIRE WESTALL

Reading Brian Lara and the traditions of Caribbean cricket poetry

> I began to have my own collection of books as well as my own bats and balls.[1]

Depicting his childhood in Trinidad in the opening pages of *Beyond a Boundary* (1963), C. L. R. James repeatedly makes clear that cricket and the canon of English literature (especially Shakespeare, Dickens and Thackeray) were connected as imperial pillars of his colonial education. He explains how his growing engagement with anti-colonial politics, including the politically aesthetic dimensions of cricket, was bound to his earlier literary development. He also articulates cricket's role in Britain's nineteenth-century domination of the Caribbean, the performative resistance of black players on the margins of the game, and how the racial divide of the plantation and its consequences were visibly enacted and challenged on the cricket pitch long after the 1833 Slavery Abolition Act. As a barrack yard author, cricket writer, Marxist activist and political agitator, James's life and writing drew together cricket, literature and the push towards independence – political, cultural and economic – that the Caribbean basin is still working through. Anthony Bateman has rightly suggested that 'the legacy of James gave rise to a significant tradition of Caribbean cricket literature, including a particularly rich body of oral and written verse'.[2] While cricket also features heavily in many Caribbean prose works, novels and short stories alike, this chapter shows that we can identify a set of cricket poems from the Caribbean and its diaspora which collectively constitute a tradition of Caribbean cricket poetry that is itself part of the canon of Caribbean writing. Much of the ground work needed to identify this field, this tradition, was laid in the 1990s by Gordon Rohlehr's 'Music, Literature and West Indian Cricket Values' and Hilary Beckles's chapter surveying cricket's appearance in Caribbean literature in *The Development of West Indies Cricket: Volume 1. The Age of Nationalism* (1998). More recently, *The Bowling was Superfine* (2011), edited by Stewart Brown and Ian McDonald, brings together an impressive array of creative pieces which demonstrate the penetrative breadth and depth of cricket's presence in the Caribbean literary imagination. Usefully, the poems presented in this chapter, as well as many more, can be found in this sizeable anthology.³ Although the chapter cannot be exhaustive, it will introduce the field of Caribbean cricket poetry and analyse several critical examples before finally evaluating the range of poems that have been written about Brian Lara, the iconic Trinidadian batsman and former West Indies captain.

Writing the field of Caribbean cricket poetry

It seems purposeful to map the field of Caribbean cricket poetry by identifying the influence of its key antecedent – cricket calypsos – and the multiple manifestations cricket poetry has taken. As has been described elsewhere, cricket and calypso music have a long history of intersection, and notable cricket calypsos emerged in the 1920s and 1930s as West Indies entered the world stage – touring England in 1923 and then again in 1928 for their first-ever Test series. As Rohlehr explains, during this period Lord Beginner composed 'Bad Selection', attacking the composition of the 1928 team, had another calypso in praise of A. E. Harragin, probably from 1932, and wrote 'MCC vs West Indies, 1935'. Meanwhile, Chieftain Douglas provided 'MCC vs West Indies' in 1929 and Atilla the Hun offered 'International Tournament: 1937'.⁴ It should not be surprising then that the first Caribbean cricket poems come from this period. In *Beyond a Boundary*, James writes of his own youthful foray into cricket poetry, describing how in 1921 he composed a poem celebrating the devastating fast bowling of Trinidadian Victor Pascall and a sonnet honouring Wilton St Hill that he 'sweated out' at the request of a fanatical St Hill supporter.⁵ The earliest poem Rohlehr identifies is the sonnet 'To Learie' (1939) by the Tobagon Eric Roach. Written following Constantine's international retirement, it praises this 'famous son' of 'our native sun' for his contribution to the West Indies and his achievements playing for Nelson Cricket Club in England's Lancashire League. Yet there is a telling, perhaps schizophrenic, tension between the exuberance of Constantine (his 'run and leap and swing') and the tight, conventional constraints of the fourteen-line English sonnet in iambic pentameter (a tension James felt composing his St Hill sonnet). The same year, 1939, Lord Caresser sang of a 'man of perpetual energy' in his calypso 'Learie Constantine', and two earlier calypsos by Beginner also registered Constantine's importance.⁶ (Interestingly, Leslie Frewin, the English editor of *The Poetry of Cricket* from 1964, wrote the poem 'On Seeing Sir Learie Constantine Return (Temporarily) from Diplomacy to Cricket' in 1963.) Later, when West Indies gained a first series win in England in 1950, Beginner and Kitchener regaled the crowd at Lord's with 'Victory Test Match' and its 'two little pals', Ramadhin and Valentine. Kitchener also penned 'Kitch's Cricket Calypso' about the same triumph and King Radio had 'We Want Ramadhin on the Ball'. Such heroic praise for Ramadhin is reflected in Cecil Gray's poem 'Sonny Ramadhin' from *The Woolgather* (1994). Since the 1950s, memorable matches, players and points of controversy have regularly featured in calypso, as in Laurel Aitken's 'Tribute to Collie Smith', Kitchener's 'Cricket Champions' and Mighty Sparrow's 'Sir Garfield Sobers' and 'Kerry Packer'. This musical tradition, rooted in Trinidad but regionally influential, brings to the fore a number of common patterns that have passed into Caribbean cricket poetry, namely: the documentation of a match or series, sometimes with substantial artistic licence, for popular memorialisation; pointed criticism of players, a team (island or regional), selectors or management via the combative and satirical tradition of picong (humour); direct intervention in domestic and international issues pertaining to the game and its popular reception; and, most often, the celebration, even deification, of specific cricketers in terms of warriorhood and as examples of masculine self-assertion that are seen to speak for the people and uplift them.

In the 1950s, Caribbean literature began to find its own shape aided by the BBC's *Caribbean Voices* series. The decade also saw West Indies go from triumphant victory over England in 1950 (winning 3–1) to disastrous loss against them in 1957 (losing 3–0). Importantly, Frank Worrell's ascendance to permanent West Indies captain in 1960 marked a watershed for cricket that was politically paralleled by independence from England, beginning with Jamaica in 1962. However, the subsequent collapse of the West Indies Federation (1958–62) ended the short-lived political embodiment of regional affiliation that had been, and perhaps still is, championed by West Indies cricket. Reflecting on this period, Kamau Brathwaite's poem 'Rites' in *Islands* (1969) was a defining moment for Caribbean cricket poetry. Although first published as a kind of poetic short story called 'Cricket' in Andrew Salkey's *Caribbean Prose* (1967), Brathwaite's alterations to the title and form worked to emphasise cricket as dramatic, communal and political ritual. Written in what he calls 'nation language', 'Rites' addresses the legacy of slavery directly and exposes the region's mid-century limbo position between colonialism and independence. It set the tone for the way poetry could explore cricket's status as a cultural vehicle for the violent expression of anti-colonial action and self-definition, while shedding light on collective ambitions and failures. Following Brathwaite, Bruce St John's 'Cricket' (1982) examines a similar period by unpacking the confluence of religiosity and cricketing reverence found by playfully relating the Trinities of the Holy Ghost, the cricketing wicket and the three Ws (Walcott, Weekes and Worrell) of West Indies batsmanship and concluding that playing cricket 'right' will lead to salvation. A host of later poems have mobilised cricket, and its representative roles and vocabulary, to probe the Caribbean's political conscience and history, as in John Agard's 'Prospero Caliban Cricket' (1993), James Berry's 'Fast Bowler' (1997), Delores McAnuff-Gauntlett's 'Cricket Boundaries' and 'Notes from a Novice' (both from 1997), William Walcott's 'Bondmen' (2005) and G. K. Sammy's 'Cricket in the Road' (which shares its name with a short story by Michael Anthony) as well as his poetic contemplation of apartheid in South Africa and recent West Indies cricket crises in 'Cricket Calypso' (2004).

Nevertheless, as with cricket calypsos, the majority of poems articulate their politicised interests through an identifiable match, ground or, most often, player. International matches are recorded in poems such as Horace Harringan's 'The Test Unparalleled in Verse' (1991), portraying the tied Test between West Indies and Australia during the 1960–61 series, Colin Shakespeare's 'England v The West Indies 1988' (1994), and two contributions from Stewart Brown, an Englishman who lived and worked in the Caribbean, 'Test Match Sabina Park' (1986) with its insight into embarrassed English nationalism and 'Counter Commentary at Kensington Oval' from 1999. Location is the anchoring force in 'Cricket Grounds, Plymouth' (1996) by Lloyd W. Brown and 'View from the George Headley Stand, Sabina' (2000) by Edward Baugh, which concentrates on crowd talk over cricketing action. Poems praising individual cricket heroes are by far the most common and include Colin Shakespeare's 'Gary Sobers' (1994), David Dabydeen's 'For Rohan Babulal Kanhai' (1988) and 'Call Him the Babu' (2000) by Sasenarine Persaud, also about Kanhai, 'Greenidge' (1986) by Faustin Charles, a cluster of poems about Viv Richards and a cycle of poems about Brian Lara, to which this chapter will return. Poems like E. A. Markham's 'On Another Field, An Ally: A West Indian Batsman Talks us Towards the Century' (1989) draw upon a multitude of West Indies heroes, and sometimes the lives of former cricketing figures are remembered, as with 'The Pulpit Eulogists of Frank Worrell' (2000) by Edward Baugh, 'Jim Allen' (1998) by Howard Fergus and 'Death of John Arlott' (1994) by Colin Shakespeare. An interesting and overtly gendered take on the heroic angle is found in Joan Anim-Addo's collection *Janie Cricket Lady with Carnival and Hurricane Poems* (2006), in which she remembers her mother, a former cricketer for Grenada, as a woman challenging the nexus of cricket, masculinity and nationalism.

Recognising the prevalent link between cricket and masculinity, there is a small but poignant group of poems that warn us about the potentially reductive and stereotypical connection between cricket and men of Caribbean descent. J. D. Douglas's 'I'm a West Indian in Britain' (1983), John Agard's 'Stereotype' (1985) and Benjamin Zephaniah's 'How's Dat' (1992) all derive from the realities of racism, social exclusion and the flattening assumptions about black men held in Britain during the 1980s, a decade in which cricket poetry grew thanks to the strength of West Indies and the diversification of Caribbean literature itself. Cricket is also used to recreate personal memories, often of childhood, as in 'Practice' (2005) by Cecil Gray. Merle Collins's 'Quality Time' (2003) and Lorna Goodison's 'For My Mother (May I Inherit Half Her Strength)' (2000) are examples that use cricketing terminology and imagery to explore relationships between children and elderly parents, especially fathers, and like many cricket poems encode death as the fall of a wicket. In addition, cricket has been deployed as an explicit sexual metaphor by Jean 'Binta' Breeze in 'on cricket, sex and housework' (2000), Milton Vishnu Williams in 'Batting is My Occupation' (1986) and E. A. Markham in his violently touching 'Not Cricket' (1995), which uses cricketing vocabulary to undercut the performance of masculinity involved in an act of rape.

This growing body of poems could be categorised according to: the chronology of their composition or publication; the poet's nationality or place of residence when writing, especially as many poems were composed in England and Canada; the poet's ethnicity, in order to identify writers of African or Indian descent (though many are mixed); or, the poet's sex, dividing poems by men, which constitute the vast majority, from those by women, which form a smaller but interesting set. This chapter cannot address each of these formulations but will instead concentrate on reading the central motifs of Caribbean cricket poetry through key example pieces that chart the historical development of West Indies cricket across the twentieth century. The century in which there was 'a succession of black goals: to get to bat, to gain places on island-wide teams and regional tours, and, as recently as the 1960s, to be named vice-captains and captains of Test teams'.[7]

The 'Rites' of Caliban and the power of heroic batsmanship

To establish his own identity, Caliban, after three centuries, must himself pioneer into regions Caesar never knew.[8]

James closes his Preface to *Beyond a Boundary* by calling upon the 'native' to push past the imperial master, working through Shakespeare's *The Tempest* and the Roman Empire. By collectively naming the Caribbean and its people 'Caliban', James registers Columbus's notion of the Caribs as cannibals, as well as their genocidal annihilation, the man-made and European nature of the Caribbean's history of slavery and servitude, and the authority of English Literature to name and thereby create a 'native' forced to enter into a new language (English) and a new language of self-understanding. By identifying Caesar as the colonial master, rather than the textual Prospero, James removes the canonically mystical from brutal oppression and identifies British imperialism with a single, human, body of empire that has already died, thereby claiming freedom from, and after, colonialism as a future certainty.

'Prospero Caliban Cricket' by the Guyanese-born John Agard is a poetic reconstruction of James's insistence upon Caliban's self-defining ability and, as Bateman states, it demonstrates that 'when viewed from the perspective of the margins of the former empire, cricket refuses to be the apolitical field it is constructed as in English literary culture'.[9] Opening with 'Prospero batting/Caliban bowling', Agard ensures that the racial divide of colonial cricket still in place at the start of the twentieth century structures his poem. Drawing upon the legacy of great West Indies fast bowling, the young Caliban is a new, quick and dangerous bowler who leaves Prospero calling upon the iconic doctor of hypocritical English amateurism 'W. G. Grace/to preserve him'. Critically, the poem is dense with aggressive references to the memories of slavery and the former master–slave relationship even as its imagery suggests the overturning of this relationship:

> Caliban arcing de ball
> Like an unpredictable whip.
> Prospero foot like it chain to de ground.
> Before he could mek a move
> De ball gone thru to de slip,
> And de way de crowd rocking
> You would think dey crossing de atlantic
> Is cricket is cricket in yuh ricketics
> But from far it look like politics.
> Prospero remembering
> How Caliban used to call him master.
> Now Caliban agitating de ball faster
> And de crowd shouting POWER[10]

The black bowler's skill, strength and 'striding' confidence speaks to and for the people, as in James Berry's 'Fast Bowler' where the ball is 'a nation's voice' and the bowler's arm 'works his nation's arm'. Agard's Caliban is the body of movement and forceful, anti-colonial action while Prospero stands for immobilising fear and imperial stasis. The crowd's collective wave-like movement, 'rocking', is reminiscent of the transatlantic passage, though here it is used to signify an anti-colonial transformation achieved as the increasing (political) 'agitation' of Caliban's bowling enables them to recognise and demand 'POWER'. This is a similar but more optimistic assessment of the transfer of energy and potential from player to crowd, from individual to society, examined in 'Rites'.

Famously, Brathwaite's 'Rites' depicts West Indies batsman Clyde Walcott and his followers, all of whom appear caught between the inescapable past of slavery and oppression and the not-yet-achieved freedom of the present. The poem unites the language of Afro-Caribbean religiosity and memory with the language of protest and an affirmation of self-entitlement (rights) but does so within a tale of 'indiscipline and irresponsibility'.[11] To Frank Birbalsingh it is the 'Rise and Fall' brought about by the mid-century 'inconsistency or fickleness' of the people, the West Indies team and the politics of the islands.[12] For Nathaniel Mackey, Brathwaite's 'linguistic replacement of umpire with "empire" underscores the centrality of slavery, the plantation system and colonialism to the history and predicaments of the region'.[13] Brathwaite conveys the pressures of history and the failures of the present through a local beach match and the destruction of Walcott and West Indies, with both narratives being relayed by a Barbadian tailor in vibrant creole/nation language. At the high point of the poem, the black batsman's recently acquired power appears to be transferable:

> Clyde back pun he back
> Foot an' *prax!*
> Is through extra cover an' four red runs all de way.
> 'You see dat shot?' the people was shoutin';
> 'Jesus Chrise, man, wunna see dat shot?'
> All over de groun' fellers shakin' hands wid each other
> as if was *they* wheelin de willow
> as if was *them* had the power;[14]

The onomatopoeic quality of '*prax!*' captures the crack of Walcott's bat in an aural reversal of the sound of Massa's whip. Brathwaite envisions a giant whose strength provides a moment of postcolonial violence, a blood-red shot of a fleeting rebellious force, as this signature shot makes the ball and English hearts bleed all the way to the boundary with the rolling *r*-sounds of its 'red runs'. This symbol of 'blood, fire and revolution' racing past existing boundaries ignites the crowd. Their sense of awe, of congratulatory adulation, soon becomes a feeling of empowerment, 'as if' Walcott's strength, carried by the ball, has passed into them. Initially, the conditional 'as if' sounds positive, as though the crowd's proxy position can become one of empowered individual and collective action, but its repetition begins to subtly mark the illusory quality of this feeling. The tailor's shift from an earlier 'we' to 'they'/'them' indicates his separation from the crowd's over-exuberance, from their false sense of achievement and glory. Further, a reader sees the division of '*prax!/*Is' as indicating that praxis itself is not yet a single, whole or knowable imperative. Thereafter, only collapse is possible, for Walcott, the team, the crowd and, it seems, the region, with no single man able to 'hole up de side'. Crucially, Brathwaite appears cautious about the heroic over-investment in Walcott and singular cricketing episodes when they are not accompanied by a sustained programme of political opposition and reform. Yet, after 'Rites', poems portraying West Indies cricketers focus on the success, especially batting success, of their aesthetic postcolonial violence, thanks to the historic pattern of world-class players and team domination. And, because of the plantation shift from slavery to indentureship, much of the same imagery is used and reused, even across lines of Indian and African inheritance, as poems about Rohan Kanhai and Viv Richards illustrate.

David Dabydeen's 'For Rohan Babulal Kanhai' and 'Call Him the Babu' by Sasenarine Persaud use Kanhai's middle name to establish an intimate bond with the cricketer, portray a cricketing 'babu', i.e. father or brother held in affection, and invoke a heroic, compensatory, Indo-Caribbean agent. Persaud recollects Kanhai's innings of 256 in Calcutta during the 1958–59 tour and presents Kanhai's prolific batting ('cutlassblade in hand') as 'bitter' retribution for his inherited severance from India and as a protest against the political suppression of Indo-Caribbeans in Guyana (with '50 + 1%/minoritied for years'). '*The Babu*' is used as a closing chant to rail against the 'great white lie' of colonial transportation and to recognise the 'unreturning', who will not see India. Similarly, Dabydeen's earlier poem establishes Kanhai as a protector and redeemer standing against the 'White Overseer' of the plantation and the 'Blackman' of nationalist bloodshed. In the first stanza, Kanhai's batting ferocity and success weighs against the empty, exhausted and seemingly sleepless figure of the 'Whiteman' as bowler, master and God. In the second, his batting is compensation for and defence against the Guyanese Prime Minister Forbes Burnham and the racially motivated killing of Indo-Guyanese citizens in 1964 at Wismar. Kanhai's cricketing work is seen to psychologically shield or 'guard' those 'coolies' who bind themselves together around the radio listening to his batting display in 'Warwick-Shire', England ('Driving sorrow to the boundary'). In both poems, Kanhai's bat is the 'cutlass' of indentureship taken up by Indian immigrants shipped to the Caribbean between 1838 and 1917 to fill the labour gap left by slavery's end. Consequently, in the poetic journey from indentureship to county cricket, Kanhai's pacey, aggressive strokeplay expresses Indo-Caribbean rebellion, self-creation and defensive hope, problematising the hegemonising force of black political power over other identities within the region, and simultaneously highlighting some of the Caribbean's continuities of suppression and their resistance through cricket.

Building a more positive picture of critical black impetus, poems about Viv Richards, the Antiguan batting legend and former West Indies captain, are laden with gestures of brilliant batting brutality as in 'Viv' (1986) by Faustin Charles, 'Conquest' (2003) by Howard Fergus and 'Massa Day Done' (2003) by Ian McDonald, which, by invoking Eric Williams's famous 'Woodford Square Speech' of 1961, lays this call for independence and political consciousness over the batting excellence of Richards. With Richards we move to an exemplar of Beckles's 'second paradigm' of West Indies cricket, characterised by the team's world dominance, roughly between 1974 and 1991, and the height of their representational value for regional nationalism.[15] Where Short Shirt's calypso entitled 'Vivian Richards' (1976) praises his intense all-round cricketing contribution, these poems focus on Richards as 'batsman-hero', a warrior or conqueror in battle defeating England and destroying the racialised imperial order of cricket.

Charles and McDonald use 'Viv' to establish a tie of familiarity between the batsman, his public and the poet, but Fergus adopts the formal, commanding, 'Richards' to make his demand for English supplication all the more imposing after the 'blackwash' of 1986 in the Caribbean and that of 1984 in England. All three poems have a strong sense of the immediacy and importance of Richards's impact at the crease and his god-like presence is repeatedly seen through associations with the natural elements (Sun, Fire, Lightning and Thunder), reinforcing his affinity with Ogun, a Yoruban deity of fire, iron and warriorhood, and Shango, the Yoruban god of thunder and lightning often linked to rebellion. The poems support Richards's right to express himself forcibly as a black man against accusations, specifically in the British media, of arrogance and to speak openly about cricket's political content. In *Hitting Across the Line* (1991), Richards writes: 'you cannot evade the point that playing cricket is in itself a political action … coming as I do from the West Indies at the very end of colonialism … I believe very strongly in the black man asserting himself in this world and over the years I have leaned toward many movements that follow this basic cause.'[16] Aligned with Black Power, Rastafarianism, regional nationalism and cricketing dominance, in these poems Richards stands for a pan-African sense of communal belief, Caribbean freedom and unity, and the individual will of a single, rebellious man who must fight and understands himself as a fighting leader.

Importantly, the violent nature of Richards's batting is at the centre of these poems. Signs of his physicality abound with the accumulation of body parts ('jaw', 'eye', 'shoulder', 'chest' and 'head'). His aggressive intention is noted from the outset in 'Massa' with his 'back-lift big' and his 'grinding' jaw reminding us of Richards's gum chewing just as it works to highlight his bone crunching, devouring determination that is reinforced by his 'stabbing the pitch' in a gesture of penetrating and striking preparation. His start is expected to be 'sudden, violent, a thunder shock', an assault on those who dare oppose him. The sound of a 'thunderous roar' is repeated by Charles as he and McDonald celebrate Richards in a god-like pose akin to Shango. This is extended in 'Massa', with Richards 'holding the bat' like an 'axe', the symbol of possession by Shango. In 'Massa', cutting is first mentioned when the poetic voice calls for the 'mightiest man' because 'Viv husk he', saving his 'best fo' the best'. The *m*-sound alliteration emphasises Richards's masculinity in contrast to the 'flight finery' he's bowled, and underlines the emasculation he will perform with the metaphorical harvesting, cutting down and back to the core, of his challenger. This motif of cutting, linked to plantation work, returns in the penultimate stanza to build a picture of the rapid ferocity of Richards's shot making. At the height of Richards's 'butchery', 'bat spill blood/and he cut like he cutting hog on a block'. The barbarism of cricket's heritage in the Caribbean is here reversed as Massa's blood is spilt. The alliteration of 'butchery'/'bat'/'blood' builds the burbling sound of the liquid of life and death which flows over onto the next line until the strong, short sounds of 'cut', 'hog' and 'block' bring it to an abrupt end. The chopping block replaces the 'altar' of the morning as Richards's batting becomes a scene of murderous sacrifice. With 'the warrior thrusts a majestic cut', Charles repeats this slicing through resistant flesh and again, as in 'Massa', the 'covers' become the area on the field of play and the blanket of suppression that is shredded as Richards slices through the past by levelling his cricketing enemy. (Charles writes of Gordon Greenidge in similar terms in the poem 'Greenidge', describing him as 'Blading the landscape with an all-conquering sweep' with his 'sword-bat'.)

These poems see Richards as having a transformative, enlivening effect on the crowd, as if his 'innings' 'could make life good', as McDonald writes. While in 'Massa' the poetic voice contends that Richards 'alone could stop slavery', all three poems suggest that the battle being waged is left unfinished. In 'Massa', the conditional closure ('could') implies that slavery, in all its guises, has not yet ended. In 'Viv', the eruption that explodes tradition brings a new life that has not yet been shaped and, in 'Conquest', Fergus highlights the plague of apartheid in South Africa as indicative of the need to fight on at home. In West Indies cricket, this need, so personally felt and publicly performed by Richards, was taken forward by Richie Richardson as the next regional captain but disintegrated under the post-nationalist pressures that were increasingly impinging upon his team and Brian Lara in particular.

'Laraism' in life and poetry

Since 1994, Brian Lara, the three-times West Indies captain and world record breaking batsman, has inspired a cycle of calypsos and poems that point to his place in the region's popular imagination. Calypso and pan tracks have included 'Lash dem Lara' by Alexander de Great, 'Signal for Lara' by Superblue and 'Four Lara Four' by de Fosto, all marking the triumphs of 1994. Rootsman's 'Lara' rang out around the Caribbean in 2004 and Lara's 400 not out was captured by de Fosto in his pan sequel 'He Strikes Again'. In terms of poetry, Breeze, Fergus, Keens-Douglas and others have all crafted pieces in commemoration of Lara and it is to these that the chapter now turns.

Jean 'Binta' Breeze's 'Song for Lara' praises Lara and the 'young generation' of the 1990s, who refuse to stand 'in awe of Wisden' (cricket's revered yearbook). While calling on dance, pan and kaiso (i.e. calypso), Breeze draws directly upon David Rudder's famous 1987 calypso 'Rally Round the West Indies', referencing the difficulties facing West Indies cricket and Rudder's call for regional solidarity in the face of generational change and defeat. However, she still chooses to concentrate on the sensational Lara as he plays himself into history. Comparably, Rajandaye Ramkissoon-Chen writes of Lara's (then) world record in 'On Lara's 375' as a moment of Caribbean carnival and concentrates on Lara's humility as 'Humbly like a hero/he bows to the wicket' and 'kisses the earth'. This image, one to be repeated a decade later and an important motif in poems about Lara, is an act of connection, of loyalty and locality being expressed to the soil and people of the region to show that he comes from them and belongs to them, that he gives thanks to them and the islands 'instinctively', as he claimed.[17] The crux of the poem becomes the emotional intensity felt by Lara (fuelled by the absence of his father) and its reflection in the crowd as he becomes the body of achievement. 'He walks the victory sign' in that now famous pose with his arms and bat held above his head and is transfigured into the (young) father and protector of the region, standing with 'arms that unite/beneath an uncertain sun'.[18]

Howard Fergus has penned four poems about Lara and entitled the collection which features three of these *Lara Rains and Colonial Rites* (1998).[19] In 'BC Lara', a poem which playfully celebrates Lara's 501 not out for Warwickshire, Fergus traces the idea that Lara brings about historical and religious transformation. Identifying 1994 as 'Anno Lari' in a play upon Queen Elizabeth II's description of 1992 as *annus horribilis*, Fergus claims that time will now be divided between before Lara and after Lara with the player's initials writing out the name of Christ. With Lara's arrival set to

Figure 10.1. Brian Lara during his 400 not out world record innings in 2004.
(© Brooks LaTouche of Barbados)

'eclipse' old empires, Fergus's double-edged attack appears to be directed
both at a Christian timeline and imperial cricketing history. Fergus's poem
about the 375, 'Lara Rains', emphasises the savage demise of England caused
by Lara's batting. Cutting the opposition 'Over and over with a blunt willow', Lara bludgeons England to death until they are buried under a 'ruin
of runs' in an 'Antiguan graveyard', i.e. the Antiguan Recreation Ground
(ARC), the site of both Lara's highest Test score records, which has St John's
Catholic Cathedral on its west side. Fergus draws upon Catholic iconog-
raphy with the umpires as priest-like 'ombudsmen' who call 'over and out'
as they enact the last 'rites' of England's cricketing and imperial superiority.
Having 'dug their hell', Lara again becomes that famous 'shape of victory',
walking with his hands aloft despite 'an uncertain resurrection/After 375

years of rain under Lara'. Like the 'uncertain sun' of Ramkissoon-Chen, the 'rain' of Lara, as the favourable life-giving weather source that breathes life into the lush Caribbean landscape, may also be the monarchical reign that must end, though Fergus writes that 'the sun will not set/On the united states of the West Indies'.

In terms of Fergus's own poetry, the 'resurrection' of Lara occurs on 15 December 2000, as recorded in 'Lara Again' in *Volcano Verses* (2003). This poem captures Lara's first innings of the third Test in Adelaide against Australia during the 2000–01 tour when West Indies were 2–0 down in the series.[20] Three days after having scored 231 against Australia 'A', Lara came in at 52-2, was 136 not out overnight and went on to make 182 the next day. Although West Indies secured a first innings total of 391 they collapsed to 114 in the second, lost the match and endured a disastrous 5–0 series defeat. In spite of this and the wider story it captures, by focusing exclusively on the first day's play Fergus is able to pay homage to Lara's spectacularly commanding performance as the batsman who makes a Christmas 'gift' like 'Santa' to his people. (Although, as Santa is an imagined fallacy of childhood innocence this may not be an entirely positive comparison.) It is noteworthy that Fergus recognises the batting efforts of a young Marlon Samuels who stays with Lara at the crease but he insists on identifying Samuels's strength as his ability to 'follow the beat of the master'. It is an irony of history that it was Marlon Samuels who ran Lara out in ignominious fashion in Lara's last international game, a one-day international (ODI) against England at the 2007 World Cup. Fergus also praises Lara's volcanic, eruptive qualities as a batsman, conveyed by his repetitive boundaries against 'terrorists' like Glen McGrath, but he also sees that a volcano is unpredictable and unreliable and this matches many reports of Lara's own youthful exuberance. In 'Lara Reach', the ordinary hero-worshipping spectator sees the arrival of Lara at the wicket as bringing a certain century while his own cricketing experience of 'singles and dots' is soon ended when he is given out. The poem offers a comedic reinforcement of the notion that almost impossible public expectations weigh on Lara and widen the gap between professional and social cricketing experiences.

Paul Keens-Douglas also addresses the batting of Lara through the hero-worshipping of ordinary folk and moves to lambaste their idolisation of him. Keens-Douglas's first engagement with Lara comes via his pivotal female character 'Tanti Merle', who is at the centre of his most acclaimed and popular cricket poem 'Tanti at de Oval'. Almost three decades after her first poetic outing, Tanti Merle reappears in 'Tanti Backin' Lara', a short story celebrating Lara's 375.[21] Markham uses a similar figure in 'Mammie', an elderly Caribbean immigrant in Britain, who insists on the need to support

West Indies as she provides her own critical reading of the game and Lara's technique in the 1995 poems 'Conversations at Upton Park iii' and 'For Brian Lara'.[22]

Keens-Douglas's other tribute, 'Lara Fans', offers a poetic critique not of Lara but of those 'die hard Lara' fan(atic)s and what Beckles has called 'Laraism', the 'unhealthy focus on Lara's persona', including his private wealth and public cricketing spats, rather than the effects of the 'Age of Globalisation', Beckles's 'third paradigm', which he embodies.[23] Keens-Douglas complains that 'Dey eh askin … bout West Indies,/Or if de wicket takin' spin' but only want to know 'how much Lara make' – as a play on both his run getting and his money making. Worshipping Lara as a kind of 'demi-god' in the way that has come to be expected for cricket heroes, they believe 'Lara alone could win dis match!' When Lara makes a duck they are discussing luck, fatigue and Obeah (folk magic or mysticism), not concentration, determination or shot selection. Keens-Douglas's poem is particularly useful in its rejection of the idolisation of a single man as he reveals his concern at the over-investment in Lara and the problems it poses for the West Indies team and regional unity in the face of capitalism, globalisation and one-man accumulation. The poem ends poignantly with his ambition for West Indies cricket:

> Ah hope West Indies start makin' runs,
> For everybody sake,
> Because ah tired hear dem askin',
> 'How much Lara make?'[24]

This hope for cricket is also Keens-Douglas's aspiration for the Caribbean as he believes that the West Indies team, and the Caribbean more generally, can and will move beyond their over-investment in the heroic individual, cricketing or otherwise, and towards a new or renewed era of unity in purpose and action.

The tone of unadulterated praise that Keens-Douglas is attacking is reflected in the two poems of Eutrice Cowie-Hope which celebrate Lara's 400, namely 'Lara the Brave' and 'Celebrating Brian Lara'.[25] Although she notes that it would have been historically crippling for West Indies to endure a 'white wash in 2004', she still rejects the importance of a series defeat against England in favour of Lara's achievement. However, after the 400 not out record Lara himself said: 'It was different last time. Then we were winning the series and you've got to look at this in the context of the series, which we've lost. So really it doesn't mean that much.'[26] Lara's mature attempt at modesty and leadership comes to the fore here. His sense of reaching back and recognising the gap between his own success and his team's position is clearly audible. His sentiment was taken up by other commentators, including Fazeer Mohammed, who did not wish to downplay Lara's achievement but rather call for it to be capitalised upon in a socially productive fashion for the people of the region.[27] Such voices wisely insist that the work of heroes such as Lara needs to be used as part of a wider socio-political uprising, part of the improvement of the masses and their communal enjoyment of the game.

Yet on his retirement Lara asked the World Cup crowd 'did I entertain?' and they responded with a resounding 'YES'. His ability to entertain, with strokes, with passion, with power, was key to his success but did not sit alongside successful leadership or collective achievement as it had done historically in West Indies cricket. Nor did it represent the dream of regional nationalism held by earlier generations. Instead, his entertaining batting spoke of contractual disputes, corporate sponsors, televisual marketing and distribution rights. It suggested, like much of the poetry in this chapter, that emancipation is an ongoing project.

NOTES

1 C. L. R. James, *Beyond a Boundary* (London: Serpents Tail, 2000), p. 16.
2 Anthony Bateman, *Cricket, Literature and Culture: Symbolising the Nation, Destabilising Empire* (Farnham: Ashgate, 2009), p. 197.
3 Stewart Brown and Ian McDonald (eds.), *The Bowling was Superfine: West Indian Writing and West Indian Cricket* (Leeds: Peepal Tree Press, 2011).
4 Gordon Rohlehr, 'Music, Literature and West Indian Cricket Values' in Hilary Beckles (ed.), *An Area of Conquest: Popular Democracy and West Indies Cricket* (Kingston, Jamaica: Ian Randle Publishers, 1994), pp. 55–102, esp. pp. 56–64.
5 James, *Beyond a Boundary*, pp. 89–90.
6 Rohlehr, 'Music, Literature and West Indian Cricket Values', p. 62.
7 Frank Manning, 'Celebrating Cricket: The Symbolic Construction of Caribbean Politics' in Hilary Beckles and Brian Stoddart (eds.), *Liberation Cricket: West Indies Cricket Culture* (Manchester University Press, 1995), pp. 269–89, esp. p. 271.
8 James, *Beyond a Boundary*, p. ix.
9 Bateman, *Cricket, Literature and Culture*, p. 194.
10 John Agard, 'Prospero Caliban Cricket' in David Rayvern Allen with Hubert Doggart (eds.), *'A Breathless Hush': The MCC Anthology of Cricket Verse* (London: Methuen, 2004), pp. 232–33.
11 Hilary Beckles, *The Development of West Indies Cricket: Volume 1. The Age of Nationalism* (London: Pluto Press, 1998), p. 107.
12 Frank Birbalsingh, *The Rise of West Indian Cricket: From Colony to Nation* (Antigua: Hansib, 1996), p. 221.
13 Nathaniel Mackey, 'An Interview with Kamau Brathwaite' in Stewart Brown (ed.), *The Art of Kamau Brathwaite* (Bridgend: Seren, 1995), p. 134.

14 Kamau Brathwaite, 'Rites' in Kamau Brathwaite, *The Arrivants: A New World Trilogy* (Oxford University Press, 1973), pp. 197–203.

15 Beckles, *The Development of West Indies Cricket: Volume 1*, p. 92.

16 Viv Richards, *Hitting Across the Line: An Autobiography* (London: Headline, 1991), pp. 186–88.

17 Brian Lara, *Beating the Field: My Own Story*, with Brian Scovell (London: Partridge, 1995), p. 100.

18 Rajandaye Ramkissoon-Chen, 'On Lara's 375' in *Ancestry* (London: Hansib Caribbean, 1997), p. 101.

19 'Lara Rains', 'Lara Reach' and 'BC Lara' are all in Howard Fergus, *Lara Rains and Colonial Rites* (Leeds: Peepal Tree Press, 1998), pp. 9, 10 & 11, respectively.

20 Howard Fergus, 'Lara Again' in *Volcano Verses* (Leeds: Peepal Tree Press, 2003), pp. 59–60.

21 Paul Keens-Douglas, 'Tanti Backin' Lara' in *Role Call: Poetry and Short Stories by Paul Keens-Douglas* (Trinidad: Keensdee Productions, 1997), pp. 33–36.

22 E. A. Markham, 'Conversations at Upton Park iii' and 'For Brian Lara' in *Misapprehensions* (London: Anvil, 1995), pp. 77 & 78, respectively.

23 Hilary Beckles, 'Brian Lara (Con)testing the Caribbean Imagination' in David L. Andrews and Steven J. Jackson (eds.), *Sports Stars: The Cultural Politics of Sporting Celebrity* (London: Routledge, 2001), pp. 243–56, esp. p. 253.

24 Paul Keens-Douglas, 'Lara Fans' in *Role Call*, pp. 8–9.

25 Eutrice Cowie-Hope, 'Lara the Brave', letters to the *Trinidad Guardian*, 26 April 2004; 'Celebrating Brian Lara', *Trinidad Guardian*, 28 April 2004.

26 Christopher Martin Jenkins, 'Scintillating Lara Peaks at 400', *The Times*, 13 April 2004.

27 Fazeer Mohammed, 'Of Misguided Celebrations and Misplaced Priorities', 30 November 2005, www.cricinfo.com (accessed 3 March 2006).

II

HILARY MCD. BECKLES

The detachment of West Indies cricket from the nationalist scaffold

West Indian people have made their greatest single cultural investment in cricket. This commitment of effort and emotion profoundly shaped the mindscape of citizens, and led to the allocation of scarce financial resources that enabled physical infrastructures to dominate the landscape of each territory. As a deeply rooted historical process it has had several implications for critical aspects of anti-colonialism and the nation-building project.[1]

While the enormity of this enterprise is generally grasped, there are important aspects that often elude general attention. Two such aspects are the historic depth and ethnic participation of the process. At the beginning of the nineteenth century, the zenith of the slavery period, masters and slaves were passionate participants in the game, and made separate preparations for its future. By the 1830s, when the regional slave system collapsed in the face of intense human-rights pressures, cricket was well on its way to becoming the first expression of Caribbean popular culture.[2]

This experience in cultural development is often narrated without specific reference to its fundamental multi-ethnic nature. While colonial white elites imported and domesticated the game, branding it for respectability with the 'whites only' tag, equally important was its appropriation by disenfranchised blacks who propelled its development as a site of racial and class contest. By the mid nineteenth century cricket had spilled out from these narrow social confines and found fertile ground in the larger communities of the emerging white and coloured middle classes, and the black labouring poor.[3]

This institutional transformation was associated with the smashing of entrenched social barriers that had hindered racial mobility for over a hundred years. Cricket culture assumed the most controversial reputation as the principal arena of colonial restructuring, a place for the public ventilation of proof that individual merit could be rewarded. No other public institution or social activity could claim this status. By the early twentieth century cricket as entrenched community culture was forcefully being democratised and its achievements linked to the broader processes of political decolonisation and euphoric nationalism.[4]

Within the context of Caribbean social and political history this is considered a seminal achievement. In 1928, when the regional team was granted Test status and set off to England for an inaugural tour, it comprised a gathering of men of all classes and colours; it was a reflection and recognition of Caribbean demographic diversity. Men of means and players from poverty walked out on the field to represent a society less than a century removed from chattel slavery. White men from elite families continued to provide leadership, and assumed the right to this role, but in no other sphere of Caribbean life was this democratising experience replicated.

Black access and prestigious participation in cricket was explained by hegemonic white elite groups in terms of the inner logic and moral imperative of the game, which emphasised the principle of player equality 'within the boundary'. Black players, however, had a different perspective, as did the leaders of political protest movements who spoke in support of their ambitions. They provided an interpretation that highlighted the radicalisation of social life 'beyond the boundary', and the achievement of attaining recognition for the principle of merit in selection to office within public institutions.

The radical political process to which black players attached their claim emphasised the role of fair competition within team selection procedures as the best guarantee in defeating the power of race prejudice. In addition, grass-roots communities were determined to gain respect for the benefits the game was enjoying as it was refashioned to suit social needs with their performance culture. It was important to inhabitants in towns and villages that they were not seen as passive recipients of English styles and methods, but as creative participants in the crafting of a West Indian genre. To this end, cricket was bent into new shapes and forms in order to accommodate the cultural and political agenda that was endemic to the anti-colonial consciousness.[5]

The social score of cricket by the mid twentieth century was quite extraordinary. West Indians, having transformed the domestic circumstance of the game, had irreversibly modified, nay, revolutionised the international game in terms of its performance and personality. A strikingly new approach came out of the West Indies with a distinct brand which audiences throughout the world admired, feared, resented and celebrated. The game had come to the colonies from England under the strained racial circumstances of slavery, and in the hands of the freed slaves and their progeny was refined, repackaged and re-exported. Some of the finest writers and most generous minds of organised sport have concluded, after experiencing the great West Indies teams of the 1950s, that the islanders had breathed youthful life into the old, dying Victorian game.[6]

A closer look at the scorecard reveals even more. Cricket, and no other activity, taught the scattered, fragmented West Indies the importance of collective organisation and collaboration. That the colonials were able to put together a West Indian team in 1886 and sustain that effort until today is remarkable if not miraculous. It is their greatest single political achievement, one that has become a model and mentor for other areas of collaboration such as the University of the West Indies, and the 'Caribbean Common Community'. Cricket, then, stands alone with ancestral pedigree as the leader of the nationalist movement for cohesion in a place of spatial and political division.

The English crowd marvelled at the early West Indies teams, as did the Indians and Australians. Unfamiliar to them were such multi-racial enterprises operating with apparent ease at a time when racial segregation and apartheid were gaining ground as approved models of social living. Teams made up of blacks, whites, Jews, Chinese, Indians, Syrians, Amerindians and every possible biological combination of these ethnicities showed a violently imperial racial world the meaning of human toleration and co-operation. And, critically, it was a winning experiment because by the mid-1960s it had defeated all-comers under the leadership of the youthful Gary Sobers, considered the best player the world had ever seen.

By 1980, West Indians were dominant in the international game. They were able to sustain this status for near twenty years. In no other area of public engagement did West Indians achieve a commanding presence in the international arena. While many sectors of regional life have emerged globally competitive, from the literary arts to the services economy, cricket remains the pivotal expression of a unified vision and action producing the effect of excellence in the global space. It is an experience that has brought the region considerable benefit in terms of pride and prestige.

The investment, then, of time, space, money and passion has paid off handsomely. Importantly, there continues to be an expectation of high returns. The game draws upon deep wells of public goodwill across boundaries of age, class and gender. It has retained its commanding iconic status within Caribbean civilisation and is inextricably linked and interwoven into the fabric of romantic idealism. While other sports enjoy considerable public attention in the region, with spectacular achievements in the area of athletics, public opinion surveys consistently show cricket as the number one organised cultural engagement. Within the global imagination the West Indies stand apart as a nation built around cricket.

In the hands of West Indians, furthermore, the game was ideologically restructured and energised to serve a purpose bigger than itself: the struggle for social justice and political freedom. West Indian supporters are generally foot soldiers of this collective historical consciousness and future expectation. In each island the game has been asked to carry a greater emotional and political burden than in other places. Here, therefore, it is not just a game; it is the heartbeat of a young nation looking into an old world, searching for a place where dignity and honour can be assured.

Along the way there have been many moments when forces beyond the boundary have determined the reactions of West Indians to developments within a game. Primarily, they have found it necessary to ventilate their political nationalism, particularly in respect to issues of racial injustice and imperial arrogance. This much is captured during the many riots that have erupted following controversial decisions by umpires. The cricket crowd, James tells us, represents a barometer of political awareness and historical sensibility.[7]

If heroes live on in the hearts of nations, the great West Indian players are celebrated in memory like no other citizens. Sir Frank Worrell remains the one beloved public figure across the region, with memorials in many places beyond Barbados, the place of his birth. In Jamaica and Trinidad, his name appears on public buildings, and in Barbados his face can be found on banknotes and in the streets. From the 1950s, following the defeat of England in a Test series, the West Indian nation have considered these heroes in much the same way that ancient Greek society celebrated warriors such as Hector and Achilles. Cricket for the crowd is their finest theatre where the turbulent past and divided present are acted out in epic, dramatic proportions.

But there was considerable opposition to these developments in the popular consciousness. Whites from elite families had opposed the abolition of slavery and the introduction of civil rights in the nineteenth century; similarly, they opposed political democracy and national independence in the mid twentieth. Likewise, they opposed the democratisation of cricket culture with the consequence that the emerging nation found it difficult to embrace them as legitimate citizens. In the sphere of cricket, while they were willing to make concessions to the principle of meritorious representation, they were unwilling to relinquish control of the leadership.

Against this background Frank Worrell emerged in 1960, after ten years of highly organised black protest, as the first black player to be appointed substantive captain of the West Indies team. Residual racism in white Barbadian society had much to do with his decision to adopt Jamaica as his home. He never felt accepted among the local elite, who considered that he had taken from them a critically important instrument of their race rule in the

West Indies. He was considered an arrogant 'black boy' in some quarters. Significant sections of these families across the region switched their support to England and Australia. At the same time it was commonly, though informally, observed that a significant migration of white Barbadians to South Africa and other 'dominions' took place after independence in 1966, where the apartheid society seemed to their liking.[8]

But nowhere was the politics of West Indian cricket more emotionally felt than among the West Indian migrants in England in the aftermath of Worrell's appointment. Cricket success was their most reliable armour in the struggle for social respect, dignity and general wellbeing in the slums of inner cities. Cricket victories revived and enlivened the politics of decolonisation and identity they had left behind in the West Indies. When England won the third Test at Edgbaston in 1963, with Frank Worrell as captain, the West Indian population in Birmingham was devastated.

Worrell, they knew, however, was laying the foundation for something grand. Winning the odd match or series was not enough to pay back on their investment. Nothing short of global domination would suffice. From enslavement to world leadership was the narrative they wished cricket to write. In this tale, the conquering of England was the principal prize. By 1980 they were well on the way. The lion of this vision was Vivian Richards, who symbolised the irrepressible West Indian; the most dominant cricketing batsman of his time. It was anti-colonialism in action in its clearest form; an ideological power struggle which was universally recognised as such.

In his autobiography, *Hitting Across the Line*, Richards explained the link in his consciousness between West Indian cricket and identity:

> I believe very strongly in the black man asserting himself in this world, coming as I do from the West Indies at the end of the colonial era. I identify with black power, Rastafarian [sic] and all the movements of black liberations. Once I was offered one million dollars to play cricket in South Africa, I could not go as long as the black majority in South Africa remains oppressed by the apartheid system. I could never come to terms with playing cricket there. I would be letting down my own black people and I would destroy my sense of self-esteem. Cricket has always been politics and especially for us in the Caribbean.[9]

Elsewhere he wrote that he would like to be remembered as a cricketer who carried his bat for 'the liberation of Africans and all oppressed people everywhere'.[10]

Before his career had ended, Richards considered himself in conflict with the conservative establishment forces that had sought to frustrate Frank Worrell some years earlier, and that were determined also to deny him access to the captaincy. In Richards's case, opposition came from the black members of the Board, led by Clyde Walcott, who saw him as a radical black power figure, who would not represent the Board's views. The extension of Lloyd's tenure of captaincy, in spite of Richards's obvious success as vice-captain, was seen by Richards as an act of hostility towards him.[11] This ideological tension between the conservative and radical traditions remained strong on account of having deep roots. In the political expressions and postures of officials and players evidence of this conflict could be found. The cricket crowd became astute in the reading of subtexts, and participated in public dialogue that assured few official cricket secrets.

West Indians were not alone in this regard. Cricket crises in the Caribbean attracted a fair share of journalistic commentary, some of which engaged the politics of issues beyond the boundary. Robin Marlar, writing for the *Sunday Times* on 4 July 1993, against the background of the change-over from the Richards to the Richardson captaincy, said:

> It is clear that the West Indies Board thought that when Vivian Richards retired it was time that the leadership of West Indies cricket shifted its centre of gravity away from black activism and back towards the mainstream of the international game. Haynes was too close to his predecessor to achieve his objective and the mantle passed to the younger, less confrontational Richie Richardson.[12]

This shifting of the ideological centre of gravity in West Indies cricket, therefore, is as much a part of the making of the modern nation as the emergence of political parties and trade unions. It is by large measure the history of the people as mirrored within the area of popular culture. It is, also, the idealistic expression of a political discourse that seeks order and coherence in a fragmented neo-colonial nation in search of sustainable political independence and a viable nationalist identity.

This magnificent edifice of performance achievement, driven as a synergistic combination of technical competence and political passion, crashed by the end of the 1990s, and was reversed as the doors to the twenty-first century were flung wide open. The West Indian Test team, invincible in the last generation, is now ranked the weakest of traditional competitors in the international arena. Critically, the team is no longer recognised as being an element within the grand pan-African project; it has no commitment to any political cause or movement. Not only is its diminished status ridiculed by old and new opponents, but it is reviled in some Caribbean and global quarters for having turned its back on the political agenda of post-nationalist radicalism.[13]

Media experts and academics have described this descent from awesomeness to awfulness as one of the most dramatic dislocations and losses of excellence in the modern history of sports. In the midst of this decline to despair is situated, as cause and effect, the rejection of cricket's relation to the radical political process and the popular consciousness. The discourse is hinged on the impact of Brian Lara and Chris Gayle, both superstars and captains of the team in the age of globalisation. While Lara is considered the batting heir to Viv Richards, beyond the boundary he is received as his antithesis, a leader who distanced himself from the political roots of the West Indian game and focused entirely on the construction of his brilliant personal career. He represents, then, the end of the nationalist paradigm in West Indies cricket, and the detachment of the game from the historical discourse.[14]

The golden patch in Lara's career as the best batsman in the world began at the end of the 1990s. It was the moment that marked the onset of deepening defeats of the West Indies team. As he broke batting records with apparent childlike ease, the team he led seemed infantile in the competitive world of adult sport.[15]

Eventually the West Indian game struck an ideological vacuum when the team, led by Lara, went on strike, suddenly, on the eve of the historic tour to South Africa, leaving President Nelson Mandela in ceremony at the airport awaiting the team that never arrived. The unimaginable had happened; the great West Indian team, whose previous members had contributed so much to bring apartheid to an end, now opted to stay in London for salary talks rather than meet a man who desperately wanted to thank them for their role in facilitating human liberation.[16]

After a decade dominated by the aura of Lara, in 2008 Chris Gayle emerged as the undisputed leader of 'the band of losers'. Critics and officials alike have been eager to agree with divided supporters that Lara's leadership and legacy laid the foundation for his successor to detach even further West Indies cricket from the sensibility of the nationalist project. Lara, his defenders retort, was just the messenger whose beheading has served to satisfy the emotions of the moment while preventing the process of sober intellectual reflection that was needed.[17]

After Lara, the WICB searched in a frenzied fashion to find a team leader who could hold his own on the field and offer West Indies cricket a lifeline to the rich performance legacy of the pre-Lara era. The mission was to find a mentality driven by commitment rather than cash, history rather than hubris. Lara, driven into exile for making it clear that it was the Board that needed to enter the twenty-first century, was not a part of the search party.

It was agreed that wherever Lara had taken the team, the new leader should take it in the opposite direction.[18]

All roads and reasoning led to Chris Gayle. Lara, unsolicited, endorsed the choice. Gale, he intimated, spoke his language and read the future from the same manifesto. A regional dialogue ensued in which post-nationalist socio-political tensions were aggressively ventilated as a crisis of cricket culture. Viv Richards stood his ground and made it clear that his successors were selling the family silver. He reminded the team of his famous refusal to play for money in apartheid South Africa and of his speech emphasising that lining his pocket with such blood money would poison the roots of West Indian cricket. Lara, however, was the first West Indian cricket millionaire, and this was the age of financial globalisation.[19]

No previous generation of West Indian cricket leaders has had as divisive an impact on Caribbean development discourse as that of Lara and Gayle. The failure of their teams to compensate for the spreading sense of despair in West Indian socio-economic decline and political disillusionment led to an intensely critical perception of both as politically unfit for the role of leadership. The public feels, furthermore, that despite its insistence on the team having an important political role 'beyond the boundary', the game has been hijacked by an uncaring cabal of mercenary money seekers, players without attachment to traditional sources of societal concerns.[20]

Fans and fraternity are not prepared to concede to Gayle a right to renegotiate for cricket a new, diminished role, even as the team struggles to be taken as a serious competitor. Lara had found the traditional values attached to the captaincy too burdensome to carry, and declared at a moment of despair that 'cricket was ruining his life'. Gayle's response to claims that he lacks the intellectual comprehension to perform the role was equally shocking and demeaning. He told the press that he didn't campaign for the job; that it was imposed upon him by his employers, and that he is willing to discard it if continually criticised.[21]

Like Lara, who tore away the nationalist scaffold, Gayle is believed to be the titular leader of a youth movement that rejects earlier conceptions of the national interest, and is in revolt against the regional socio-political and economic establishment. The political independence project, despite its many achievements, did not succeed in uprooting institutionalised ghetto poverty, and players drawn from such communities, such as Gayle, do consider the state and its affiliate governance systems the enemy rather than the enabler.[22]

Meanwhile, the general fear at the level of regional leadership is that cricket culture will fall fully into the monetary embrace of foreign controlled globalised market forces. Citizens are generally satisfied with the idea of the cricket millionaire, but the image of the cricketers as a freelance agent on the money market with no sincere attachment to national emotions is considered a price too high to pay.[23]

Lara was keenly aware of the public vexation associated with the discourse that surrounded his leadership. He often spoke candidly about the challenges he faced in socially integrating his 'guys' from different 'islands' into a West Indian team. At the same time he resisted the 'entrapment' of the historical social construction of the cricket hero, and team, as political ambassadors of the West Indian 'nation'. No one, it appeared, was more hyper-sensitive to the ideological imprisonment of the category. He considered himself politically framed and socially hung; and he broke free.[24]

The perfect picture of Frank Worrell did not hang comfortably on the walls of Lara's mind. Behind him was a stream of financially compromised, and socially abandoned, superheroes. For him Gary Sobers's financial discomfort was a sobering example of the fickle and unreliable sentiments that constitute the national ambition in the Caribbean. The majority of his cricket mentors, in his estimation, were never financially compensated with hard currency at a level commensurate with the degree of hero-worship they attracted.[25]

Cast aside and cash-challenged, it appeared to some spectators that old stars were looking in envy at the glitter of gold that symbolised the new commercial order of West Indian cricket. Lara's stand constituted the new West Indian brand; he was global, and his image was golden. With this armour he protected himself from the political swords drawn to suppress his alleged mutiny. With his wealth he bought protection and surrounded himself with foot soldiers and surrogates to ensure his safety. He won his battle and is about to be rehabilitated by the establishment that now sees him as what he was – the messenger of a new age and not the designer of the debacle.[26]

Gayle's recent aggression towards the West Indies Cricket Board, and his apparent general disregard for public opinion, is indicative of the widespread youth disillusionment that characterises the post-national Caribbean society. The official relationships between 'star' and state in most cases are sour, sullen and not likely to be mutually supportive. The attitudes and allegories of dejected former stars that shaped the social landscape which produced Gayle and his cohorts constitute an energy source that drives their determination to defeat the employers and resist public judgements by all means necessary.[27]

What has happened in the post-Lara era is that the anti-colonial dream of building a legitimate, sovereign West Indian nation as a supportive environment for the West Indies team has eluded political leadership, collapsed under the weight of a cocktail of crass opportunism and mind-boggling mismanagement. The political consequence of this reality has been the emergence of a string of impoverished micro-states that cannot, after thirty years of independence, legitimise their existence in serious, sound and rational ways. As retreating regimes, they are insecure and pessimistic about the future. The price tag for this new commodity has been placed around Gayle's neck.[28]

The severe implication of this new circumstance is that traditional leadership forms and styles no longer appeal to youth. If, for example, with respect to the West Indies cricket team, Sir Frank Worrell was the Founding Father, Sir Gary Sobers the King, Clive Lloyd a Statesman, Sir Vivian Richards a General and Brian Lara a Prince, then Chris Gayle is undoubtedly the Don of the posse – unchallenged leader of the 'gang'. Gayle is the man his team wants, though the West Indian community is deeply divided as to whether he is who it needs.[29]

West Indies cricket is now challenged to free itself from the anti-social values of the street gang culture that rocks the development efforts of communities across the region. The islands, large and small, and Guyana, are struggling to produce youth leadership that does not celebrate the community 'don'. Church and state speak of the importance of a rescue act. Cricketers are accused, for the first time in the history of the game, of setting a bad example to youth, one that typifies indiscipline, greed and selfishness.[30]

The ability of Gayle to command the loyalty of players from across the region attests to the proliferation and regional acceptance of Jamaican-style street culture; its music and imagery, dance and demeanour, macho and money-first mentality. While there remain positive values for youth development in aspects of this culture, such as the willingness to engage with, rather than fear, the global, its inability to promote the learning systems necessary for international competitive standards suggests its general inadequacy as a pillar on which West Indies cricket can rise.[31]

The idea of playing for one's country as an ultimate status that drives player motivation has become obsolete on the streets of Caribbean towns and rural villages. Players drawn from economically dispossessed communities that have been exposed to no experience but high unemployment, police brutality, drug trading and endemic violence have asked the question 'What has my country done for me?'. In so asking, they point to the political concept of 'failed nations' that dominates social science discourse on postcolonial developing countries, and identify themselves as targeted victims of the nation they are expected to represent.[32]

For them, the benefits of nationhood neither poured into, nor trickled down to, their households, while official fiscal and monetary policies left them exposed to corrosive unfettered market forces. They now wish to engage and benefit from these very forces that once held them as captives. While corporate commercial elites defined them as 'unemployable' and middle-class-led political parties consider them a 'social problem', the market economy of cricket welcomed them as free, empowered persons in charge of their personal destinies.[33]

Not surprisingly, there is frequent assertion that the team is populated by pariahs and pirates who should be cast out with their cash. For such critics there remains an enduring hope that a new mentality, connected to the earlier dispensation, will emerge, bringing with it a familiar commitment to high performance and broad-based leadership excellence. Much of this, however, rings hollow. The West Indies today, like other parts of the world, is participating in a process whereby political discourses are being refashioned to accommodate both the positive and negative aspects of social and financial globalisation in a post-imperial setting.

While the success of earlier teams had much to do with their willingness to draw upon and connect to public discourses as a source of motivation and discipline, their excellence was a direct result of extraordinary skills and the capacity to innovate. The de-skilling of contemporary cricket, and the reduced capacity of young players to learn the postmodern game, has more to do with the leadership crisis of the cricket establishment than the social condition and consciousness of young players. The West Indies have made the least provision for the training and professional development of their players. In a game where talent needs to be honed by programmes for team development, the region chronically requires major investment in the human and material resources that will allow it to yield future returns. This is a strategic choice that needs to be made within the boundary.[34]

NOTES

1 C. L. R. James, *Beyond a Boundary* (London: Hutchinson, 1963); James, 'Garfield Sobers' in Anna Grimshaw (ed.), *The C. L. R. James Reader* (Oxford: Blackwell, 1992), pp. 379–89; Anthony Bateman, *Cricket, Literature and Culture: Symbolising the Nation, Destabilising Empire* (Farnham: Ashgate, 2009); Farrukh Dhondy, *C. L. R. James: Cricket, the Caribbean and World Revolution* (London: Weidenfeld and Nicolson, 2001).

2 James, 'Cricket and West Indian Culture' in Anna Grimshaw (ed.), *C. L. R. James: Cricket* (London: Allison & Busby, 1986), pp. 118–24.

3 Learie Constantine, *Cricket and I* (London: Philip Allan, 1933); Gerald Howat, *Learie Constantine* (London: George Allen and Unwin, 1975); Vivian Richards, *Hitting Across the Line* (London: Headline Books, 1991); Hilary Beckles, 'The

Most Deeply Democratising Force', *ICC Cricket Quarterly*, 7(3), 2009, pp. 8–9.

4   Beckles, *The Development of West Indies Cricket: Vols. 1 and 2* (London: Pluto, 1998).

5   Beckles, *A Nation Imagined: First West Indies Test Team, The Tour of 1928* (Kingston: Ian Randle, 2003); Beckles, *The First West Indies Cricket Tour: Canada and the United States in 1886* (Kingston: University of the West Indies Press, 2006).

6   John Figueroa, *West Indies in England: The Post-War Tours* (London: Kingswood Press, 1991); Hilary Beckles and Brian Stoddart (eds.), *Liberation Cricket* (Manchester University Press, 1998).

7   James, *Beyond a Boundary*.

8   Plantations were left in trust with lawyers. In the 1970s many were urged to return by the then mixed-race Prime Minister Tom Adams, though the strengthening of white economic hegemony that resulted from this 're-migration' caused problems for Adams's political position.

9   Quoted in Beckles (ed.), *An Area of Conquest: Popular Democracy and West Indies Cricket Supremacy* (Kingston: Ian Randle, 1994), pp. 52–53.

10 Viv Richards, 'Foreword' in Beckles and Stoddart, *Liberation Cricket*, p. vii.

11 Richards, *Hitting Across the Line*, pp. 146–48.

12 Ibid., p. 53.

13 Colin Croft, 'Brian Lara: Prince or King?', *Cricinfo Interactive Magazine*, 2 April 1999; Peter Roebuck, 'How Our Man in Washington Made Lara a Winner Again', *Electronic Telegraph*, 4 April 1999.

14 Beckles, 'The Strife of Brian' in Rob Steen (ed.), *The New Ball: Universal Stories Volume 2* (London: Mainstream Publishing, 1998), pp. 79–95.

15 V. Lokapally, 'Brian Lara out on a Mission', *The Hindu*, 19 May 1996.

16 A. Brown, 'Richards and Sobers Defend Primacy of Test Cricket', *CricInfo*, 16 May 2009.

17 Brian Lara, *Beating the Field: My Own Story* (London: Corgi, 1996).

18 Hilary Beckles (ed.), *A Spirit of Dominance: Cricket and Nationalism in the West Indies* (Kingston: University of the West Indies Press, 1998).

19 Wes Hall, 'Manager's Report on West Indies Tour to England', *Trinidad Guardian*, 8 and 12 December 1995.

20 Beckles, 'The Strife of Brian'.

21 'Why Brian Lara is a Loser', *Sydney Morning Herald*, 6 November 1998.

22 'Gayle Picked is Blasted', *Daily Nation* (Barbados), 5 November 2009.

23 P. J. Patterson, 'Report of the Governance Committee on West Indies Cricket' (Kingston: West Indies Cricket Board, 2007).

24 See 'Brian Lara' at wikipedia.org (accessed 4 November 2009).

25 Tony Cozier, 'West Indies Cricket Board, Players Face Off Today', *Daily Nation* (Barbados), 4 November 1998; T. Becca, 'South African Boss Pledges Full Support to Tour', *Jamaica Gleaner*, 5 November 2009.

26 Hilary Beckles, 'The Unkindest Cut: West Indies Cricket Culture and Anti-Apartheid Struggles at Home and Abroad, 1893–1993' in Beckles, *A Spirit of Dominance*, pp. 89–122.

27 'Message from the President, WICB, Hon Dr Julian R. Hunte', *Weekend Nation* (Barbados), 11 September 2009.

28 'Gayle Ponders Test Future', *CricInfo*, 13 May 2009.

29 P. J. Patterson, 'No Action on West Indies Report', *Sunday Sun* (Barbados), 30 August 2009.

30 Michael Manley, *A History of West Indies Cricket* (London: Andre Deutsch, 1998).

31 T. Hector, 'On Lara and the Captaincy', *Trinidad Express*, 10 December 1997.

32 'Lara Backs Gayle as Windies Captain', *Weekend Nation* (Barbados), 13 November 2009.

33 Tony Cozier, 'WICB, Players' Association, Needs to Step Back', *Midweek Nation* (Barbados), 15 July 2009.

34 Ibid.

12

BORIA MAJUMDAR

The Indian Premier League and world cricket

In the contemporary sporting world, few would doubt that India is the new cricketing superpower. It is more often than not that Indians lead, the others follow. Without exaggeration, Indian cricket is a mirror in which nations, communities, men and women now see themselves. That reflection is sometimes bright, sometimes dark, sometimes distorted, sometimes magnified. Cricket for a billion plus Indians is a source of mass exhilaration and depression, security and insecurity, pride and humiliation, bonding and alienation. In fact, for many in India, cricket has replaced religion as a source of emotional strength and spiritual passion and, since it is among the earliest of memorable childhood experiences, it infiltrates memory, shapes enthusiasms and serves fantasies.

India's position as the new nerve centre of world cricket, completing what I call the 'decolonisation of Indian cricket', has been strengthened in recent times thanks to the impact of the IPL on world cricket. The first edition of the IPL, played to packed houses for forty-four days between 18 April and 1 June 2008, was a resounding success by all yardsticks. So much so that there was talk of a withdrawal syndrome among cricket fans once the spectacle was over. In most metropolitan cities across India, as also in many cities across the world with large Indian diasporas, religiously watching IPL action had become a must in April and May 2008.

As the clock struck 8 p.m. Indian time, it was IPL time. It was a passion that was seductively intense and one that cut across age and gender. Spread over forty-four days, the tournament was full of manic moments of drama, spectacle, ecstasy and agony. At the cost of giving favourite soaps and serials a miss, entire Indian families were converted to the heady mix of cricket and entertainment on offer, a package unprecedented and one that transformed the face of Indian and world cricket. That similar passions were witnessed in 2010 during the third edition of the tournament helped demonstrate that the IPL, as a phenomenon, is here to stay, lending credence to the belief that India is truly world cricket's new nerve centre.

The IPL has also resulted in an unprecedented windfall for the BCCI and franchise owners of the eight competing teams. Contrary to fears, the board earned Rs 350 crore from the inaugural edition, much more than its entire profit of Rs 235 crore in 2007. Even before the semi-finals were played, ninety-nine million viewers had tuned in to watch IPL matches. Several franchise owners such as the leading Bollywood star Sharukh Khan had broken even in year one itself. It is this unprecedented success of the IPL, repeated in 2009 and 2010, that helped consolidate India's position as world cricket's centre of gravity and completed the process of Indian cricket's 'decolonisation'.

Pre-tournament fears

The IPL administrators' decision to put the cricketers under the commercial hammer met with vociferous opposition from more than one quarter. Moralists and politicians throughout India were up in arms against this public auctioning in February 2008, even threatening to raise the issue in Parliament. Gurudas Dasgupta of the Communist Party of India claimed that the auction had sounded the 'death knell' of the gentleman's game. Over in Mumbai, Shiv Sena supremo Bal Thackeray castigated then BCCI President Sharad Pawar for turning cricketers into 'commodities'.

Other key questions that confronted organisers before the start of the IPL were as follows: will the benefits of monetisation truly filter down to the grass roots and contribute to improving domestic cricket superstructure? Will fans come out to spend their hard-earned money to watch games in the oppressive heat of April and May?

Indeed, the question of fan participation was pertinent because in India fans generally only ever attend international cricket contests, pitting countries against each other. Nationalism, in other words, has been at the core of cricket-watching in India. Meanwhile, Indian domestic contests such as the Ranji or Duleep Trophy, even when major Indian stars like Rahul Dravid or Sourav Ganguly are playing, hardly attract more than 1,000 spectators per match.

It was also conjectured that, faced with teams made up of random conglomerations of players, the draw for most spectators was less the game and more the entertainment on offer. But will fans really want to be merely 'entertained' for forty-four straight days? Even in terms of television viewership, the IPL – pitted against soaps and reality-television shows – faced stiff competition. Finally, it was hotly debated whether the benefits of the new league would trickle down to the grass roots of cricket and whether the tournament could ultimately serve as a supply line for future national stars.

Post-tournament reality

When the legendary Arthur Morris, key member of Don Bradman's invincible team of the 1940s, was asked what he got out of playing cricket, his answer was startling. Morris negotiated the question with a single-word retort, 'Poverty'.[1] With the onset of a cricketing revolution courtesy of the Indian Premier League, contemporary cricketers will have a radically different answer to a similar question. Most, it can be conjectured, will suggest with a welcome smile, 'We became millionaires.'

One billion dollars in TV rights for a ten-year period, 12,700 advertisement slots on Sony Entertainment Television (the host broadcaster) for the fifty-nine games between 18 April and 1 June 2008, all sold, hitherto unthinkable players' earnings, $3 million in prize money, $5 million for title sponsorship rights for five years, unprecedented television ratings and capacity crowds in practically all the games in its first year of existence – what the IPL has unequivocally driven home is that the shift of the nerve centre of cricket to the subcontinent is now complete.

There is little doubt that 18 April 2008 will go down in cricket history as the date when cricket changed forever. Even if subsequent editions of the IPL fail to deliver – possible if its economics go haywire – it has proved beyond doubt that cricket sans nationalism can also be made into a lucrative market proposition.

Modelled on Major League Baseball and the National Football League, IPL has come at a time when the Indian economy has opened itself to global riches, and the big corporates trying to make India home are in search of lucrative investment platforms across the country. IPL, for many, is the ideal answer. At one go, it has given them a foothold in a market of a billion plus and has generated eyeballs that millions spent on advertisements won't garner.

Add to this the fact that, for a billion plus cricket fans, filling stadiums was hardly difficult with proper marketing and hype. With celebrity owners like Sharukh Khan, India's leading Bollywood star, doing his bit in earnest, fans had more than cricket on offer for a couple of hundred rupees. With fans thronging the grounds or picking their seat in front of the TV set, sponsors queued up and paid millions for ten-second slots on Set Max, on in-stadia hoardings and team apparel.

IPL impact

With IPL 2010 also a major success, each match across India was sold out, and with national cricket boards seemingly making room for it already, it will be of interest to note if the ICC soon creates a window for the billion dollar league. The one time the ICC clashed with innovative private entrepreneurship in the 1970s, it was humiliated at the hands of Australian media tycoon Kerry Packer. If the IPL humiliates it again, control of the game's most lucrative version may well slip from the ICC's hands, because the IPL is that unique tournament that inspires English players to revolt against their own Board and for which Australian cricketers contemplate giving up the coveted baggy green cap.

Interestingly, even when the League had to move to South Africa in 2009 at short notice because the government was unable to provide necessary security during India's national elections, its popularity hardly waned. Half-full grounds or less than animated spectators in Durban or Cape Town could be perceived as blips only when IPL season two was compared to packed stands and wild spectators back home in IPL's inaugural edition.

For South Africa, however, the tournament was a success. Anyone with any knowledge of South African sport will agree that the IPL, a foreign import, did much to present South Africa as a perfect sporting destination before the 2010 FIFA World Cup. Social integration, still far from complete in mainstream South Africa, received a significant boost thanks to the IPL. And sports organisers, fearing a Western backlash citing under-preparedness for the FIFA event, had their hands hugely strengthened.

IPL season two was also a successful experiment with globalisation. It was India's first truly global sporting export and helped create India's first international sporting brand. Unlike most sports still controlled and dominated by the West, the IPL is an example of 'atypical' globalisation, where the West has to look to the East. It has led to the possibility wherein Indian administrators can justly claim that, in cricket at least, an Indian hegemony is finally about to commence. Unifying the global cricket world under its aegis, India has successfully consolidated its commercial hold atop cricket's global hierarchy. With leading exponents of the game like Shane Warne, Chris Gayle and others urging the International Cricket Council to create a window for the IPL, it is expected that this 'grip' over world cricket will grow stronger in years to come.

Also, the lasting gain from IPL's second edition was evident once the tournament returned home in March 2010, when it again played to packed houses. The IPL came back to its home base having established itself as a leading global sports brand with multiple global enclaves and constituencies, carefully created and nurtured in the course of the second edition of the tournament.

At a time when the actions of some global sports administrators such as the Australian Tennis Federation tried to identify India as an unsafe sports destination, the IPL was India's best bet in reversing this unfortunate trend. Having received rave reviews in South Africa and having done much to woo the world's best, IPL 2010 continued to bring together the most impressive assemblage of the world's leading cricketers. And with resolute government support coming to its help in 2010, there's little doubt that it did much to strengthen India's claim to being a safe sporting destination months before the New Delhi Commonwealth Games in October 2010.

IPL and the race question

Besides consolidating India's position as world cricket's financial capital, the IPL also played its part in countering the racial problem, one that continues to plague international sports contests. The discourse on 'race' in India has been historically predicated upon a position of relative underprivilege. India, considered a 'white man's burden'[2] during its colonial conditioning, fought for nearly two centuries to free itself of this position of inferiority. While discrimination based on conditions of colour and economic pre-eminence was a regular practice in colonial India, its vestige continued for decades after independence. Hence, every time an Indian was/is questioned by an immigration official on entering a Western country, it is immediately perceived as a deliberate act of racial discrimination. To go a step further, most Indians settled in the West were, until a couple of decades ago, expected to be living in a ghettoised urban space, hardly ever integrated into the mainstream of Western society. This understanding of the West as 'superior' made for divisions between the Occident and the Orient and allowed for the perpetuation of the doctrine of 'orientalism'.

Such a common man's understanding of race has been substantively transformed in recent times, and the Indian Premier League, a hugely successful Indian innovation, has certainly helped mediate this change. Race, in contemporary India, is no longer a discourse predicated upon notions of inferiority. Rather, of late at least, it is built upon a notion of privilege, which has largely to do with India's new-found status as a world player in an era of globalisation. At no point am I trying to claim that the IPL is a singular mover in heralding this transformation. Rather, it is my contention that the IPL has significantly enhanced the process, which, in the sporting domain, was spearheaded by India's takeover of world cricket's finances from the middle of the 1990s. With the nerve centre of cricket moving to India, a process the IPL has finally completed, there occurred three significant changes:

1. The West was much better co-opted and appropriated within the Indian imaginary.

2. It brings to light the complex and also exceptional nature of India's racialised modernity.

3. An aggressive hyper-jingoistic nationalist sentiment has emerged in India and it often results in a complete overturn of the conventional racial ideology.

This transformed race reality is borne out by an ethnography of spectator behaviour across IPL matches in South Africa in 2009. For example, when Shane Warne rushed to congratulate Yusuf Pathan after his super-over heroics against the Kolkata Knight Riders, the large Indian diasporic crowd was spontaneous in applauding Warne for his gesture. The Australian super-hero, taken out of his nationalist context, had suddenly been appropriated and indigenised and was a key member of the Rajasthan Royals side. In the first edition of the IPL, too, this feature was prominent. David Hussey, the most consistent batsman for the Kolkata team in IPL season one, had soon become 'Hussey da', meaning elder brother in the vernacular. However, this co-option rests on unstable foundations, a fact evident from the venom spat at coach John Buchanan each time the Kolkata Knight Riders failed to deliver. Each failure was greeted with murmurs of a 'white man here in India just for the money'.

This behaviour, it needs to be stated, is an exact throwback to a century earlier, when the British reacted in an exactly similar manner to Kumar Shri Ranjitsinhji, Indian cricket's first superhero. 'Ranji', a native chief who had no rightful claim to the throne of his principality, finally became *Jamsaheb* thanks to the British support that came his way.[3] This support, it can be argued, was largely a product of Ranji's cricketing prowess. Educated at Cambridge, Ranji went on to represent England against Australia with distinction and thus captured the public imagination of his peoples back home. When Ranji scored a century on his debut for England against Australia in 1896, his performance had a multi-layered impact. In England he became the people's darling and roused a 'Ranji fever'. In India, contrastingly, Ranji's batting was declared a triumph of nationalism on the sporting field, disregarding the fact that Ranji was playing for England, the 'white master'. For the colonial Indian imagination, the political reality of colonialism was relegated to a lower rung in the hierarchy, below the cardinal question of 'race'.

British administrators in India also tried to bail Ranji out of his financial difficulties on the grounds that it was unworthy of a great cricketer to suffer such ignominy. For the British in India, Ranji was a hero, having performed well against arch-rivals Australia. The British rulers saw him as proto-British and used him as a trump card in sports contests against Australia. However, every time he failed, it didn't take much time for the spectators to label him 'dirty nigger', displaying how sports as a social practice has always been used to signify far deeper and more significant cultural attitudes and political contours.[4] Another issue comes into the reckoning here. For more than two decades now scholars of postcolonialism have sought answers to the question raised by Gayatri Chakravorty Spivak: 'Can the subaltern speak?'[5] While it would be foolhardy to suggest that the IPL's position in world economic and political relations is anything but slight, it might nonetheless be seen in some sense as a sign of change.

Controlling the cricket economy

Once the second edition of the IPL was over on 24 May 2009, action shifted to the UK for the world Twenty20, which was played out in June 2009. Unlike the domestic Twenty20 circuit in the UK, which is gradually falling by the wayside, an international competition like the ICC Twenty20, which is rooted in nationalism and nationalist sensibilities, it was argued, will always thrive in multi-cultural London and its surrounds.

And this is where the subcontinent comes into the equation. Put bluntly, the huge Indian and Pakistani cricket markets, both at home and in the British South Asian diaspora, held the key to the organisers making substantial profits from the competition. In fact, soon after ESPN-Star Sports (ESS), the host broadcaster, acquired the ICC telecast rights for a staggering billion plus dollars in early 2007, ESS Managing Director Jamie Davis declared: 'This acquisition affirms our commitment to the Indian subcontinent and the world and we are absolutely delighted to bring the exciting line-up of ICC events to millions of cricket fans globally.'[6]

Inherent in this statement is the root of the problem. For the recovery of more than 80 per cent of the $1.1bn spent, ESPN was/is banking on the cricket craze in India. Intrinsic to Mr Davis's statement is the notion that cricket continues to be a licence to print money for broadcasters in the subcontinent. However, the reality, as Peter Hutton, veteran television broadcaster, suggests, is that 'the price being paid is linked to equity valuations, mergers and acquisitions. It is a dangerous time, when advertising income doesn't cover the rights fees being paid and there is every danger of the cricketing bubble economy going bust.'[7] With the economic downturn continuing to seriously affect the Western world, the cricket economy too, it is expected, will take a hit. With people's spending powers limited and with companies shutting down every month, in-stadia advertisers are counting their pounds before agreeing to be a part of the spectacle. Even advertising rates are being tailored to suit the downturn, and this is where the reliance on the subcontinent, relatively stable in comparison, increases.

In effect, this means that India and Pakistan need to play well all the time if the huge amounts invested by the broadcasters are to be recovered. In fact, if India or Pakistan crash out at the group stage, as had happened in the Caribbean in the 2007 World Cup, advertisers' interest in the tournament nosedives. In fact, it can be argued that the World Cups in 1999 and 2003, in England and South Africa respectively, were economic success stories because Pakistan (1999) and India (2003) made it to the finals. During the 2003 World Cup, market consultants in India had estimated a total advertising spend over the six weeks as something like $222 million – more than the net profit that India's largest private sector company, Reliance Industries, posted in the first quarter of the financial year 2002–03.

Interestingly, in a timescale less than the length of Sachin Tendulkar's career, the nature and economy of world cricket has fundamentally changed. In 1992, the BCCI, now the richest cricket body in the world, had a deficit of $150,000. And in 1997, the ICC, cricket's apex body, had little more than $25,000 in its coffers.[8] Once cricket administrators decided to marry cricket with television, the scenario changed. The cricket market became an Indian monopoly and within months the schedule of cricket worldwide was driven by the needs of multiple television players each wanting a share of the Indian pie.

Indian cricket and the satellite television revolution

Cricket's emergence as a prime driver of entertainment television in India is a relatively new phenomenon. Until 2002, at the time when Sony Television first made its mark with the telecast of the ICC Champions Trophy played in Colombo, cricket was hardly ever covered by non-news and non-sports channels in India. Until then cricket was not entertainment; it was sport, which was profoundly different and had a distinctive sphere of its own. Then came what can justifiably be termed the *broadcast* revolution. Just like most things novel, the first attempt to promote cricket with star divas as anchors in September 2002 was a failure.

Unlike most novel Indian experiments, however, the plan was persisted with. And the biggest surprise of World Cup 2003, an even bigger surprise perhaps than India's qualification for the final, was the runaway success of the Mandira Bedi phenomenon. A minor Bollywood star, the stunningly attractive Bedi's conversion to cricket commentary proved decisive in the TV rating wars. The success was such that during the World Cup Sony Max showed a 24 per cent growth while rivals like Star Plus lost out on 47 per cent of its viewers. Said Kunal Dasgupta, CEO, Set India: 'The TAM [television audience measurement] ratings for the week ending 15 February [2003] revealed that Max was the top channel and garnered the highest channel share amongst all C&S channels.'[9] Statistics showed that for the first time in its history in the week ending 15 February 2003 Sony Max was the top channel with a channel share of 16.8 per cent as against 11.1 per cent of the second placed Star Plus.

What added to the Sony Max success was that it had returned excellent ratings across all markets and cities. While Kolkata returned a high average rating of 10.3 for all seven World Cup matches played that week, the ratings skyrocketed to a spectacular 20.2 during the India–Australia game on 15 February 2003. Mumbai, Delhi and Chennai all achieved a near 10 rating, making the week immensely successful for Sony Max. As reported by the Sony Max press release issued on 24 February 2003: 'The cricket telecast on *Max* attracted a whopping 48.6 million C&S individuals across the TAM markets. Further, even before India played its first match, *Max* had already attracted 38.4 million viewers, vindicating the appeal of its cricket presentation to every kind of cricket lover in India, including the die hard purists.'[10] 'Extraa-Innings', Sony Max's pre-, mid- and post-match wraparound programming, on its own managed to bring in an unprecedented 25.1 million individuals even before India played its first match. This further shot up to 36.9 million individuals by the end of week one of the tournament.

Interestingly, the cricket coverage also had an impact on the channel's overall performance. During the World Cup, twenty of the top hundred programmes of the month were from Sony Max, including four programmes in the top twenty and twelve in the top fifty. The success of Sony Max's cricket coverage also made possible other major business tie-ups for the channel. As reported by *Business Line*, the financial daily of the *Hindu*, Aaj Tak and Sony entered into a tie-up on the eve of the Videocon Super Challenge in Amsterdam in August 2004. According to the tie-up, Sony Max was to provide Aaj Tak access to its commentators and other panellists for its half-hour cricket capsule, 'Runbhoomi'. Tushar Shah, Vice-President of Sony Max, justified this tie-up, suggesting: 'This marks a new era in marketing in the television domain. *Max* is known for innovation, creativity and attitude, and this tie-up is an example of all three coming together to create a win-win situation for both *Aaj Tak* and *Max*.'[11]

Many ask whether this unique blending of entertainment with sport dilutes the essence of cricket. In other words, whether such a blending, which is anathema for the cricket purist, can ever take the game forward. Such questions, I wish to suggest, are missing the point completely. As Amartya Sen mentioned in an interview soon after winning the Nobel Prize, it is not relevant whether one likes globalisation or not, it is the defining feature of our age and we have to live with it. The pertinent question is how far we are able to tame it to suit our needs. Similarly, after the success of the 'Set Max' brand of IPL cricket coverage, the important question is no longer whether this form of coverage is proper.

Rather, the question is, or should be, how the nature of the coverage can be made more interactive – thus widening the ambit of cricket spectatorship. One simple statistic is enough to substantiate the above point. In 2003, most cricket magazines and portals had rallied against the 'invasion of the dumb belles', but by the end of the World Cup, Sony Max's managers themselves were surprised by the ratings: 2.2 crore had tuned in and this amounted to a massive 46 per cent of the total viewership. 'Set Max' had success-fully become the 'voice of the cricket-widows'. At the same time the die-hard cricket purist had not condemned the Sony Max brand of coverage. As Rajat Jain, a senior Sony Max official, had suggested: 'A purist is someone who will watch cricket regardless of whether or not India is playing. And remember even before India had played its first match "Extraa Innings" had reached out to 25.1 million individuals. We believe that a majority of them were purists.'[12]

As far as TV advertising was concerned, media buyers suggested on the eve of the 2003 World Cup that Sony Max had already managed advertising worth Rs 2.1 billion, and Nimbus, which was commissioned to produce the 'Extraa-Innings' programme, had garnered 1.3 billion. In fact, a relatively unimportant match like the India–Zimbabwe encounter attracted 4,760 sec-onds of advertising. According to the findings of a TAM-S group, Sony Max had the opportunity to telecast approximately 250 commercials in these 4,760 seconds.[13]

Another interesting Sony Max innovation was the unique blending of Bollywood with cricket, something the channel has significantly advanced with the IPL. Given that cricket and Bollywood have been crucial in fash-ioning people's identification with a consumerist ethos within a liberalising society and economy, this was a masterstroke. Sony used its feature film *Lagaan*, a film with a cricket theme and one nominated for the Oscars in 2002, effectively to build its mass base on the eve of the World Cup. *Lagaan*, which starred Bollywood superstar Aamir Khan, used cricket to showcase the Indian nationalist struggle and raked in unprecedented sales in the box office. The *Sony-Lagaan* contest, held during the screening of the film, was promoted with the interesting catch line, 'Watch India vs England on January 26; watch India vs England on February 26!' The contest invited viewers to answer a simple question from their mobile phones and to call the designated Sony number or to log on to its website.

As reported by Indiantelevision.com: 'the contest promised to take eleven lucky winners to South Africa and enable them to watch the World Cup cricket 2003 league match involving the Indians and the English players. Consider the following statistics: a total of 68,000 messages were received during the five hour period (starting 1 pm) when the movie was screened. There were 29,075 correct answers which only showed that viewers – purists and masses – were participating in a big way.'[14]

What has helped the new brand of cricket broadcast is cricket's newest avatar, Twenty20 cricket. The similarities are indeed palpable – both have raised the eyebrows of the purists, both have proved to be runaway successes and both, to go a step further, seem defining aspects of the game's future.

In April 2003 the London *Daily Telegraph* published a poignant picture the day after the start of the English domestic cricket season. A six-column, almost half-page picture, it showed a solitary spectator watching county cricket in an otherwise empty stand. The bottom line was clear: English cricket needed a new infusion of oxygen to survive, with the very existence of county cricket in peril. This oxygen was first supplied on 13 June 2003 at the Rose Bowl in Hampshire, when Sussex Sharks played Hampshire Hawks.

Nearly 15,000 people enjoyed the action and a new phenomenon in Twenty20 cricket was born. Present at the Rose Bowl on that fateful day, I was amazed to see the high percentage of children who had come along with their parents to enjoy the action. Not many, I must confess, watched cricket. However, they did have a good time. With games, toys and a concert to follow it was a perfect summer evening out for the family. Having just watched a few baseball games at Wrigley Field in Chicago, home of the Chicago Cubs, it all seemed familiar – the music, short duration, loud drawling announcements, a little break between innings, two-word alliterating names, frenzied action and, above all, non-stop fun. Anathema for the cricket purist, it was, simply put, the 'baseballisation' of cricket. If asked to describe the origins of Twenty20 cricket in a single sentence, the best answer would be: it was a survival mechanism. The unique blending of cricket and entertainment achieved by the IPL in the Indian context is yet another survival mechanism.

Most cricket fanatics, leave alone the occasional ones, are saturated by the amount of one-day cricket being played. In such a situation it is almost imperative for television broadcasters to introduce innovations, newer techniques of coverage that will continue to attract eyeballs to the nation's most perceptible passion. More than making profits, it may be suggested, the broadcaster is entrusted with the duty to ensure that Indians don't get bored with one-day cricket. And women anchors, noodle straps, tarot cards and models amidst the fans are all such innovations, which have successfully made cricket coverage more viewer-friendly and more interactive.

The success of entertainment-focused cricket programming has led other Indian news and even global sports channels to replicate the same model. In fact, the strategy – special programming with women anchors and other innovative attractions – has become the standard way of covering cricket in India and also in some other countries. With cricket across the world in need of the infusion of new innovations, it is only a matter of time before it becomes the standard global norm. Amidst all the euphoria generated by the IPL, and more broadly Twenty20 cricket, there are some issues which Indian cricket needs to grapple with to consolidate its position at the top of the global cricket hierarchy.

We still play to empty grounds: Test cricket in India

This question is especially pertinent in the backdrop of the recently con-cluded Test series between India and South Africa played in India in February–March 2010, labelled in the media as the unofficial world Test championship played between the number one and two ranked teams in the world. While the second Test match at the historic Eden Gardens had it all, high-intensity drama, thrills until the second-last ball of the penultimate over, fantastic batsmanship and bowling, weather disruption and, finally, controversy over the playing surface, it also had what is now considered a disappearing breed from the Test match arena in India – an almost capacity crowd on all five days of play. It wouldn't be wrong to suggest that India's best was brought out by the high voltage screaming of the 35,000-strong Eden crowd. It was truly a contest that lived up to the billing of the unoffi-cial Test championship. This is especially so after Nagpur, where the first Test match saw no more than 1,000 spectators per day. This despite the Vidarbha Cricket Association (VCA) making free tickets available to lure a decent enough crowd to the stadium at Jamtha, some sixteen kilometres from Nagpur city.

While some ascribe the empty stadium to distance, the very same venue was packed to capacity during an India–Australia one-day international in early November 2009. At Nagpur, India's home advantage was nullified with the match being played out in an empty stadium. Cricket is not just a con-test between the twenty-two players out in the middle. What makes playing cricket at the MCG in Melbourne all the more intimidating is the 60,000 plus Australian fans screaming down your throat. A similar experience awaits visiting teams at Eden Gardens, something Steve Waugh's legendary Australian team of 2001 and Graeme Smith's South Africans will testify to. The lesson Eden Gardens holds is that there should be designated heritage Test centres in the country. These are cities and venues where cricket fans still flock to watch Test cricket, considered by a minuscule minority of fans across the world as the real test of a player's ability. There was a sizeable crowd when India played Sri Lanka at the Cricket Club of India in Mumbai in November 2009, a near full Chepauk when England returned to play Tests after the Mumbai terror attacks in November 2008, and a healthy 20,000 watched India play Australia at the Chinnaswamy in Bangalore in October 2008. The common thread between all these centres: the venues have hosted Test cricket for over half a century. In contrast, relatively newer stadiums – the VCA stadium in Jamtha and the PCA stadium in Mohali are cases in point – bear a deserted look every time the Test match caravan moves in. Even Sourav Ganguly's retirement Test match in November 2008, which could have brought Kolkata to a standstill, did not attract more than 2,000 spectators in Nagpur. Sachin Tendulkar was forced to score his 12,000th Test run in front of 500 schoolchildren at Mohali.

The BCCI must act. Kolkata and Eden Gardens have helped provide enough evidence. It is essential to have designated Test venues while other venues can continue to host shorter versions of the game. This is imperative given the vast difference in cricket-watching cultures across India, and more so because India wants to be looked upon as world cricket's real nerve centre. In England and Australia, Test matches are played only in certain venues. 'Down under', all leading international sides play Test cricket in Melbourne, Sydney, Brisbane, Adelaide or Perth. In England, too, Test matches are played at Lord's, the Oval, Trent Bridge, Old Trafford, Edgbaston, Headingley and, more recently, Cardiff. While it is a bold attempt to spread Test cricket to relatively newer centres in India, evidence suggests the experiment is premature and needs to be abandoned immediately. The point is simple: if we host a Test match between the world's number one and number two sides in an empty stadium, there's no way India can justify its tag as world cricket's centre of gravity. Just a year or so earlier, an entire Ashes series was played to packed stadiums in England and a pedigree Boxing Day Test at the MCG easily gets 50,000 plus spectators on most days. Unless Indian fans develop a composite appreciation of all forms of cricket, England, and to a lesser extent Australia, will continue to look upon India as the brash new rich kid on the block. Appreciation of Twenty20 cricket cannot elevate India to being the game's real arbiter.

India should fall back on its tried and tested venues, assured of decent crowds to cheer for the home team. This ensures shorter formats are always played to capacity. It will also help cement India's place among the world's best destinations for Test cricket. Not without reason do players of all countries look upon Eden Gardens as cricket's mecca. By providence, in February 2010 Eden Gardens yet again played host to one of the most sensational

Test matches ever, with the home side coming out on top at the very end against South Africa.

Conclusion

Regardless of the hubbub generated by the lack of audiences in Test match grounds, it is time to accept that Indian cricket, thanks to the IPL and the advent of Twenty20 cricket, is an exciting proposition, if for no other reason than its success in commercialising cricket in a manner unthinkable just a few months ago. In the future, balancing between the needs of the market and the needs of the fan base will undoubtedly decide how well these formats are able to sustain the hype they have generated. And until a final verdict can be made on that score, observers of cricket as a phenomenon would do well to support these incarnations of the game and agree that they are indeed a breath of fresh air, which has converted the game into a multi-billion-dollar enterprise and India into the real nerve centre of the gentleman's game, completing the process of Indian cricket's decolonisation.

NOTES

This chapter was written before former IPL chairman Lalit Modi was ousted on charges of financial embezzlement, and two IPL teams, Rajasthan Royals and King XI Punjab, were banned for flouting the rules, a ban that was subsequently revoked by the Indian law courts. The BCCI was forced to accept the court ruling. However, these events did not deter the organisation of IPL season 4 and had little effect on its popularity.

1 Boria Majumdar, interview with Arthur Morris, Sydney, 4 January 2008.
2 Rudyard Kipling, 'The White Man's Burden', *The Times*, 12 February 1899.
3 Boria Majumdar, 'Ranji's Leg Glance to the Throne' in *Lost Histories of Indian Cricket* (London: Routledge, 2005).
4 Ibid.
5 Gayatri Chakravorty Spivak, 'Can the Subaltern Speak?' in Cary Nelson and Lawrence Grossberg (eds.), *Marxism and the Interpretation of Culture* (Urbana: University of Illinois Press, 1988), pp. 271–313.
6 Jamie Davis, ESPN-Star Sports media release, 12 February 2007.
7 Boria Majumdar, interview with Peter Hutton, 8 March 2008.
8 Interview with Jagmohan Dalmiya.
9 Interview with Kunal Dasgupta, 6 May 2008.
10 Sony Max press release.
11 Ibid.
12 Set Max press release, 15 March 2007.
13 Ibid.
14 Rajat Jain media release, 12 March 2007.

13

PRASHANT KIDAMBI

Hero, celebrity and icon: Sachin Tendulkar and Indian public culture*

When he completed twenty years in international cricket in November 2009, Sachin Tendulkar reaffirmed his status as one of the greatest public icons of post-independence India. Ever since his genius was first glimpsed on the *maidans* of Bombay over two decades ago, Tendulkar has reigned supreme as a sporting idol, his popularity cutting across the boundaries of caste, class, gender, region and religion. Curiously, however, there has been relatively little scholarly scrutiny of the Tendulkar phenomenon and what it might tell us about the changing nature of Indian public culture.

This chapter attempts to understand, and account for, Sachin Tendulkar's enduring hold over the Indian public imagination by exploring three facets of his remarkable career. The first section considers, in historical context, Tendulkar as 'hero': someone who displays superlative skills and performs spectacular feats. An analysis of popular sporting figures needs to reckon with the ways in which their attributes and accomplishments on the field of play are crucial to their elevation as heroes. However, the analytical prism of the 'hero' is insufficient in itself in accounting for Tendulkar's fame. The second section suggests that Tendulkar's celebrity is an attendant effect of the intensified relationship between cricket, television and money in contemporary India. At the same time, the immense power and resonance of Tendulkar's image within Indian society makes him more than a frothy confection of the sport–media nexus. The final section argues that as a national icon Tendulkar embodies the aspirations of millions of Indians. The symbolic meanings they have invested in his persona derive their charge from the interplay between cricket, nationalism and the middle classes in contemporary India.

The cricketer as hero

In the pantheon of Indian heroes, the sportsman has not always constituted a discrete entity. Prior to the colonial period, the paradigmatic hero figure was generally a warrior, who displayed martial prowess and earned renown on the battlefield, often sacrificing his life in a lost cause.[1] Of course, warrior-heroes were also known to excel in sports such as archery, swords-manship, wrestling and hunting. But their sporting pursuits were an intrinsic part of the elite martial culture of the period and 'symbolised the expansive powers of the king, particularly at important moments in the public ritual of the court'.[2]

As the British disarmed and pacified Indian society during the course of the nineteenth century, the martial ethos of the pre-colonial social order began slowly to diminish in significance. Simultaneously, the archetypal warrior-hero began to make way for other kinds of heroes. Perhaps the most notable development in this regard was the emergence, within the sphere of civil society, of a new embodiment of heroism: the selfless, public-spirited individual who dedicated his life to the service of others.

But the ideals of heroism associated with the martial culture of the war-rior did not disappear. On the contrary, the hero as an embodiment of phys-ical prowess and skill was reconfigured within a newly demilitarised context and reappeared within the modern public sphere in the distinctive figure of the sporting hero. In this context, four developments in the late nineteenth and early twentieth centuries were crucial. First, in a bid to inculcate in some of their Indian subjects a version of the Victorian games ethic, the British introduced sporting activities in the schools and mission colleges that they established in the subcontinent.[3] Games like cricket, football and hockey acquired a foothold in educational institutions, thereby enabling Indians who excelled in them to become well-known sportsmen. Second, sport was also an integral part of life in the British Indian army and this afforded the opportunity for some Indian soldiers to make a name for themselves as sportsmen. Third, the need to refute colonial stereotypes about the effemin-acy of educated Indians, anxieties about racial decline and a desire to engage in forms of national self-strengthening, all combined to prompt elements within the emergent Indian middle classes to take a new interest in physical culture and sporting activities.[4] Finally, even though they had been stripped of their substantive military power, the Indian princes continued to uphold the culture of physical prowess that had once been integral to the royal courts by offering substantial patronage to a variety of sporting activities from cricket to wrestling.[5]

In one way or another, these developments opened up the space for the emergence of the modern Indian sporting hero at the turn of the twentieth century. The most famous of these was undoubtedly Kumar Shri Ranjitsinhji, whose dazzling batting exploits on the cricket fields of England made him one of the most recognised public figures within the British Empire during the late Victorian and Edwardian eras. And, coming from the opposite end of the social hierarchy, there was Palwankar Baloo, a Dalit, who was the most famous bowler in India prior to the First World War.[6] But sports other than cricket also furnished heroes. Thus, we have Jamsetji Marker, the Parsi squash player from Bombay, who was the world champion in his sport during the first decade of the twentieth century. Likewise, the legendary Gama, an illiterate Muslim wrestler from the Punjab, acquired national and international renown as a fighter in the early twentieth century.[7]

From the 1930s, however, cricket began gradually to outstrip other sporting activities in popularity. Even though India achieved significant sporting successes in games like hockey, and other pastimes continued to attract a sizeable following among the subaltern classes of the provincial towns and villages, cricketers such as C. K. Nayudu and Lala Amarnath (among others) were increasingly the most prominent sporting heroes.

The cricketer continued to dwarf other sportsmen in the national imagination in the immediate post-independence decades, even though India's performance in international cricket in these years was scarcely worth trumpeting. By the 1970s the premier status of the cricketer was well established, with the emergence of a new generation of heroes who played a key part in India's memorable cricketing triumphs in that decade: the batting duo of Gavaskar and Vishwanath; the famed spin quartet of Bedi, Chandrasekhar, Prasanna and Venkataraghavan; and the trailblazing Kapil Dev. A number of developments in the 1980s – the Indian cricket team's improbable victory in the 1983 World Cup, the failures of the Indian hockey team and the country's continued poor performance in international sporting events – only served to reinforce the pre-eminence of the cricketer as hero. It is against this historical backdrop that we need to set the emergence of Sachin Tendulkar.

The career of sporting legends has often been marked by an extraordinary performance at the outset that presages what is to follow. Tendulkar announced himself with a series of astounding feats that are now an essential part of the folklore of contemporary India. Indeed, C. L. R. James's words about W. G. Grace could easily apply to the Tendulkar phenomenon in its early years: 'He was news, and as he continually broke all precedents … before he had passed the middle twenties, each amazing new performance told the public, cricketing and otherwise, that here was one of those rare phenomena, something that had never been seen before and was not likely to be seen again.'[8]

Tendulkar first stirred the public imagination as a precocious fourteen-year-old schoolboy in February 1988, when he compiled a world record batting partnership of 664 runs with his schoolmate Vinod Kambli in the

Harris Memorial Challenge Shield, Bombay's oldest inter-schools cricket tournament. Before the end of that year, he became the youngest player to play first-class cricket for the city, known for its competitive and hard-nosed cricket culture, marking his Ranji Trophy debut against Gujarat with an assured century. In November 1989, aged sixteen, he made his international debut at Karachi against Pakistan, becoming in the process the youngest Indian to play Test cricket. Two months later, on India's tour of New Zealand, he narrowly missed becoming the youngest centurion in the long history of Test cricket. Shortly thereafter, he scored his first century against England at Old Trafford, a match-saving performance that marked him out as a special talent on the international stage. But it was the two thrilling centuries that he reeled off at Sydney and Perth during India's ill-fated tour of Australia in 1992 that conclusively sealed his reputation as a player destined for cricketing immortality.

From the outset, Tendulkar manifested different aspects of the 'heroic ideal' in cricket. For one, he faced fast bowling with reassuring certitude and confidence. This was significant in a sport where, even after the introduction of modern protective equipment, the reputation of batting heroes has crucially depended on their ability and skill in coping with genuine pace. In India especially, as Mukul Kesavan has noted, 'being suspect against fast bowling isn't just a weakness; it is a moral defect, a stigma'.[9] Tendulkar easily passed this test of 'manhood' in his debut series. Thus, even though his overall performance in the series was hardly spectacular, the physical courage and poise that he displayed against the daunting Pakistani pace attack elicited praise from all quarters.

The unbridled ferocity with which he assailed opposing bowlers also captivated spectators. In this respect, he was a startling departure from the restrained orthodoxy that had traditionally defined the 'Bombay school of batsmanship'. An early demonstration of this aspect of Tendulkar's play came in that epochal debut series in Pakistan. In a friendly exhibition match at Peshawar, the teenager launched a breathtaking assault on the great Abdul Qadir, one of the craftiest spin bowlers in the world. The encounter quickly entered cricket folklore when it transpired that Qadir had challenged Tendulkar to demonstrate his prowess; the suitably chastened bowler prophesied that the boy was going to be a fearsome tormentor of bowlers.

Over the course of the next decade, Tendulkar confirmed Qadir's assessment as he repeatedly destroyed bowling attacks in a manner that enthralled cricket followers across the world. His batting in these years was a heady cocktail of risk-taking intent and daring improvisation, frequently in circumstances where the rest of his team had failed. Indeed, the explosive drama of a heroic Tendulkar performance could simultaneously evoke collective awe and anxiety. After a dazzling, but doomed, batting display against the Australians in the 1996 World Cup match at Bombay, one cricket writer described the experience of watching him play: 'Each stroke was like a shot of adrenalin, yet each was accompanied by fear and trembling. There would be one too many daring shots, and it would all end, suddenly and catastrophically.'[10]

In the second decade of his career, however, there occurred a notable change in Tendulkar's batting approach. The swashbuckling boy wonder gradually gave way to a more circumspect elder statesman, prone to ponderous bouts of self-denial in the larger team interest. In 2005, *Wisden* declared that 'watching Tendulkar became a colder experience' and that 'he seemed to reject his bewitching fusion of majesty and human frailty in favour of a mechanical, robotic accumulation'.[11]

At the same time, after a decade in which his batting performances had seemingly defied the law of averages, Tendulkar began to appear more susceptible to the vagaries of form. Moreover, a series of niggling injuries raised the prospect of a tame end to a spectacular career. Increasingly, too, his fans began to grow restive with their hero's faltering performances. In 2006, after yet another failure against the touring English side, he was greeted with jeers at his own home ground in Bombay. And when India made an inglorious exit from the World Cup held in the Caribbean the following year, a growing number of critics believed that it was time for Tendulkar to quit.

Fortitude in the face of failure and the quest to reclaim a lost domain are also integral elements of the heroic ideal. In the final stretch of his long career, Tendulkar also fulfilled this requirement in ample measure. In the three years after the disappointing 2007 World Cup, he rediscovered his touch and scored prodigiously in both Test matches and one-day internationals. But more than the sheer number of runs that he scored, it was the manner in which he did so that was significant. Cricket fans were treated once more to the sight of a rejuvenated Tendulkar batting with the aggressive intent of yore. Two incandescent exhibitions of batsmanship, on the threshold of his third decade in international cricket, stand as testimony to his astonishing resurgence as an attacking batsman. In a one-day international against Australia at Hyderabad in November 2009, he scored an epic 175 as India chased a monumental score of 350. Barely three months later, against South Africa at Gwalior, he became the first batsman to score a double-century in the history of one-day international cricket.

Allen Guttmann has noted that 'the unsurpassed quantified achievement, which is what we mean by "record" ... is a constant challenge to all who strive to surpass it and thereby to achieve a modern version of immortality'.[12] Measured by this yardstick, Tendulkar's immortality is assured since it is certain that he will exit the international stage in secure possession of almost all the major batting records in the game. But, as a cricketing hero, Tendulkar will be remembered not so much for the incessant toil that he inflicted on cricket statisticians, as for the sense of enchantment that his wondrous skills induced in those who watched him play.

The hero as celebrity

In order to understand how Tendulkar's image came to dominate the Indian public imagination, however, it is necessary to look beyond the boundary and engage with his celebrity. Like many contemporary sporting super-stars – David Beckham, Tiger Woods, Michael Jordan, among others – the key to Tendulkar's singularity as a modern sporting celebrity lies in the highly intensified interplay between commercial sport, the entertainment media and consumer capitalism.[13]

Two factors, acting in conjunction, provided the matrix within which Tendulkar's image as a sporting celebrity came to be fashioned in the 1990s. The revolution in the sport–media relationship triggered by the entry of sat-ellite television into India played a critical role in constituting the star status of leading international players like Tendulkar. Relatedly, the growing reach and popularity of cricket aroused the interest of corporate sponsors keen to market their products and brought money flooding into the game. These twin developments propelled the commodification of the cricketer as celeb-rity, of whom Tendulkar is the supreme exemplar.

The history of the cricketer-celebrity in India is integrally linked to the role of the modern mass media in the 'vernacularisation' of the game. Mass-mediated forms of communication – print, radio and television – enabled 'large numbers of Indians to experience cricket as a linguistically familiar form, thus liberating cricket from the very "Englishness" that first gave it its moral authority and intrigue'. In the process, they also created a large cricket-obsessed public that followed the game and its players with 'the pas-sion generated by reading, by hearing and by seeing'.[14]

Newspapers began to report cricket extensively in the early twentieth cen-tury, and the process accelerated even further after 1947. Until the 1970s, the bulk of this coverage was in English and catered largely to the metro-politan middle classes. But by the end of the twentieth century, a growing body of mass vernacular literature – newspapers, magazines, pamphlets and books – also came to be devoted to cricket. Saliently, by focusing on the 'lives and styles' of great cricketers in the form of information, anecdotes and gossip, this burgeoning print culture contributed to the construction of their celebrity status.[15]

Radio broadcasts of cricket in India began in the 1930s and were in English during the first two decades.[16] However, from the 1960s onwards, All India Radio, the public service broadcaster, began to air commentary in Indian languages such as Hindi, Tamil and Bengali. Multi-lingual commentary was not only an 'important instrument in the socialization of the Indian mass audience into the subtleties of the sport', but also a crucial factor in making cricketers famous across the land.[17] At one level, because the action was heard, and therefore necessarily *imagined*, radio accentuated the mystique surrounding its stellar performers. At another level, however, by closely describing the activities on the field of play and fostering a sense of collective intimacy, radio commentary simultaneously rendered the leading cricketers *familiar* figures to their listeners.

From the 1970s onwards, cricket became a major cultural spectacle when Doordarshan, the state-owned broadcasting corporation, began to telecast Test matches. Cricket was ideally suited for television for a number of reasons: the restricted spatial confines within which the main action took place; the number of pauses and breaks in the play; and the fact that camera technology made it easier to watch the game on screen than in the stadium.[18] Importantly, in a country where cinema stars had hitherto been the most prominent celebrities, television lent 'cinematic authority to sports spectacles'. It thus turned cricketers into major celebrities by enhancing and intensifying their star appeal.[19]

At first, the role of television in transforming cricket into a spectacle was not readily apparent. In the 1970s, the live telecast of cricket matches was restricted to the biggest cities and its audience was relatively small.[20] However, by the time Tendulkar made his debut at the end of the 1980s, the role of television in broadening the mass appeal of the game was undeniable. Two concurrent developments were responsible for this transformation. First, the growing affordability of television sets and the rapid extension of Doordarshan's broadcasting network took the game to a mass audience that was historically unprecedented in its size. Second, the expansion of television coverage coincided with, and fed off, a new phenomenon that gripped the Indian public: one-day cricket.[21]

The shorter format of the game had grown increasingly popular in Australia and England in the late 1970s, following the revolution wrought by Kerry Packer's World Series Cricket. In India, its impact was relatively muted until a glorious summer day in June 1983, when an unheralded Indian cricket team pulled off a stunning victory over the mighty West Indians in the finals of the World Cup. Two years later, the Indian team scripted yet another improbable triumph, winning the World Championship of Cricket in Australia. Suddenly, the Indian public, whose innate cultural dispositions had allegedly predisposed it to the slow rhythms of Test cricket, demonstrated an insatiable appetite for the frenzied rhythms of limited-overs cricket. The panjandrums of the Indian cricketing establishment were only too happy to follow where the crowds led them. Between 1974 and 1979, India had played thirteen one-day internationals; in the years between 1980 and 1989, however, the figure shot up to 155. Millions were transfixed by the live telecasts of these matches, which proved beyond doubt that one-day cricket was India's most popular sporting spectacle.

It was in this situation that satellite television made its entry into India in 1991. From the very beginning, cricket was the principal focus of the slick new channels that challenged Doordarshan's monopoly of sport. Their impact was immediate and radically transformed cricket coverage. For one, they deepened the hold of cricket in remote towns and rural areas that had previously been lightly touched by it. At the same time, they also repackaged cricket (especially the one-day game) as a spectacle in novel ways, ranging from innovative camera angles and slow-motion replays to the role of expert commentators who explained rather than merely described the unfolding action. Furthermore, the 'individualizing production aesthetic' that governed the culture of satellite television had at its core a relentless focus on star performers – like Sachin Tendulkar, Shane Warne and Brian Lara – who became the most visible symbols of the sport.[22]

Tendulkar's larger-than-life image was carefully nurtured and ceaselessly celebrated by these new sports channels. The sense of visual intimacy engendered in viewers by the new technologies, and the modes of presentation that they deployed, consolidated his star status. His presence thus attracted vast audiences to the one-day games (often played at night under floodlights) that quickly became the staple fare of these channels; in turn, the televised coverage of his exploits made him India's greatest sporting celebrity.

The growing popularity of cricket in the 1990s, and the commercial possibilities inherent in this development, made it an increasingly attractive proposition for corporate capital. In turn, the rapid influx of big money into the game turned leading cricketers into marketable commodities. Of course, corporate engagement with Indian cricket was by no means an entirely new development. Indeed, after 1947, when princely support for cricket began to diminish in significance, commercial firms in the public and private sector emerged as the biggest patrons of the game. But until the 1970s their role was largely restricted to offering secure employment to cricketers with a view to garnering favourable publicity and goodwill for their business.[23]

The first signs of enhanced corporate involvement in cricket became manifest in the 1980s, when the mass base of cricket in India began to expand rapidly. Thus, the 1987 World Cup was sponsored by Reliance, one of India's biggest business companies. Simultaneously, leading cricketers such as Sunil Gavaskar, Kapil Dev and Ravi Shastri began to appear in advertisements for a range of products from suits to shaving cream. Indeed, these cricketers were the first to pursue actively the commercial possibilities opened up by the game's growing popularity in the subcontinent.

However, it was only in the 1990s that the structural relationship between cricket and commerce was decisively transformed. The context within which this shift occurred was a momentous one. In 1991, India began to dismantle the 'licence-permit raj' and embarked on a path of economic liberalisation. With the opening up of the Indian economy and its closer integration with the world market, foreign firms began to eye the country as a major growth area for their products. Faced with the challenge of gaining a foothold in an unfamiliar terrain, and quickly recognising cricket's status as a national passion, multi-national corporations – most notably, Pepsi, Coca Cola, Nike and Adidas – latched on to it as an ideal promotional vehicle. To this end, they sought to tap into the popular appeal of leading Indian cricketers, who now came to dominate their lavish advertising campaigns.[24]

A number of other companies also followed suit and sought to associate themselves with cricket. Some paid out vast sums of money to sponsor one-day cricket tournaments; others clamoured for the right to advertise their products at cricket stadiums or else to emblazon their logos on the players' apparel; and yet others sought to sponsor the team, its kit or, all else failing, its travel and accommodation. Cricket's potential as a generator of massive advertising revenues prompted media companies to engage in frenetic bidding wars to procure the exclusive rights to telecast major one-day tournaments. Huge sums of money now began to be proffered for television rights. In 2006, for instance, Nimbus Communications, a leading Indian television company, paid $612 million for four-year rights to telecast India's domestic and international matches.

The major beneficiary of this financial bonanza was the BCCI. In 1992, the BCCI was faced with a deficit of $150,000; by 2007–08, its revenues were a staggering $213 million.[25] It had in the process become, by some distance, the richest organisational body in the sport. But leading Indian cricketers too reaped the rewards of this commercial revolution. Their match fees rose exponentially from the early 1990s, as did their earnings from endorsements. In turn, the growing involvement of star cricketers in commercial activities led to the emergence of professional sports management companies to look after their public relations and endorsement portfolios.

Sachin Tendulkar was the biggest brand name of them all. From the very early years of his career, he was much sought after by corporate firms eager for him to endorse their products. The reasons are not far to seek: he was young, dynamic, successful, scandal-free and possessed a fan following that numbered in the millions. Saliently, too, these companies quickly grasped that Tendulkar's recognisably middle-class social background made him highly appealing to the principal consumers of their products. Tendulkar's commercial value became clear in 1996, when he signed a five-year deal worth $6 million with World-Tel, a sports management company. When the contract was renewed in 2001 for another five years, Tendulkar's pay cheque had more than doubled, making him the highest earner in the game. The deal with World-Tel made Tendulkar an omnipresent celebrity, his cherubic face beaming out of billboards and television screens across the length and breadth of the country, endorsing everything from cars to colas.

'When a man appears as a hero and/or celebrity, his role as celebrity obscures and is apt to destroy his role as hero', observed Daniel Boorstin in an oft-cited essay on the modern culture of fame.[26] In one sense, at least, the remark could well apply to Tendulkar's career as a celebrity. Arguably, his very ubiquity, and the sense of familiarity produced by this, has meant that Tendulkar has been divested of the romance and mystique that surrounded sporting heroes of previous eras.[27]

The celebrity as icon

Seen from another perspective, however, Sachin Tendulkar is a unique national icon who has dominated Indian public life in a way that none of the great cricketers of the past ever did. As we have seen, the production and marketing of his image as a celebrity played a crucial part in this regard. But to understand fully the Tendulkar phenomenon, it is necessary to explore the popular reception of his image and the ways in which this has been shaped by the changing politics of nationalism and class in contemporary India.

Tendulkar's iconic status was a function of two interlinked developments. As cricket was transformed into a money-driven mass spectacle in the 1990s, the Indian cricket team became a prime vehicle for the expression of an increasingly bellicose nationalism that demanded constant success on the playing field. And, as the team's most accomplished performer, Tendulkar was the gleaming receptacle into which were poured the steaming expectations of the Indian public. This, in turn, was related in important ways to the profound transformation in the nature of the Indian middle classes, who have traditionally constituted the most significant and vocal followers of cricket in the country. In particular, Tendulkar came to symbolise the globalising ambitions and cultural self-assertion of the rapidly expanding Indian middle classes.

Cricket and politics have been mutually implicated from the very beginnings of the game in the Indian subcontinent. Since colonial times cricket has served as a site for the expression of the principal 'values, prejudices, divisions and unifying symbols' of Indian society.[28] In the late nineteenth and early twentieth centuries, it was the fissures that were most apparent, most notably in the communal basis of prominent cricket tournaments like the Bombay Pentangular and the overt discrimination that players from the lowest rungs of the social hierarchy had to confront.

However, from the early twentieth century cricket had also begun to engender nationalist sentiments and to bring together Indians of different communities. As anti-colonial nationalism became a mass phenomenon in the inter-war years, cricketing encounters with the English increasingly became occasions for patriotic self-expression. Moreover, even though 'cricket nationalism and official nationalist politics were rarely wedded in conscious public debates or movements ... they affected the lived experience of play, skill, space, and rights for many young Indians in the small towns and playing fields of India before independence'.[29]

The link between cricket and nationalism continued to endure even after the British left India in 1947. The rare victories that the Indian cricket team achieved in international encounters in the first two decades after independence were occasions for decorous national rejoicing. Indeed, they were treasured precisely because of the fleeting nature of the triumph that they represented.

The 1970s marked a watershed in the relationship between cricket and nationalism. The catalyst here was the series of famous overseas wins that the Indian team pulled off against the dominant cricketing powers of the time: England, West Indies and Australia. These victories have been widely interpreted as India's coming of age as a cricketing power. The lustre of the Indian cricket team was further enhanced in the 1980s, following its extraordinary success in major international tournaments.

The public response to India's cricketing conquests in these two decades heralded important changes in the nature of sporting nationalism. Perhaps its most benign manifestation was the sense of patriotic pride that the achievements of the Indian team evoked, in a context where the country otherwise had very little to cheer about in the sporting sphere. More worryingly, though, Indians now came to *expect* victory in international cricket encounters as a matter of course. But the most ominous trend of all was the extent to which the cricket team gradually came to be equated with the nation itself. When India won on the cricket field, the victory was celebrated as a national triumph; when it lost, the defeat was treated as nothing less than a national calamity.[30]

Sachin Tendulkar's career unfolded against the backdrop of a dramatic intensification in the interplay between cricket and popular nationalism. On the one hand, this development was spurred by cricket's transformation in the 1990s into a highly commercialised and commodified form of mass entertainment. Commercial promoters, advertisers and media interests associated with the game insistently mobilised the idea of the nation in their marketing strategies and inflated the expectations that were placed on the Indian cricket team.[31] On the other hand, this sporting nationalism was sharply accentuated by the tumultuous changes in the larger political landscape. Even as India began to assert itself more stridently on the world stage on account of its growing economic clout, the *fin de siècle* witnessed a profound political churning in which many of the founding ideals of the republic were ferociously contested. A nation buffeted by political turbulence increasingly looked to its cricketers for succour.

Together, these two developments generated a shrill cricket nationalism that was wildly exuberant in victory and savagely vituperative in defeat. This belligerent chauvinism was most visibly on display when India met Pakistan on the cricket field. As political relations between the two nations steadily deteriorated in the 1990s, the cricketing contests between them became 'war minus the shooting'.[32] But the prickly intolerance of Indian cricket followers was also expressed in other ways, from rioting to stop contests in which their team was headed for defeat to the studied refusal to applaud opposing teams.

Tendulkar's image as a national icon crystallised in this volatile context. His heroic performances during the 1990s electrified a cricket-obsessed nation and offered the reassurance that it could produce genuine world champions in the sporting arena. Moreover, in a politically fraught era, his significance transcended the realm of sport. His assertive style of play resonated well with those who were keen to contest their own marginal status in the world. Some saw him as a rare symbol of unity in a nation racked by divisive political conflicts. For others, he was a ray of light in a horizon darkened by national failures on every front. In the words of the writer C. P. Surendran: 'Every time Tendulkar walks to the crease, a whole nation, tatters and all, marches with him to the battle arena. A pauper people pleading for relief, remission from the lifelong anxiety of being Indian, by joining in spirit their visored savior.'[33]

This is an evocative image that conveys the enormous burden of public expectation that Tendulkar has to shoulder. However, it is inaccurate in one crucial respect. It was not the 'whole nation' but a particularly vocal section of it that figuratively accompanied – clad, it is worth noting, in the shiny accoutrements of modernity – Tendulkar every time he went out to do battle.

For above all, it was the nation's middle classes who gloried in Tendulkar's achievements and came to venerate him as a secular version of divinity.

The middle classes have formed the core constituency of Indian cricket for the better part of its history. During the colonial period, even though the major patrons of cricket were princely aristocrats, it was the English-speaking, urban middle classes who took most enthusiastically to the game and its rituals. This trend was consolidated even further after 1947. A vast majority of the players who have represented India at the international level have been from middle-class backgrounds.[34] Moreover, while the mass appeal of cricket has expanded exponentially, it is this 'conveniently elastic category' that has furnished the most sizeable chunk of the game's following in India.[35] The changing values and orientations of the middle classes have thus crucially shaped the culture of Indian cricket.

Prior to the 1980s, the Indian middle classes (especially the salariat that constituted its dominant element) were economically constrained, cultur-ally conservative and politically moderate. This influenced the manner in which they engaged with the game. Driven by the requirements of stability and gentility, the middle classes played cricket in a '(sh)amateur' fashion.[36] Their relatively modest financial circumstances also placed strict limits on the extent to which they could patronise the game.[37] And, most importantly, the middle-class followers of cricket had internalised its Victorian governing conventions and traditions.

Sachin Tendulkar's career coincided with a fundamental transformation in the nature of the Indian middle classes. This development is widely linked to the policies of economic liberalisation initiated in 1991. The deregulation of the Indian economy and its subsequent receptivity to the forces of glo-balisation had a profound impact on its middle classes. Most notably, even as they grew in numbers and affluence, the middle classes became more internally diverse, upwardly mobile and hungry for recognition on the inter-national stage.[38]

In turn, the remaking of the middle classes had decisive consequences for the culture of Indian cricket. The new claimants to middle-class status raucously embraced cricket in their eager quest to acquire the trappings of metropolitan modernity.[39] For these elements, the consumption of cricket afforded a 'sense of cultural literacy in a "world" sport ... and the more dif-fuse pleasure of association with glamour, cosmopolitanism, and national competitiveness'.[40] Simultaneously, as a growing number of middle-class Indians migrated and settled abroad, cricket became a means of affirming their ties with the country that they had left behind. The spread of satel-lite television and the arrival of the Internet facilitated and consolidated these trends.[41] It was thus the new middle classes who were most visible and voluble – at cricket grounds, on television and on the Internet – in their support for the Indian cricket team.

As the nation's most consistently successful performer in its most popular game, Tendulkar became a totemic figure for India's new middle classes in the era of economic liberalisation and globalisation. For one, his life story powerfully encapsulated the emergent middle-class aspirations of upward social mobility: a boy from an ordinary service background who succeeded in gaining entry, through his talent and hard work, into a rarefied world of money, power and fame. Moreover, consuming the alluring images of the global brands that Tendulkar endorsed allowed Indian middle-class males to experience 'the pleasure of being a modern consumer-citizen'.[42]

But, above all, it was the poise with which Tendulkar was perceived to have coped with the pressures and perils of modernity that made him an ideal role model for the new middle classes. On the one hand, as one writer noted, he was admired as a 'modern man playing a modern game in a modern style in the modern world'.[43] On the other hand, his conduct was seen to epitomise traditional middle-class values and morality.[44] Thus he was lauded for being a devoted family man, and for remaining humble and restrained in his public conduct despite being a globally recognised sporting celebrity.

Two events at the turn of the century served to confirm Sachin Tendulkar's status as an exemplary middle-class icon. In April 2000, the Delhi police produced startling evidence that implicated major South African and Indian players in a scandal involving the fixing of cricket matches. The controversy severely eroded the game's public image and abruptly terminated the career of a number of leading international cricketers. Tendulkar, however, emerged unscathed from this distasteful episode, which further enhanced his reputation as an honest and trustworthy public figure.

The extent of the public faith in Tendulkar's probity was vividly demonstrated a year and a half later, on India's tour of South Africa. During the second Test, Mike Denness, the English match referee, penalised six Indian players for illegal conduct. Among the accused was Sachin Tendulkar, who was held to have tampered with the condition of the ball. The incident triggered a major furore, with the Indian public rushing angrily to defend their hero. Repeatedly, in newspaper columns, in television studios and in countless Internet 'chat rooms', middle-class India lashed out at those who had dared to question Tendulkar's integrity, and repeatedly invoked his unblemished track record on and off the field of play. The controversy, wrote Ramachandra Guha, highlighted 'Sachin Tendulkar's status as the only flawless Indian'.[45]

Ashis Nandy once observed that in contemporary South Asia 'popular heroes of the worlds of sports and entertainment are expected to be exemplary social beings but they are also continuously suspected of being severely flawed'. This was because such heroes embodied 'the secret fears, anxieties, ambitions, hopes and especially, the unfulfilled temptations to deviate from social norms' of ordinary citizens. Inevitably, given his exalted status in Indian public life, Sachin Tendulkar has been the object of such intensely contradictory attitudes throughout his playing career. But he has also been more successful than most of his ilk in negotiating the 'ambivalence in the middle-class culture towards its heroes'.[46] This is perhaps his most remarkable achievement.

NOTES

* I would like to thank Anthony Bateman, Scyld Berry, Jeffrey Hill and Samira Sheikh for their valuable comments and suggestions. I am also deeply grateful to the Leverhulme Trust for the grant of a research fellowship that allowed me the time to prepare this essay for publication.

1 Heidrun Brückner, Hugh van Skyhawk and Peter Claus Zoller (eds.), *The Concept of Hero in Indian Culture* (New Delhi: Manohar Publications, 2007).

2 Rosalind O'Hanlon, 'Military Sports and the History of the Martial Body in India', *Journal of the Economic and Social History of the Orient*, 50, 2007, pp. 490–523.

3 J. A. Mangan, *The Games Ethic and Imperialism: Aspects of the Diffusion of an Ideal* (London: Routledge, 1998).

4 John Rosseli, 'The Self-Image of Effeteness: Physical Education and Nationalism in Nineteenth Century Bengal', *Past and Present*, 86, 1980, pp. 121–48; Paul Dimeo, 'Sport and the "Civilizing Mission" in India' in Harald Fischer-Tine and Michael Mann (eds.), *Colonialism as Civilizing Mission: Cultural Ideology in British India* (London: Anthem Press, 2004), pp. 165–78.

5 Joseph S. Alter, 'Gama the World Champion: Wrestling and Physical Culture in Colonial India', *Iron Game History*, 4, 1995, pp. 3–9.

6 Ramachandra Guha, *A Corner of a Foreign Field: The Indian History of a British Sport* (London: Picador, 2002), pp. 81–147.

7 Alter, 'Gama the World Champion'.

8 C. L. R. James, *Beyond a Boundary* (London: Serpent's Tail, 1996), p. 174.

9 Mukul Kesavan, *Men in White: A Book of Cricket* (New Delhi: Penguin, 2007), p. 171.

10 Mike Marqusee, *War Minus the Shooting: A Journey through South Asia during Cricket's World Cup* (London: Heinemann, 1996), p. 117.

11 'The Wisden Forty' in Matthew Engel (ed.), *Wisden Cricketers' Almanack, 2005* (London: John Wisden, 2005), www.cricinfo.com/wisdenalmanack.

12 Allen Guttmann, *Games and Empires: Modern Sports and Cultural Imperialism* (New York: Columbia University Press, 1995), p. 3.

13 David L. Andrews and Steven J. Jackson (eds.), *Sport Stars: The Cultural Politics of Sporting Celebrity* (London: Routledge, 2001), pp. 1–19.

14 Arjun Appadurai, 'Playing with Modernity: The Decolonization of Indian Cricket' in Carol Breckenridge (ed.), *Consuming Modernity: Public Culture*

in a South Asian World (Minneapolis: University of Minnesota Press, 1994), pp. 34–39.

15 Ibid., p. 36.

16 Richard Cashman, *Patrons, Players and the Crowd: The Phenomenon of Indian Cricket* (New Delhi: Orient Longman, 1980), pp. 141–42.

17 Appadurai, 'Playing with Modernity', p. 34.

18 Cashman, *Patrons, Players and the Crowd*, pp. 149–50; Appadurai, 'Playing with Modernity', p. 35; Kesavan, *Men in White*, pp. 28–29.

19 Appadurai, 'Playing with Modernity', p. 35.

20 Cashman, *Patrons, Players and the Crowd*, pp. 149–50.

21 Guha, *Corner of a Foreign Field*, p. 329.

22 Andrews and Jackson (eds.), *Sport Stars*; Satadru Sen, 'History Without a Past: Memory and Forgetting in Indian Cricket' in Stephen Wagg (ed.), *Cricket and National Identity in the Post Colonial Age* (London: Routledge, 2005), pp. 94–109.

23 Cashman, *Patrons, Players and the Crowd*, pp. 48–74.

24 Marqusee, *War Minus the Shooting*, pp. 189–206.

25 Osman Samiuddin, 'The World Money Made', www.cricinfo.com.

26 Daniel Boorstin, *The Image: A Guide to Pseudo-events in America* (New York: Atheneum, 1971), p. 73.

27 Ramachandra Guha, *The States of Indian Cricket* (New Delhi: Permanent Black, 2005), p. 12.

28 Guha, *Corner of a Foreign Field*, p. xiv.

29 Appadurai, 'Playing with Modernity', p. 33.

30 Ashis Nandy, *The Tao of Cricket: On Games of Destiny and the Destiny of Games* (New Delhi: Oxford University Press, 2000), pp. 107–108; Guha, *Corner of a Foreign Field*, pp. 340–55.

31 Appadurai, 'Playing with Modernity', pp. 38–43; Guha, *Corner of a Foreign Field*, pp. 404–406.

32 Marqusee, *War Minus the Shooting*; Guha, *Corner of a Foreign Field*, pp. 397–433.

33 Quoted in Guha, *Corner of a Foreign Field*, p. 352.

34 Cashman, *Patrons, Players and the Crowd*, pp. 75–107.

35 Kesavan, *Men in White*, p. 34.

36 Ibid., p. 237.

37 Sen, 'History Without a Past', pp. 99–100.

38 Ibid., pp. 102–103.

39 Ibid., p. 103.

40 Appadurai, 'Playing with Modernity', p. 46.

41 Sen, 'History Without a Past', p. 103.

42 Ibid., p. 104.

43 Mike Marqusee, 'A Singular Icon', www.cricinfo.com.

44 Abilash Nalapat and Andrew Parker, 'Sport, Celebrity and Popular Culture: Sachin Tendulkar, Cricket and Indian Nationalisms', *International Review for the Sociology of Sport*, 40, 2005, pp. 433–46.

45 Guha, *Corner of a Foreign Field*, p. 355.

46 Nandy, *Tao of Cricket*, p. xxii.

14

MIHIR BOSE

Conflicting loyalties: nationalism and religion in India–Pakistan cricket relations

The story of India and Pakistani cricket relations is not a bilateral one but a triangular one. It involves not only the cricketers and administrators of the two countries but also India's huge Muslim population. Their position, and in particular what the majority Hindu community perceive to be their attitude, is part of this three-sided story.

Early personalities and rivalries

Early India–Pakistan cricket relations were shaped by two individuals who went back to the era before the British withdrawal from the subcontinent in 1947. Both had played for India and both hailed from Lahore. The first of them, Lala Amarnath, was one of India's most celebrated and controversial cricketers, the first Indian to score a Test century and the first to be sent home from a tour, following clashes with the team manager on the 1936 tour of England. On the Pakistani side was Abdul Hafeez Kardar, who had played for India before partition, being a team-mate of Amarnath on the 1946 tour of England. Then, Muslims had formed a sizeable proportion of the Indian Test team. Nearly all of them were from Punjab, a northern Indian state, and nearly all of them were from the Indian lower-middle classes. India's partition resulted in the division of Punjab, with Lahore going to Pakistan, and the loss of a great many Muslim cricketers, particularly fast bowlers. Kardar, a strong supporter of Pakistan's founder Mohammad Ali Jinnah and a believer in the two-nation theory that Muslims needed their own homeland, played a huge part in creating and developing Pakistani cricket. He was not only Pakistan's first captain but became an administrator and then a politician.

Appropriately, both Amarnath and Kardar were captains of their countries when the two nations met for their first ever series in India in 1952. The series also marked Pakistan's debut as a Test playing country. The series featured several other firsts. For the first time India won a Test series 2–1, winning the first and third Tests in Delhi and Mumbai but losing the second Test in Lucknow. That victory set a trend for the Pakistani team, who henceforth always managed to win at least a Test in their first series against an opponent. Two years later, in 1954, on their first visit to England, they won the last Test at the Oval. No other country has ever achieved this on their first visit to England (it took India seven visits to win a Test in England). Pakistan repeated this feat against West Indies three years later, whereas it took India six series to win its first ever Test against West Indies, the victory eventually coming in the Caribbean in 1971.

In his biography of his father, *The Making of a Legend*, Lala Amarnath's son Rajender, giving his father's side of the story, describes how in constructing his win over Pakistan Lala had had to overcome the machinations of his own team members. Lala was in no doubt what caused the defeat in Lucknow. The Indians, probably to make their visitors feel at home, had chosen this as a venue, the city having been one of the great centres of Muslim culture and power. It also had a matting wicket, on which Pakistani players were more used to playing. Their opening bowler, Fazal Mohammed, made the most of it. To add to Indian problems they were without two of their main batsmen, Vijay Hazare and Hemu Adhikari, and their great all-rounder Vinoo Mankad. All three had major roles in the victory in the opening Test in Delhi. Rajender quotes Lala as saying that the players had opted out because they wanted to damage Amarnath, reflecting the bitter internal battles that have always marked subcontinental cricket. These players, Lala alleged, did not 'understand the mental trauma that had affected the displaced players due to Partition. I could because it had affected me.'[1] Whether Lala was right in making this charge is impossible to assess, as all the participants are dead, but the Lucknow crowd did not take kindly to defeat. The Indian team bus was stoned and Lala had to wade into the crowd with a lathi, an Indian stick, to rescue his players.

India rectified matters in the third Test and, according to Lala's version of events, he played a major part in this. On looking at the Mumbai wicket, and anticipating it might help the bowlers due to early morning moisture, he fooled Kardar into thinking the Indians would bat. Kardar won the toss and batted, Lala himself bowled beautifully and Pakistan's first innings score of 186 meant they were never in the game and lost. With the fourth and fifth Tests drawn the Indians held on to their 2–1 series lead.

The Indians went to Pakistan in 1954–55 to play another five Tests. Not only were all the matches dreadfully dull, boring draws, there were several other problems on the tour. Amarnath, now manager, fell out publicly with Kardar and the two men exchanged blows in a Lahore hotel. Earlier the arrangements made for the team at Bahawalpur were so bad that Amarnath threatened to take the team home. If the cricket on the field was often unmemorable there was many an off-the-field diversion. Vinoo Mankad, captain for the tour, fell in love with a Pakistani singer and was often distracted. Then, just before the last Test, Amarnath went to have tea with Kardar as a goodwill gesture and claimed he had discovered a plot by the umpire Idris Begh. Begh had come into the room and not realising Amarnath was there asked Kardar, 'Any instructions for tomorrow's game skipper?' When Amarnath revealed himself Begh fled and later claimed it was a misunderstanding. Amarnath insisted the umpire be changed and Begh, who had officiated in all the previous four Tests, was replaced by Masood Salahuddin. All this meant neither country was keen to have another visit and in any case, after 1954, political relations between the two countries progressively deteriorated. Pakistan became more closely involved with the American-sponsored alliances, while India became a champion of the non-aligned world and drew closer to the Soviet Union.

Pakistan finally revisited India in the winter of 1960. The series saw all five Tests end in draws, as it had done in 1954–55. But if the cricket was again fairly routine this was the series where the third element in this relationship – Indian Muslims and their relations with Pakistan – came into play. The first Test was played in Mumbai and was a sell-out long before it started. I was a schoolboy in Mumbai and persuaded my parents to let me visit the flat of one of their friends, which happened to overlook the Brabourne stadium where the Test was staged. The route to the friend's flat passed Churchgate railway station and the entrance to the East Stand of the stadium. On the first day of the Test I walked towards the flat and saw a whole crowd of very Muslim-looking people entering the stands. One passer-by observed the rush of the Muslims and commented, 'No wonder these *Meibhais* [as some Muslims are called] come crawling out now. It is their team that is playing. No prizes for guessing who they are supporting.' This bitter remark reflected the feeling of many Hindu Indians during the series – that Muslims in India were all supporting Pakistan. It was this feeling that was to prove the undoing of Abbas Ali Baig, a Muslim.

Baig had come into prominence when Indian cricket desperately needed a saviour during the 1959 Indian tour of England. He played so well for Oxford University at the start of the 1959 season that, when the main Indian batsman Vijay Manjrekar withdrew from the team because of a knee injury, the young Muslim cricketer was drafted in. He proved a splendid choice and was one of the few successes for the Indians on that dismal tour which saw India lose all five Tests. Playing in the fourth Test he repeatedly hooked the bouncers of India's nemesis Fred Trueman. The fiery Yorkshireman had been a horror figure for Indian cricket ever since the England tour of 1952 when Indian batsmen had failed miserably against him in that series, the nadir coming in the first Test when they were reduced to 0 for 4, still the worst start to an innings in Test history.[2] Though Baig was hit on the head by a bouncer, and had to retire hurt, he came back to complete a fighting century – joining a select band of Indians who had scored a century in their first Test.

Baig's status as India's up-and-coming batsman was further reinforced the following winter when the Australians under Richie Benaud toured India. Though India lost the series, they won a Test match against Australia for the first time and Baig was a central figure in the Indian batting revival. In the third Test at Mumbai he scored a fifty in each innings and was rewarded by being kissed by a girl who rushed out of the stands to the middle of the pitch to peck him lightly on the cheek. Within a year, however, Baig's cricketing world had been reduced to dust. The reason was his slump in form against Pakistan.

A failure in a non-Pakistan series, or by a Hindu in that series, might have been overlooked. But against Pakistan the natural, albeit libellous, conclusion was that Baig had sabotaged his own chances so that the good of Islam, in the form of the Pakistan cricket team, could triumph. His scores in that series were: 1, 13, 19 and 1. As the magazine *Current* put it, in a review of India and Pakistan Test cricket between 1952 and 1984, 'Confidence was further shaken by a torrent of poison pen letters, telephone calls and telegrams. He opted out of the Indian team after the Kolkata Test.'[3] Baig never recovered from the libellous accusations made against him during that series. After the 1960 Pakistan tour he became the forgotten man of Indian cricket and played just two more Tests, seven years later. A number three batsman who looked like becoming one of the Indian greats, Baig's fall was tragic.

The Muslim factor

It is, perhaps, not surprising that India's Muslims should have become part of this cricket story. Of India's population of nearly 1.2 billion, some 120 million are Muslims. The great majority of these are descendants of converts to Islam from Hindu society. A small minority could, possibly, claim descent from the Muslim conquerors that arrived in India in a wave of invasions that started in the Middle Ages. The Muslim conquest of India was a long, gradual process which started in Sind in the eighth century, and ended with the Mughal rule in Delhi between the fifteenth and the eighteenth centuries. The Muslims never conquered the whole of India, or even ruled over all of it, not even at the height of the Mughal Empire. As D. P. Singhal says in *A*

History of the Indian People, while the Turki Afghan invaders were mainly interested in loot and plunder – destroying innumerable Hindu temples and icons, carrying off immense wealth and appropriating businesses – the later Muslim rulers were woven into the India pattern 'drawn by the tolerance and responsiveness of the Indian mind and their own capacity for absorption and imitation. Throughout India, an initial clash was followed by fusion and synthesis.'[4]

While many of India's Muslims are poor and live in ghettos, there are many who have prospered in independent India. India advertises itself as a secular state and Muslims have occupied high positions within politics and civil society. In the years since Indian independence, India has had three Muslim presidents, a Muslim chief of defence staff, several Muslim judges, two Chief Justices of the Indian Supreme Court, a great number of Muslim politicians and ministers in central and state politics, and several senior Muslim civil servants. In addition, two of India's cricket captains have been Muslims and several prominent Muslims have played for India, including two of its most loved cricketers, the Nawab of Pataudi junior and Salim Durrani.

Their heyday came during that seventeen-year period between 1961 and 1978 when India and Pakistan did not play each other. Such breaks in cricket are not entirely unknown. Australia played its first ever Test with New Zealand in 1946, then did not play their neighbours again until 1973. But in this case of India and Pakistan wider political issues were involved. In 1965 the two nations went to war over Kashmir, and in 1971 Pakistan and India were again at war, a conflict that eventually led to the division of Pakistan and the creation of Bangladesh.

It is interesting to speculate how the popularity and evident appeal of either Pataudi or Durrani would have fared had they failed against Pakistan. Pataudi, or 'Tiger' as he is more popularly known in India, arrived on the Indian cricket scene in 1961 after exploits at Winchester School, Oxford University and Sussex and seemed to recall Indian cricket's first great superstar, K. S. Ranjitsinhji. His father had played for both England and India and had captained India. Pataudi junior did much to rescue Indian cricket from the 'dull dogs' tag it had earned in the 1950s. He led India for much of the 1960s and there was always something challenging and romantic about his cricket, as there was with Salim Durrani. Salim is a magical name in India, the name that the Mughal Emperor Akbar gave his son from his Hindu wife. Though Salim took the name Jahangir when he became Emperor, it was as Prince Salim that he created some of the most enduring Mughal legends, legends strong enough to become translated into films like *Anarkali* an epic *Mughal-E-Azam*. The name Salim evoked romance, valour lessness and Durrani's cricket symbolised all that. As N. S. R to write in *Indian Cricket*, 'Durrani broke hearts not records'.[5] Handsome enough to be lured by films (in which he was not very successful), there was always something glamorous about his cricket. As an orthodox left-arm spinner he was not in the class of the great Bishan Bedi, but he bonded with the crowd, particularly when batting. 'We want six, we want six, Salim', the Indian crowd would shout, and sure enough Salim Durrani tried to oblige.

By the time India resumed cricketing relations with Pakistan in the form of a tour of the country in the winter of 1978–79, Pataudi and Durrani had long retired. The only Muslim in the side was Syed Kirmani, and he was so established as a wicketkeeper that few would dare to ascribe his failures to religious feelings. This phase of India–Pakistan cricket was to see the rise of great fast bowlers in Pakistan who destroyed India's batting. The Indian visit to Pakistan also marked the end of the four great spinners who had dominated Indian cricket for much of the late 1960s and 1970s: B. S. Bedi, E. A. S. Prasanna, S. Venkataraghavan and B. S. Chandrasekhar. The Pakistani batsmen treated them so roughly they were never a force again. In 1978–79 India lost a three Test series 2–0. The only consolation was that the series saw the emergence of Kapil Dev, an all-rounder who could also bowl fast and who was to play a dominant part in Indian cricket over the next decade. But although he was a vital part of the Indian team that went to Pakistan in 1982–83, the Indians lost three of the five Tests, two by an innings, one by ten wickets. Their batsmen were put to the sword by Pakistan's Imran Khan who, on supposedly lifeless subcontinental wickets, took forty wickets at a staggeringly low cost of 13.95 runs each. While the Indians did not know how to cope with Imran, the Pakistani batsmen could not stop making runs. They rarely had to bat more than once in a match and their scores in the first four Tests were 485, 452, 652 and 581 for 3 declared.

Both defeats led to changes in the Indian captaincy. Bedi lost the job after 1979, and Sunil Gavaskar, who had taken over from Bedi, lost his after the 1983 series. But in between these defeats Gavaskar did lead the Indians to their first series victory at home since Amarnath's inaugural series in 1952. This victory in the winter of 1979–80 by 2–0 was convincing enough, though the tour was marked by allegations that Pakistani cricketers had taken their eye off the ball by partying with Bollywood starlets. During the controversial third Test in Mumbai, which was the first of the two Indian victories, there were Pakistani allegations of Indian skulduggery with the pitch. This Test had seen the lone Muslim in the side, Kirmani, put on ninety-five for the seventh wicket with Kapil Dev, helping India reach 334 in the first innings and playing a crucial part in its victory.

The controversy arose from the nature of the pitch. The scrupulously objective reports in *Wisden* admitted the pitch presented problems from the first day, so much so that Gavaskar, who had decided to bat on winning the toss, was out for four by a ball that 'stopped' (did not bounce as he expected due to the poor quality of the pitch). The Indians secured their initial advantage because they won the toss, but the Pakistani failure was caused by the number of dubious lbw decisions given by the umpires against their batsmen. Four of them were out lbw in the second innings, as against only one, Viswanath, in the Indian second innings. *Wisden*, describing Miandad's lbw, said: 'considering that the ball was turning so readily, he might have been unfortunate to be given out.'[6]

The Pakistani cricketers also claimed that the ground authorities in Mumbai had doctored the pitch after the match had started. Not long after the match finished the following graffiti appeared on the walls of certain parts of Mumbai. It read: 'INDIA PLAYS WITH THIRTEEN PEOPLE – ELEVEN PLAYERS AND TWO UMPIRES.' The graffiti had appeared mostly in the Muslim areas of Mumbai. For some Indians, the fact that the views of some Indian Muslims appeared to agree with those of the Pakistani cricket team raised all the old doubts. By the time I visited Mumbai almost a year later I not only saw the graffiti but became aware that the entire series had reopened many of the arguments I had personally experienced back in 1960–61. Then the debate had taken place behind closed doors. Now it was the subject of cover stories. Very simply it was: When India played Pakistan, what was the position of the large Indian Muslim minority? Did they support India, Pakistan or remain neutral? Yet despite this backdrop, cricket between the two nations continued. Pakistan's visit to India in 1983–84 saw all three Tests drawn and India's return visit in the winter of 1984 was cut short after two drawn Tests, by the assassination of Mrs Indira Gandhi.

The impact of one-day cricket and the 1996 World Cup

In the meantime, a different dimension was coming into play, created by the rise of one-day cricket. It was India's unexpected victory in the 1983 World Cup which triggered this. The victory owed much to India's captain Kapil Dev and the team he had forged and the result was that India, supposedly devoted to Test cricket, suddenly placed enormous emphasis on the one-day format. Furthermore, India leveraged their victory to stage the World Cup outside England for the first time.

In 1987, India and Pakistan jointly hosted the World Cup, and while neither country reached the final it showed how the cricket administrators of the two nations could work together. By then, for various reasons, there had been a growth of one-day matches, an expansion that was to increase during the 1990s. This saw one-day series between India and Pakistan in such unlikely cricket places as Sharjah, Singapore and Toronto. The Indians call these 'masala' matches, 'spice' matches – something made-up and not quite real. Sharjah had started as a venue for benefit matches for Indian and Pakistani cricketers who have no English-style benefit system. Toronto provided a North American haven for India versus Pakistan matches, often not possible for political reasons in the subcontinent. Singapore and other tournaments represented the commercial opportunities that one-day cricket provided to those seeking to reach the new emerging Indian middle classes.

Many of these mini-series were sponsored by firms such as Singer and Pepsi, with extensive interests in South Asia, who saw the marketing advantages of being associated with Indian cricket. Rupert Murdoch's Star television and Disney's ESPN were also keen to reach this important economic group. With estimates that every second person watching cricket in the world is an Indian, this was a market worth cultivating. All this stimulated the ambitions of the region's cricket administrators, illustrated in the decision to stage the 1996 World Cup in the Indian subcontinent. While the decision was controversial, the event proved a marketing bonanza for the game there.

Just as India's victory in 1983 had brought the World Cup to the subcontinent, so the springboard for its return in 1996 was Pakistan winning the 1992 World Cup held in Australia. However, the way the 1996 tournament was secured for South Asia and then run was a vivid illustration of the partnership forged by its various cricket administrators. The crucial meeting was at Lord's in 1993, in what is seen as the most unpleasant meeting ever of the ICC. England came to the meeting confident it had a gentleman's agreement to host the 1996 tournament. Throughout the meeting they behaved as if this was an old boys' gathering. In contrast India, Pakistan and Sri Lanka, bidding jointly for the competition, had looked up the rules, wheeled in politicians and lawyers and treated the event like a political election contest. They targeted the ICC's Associate Members. In the past they had been shunned by cricket's big nations. Each of the associates was promised £100,000, £40,000 more than England offered. And after their victory, led by the Indians, the subcontinent made the most of the prize they had won.

At that stage, unlike the Olympic Games, football's World Cup and European Football Championships, the cricket World Cup was not owned by the international authority that runs the game. The country staging it owned the competition. In five previous World Cups the host country had made little money. The 1996 World Cup changed everything.

The subcontinental alliance began exploiting the competition as never before. They auctioned the television rights for a then staggering US$14 million, using an unknown agent, Mark Mascarenhas, an Indian born in

Bangalore who was based in the USA. The UK rights fetched $7.5 million, compared to $1 million in 1992. In addition, the tournament had official sponsors for almost every conceivable product, including the official World Cup chewing gum. Coca-Cola and Pepsi Cola both wanted to be the official drink supplier. Coke won by paying $3.8 million, more than Benson and Hedges had paid the Australians to be the main sponsor for the 1992 World Cup. The main sponsors Wills, the Indian tobacco offshoot of BAT, paid four times as much: $12 million. The organisers knew the competition meant money. They could keep all the profits, once they had met expenses. This meant paying £250,000 to each of the competing Test countries, though the amount did not even cover the expenses of some of the teams. But India and Pakistan made a profit of almost $50 million. During the same year, the 1996 European Soccer Championship in England saw UEFA, owners of the competition, make a profit of £69 million, while England, the hosts, lost £1.7 million.

Not all subcontinental countries financially benefited from the 1996 World Cup. The Sri Lankans were co-hosts with India and Pakistan but, worried that the competition might make a financial loss, did not agree to underwrite the costs and did not therefore participate in any of the profits. The Sri Lankan consolation was that their team won the competition. India, drawn in a tough group featuring Australia, appeared to have done all the hard work when they won their quarter-final in Bangalore against Pakistan. But they came badly unstuck in their semi-final against Sri Lanka. Not only did they lose but, with defeat imminent, the Kolkata crowd became so incensed they threw bottles and set seats on fire, and Clive Lloyd, the match referee, abandoned the match, giving Sri Lanka the game by default. However, all this did nothing to derail the bond the cricket administrators of India and Pakistan had formed. The countries could go to war and their people found it difficult to visit each other, but in cricket they could come together and make money.

Dalmiya and power struggles

The Pakistani administrators readily acknowledged that the money machine was driven by Jagmohan Dalmiya. Known to all as Jugu, his official title was Convener of the Pakistan–India–Sri Lanka Organising Committee (PILCOM). Dalmiya hails from the Marwari community of India, whose business skills are both feared and respected. By making a financial success of the World Cup Dalmiya furthered his international ambitions and ensured the India–Pakistan coalition was intact as he sought world power. The suggestion that he should go for the top job in cricket had come just before the World Cup and was made by Anna Puchi Hewa, President of Sri Lankan cricket. As they stood in Kolkata's Taj Bengal hotel, the sumptuous Kolkata hotel just opposite the city's zoo, he said to Dalmiya: 'We should have an Asian as the next President of the International Cricket Council.'[7] The idea had been triggered by Australia's refusal on security grounds to go to Colombo to play their World Cup group matches. The ICC could not force Australia to go and the Asian organisers were furious yet could do nothing. The opening ceremony in Kolkata was only days away and the Asians felt it was time they took over from the old powers, England and Australia.

The idea was immediately supported by Joe Bazalio, representative of Gibraltar, and Dalmiya ran his election as if it was an American presidential race, energetically wooing the associates. But despite Dalmiya twice winning the vote of the ICC members, the old powers were reluctant to accept him. The result was a brown versus white (and black) battle with England, Australia, New Zealand and West Indies against the subcontinent. It was so bitter it created scars that have never healed. The old powers felt that the new kids on the block were not following gentlemanly ways or doing anything about cricketing corruption, which had begun to rear its head. The Asians resented the fact that England and Australia would not accept them as equals. As one Asian official put it to me: 'We do not want to come to Lord's for the ICC meetings and just nod our heads like little schoolboys as we used to. Now we come with fully prepared plans and want to be heard as equals.'[8] This war was to see many battles. The first took place at the annual ICC meeting at Lord's in July 1996. The former West Indies batsman Sir Clyde Walcott was coming to the end of his term of office as chairman. Dalmiya stood for the chairmanship, as did Malcolm Gray from Australia and Krish Mackerdhuj of South Africa. The first round saw Dalmiya ahead of Gray and Mackerdhuj, with thirteen associates and three Test countries, India, Pakistan and Sri Lanka, voting for him. Mackerdhuj dropped out and in the second round Dalmiya got the vote of a fourth Test playing country, Zimbabwe, although South Africa abstained. Dalmiya also received more associate votes, eighteen in all, and was ahead of Gray. But the ICC rules required a majority of Test playing countries and he did not have the support of England and Australia, who had the veto. The rules were not very clear. The Indians, having taken legal advice, argued that the election should be decided by a simple majority. Walcott countered by saying a chairman required the backing of a two-thirds majority of the Test playing countries: six out of nine. It was clear the old powers feared what a Dalmiya chairmanship might do to the game, whilst the Asians saw racism at play.

Not long after this inconclusive battle, Eshan Mani, the Pakistani representative, David Richards, chief executive, Dalmiya himself and Sir John Anderson, representing New Zealand, flew to Singapore. It was agreed Dalmiya would be chairman but of a restructured ICC. It would now be an incorporated body, with an executive board and other committees, and Dalmiya's title would be President not Chairman. The old colonial powers felt they were fencing in the new boy. Mani's suggestion of rotating the presidency was accepted. So Dalmiya would be succeeded by Gray. But the big question was: How long would Dalmiya serve? Walcott had had three years, Dalmiya wanted three. Anderson and Richards said no: only two. The matter was only resolved a few months later in Kuala Lumpur when Mani successfully proposed that both Dalmiya and Gray should serve three years and that thereafter the term of presidency should be two.

While all this negotiation was taking place off the field of play, on the field India–Pakistan cricket relations in the late 1980s and early 1990s were often rocky. The one-day matches in Sharjah ran into trouble, with the Indians having the worst of the largely expatriate Pakistani crowd and the results on the field. The most searing defeat for them came in 1986. A brilliant innings by Javed Miandad meant that Pakistan, requiring four to win, won with Miandad hitting the last ball of the match, bowled by the hapless Chetan Sharma, for six. Two years later, in the winter of 1986–87, Imran Khan led Pakistan to their first series win in India, winning the last and most gripping Test of an otherwise dull series. The Indians did manage to avoid defeat when they went to Pakistan two years later and drew all four Tests. The series was more memorable for the use of neutral umpires for the first time in Tests, and the debut of sixteen-year-old Sachin Tendulkar. Until then Pakistan had rarely been a stage for great Indian cricket but the tour marked the start of the career of India's, and one of the world's, greatest cricketers.

Resumption of Test matches

That series also marked another interruption to the two neighbours playing each other at home. They met in World Cups and one-day matches in far-distant lands but they did not meet in a Test series for a decade, until the winter of 1998. By this time Sachin Tendulkar had come and gone as captain and Mohammad Azharuddin had once again taken over. Azharuddin, a Muslim, had led India against Pakistan before, but this was the first time in a Test series. For a time it seemed the series might not take place. The threat of violence from Hindu extremists had cancelled tours in 1991, 1993 and 1994. As in 1991, when the pitch at Wankhede was dug up, this time it was the one at Kotla but, with the government determined to resist fanatics, the tour went ahead amidst unprecedented security.

The first Test at Chennai saw Pakistan set India a target of 273. The match looked all over at 82 for 5 but among the unbeaten five was Tendulkar. His 136 nearly brought victory, India failing by 12 runs. The second Test at Kotla not only brought India victory but made history. Pakistan, set 419, had made a good start, getting to 101 for no loss at lunch on the fourth day. But after lunch the Indian spin bowler Anil Kumble changed ends, from the Football Stand End to the Pavilion End. In nineteen overs and three balls he took all ten wickets, only the second time since Jim Laker (against Australia in 1956) that a Test bowler had done so.

Although this marked the end of the two-Test series, India and Pakistan played a third match in what was billed as the Asian Test championship. This match showed the destructive passions India–Pakistan cricket can generate. India, after making a great start by reducing Pakistan to 26 for 6 on the first day, had a fight on its hands, being set 278 to win in their fourth innings. How explosive this fight could be was soon demonstrated. There occurred two incidents which ignited the Kolkata crowd and shamed Indian cricket. Tendulkar, on 9, hit a ball to the boundary and in going for a third – his second had taken him past 5,000 Test runs – he collided with Pakistan's Shoaib Akhtar at the bowler's end and was run out. The crowd felt Akhtar had deliberately blocked him and forced the game to come to a stop. Tendulkar and Dalmiya, the ICC President, had to appeal to them before play could resume. But the crowd was on edge and on the final morning, when their hero Sourav Ganguly failed and with India facing certain defeat on 251 for 9, they rioted. The police evicted all the spectators and, with only about 200 VIPs, officials and journalists present, Pakistan won by 26 runs. After Kumble's deeds at Delhi, the behaviour of the fans and the incompetence of the authorities represented a sad and dishonourable episode for Indian cricket. The defeat also meant that in effect two successive Pakistani visits to India had resulted in their going home victors. But the tide was about to turn for India and it was Ganguly, the man at the centre of the drama in Kolkata, who engineered it.

It was another three years before India and Pakistan resumed Test cricket relations. Ganguly led the side to Pakistan and did what no other Indian captain had previously done there, namely win both a Test *and a Test series*. Injury meant Ganguly could not captain the side during the first Test at Multan and Rahul Dravid led the team, but for the Indians the match set all sorts of records. For the first time in twenty attempts India won a Test in Pakistan and Virendra Sehwag became the first Indian to score 300 runs in a Test innings. India lost the second Test but Ganguly returned to lead India to victory in the third.

There have been three further series since then, with India winning one at home, drawing the other and Pakistan winning one at home. But unlike previous encounters where draws have predominated – 64 per cent of all Tests between the two sides have been drawn – more recent series have been more result-oriented, with both sides willing to go for victory rather than settle for draws. However, there has been no series since the last one in India in 2007–08, with terrorism casting a vast shadow. The terror attack on the visiting Sri Lankan team in early 2009 has put Pakistan out of bounds for international cricket. That attack came in the wake of the terror strike on Mumbai in the winter of 2008, organised by groups from Pakistan. All this has so soured relations between the two countries that it makes any cricket contact impossible. So much so that the 2010 IPL cricket season saw no Pakistani players take part.

Relations between the Boards of Control

The exclusion of the players created much controversy in India, leading to televised debates on the subject, with some IPL franchise-holders expressing unhappiness about the decision. They included the Bollywood super-star Shahrukh Khan, who owns an IPL franchise. However, with Khan being a Muslim, his comments in favour of Pakistani players so incensed Hindu fanatics that they attempted a boycott of his film *My Name is Khan* in Mumbai, the centre of the Bollywood film industry.

One reason for the IPL exclusion of Pakistani players was the breakdown in relations between the two Boards. Indeed, matters had reached such a pitch that Indian Board officials privately told the President of Pakistan, Asif Zardari, who is also the Patron of the country's cricket, that the situation could only improve if he sacked Ijaz Butt, the head of Pakistan cricket. One very high-placed Indian Board official told me: 'We have approached the Pakistani President and told him that, for the sake of sub-continental cricket, he should exercise his power as patron and sack Butt. Without Butt's removal our two boards cannot work together. In the past, despite political problems between our two countries, and even with the armies squaring up to each other, the two cricket boards worked together. But now we cannot because of Butt.'[9]

Butt and the Indians had never had good relations. They had differences dating back to 1987, but the present crisis originated in early 2009 when, following the terrorist strike against the Sri Lankan cricketers in Lahore, the ICC decided that Pakistan would not stage 2011 World Cup matches. They were meant to host the tournament along with India, Sri Lanka and Bangladesh. The fourteen matches due to be played in Pakistan were thus reallocated, with India taking the lion's share.

The Indians have argued that, had they not done so, the World Cup would have been moved from the subcontinent to Australia and New Zealand, the reserve venues for the 2011 competition. But Butt has never forgiven the Indians for what he feels was an act of betrayal and an instance of India taking advantage of the terrorist strike in Lahore. He made public and private comments blaming the Indians for isolating Pakistan's cricket and forcing it to play all its home matches overseas.

The breakdown in relationship between the two Boards is said to be so complete that I am told the Indian cricket officials are not on speaking terms with Butt. It also led to Lalit Modi, the Indian Board official who organises the IPL, writing to David Morgan, the chairman of the ICC, registering a complaint against Butt and demanding that he be brought before the ethics commission of cricket's governing body for damaging his reputation and that of the Indian Board.

This followed public exchanges between Butt and Modi. In December 2009 Modi declared no Pakistani player would play in the IPL on the grounds that they had failed to obtain their visas before the deadline for confirmation of participation. Butt immediately contested Modi's version saying, 'The players have applied for visas but the clearance hasn't come from the Indian side. The ball is not in our court.'[10] The issues concerned were not insoluble and from talking to Indian officials it is clear that their antagonism for Butt played no small part in keeping the Pakistani players out.

As this is being written, with the IPL under intense scrutiny by both the Indian Board and the Indian authorities, and Modi, the creator of the IPL, forced out of the organisation and asked to explain himself for alleged financial irregularities, it is hard to see how the issues can be resolved. But given the way these two countries have kept their cricket relations going when so much between them does not work, the hope must be that before too long the cricket will resume.

NOTES

1 Rajender Amarnath, *The Making of a Legend* (New Delhi: Rupa, 2004), p. 192.
2 Mihir Bose, *The Magic of Indian Cricket: Cricket and Society in India* (Abingdon: Routledge, 2006), p. 227.
3 Ibid., p. 215.
4 D. P. Singhal, *A History of the Indian People* (London: Methuen, 1983), p. 157.

5 Bose, *The Magic of Indian Cricket*, p. 213.
6 Ibid., p. 202.
7 Mihir Bose, *A History of Indian Cricket* (London: Andre Deutsch, 2002), p. 441.
8 Ibid., p. 443.
9 Mihir Bose, 'Pakistan Snub Raises Fears of IPL Terrorism', *Independent*, 26 February 2010.
10 Ibid.

15

ANDRE ODENDAAL

Cricket and representations of beauty: Newlands Cricket Ground and the roots of apartheid in South African cricket

In January 2010, England played South Africa in the traditional New Year's Test at Newlands in Cape Town. Former England captain Michael Atherton led his story in the London *Sunday Times* with an ode to the beauty of the stadium:

> A new year of Test cricket dawns for England at one of the most stunning venues in the world game. Newlands was shimmering on Friday morning under the shadow of Table Mountain, Cape Town's defining feature, as both sets of players prepared for the pivotal Test of the series.[1]

England captain Andrew Strauss was equally respectful of the venue and throughout the match the media framed the ground as 'picture perfect'. The *Times* from Johannesburg, its front page dominated by a colour photograph of Newlands, dubbed it the 'Field of Dreams'.

Even the Canon Chancellor of Blackburn Cathedral, Chris Chivers, joined in the reification of this space. In a thoughtful article in the *Cape Times*, he mused on how epic battles on the sports field mirror the real-life struggles against fear, failure and pain that every individual is engaged in. Newlands was his starting point: 'nothing beats a Test match played at Newlands, beneath one of the most spectacular mountains in the world.' Furthermore, watching a game here provides a perfect setting for understanding deeper things about life, for 'aesthetics – as the Ancient Greeks knew only too well – sets the stage for contests which are often of the most epic proportion'.[2]

Newlands and the mountain that towers over it have been lyricised for over 120 years in this way. Ground and mountain have become part of the romance and folklore of South African and international cricket.

This chapter reflects on the way the Newlands Cricket Ground (today named Sahara Park Newlands for commercial reasons) has been represented in travel descriptions of South Africa by English cricketers and cricket writers since the first Test match there in 1889, less than five years after Lord's hosted its first international game. It is argued that a subtext of this genre of writing is the representation of Newlands as a place of colonial idyll. Just as a large body of cricket writing has romanticised the village and rural roots of cricket in England (partly as a conservative response to change in the game and in the world),[3] so the geography and customs of this cricket ground and the way it has been described came to represent all that was good (and superior) about being 'British' in the colonies. From the start, the stadium and those who ran it developed the most intimate of relationships with 'Home'. These associations were reinforced by close connections between the respective political and cricket establishments, and also the many English professional cricketers who came to winter in Cape Town every season from the late 1880s onwards. Not for nothing did the Club that owned the ground become known as 'the MCC of the Cape Colony'.

However, behind this romanticised view of the Newlands Cricket Ground, its surroundings and its obvious beauty, there was a shadow side that needs to be explored. Those in charge of this most English of social spaces were deeply part of the institutionalised violence of not only colonialism, but also apartheid. In later years, it became fashionable to blame the 'crude' Afrikaners for apartheid (an idea itself rooted in Social Darwinism and imperialistic thinking), but the Newlands-based cricket establishment were in fact directly responsible for racial segregation becoming official policy in South African cricket.

Visiting the colonies

The origins of the cricket ground in Newlands go back to the mid-1880s, when the Wynberg-based Western Province Cricket Club decided to hire and turn into a cricket ground a piece of farmland – bordered by marshes, the railway line and the brewery – in one of the neighbouring suburbs, Newlands. A rugby ground, which also became famous as an international venue, was built at roughly the same time on the other side of the tracks. The cream of colonial society was involved in these parallel developments, including Cape Dutch leaders such as 'Onze Jan' Hofmeyr. Two of the people on the Committee responsible for the developments of the new cricket ground were Major Robert Wharton, who went on to organise and manage the first international team to visit South Africa in 1888, and William Milton, who was to captain South Africa in that series. Both were civil servants from England. Milton, who was educated at Marlborough College and had played rugby for England, became private secretary to Cecil John Rhodes, Prime Minister of the Cape Colony.

The first match at Newlands was the annual fixture between Home Born and Colonial Born on 2–3 January 1888. This match was a highlight in the colonial cricket and social calendar. At that stage 'Home Born' meant English in colonial discourse. The locals won. The Royal Inniskilling Fusiliers band and a good crowd of spectators were in attendance.[4]

In December 1888, the first English touring team arrived. They were captained by Aubrey Smith (who was to become a Hollywood film star famous for playing the quintessential British gentleman). The whole of Cape Town turned out to greet them and the tourists played the first game involving an international team in Africa at Newlands. The English captain described the scene as follows:

> Newlands Cricket Ground was a picture to be remembered, with its surrounding mass of pines, overtopped by the great table mountain on one side, the new stand covered with red cloth standing out prominently against the green background. The picturesque effect given on our own grounds being enhanced by the bright and varied colours of many Malay women in their holiday attire.[5]

Smith estimated the crowd to be 4,000 strong, 400 of whom were accommodated on a temporary grandstand erected especially for the occasion. 'The weather was beautiful and an excellent matting pitch was laid in the centre of the good grass ground.' He noted that, 'Hundreds of people arrived by train every ten minutes to Newlands'. Women constituted 'a very large percentage' of the crowd that watched the English lose by seventeen runs to the Western Province XXII.

The English returned to Newlands in March 1889 before they took the boat home. England destroyed South Africa thanks to match figures of 15 for 28 by the Lancashire professional Johnny Briggs, which enabled the tourists to win by an innings and 202 runs.

English tours to South Africa became regular occurrences after 1888–89. South Africa (not yet formally a country) now started establishing itself as one of the handful of test-playing sides. Newlands's reputation as a cricketing paradise soon became recognised throughout the cricketing world. During the 1905–06 tour, MCC captain Sir Pelham Warner noted that:

> ... there was a tremendous crowd on Saturday last, when the M.C.C. and South Africa again faced each other. And never did the Newlands ground look prettier. It was a perfectly glorious day, the sun shining with brightness and warmth from an almost transparently blue sky, while above the thousands who sat packed on the terraces and under the oaks towered the great mountain.[6]

The Western Province Cricket Club (WPCC or simply the Club), which built Newlands and organised the first English tour, now found other clubs reacting to their privileged position. In 1890, the Western Province Cricket

Union (WPCU or the Union) was formed by clubs who 'wished to wrest away control from the Western Province Cricket Club the apparent monopoly which they held in the administration of cricketing matters in the Western Province and obtain equal representation for all first-class local clubs on a duly constituted board'.[7] The WPCU now became responsible for the organisation of Tests and representative matches at Newlands. Although the Club and the Union sometimes had an uneasy relationship, they were nevertheless in broad agreement about how the ground and cricket in South Africa should be run.

One of the purposes of these early tours, as recent studies have shown, was to extol the virtues of colonialism and the links with Britain. They were accompanied by elaborate social programmes and speeches by political figures emphasising this.[8] So closely were the projects of cricket and colonialism combined that Monty Bowden, who captained England during the 1888–89 tour, accompanied the Pioneer Column which colonised Rhodesia (Zimbabwe) as a celebrity guest in 1890. William Milton became the Administrator of Rhodesia, and many of his cricket friends became leading officials in the new administration. So brazen were the cricket and political connections that Lord Hawke's team in 1896 visited the ringleaders of the Jameson Raid in Johannesburg where they were imprisoned following their abortive attempt to overthrow the government of the Transvaal. Moreover, the influential Lord Harris, for a long time an autocratic secretary of MCC, soon afterwards became Chairman of the South African mining company Consolidated Gold.[9]

Sir Pelham Warner, a great figure in English cricket history, was one of those who over several decades developed intimate links with Cape Town. After he had fallen ill with 'a virulent form of poisoning' in 1930, he embarked on a holiday to Cape Town and his later description of it clearly shows the friendships that existed between the British and colonial establishments on political, cricket and social levels in the nineteenth and twentieth centuries.

As Warner put it: 'A voyage to South Africa in company with my daughter followed, and the sea-breezes, plus Jack Rennert's daily glass of champagne, quickly restored me to health.' One of his fellow passengers was the magnate and cricket sponsor Sir Abe Bailey, who 'had brought with him a library of books, to which he kindly gave me access'. Once arrived in Cape Town, J. J. Kotze, the former South African fast bowler, and the then groundsman at Newlands, who had recently laid the first turf there, came on board and 'insisted on driving me there and then in his car to Newlands to see the grass wicket for which he was responsible'. Warner explained:

> We had a glorious time in Cape Town. At first we stayed at a hotel, and later
> both Sir Abe Bailey and Colonel and Mrs J.J. of my old friends the Van der

Bijls, Mr and Mrs Syfret, and Mr and Mrs Young – made the days pass all too quickly. The Van der Bijls I had known since my first cricket tour in South Africa under Lord Hawke in 1898–99, and I had played cricket on Bearsted Green and in the dockyard at Gibraltar against a son of the Syfrets, now a distinguished Admiral. We went for several motor drives in and around the Cape Peninsula, on one occasion lunching with the Pickstones in their lovely old house, Lekkerwign, at Groot Drakenstein, in the Paarl Valley.

Warner mixed with leading local celebrities during his visit. He met members of the famous 1906 Springbok rugby team and the Cabinet Minister Piet Grobler. He visited Sir Lionel and Lady Phillips at Vergelegen, 'the original residence of the first Dutch Governor, with its famous library and organ which Sir Lionel played for us'. He had lunch at Admiralty House in Simonstown with Admiral Rudolf Burmester. He played tennis at the Knollys' with his Oxford contemporary Charles 'Strugs' Strubens and was entertained by the Cartwrights at Fernhurst, 'with Table Mountain behind the house', a 'delightful garden ... round the bathing-pool and zinnias as big as sunflowers'. Warner concluded:

> Those happy days in South Africa seem like a dream. Bathing in the sea at Muizenberg, fishing from Sir Abe Bailey's motorlaunch, tennis at the Van der Bijl's, and the race-meetings, at one of which we met Captain Bonham-Carter, one of the heroes of Zeebrugge [who] ... invited us to lunch in his ship, H.M.S. Carlisle, and there I renewed my friendship with R.B. Cunliffe and K.A. Sellar, who had played in the Navy v. M.C.C. match at Portsmouth.[10]

The great English cricketer Walter Hammond toured South Africa several times and also spent a recuperative summer in Cape Town, raving about its beauty and the climate. He noted that:

> Cape Town is one of the few places I have been in that seems to have a definite strata of society which one might term the 'cricket set', just as some places have a 'bridge set'. They were charming to me, and as hospitable as only Colonials can be; one way and another, my enforced visit to Cape Town was one of the pleasantest periods of my life.[11]

Famous English cricketers such as Lionel, Lord Tennyson, Ian Peebles, Bill Edrich, Godfrey Evans, Alec and Eric Bedser, Denis Compton, Colin Cowdrey, Trevor Bailey, Doug Insole and Ken Barrington all duly reinforced the positive accounts of touring South Africa, visiting Cape Town and playing at Newlands given above by Smith, Warner and Hammond. In many of these accounts, South Africa is described as the most enjoyable country to tour and Newlands as the most beautiful ground in the land.[12]

After the Second World War, some of England's greatest cricket writers added to the chorus of unrestrained admiration for Newlands. John

Arlott, not the greatest admirer of South Africa, nonetheless described Newlands as 'one of the loveliest of all cricket settings'.[13] E. W. Swanton claimed that 'no cricketer could wish for a happier New Year than to play in or watch a game on the most perfect and most comely of all cricket fields. Newlands ... is a beautiful survival among the world's great cricket grounds.'[14] The poet and cricket writer Alan Ross painted this picture in his literary way:

> Newlands is so certainly, in the popular imagination, the most beautiful Test ground in the world that one half hopes to disagree. But in honesty one cannot. Separated from the sea and the city by Table Mountain, it lies deep under the rocks of Devils Peak. The mountain line is no distant prospect, but an immediate backdrop up to which one has to raise one's head. The pavilion is full of flowers, the stands painted the blue of the sightscreens at Lord's. If you sit among the plane trees, with your back to Table Mountain and the railway, you look across at a thick line of oaks, the people under them light as in a painting by Pissarro or Seurat. From every other position Table Mountain flowing into its foothills dominates the eye.[15]

The beauty of the ground and its setting has been undisputed for more than a hundred years. The radio commentator Charles Fortune, the voice of cricket for generations of South African cricket enthusiasts in the age before television, summed up the adoration felt for it in South Africa when he said that 'Newlands has contrived the miracle that can encompass a test [sic] match crowd yet still maintain the image and the atmosphere of a village cricket match ... Peace more perfect than with a glass of beer in hand, looking out across Newlands, you will not find.'[16]

This idyllic theme in relation to Newlands recurs over and over again in cricket literature, going beyond mere geographical descriptions to reinforce notions of what was beautiful and civilised about cricket and colonial life, and the relationships and experiences and attitudes that went with this.

The shadow side of Newlands

The people who ran the postcard-pretty Newlands Cricket Ground endlessly extolled cricket's notion of 'fair play', but chose not to practise it. The beautiful place under the mountain, celebrated in the literature of cricket for over a century, also has a shadow side to it. Professed cricket protocols and standards did not apply to those who were not white or 'European' here. The underclasses were allowed into Newlands only on certain strict conditions. They could not sit on the grandstand, for example. And, after initially being allowed to play there, they were soon completely excluded from doing so. Their role was mainly to fulfil menial tasks and stay inconspicuous. An institutional culture of racial and class superiority became infused into the very fabric of the place, and into the muscles and minds of those who played in flannels on its grass.

Jan Morris noted that in Britain's colonies the Club was the place that most represented the superiority of the colonists over the unadmitted millions. Nowhere was this more so than at Newlands.[17]

Both the Union (WPCU) and the Club (WPCC) openly practised segregation and racism. For a hundred years the logic of colonialism and apartheid ruled at Newlands. Unlike India or the West Indies, where discrimination in a colonial society evolved into opportunities for the indigenous people to represent their country, by the 1920s and 1930s South Africa followed the opposite direction, hardening the system of racial discrimination rather than gradually relaxing it.

If a more tolerant approach had been followed, things could have been very different at Newlands. The surrounding suburbs of Newlands and Claremont were mixed residential areas at the turn of the twentieth century and flourishing cricket cultures emerged in the Muslim and coloured Christian communities (often lumped incorrectly together as 'Malays' at the time) who lived there.

Aubrey Smith specifically commented on the enthusiasm for cricket in the black communities of Cape Town at the time. Black enthusiasts were among the large numbers that greeted the first English team at the Docks in December 1888 and many turned up to watch the first international game at Newlands.[18] Coming back from Christmas lunch with Admiral Wells on HMS Raleigh moored in Simonstown, Smith observed: 'On our way home we saw as quaint a site as ever cricketers saw at Mowbray. Two or three cricket matches were being played by Malays and Kaffirs and hundreds of Malay women in their many coloured costumes were there to do honour to the friends.'[19]

Many of these players and spectators lived in the shadow of the Newlands Cricket Ground. However, because they were not allowed to join the whites-only Club and Union they had to play separately. As early as January 1890, the same month the first-ever white Western Province team took to the field against Natal at Newlands, the local black cricketers hired the ground for an inter-town tournament. Claremont and 'Cape Town Union' played against Port Elizabeth and Johannesburg, which was then only a five-year-old settlement.

Matches were played over three weeks, every Monday and Tuesday when not being used by white cricketers. The *Cape Times* described the scene in a vivid way:

The visage presented to the visitors at Newlands yesterday, could hardly have been rivalled by the most gorgeous of Eastern spectacles, whilst the beautiful background of trees and the lofty mountain rising beyond toned down the daring blaze of colour, the whole forming a picture which must have printed itself indelibly upon the retina of all who made the journey to the ground. The whole of the Malay population appeared to have deserted Cape Town for the sylvan pastures.[20]

But this event was unfortunately one of the few exceptions. Within a few years the ground became off limits to black cricketers. Excluded from the mainstream, they went on to form their own Western Province Coloured Cricket Union (WPCCU) and in 1898 Western Province won the first inter-provincial tournament for black cricketers in Port Elizabeth. Dr Abdullah Abdurahman, the first black medical doctor in South Africa and a City Councillor for forty years, was the first president.

Palmboom Road in Newlands was one of the venues for meetings of the early WPCCU. Today this is a gentrified area with no trace of its history, but in 1900 Palmboom Road was 'particularly mixed with a high proportion of Coloured residents at the top end'. There was a school for coloured children in Palmboom Road and at the bottom end (near today's Blue Cross Hospital) a Gandhi Memorial School was later built. In 1902, according to Beatrice Law, 'about half of the population [of Newlands village] were Coloured and about half White'. Claremont was similarly mixed. A mosque was built in Claremont Main Road in 1894. (It is still in active use today, although dwarfed by the sea of concrete commercial buildings going up there currently.) A little further down Main Road there was a school attached to St Saviour's Church.[21]

The Western Province Coloured Cricket Union was geographically separated into a 'Town Section', covering the District Six, Bo-Kaap and City areas playing mostly at Green Point Common, and a 'Suburban Section' based in Claremont and Newlands. In the twentieth century, flourishing clubs emerged here, including Vineyards, Violets, Pirates, Alphenians, Primroses and Green Roses.[22] These 'Suburban Section' clubs played mostly at Rondebosch Common, a mile or so away from the Newlands ground.

Although discriminated against, the locals remained passionately involved with Newlands. Sir Pelham Warner vividly described the atmosphere at the match in 1898 between Lord Hawke's team and Western Province:

On Boxing Day there was a crowd of over 8000 spectators and the parade during the luncheon interval reminded us of an Eton v. Harrow or Varsity match. The bands of the King's Royal Rifles and the Liverpool Regiment played on the ground, while amongst the crowd there were a large number of

Malays, many of whom are engaged as bowlers by the clubs in Cape Town. They could easily be recognised by their red fez. Some of them bowl well and their keenness is beyond doubt.[23]

In his book on the 1905–06 MCC tour, Warner speaks of how the locals participated in the English team's net sessions and how C. J. Nicholls, 'a young Malay with a fast left-hand action hit my middle stump nearly every other ball'.[24]

A tantalising autobiographical profile of one of these cricketers, known only as Isaac, which appeared in the *Cape Times*, neatly summarised the Newlands and South Africa's colonial cricket set-up in those years. From 1901 onwards, 'Isaac' was closely involved with the Club and helped out the white Western Province and South African teams and their international opponents. As a youngster he would go to Newlands every day after school to 'help to field and pull out the grass'. In addition, 'Isaac often clean[ed] the secretary, Mr Bissett's cricket togs, and this makes it a extra 6 [pence]'. By 1907 he was the 'net boy' at the club. The club's English professional there, F. Tate (father of Maurice), taught him how to bowl 'six different balls'.[25] He became 'of great value as a groundsman', ran the scoreboard and 'bowled for 15 years in the nets for Western Province'. Those he bowled to included Jack Hobbs, Jimmy Sinclair, E. H. D. Sewell and Frank Mitchell, the South African captain. According to Isaac, the overseas teams 'whispered that Isaac will be an expert bowler one day'. He 'became a good bowler in the Western Province and his salary was also increased to 10s[hillings] a week besides his other tips'.[26]

In his other life, away from the master–servant world of Newlands, Isaac was selected for the Western Province Coloured Cricket Union provincial team that played in the Barnato tournaments. This aspect of his career, however, rates no further mention in a long article; his story was only of value to the *Cape Times* because of his novelty value to whites.

After finding work in the then Southern Rhodesia, where he became groundsman at the Queens Club in Bulawayo, Isaac returned to Cape Town to resume his duties as baggage master and 'massage man' of the Western Province team, travelling away with them as well. Isaac is still there in 1946, standing back right, in the team photograph of the first post-Second World War whites-only Western Province team captained by Tuppy Owen-Smith.

This fifty-year-long cricket love story involving a scarcely literate man with no surname was replicated in many different ways by other individuals at sports clubs in Cape Town. The local people became part of the furniture at Newlands, employed as net bowlers, scorers, baggage men, barmen and 'boys' on the ground staff by the ruling classes. And on match days they would be present in their segregated enclosure following play with colourful mannerisms.

The closeness of locals like Isaac to the white establishment cricket scene as 'skivvies' is reminiscent of the West Indies experience. C. L. R. James, as well as Brian Stoddart and Hilary Beckles, have described how a layer of very skilled black working-class cricketers consisting of 'groundsmen, young men employed as grounds bowlers, and occasionally helpers and hangers on' emerged in Barbados and Jamaica from the 1890s onwards. They were excluded from the Challenge Cup competitions, but a few clubs (like Spartan) gave some opportunities and gradually top black players emerged.[27] Similar practices and talent emerged in South Africa as well. But instead of these players becoming South African versions of George Headley and Learie Constantine, their achievements became more invisible over time. In an age where the 'amateur' was idealised as a leisured gentleman, the fact that the black workers at clubs in the Caribbean were 'professionals' was sometimes given as the reason for their exclusion. In South Africa, the white establishment made no attempt to hide the fact that race was the reason.[28]

Nevertheless, the number of black cricketers in Cape Town continued to grow and by the mid-1940s the Western Province Coloured Cricket Union had thirty-seven teams participating in its first and second divisions.[29] In addition to the Muslim-dominated WPCCU clubs, there were also clubs in Claremont playing in the Cape and District Cricket Union, made up mainly of Christian cricketers. They were affiliated to the rival Peninsula and Western Districts Cricket Board (PWDCB), which claimed to have even more players than the WPCCU in Cape Town – over fifty teams in the early 1950s.

Many of these cricketers lived in very close proximity to Newlands. Rushdie Magiet, who became convenor of the national selectors after democracy, remembers that Fridays were a big day in Claremont. First there was mosque and later all the cricketers would walk down Main Road (only a few hundred metres from Newlands) dressed in their whites and blazers in delicious anticipation of the weekend games ahead.

Despite this enthusiasm, the local cricketers could only be part of the sideshow at Newlands, working in menial positions or watching from the segregated enclosures. Black cricketers could not play for official clubs, provinces or national teams, or share facilities with white cricketers. The handbook of the WPCU made this clear. It contained a paragraph with a specific prohibition: 'No coloured professionals or members shall be allowed to compete in any matches under the jurisdiction of the Union.'[30] South Africa was well on the way to apartheid. There was little the local fans could do to change this situation at Newlands, but they did find ways to show their dissatisfaction with the way they were treated.

Fixing the colour bar in South African cricket

The Western Province Cricket Club which owned Newlands and the Western Province Cricket Union which organised big matches there not only adhered to the 'traditional' way of doing things, they were also more than anyone else responsible for officially introducing the colour bar into South African cricket in 1894.

The trigger was a once-only match in March 1892 between a local 'Malay' team and W. W. Read's second English touring team at Newlands. After South Africa were thrashed in two days, the local cricketers challenged the tourists to a match before the boat left. H. 'Krom' Hendricks, who had been picked for the first-ever South African Malay team at the inter-town tournament in Kimberley the previous year, so impressed the English that they compared him with 'The Demon' Spofforth, the great Australian fast bowler of the time. They suggested he be picked for the first South African tour in England in 1894. When the time arrived Hendricks was, indeed, included in the fourteen-player squad by the national selectors. Influential sections of the colonial cricket establishment – most notably the journalist and First Secretary of the South African Cricket Association (SACA), Harry Cadwallader – recognised Hendricks's talents and supported his selection. But William Milton, President of the Club and the Union and past South African captain, who was also the selection convenor, made sure Hendricks was omitted. He did so after consulting Cecil Rhodes, with the full backing of both the Club and the Union.

Jonty Winch has detailed, step by step, how Rhodes's supporters in the Club and the Union systematically plotted against Hendricks, despite those arguing in favour of a merit-based system in cricket.[31] After barring him from the first tour overseas in 1894, the exclusionists again held firm in 1895–96 when Lord Hawke's team made a return visit. They also barred Hendricks from the top local match between Home Born and Colonial Born (1894), the Western Province team to play in the Currie Cup (1895) and, eventually, from local league matches (1897), although he had performed outstandingly at this level before for Woodstock.

The ugliness of the Hendricks case lies in the systematic insistence of the Newlands establishment over a long time that he be excluded. It was not a one-off headline story. Hendricks was still trying unsuccessfully in the early 1900s, ten years later, to get permission to play in the WPCU leagues.

Harry Cadwallader, too, paid a heavy price for supporting Krom Hendricks. Although he had been the main organiser of the tour to England and it was assumed he would be manager, Milton had him ditched and replaced by an official from Milton's circle. Cadwallader subsequently also lost his position as the First Secretary of the South African Cricket Association. He was so sidelined that when Luckin's monumental *History of South African Cricket* was published in 1915, his name was not even mentioned. The cricket establishment airbrushed him out of history as surely as Stalin did Trotsky.

According to Winch and his co-authors, 'Cricket was a key element of the cultural expression of the Colonial establishment' and those in charge had decided unambiguously that cricket in Cape Town and South Africa must be kept lily-white.[32] These moves to impose segregation in sport were part of the broader political agenda of Prime Minister Rhodes and Milton, his private secretary and drafter of legislation. They happened at the very same time that Rhodes and his allies set out politically to replace mid nineteenth century 'Cape liberal' notions of individual opportunity and advancement with a clear segregationist policy (via the Glen Grey Act and other measures) that sought to restrict rather than encourage an emerging black middle class. This growing group of black propertied, educated and therefore increasingly skilled people, twenty thousand of whom qualified to vote in the Cape, were now seen as a threat to rather than a precondition for future progress. Following the discovery of diamonds and gold to the north, Rhodes's priority was to secure cheap black labour rather than promote social and political equality.[33]

With hindsight, it can be seen that the action against Hendricks fatally fixed the colour bar in cricket. This, in turn, led South African domestic and international cricket into a long cul-de-sac. The pattern for the future was established. Instead of increasingly accommodating black cricketers, as in other British colonies, the white cricket establishment increasingly excluded them. Segregation and later rigid apartheid became the norm.

The Hendricks case coincidentally happened at almost exactly the same time that Western Province Cricket Club also barred women from becoming members. A proposal that they be admitted was put at the Annual General Meeting in 1893 but the stiff upper lip of colonial patriarchy hardly twitched. The club historian's description of the event speaks volumes:

Occasion, annual general meeting. Year, 1893. Attendance, twenty-six.

A TIMID VOICE: 'Mr Chairman, before we close may I propose that – er – ladies be admitted to – er – this club – er – as members? Er – of course – on payment of a small subscription.' A stunned silence. Then growls of 'Heavens ... Ladies ... in a CRICKET club ... What's the man ...?'
CHAIRMAN: 'THE PROPOSAL IS OUT OF ORDER.'[34]

Newlands and apartheid

In 1948 the National Party won the whites-only general election, inaugurating a new era of intensified institutionalised racism in South Africa. A raft of legislation followed to give effect to the policy of apartheid. The coloured communities in Cape Town were particularly hard hit by the Population Registration Act, which introduced humiliating forms of racial classification, the Separate Representation of Voters Act, which disenfranchised them, and the forced removals under the Group Areas Act, one of the most destructive of all apartheid laws.

On 5 July 1957, Proclamation 180 was printed in the Government Gazette dividing the Magisterial Districts of Cape Town, Wynberg and Bellville into different 'Group Areas' for Whites, Coloured, Indians and Malays. People who had lived in Claremont and Newlands for generations were given notice to sell, pack up and leave. The legal letters followed:

> Under the provision of this proclamation it becomes illegal for you to occupy, and illegal for us to allow you to reside on such premises after the 6th July 1959.
>
> Under these circumstances the law compels us to give you formal notice which we hereby give you, to vacate the premises you occupy by the 31st October 1959.[35]

Beatrice Law explained in her history of Newlands:

> People of the non-White race groups were given two years from the date of the proclamation after which they would be considered illegal residents. Houses were valued and Coloured owners were forced to sell up and move. Getting another house was difficult. There were interviews to be endured and Government approval to be won, even for homes in the new areas like Heideveld. If they managed to sell their property at a price above the official valuation, half of the excess was claimed by the government.[36]

Some 44,000 families were removed from District Six and tens of thousands more from other parts of the City. People went through unspeakable pain, including suicide, rather than leaving their home, and settled communities with their churches, mosques, schools, sports clubs, bioscopes and distinct cultural life were broken up and scattered on to bare patches of land which have become today's depressed, gang-infested Cape Flats townships.[37]

Many cricketers were forced out of their homes by the removals under the Group Areas Act. The Conrad family, which has produced three generations of Western Province cricketers, had to move from Poplar Street

Newlands (now renamed Arbor Road), right next to the rugby stadium. Nazeem Smith, Western Province women's provincial coach, grew up at number 6 Dreyer Street, Claremont and he had to watch as the landmark Cavendish Square was built over his home. The entrance is on the exact spot, so every time he goes through the front door of this top-end-of-the-market shopping mall he is reminded of the childhood home his family was forced out of. The Magiet brothers, Rushdie and Saaiet, brought up in Stegman Road, a few hundred yards from the stadium, had to pack their bags and the taste it left was bitter. The young Rushdie decided not to watch again at Newlands until he was recognised as a human being with the same rights as everyone else – and he stuck to his word, for thirty-two years, until unity happened in 1991. Rushdie Magiet recalls that what made it hurt even more was the fact that every day he followed what was happening at Newlands in the newspapers, and that the sports columns were a daily reminder of what he had lost. After democracy, he went on to become con-venor of the national selectors. The Behardiens lived in a street near today's lovely Norwich Oval and the Galants were from Draper Street. The Vallie brothers, Ebrahim and Ahmedi, remember their big garden with pomegran-ate trees where the Newlands Sun Hotel (temporary home to many rugby and cricket teams playing at Newlands) now stands. The list of those who had to leave goes on and on.

Former team-mate [of the author] and Western Province bowler Salie Green told me with tears in his eyes in 2009 how he and his mother went around to say goodbye to old neighbours when they had to leave and, 'I can still see the pain in my mother's face as if it were yesterday. That pain also went into my body. She was never the same again and soon got sick out there in the sticks at Grassy Park.'[38]

All over Cape Town, Claremont included, clubs with long histories col-lapsed as people were scattered. The black cricket community had totally to reorganise itself in spatial terms and many long-established clubs went out of existence or had to merge with others. The white Western Province rugby and cricket unions made no attempt to defend the rights of the fans being forcibly removed around them; indeed, at an exhibition commemorating the forced removals, a letter from the Western Province Rugby Union supporting the evictions was displayed. For the white sporting establishment life went on as usual.

The cavalier Keith Miller, one of the most flamboyant Australian crick-eters of all time, and his ghost writer, R. S. 'Dick' Whitington, observed astutely the protocols that overlay the lifestyle and power relations in this setting in the early apartheid period. Effusive in their praise of South Africa, to the point of admiring colonial paternalism and racism, they describe in an account of the early 1950s the lifestyle that went with the setting:

> The sun is shining brightly on the green grass, and black waitresses are wait-ing upon white people at the white tabled-clothed tables under the elm and oak trees.
>
> A cup of tea and a cake or sandwich is one of the essential preliminaries to many people's day's cricket at Newlands.
>
> [After play,] society people pause for a cocktail at the fashionable Kelvin Grove Club before collecting their American automobiles.

However, if one reads a little further in Miller's description, you see there was also a hint of menace beneath the pretty picture of Newlands:

> Young Cape coloured natives sing as they stroll home in the gathering dusk through the green winding lanes. These natives are happy because the South African whites are getting beaten. They have been cheering for Australia all through the heat of the day. Dark curly-haired Neil Harvey, not blond-headed Cuan McCarthy, is their hero. And tomorrow is another day.[39]

This resentment, which initially expressed itself in an almost carnivalesque way, started hardening into something tougher after the advent of apartheid, particularly after the devastation of the Group Areas Act.

Given the context, it was no coincidence that the various black cricket bodies in Cape Town amalgamated into a new Western Province Cricket Board with clear non-racial principles in 1959. The new Board dropped all racial labels. It started to become openly 'political' about sport and its relationship to apartheid. It emanated as a reaction to intensifying apartheid.

While all this was happening, the white establishment carried on compla-cently in its old ways. In 1964, the Western Province Cricket Club celebrated its centenary. For the season's highlight – the Test against England – the Club invited Dr H. F. Verwoerd, the architect of apartheid, to be the guest of honour. This was the same year that Nelson Mandela, then universally viewed as a terrorist by white South Africans, was sentenced to life impris-onment for his opposition to apartheid.

Melvin Wallis-Brown, a teacher for nearly half a century at the nearby Diocesan College (Bishops), which produced the most South African schools caps during the whites-only era, recently recalled some of the authoritarian culture and thinking that existed in the early sixties in the close-knit English milieu in Cape Town that the Club was part of. He explained that when he arrived at Bishops the teachers were nearly all men, either old boys or Oxford graduates, and that caning and other Victorian conventions were strongly adhered to. Even the fact that he had a German car was questioned.

It was made clear to him: 'Young man, we at Bishops drive British Motor Corporation (BMC) vehicles.'[40]

Four years after the centenary of the Club, one of the greatest crises in the history of cricket broke out. The former Capetonian, Basil D'Oliveira, was forbidden from entering the country as a member of the MCC team because of the colour of his skin, leading to the cancellation of the tour and twenty years of isolation from international cricket. On 16 September 1968, the South African Prime Minister declared he would not accept the team with D'Oliveira in it. He said: 'The MCC team as constituted now is not the team of the MCC but the team of the Anti-Apartheid Movement.' Next day, E. L. McKay, President of the Western Province Cricket Union, declared emphatically: 'I am disappointed, but I support Mr Vorster on this.'[41]

The Western Province Cricket Club (owners of the ground), the Western Province Cricket Union (the representative regional organisation) and their national body, the South African Cricket Association, actively upheld apartheid and were deeply part of that system. Apartheid was enforced rigidly at Newlands. When Dik Abed asked for press accreditation in the 1970 series against Australia he was refused access to the press box. Instead he was given a table in front of the small 'Non-European' section of the ground. Apartheid signs were put up at the ground to indicate where 'Non-Europeans' could watch. The first rows of seating were installed in this 'Non-European' section only in 1972, as the white establishment sought to counter growing isolation and political condemnation.

One of the fundamental dishonesties still commonly propagated by old SACA players and administrators during the apartheid years is that they were against apartheid. As this chapter shows, that organisation in a deep sense enforced apartheid. Only when faced with isolation after the D'Oliveira Affair did some within its ranks belatedly start questioning apartheid in cricket and start tinkering with it (while still blaming those calling for non-racial cricket and equal rights as troublemakers and 'politicians').

In the modern post-1994 context, this hypocrisy has been perpetuated by criticism in injured tones directed at previously disadvantaged cricket people who support transformation and affirmative action. These attitudes show not only an inability to self-reflect, but also a state of denial that somehow hopes to wish away unpleasant facts so things can continue as 'normal'.

Cricketers and administrators in England were equally complacent and enjoyed a cosy relationship with the apartheid-supporting South African Cricket Association. In a way, this was a natural outflow of the Victorian-rooted 'culture' of cricket and the close cricket contacts between the two countries over the years. Peter Oborne describes 'the identity of interest, prejudice and approach between white South Africa and the British establishment in the 1960s'. He shows how culpable both the English and South African cricket establishments were in colluding with Prime Minister Vorster and the apartheid government to keep Basil D'Oliveira out of the 1968 MCC touring team. Some of them, like one-time MCC President Lord Cobham, had extensive business interests in South Africa and were sympathetic to the apartheid-supporting white cricket body. Drawing on official and private correspondence from recently opened archives, Oborne convincingly argues that 'The South African Cricket Association – to all intents and purposes an arm of the South African government throughout 1968 – was party to the intrigue [by the Prime Minister]. At Lord's, the MCC, advised by the former Conservative Prime Minister Sir Alec Douglas-Home, helped make Vorster's life as easy as it could.'[42]

Wisden Cricketers' Almanack has only recently belatedly acknowledged the role played by the cricket establishment in England in giving succour to apartheid sport. In the *Wisden Anthology: 1978–2006*, editor Stephen Moss wrote:

> Hindsight is a wonderful thing. With hindsight we can see that the isolation of apartheid South Africa in the 1980s and 1990s did the trick – it helped bring that wretched regime founded on ignorance, stupidity and selfishness to heel. With that hindsight we can also see that Wisden was on the wrong side for much of the period. It believed that visiting cricketers, repositories of enlightenment (sic), could bring illumination to that benighted land. Phooey! Wisden's line – with that blessed hindsight – was misconceived. Apartheid in South Africa couldn't be tempered; it had to be dismantled.[43]

Indeed, it is important for building new inclusive identities in post-apartheid South Africa that we understand and acknowledge the ugly past of the game in South Africa. This includes the harshness that underlay the beautiful pictures drawn about Newlands. The captivating beauty of the ground was not all that it seemed.

Afterword

In 2002, the Western Province Cricket Association (WPCA), the new governing body for cricket in the province following democracy, bought the Newlands Cricket Ground from the Western Province Cricket Club which had owned it for 114 years. Founded in 1991 on the principles of inclusivity and equal rights with the aim of uniting all cricketers in Cape Town for the first time, the WPCA is made up of 69 per cent black cricketers. Today all young cricketers can aspire to play at Newlands and their history is recorded in the President's Suite. Western Province has produced nearly half of all the black players so far selected for South Africa. In October 2009, the Cape Cobras, whose headquarters are at Newlands, reached the semi-finals of the inaugural Champions League Twenty20 tournament in India, the new world 'club' championships for cricket. When the Cobras beat the powerful Bangalore Royal Challengers in front of 40,000 Indian fans to qualify, no fewer than eight of the eleven players on the field were black. They would not have been eligible to play at Newlands in the past. The meaning of a place which symbolised in a deep way the dispossession which occurred under colonialism and apartheid is slowly being re-appropriated and changed by those who were marginalised before, even if in uneven and sometimes contradictory ways.

NOTES

1 Mike Atherton, 'Wilting Proteas Must Take Bloom off Flower's England', *Sunday Times*, 3 January 2010.
2 C. Chivers, 'Epic Battles on the Sports Field Mirror Private Struggles with Fear and Pain', *Cape Times*, 5 January 2010.
3 Derek Birley, *A Social History of English Cricket* (London: Aurum Press, 1999), pp. 354–55.
4 A. C. Parker, *Western Province Cricket 100 Not Out* (Cape Town: WPCU, 1990), p. 16.
5 Jonty Winch, *England's Youngest Captain: The Life and Times of Monty Bowden and Two South African Journalists* (Windsor: Windsor Press, 2003), p. 71.
6 Pelham Warner, *The M.C.C. in South Africa* (Cape Town: J.C. Juta and Co., 1906), p. 2.
7 Parker, *Western Province Cricket*, p. 11.
8 For example, Winch, *England's Youngest Captain*, pp. 68–70.
9 B. Murray and G. Vahed (eds.), *Empire and Cricket: The South African Experience 1884–1914* (University of South Africa: Unisa Press, 2009), pp. 225–27, 266.
10 Pelham Warner, *Long Innings: The Biography of Sir Pelham Warner* (London: George G. Harrap, 1951), pp. 132–35.
11 Walter Hammond, *Cricket My Destiny* (London: Stanley Paul, n.d.), p. 31.
12 Lionel Tennyson, *Sticky Wickets* (London: Christopher Johnson, 1950), pp. 72–77; Ian Peebles, *Spinner's Yarn* (London: Collins, 1977), pp. 39–52, 79–84; W. J. Edrich, *Cricket Heritage* (London: Stanley Paul and Co., n.d.), pp. 78–85; Godfrey Evans, *Behind the Stumps* (London: Hodder and Stoughton, 1951), pp. 194–213; Alec and Eric Bedser, *Our Cricket Story* (London: Evan Brothers Ltd, 1951), pp. 160–205; Denis Compton, *End of an Innings* (London: Oldbourne, 1958), pp. 48–52; Colin Cowdrey, *Cricket Today* (London: Arthur Barker, n.d.), pp. 38–47; Trevor Bailey, *Wickets, Catches and the Odd Run* (London: Willow Books, 1986), pp. 178–84; Doug Insole, *Cricket from the Middle* (London: Heinemann, 1960), pp. 150–90; Ken Barrington, *Playing it Straight* (London: Sportsman's Book Club, 1969), pp. 68–84.

13 John Arlott, *Gone with the Cricketers* (London: Longmans, 1950), p. 64.

14 E. W. Swanton, *Report from South Africa with P.B.H. May's M.C.C. Team 1956/57* (London: Robert Hale, 1957), p. 105.

15 Alan Ross, *Cape Summer, and the Australians in England* (London: Hamish Hamilton, 1957), p. 180.

16 Andre Odendaal Collection: photocopied quotation in 'Newlands, 1888–2010' file in author's possession.

17 Andre Odendaal, 'South Africa's Black Victorians: Sport and Society in South Africa in the Nineteenth Century' in J. A. Mangan (ed.), *Pleasure, Profit and Proselytism: British Culture at Home and Abroad, 1700–1914* (London: Cass, 1988), pp. 202–203.

18 Winch, *England's Youngest Captain*, p. 71.

19 Ibid., p. 76.

20 'Sporting Intelligence: The Malay Tournament', *Cape Times*, 14 January 1890.

21 B. Law, *Papenboom in Newlands, Cradle of the Brewing Industry* (Cape Town: by the author, 2007), p. 60.

22 'Western Province Coloured Cricket Union', *The Cape Standard*, 31 December 1945.

23 Pelham Warner, *Cricket in Many Climes* (London: William Heinemann, 1900), pp. 191–92.

24 Warner, *The M.C.C. in South Africa*, p. 2.

25 F. Tate was in fact the WPCC's professional in 1898–99, so Isaac either started earlier than 1903 or the names of the professionals were confused.

26 Andre Odendaal Collection: undated *Cape Times* newspaper cutting [c.1935].

27 Hilary McD. Beckles and Brian Stoddart (eds.), *Liberation Cricket: West Indies Cricket Culture* (Manchester University Press, 1995), pp. 40–41.

28 See foreword of Peter Oborne, *Basil D'Oliveira, Cricket and Conspiracy: The Untold Story* (London: Little, Brown, 2004).

29 'Western Province Coloured Cricket Union', *The Cape Standard*, 31 December 1945.

30 'Handbook of the Western Province Cricket Union', 1 October 1928.

31 Jonty Winch, '"I Could a Tale Unfold": The Tragic Story of "Old Caddy" and "Krom" Hendricks' in Murray and Vahed, *Empire and Cricket*, pp. 3–17.

32 Ibid., p. 3.

33 This section is taken directly from the author's foreword in Murray and Vahed, *Empire and Cricket*.

34 Quoted in Jonty Winch, *Cricket in Southern Africa: Two Hundred Years of Achievements and Records* (Windsor: Windsor Publishers, n.d.), p. 270.

35 Y. Fakier, 'Group Areas Took Away My Life', *Cape Times*, 16 April 1997.

36 Law, *Papenboom in Newlands*, pp. 67–68.

37 Ibid., pp. 67–71; A. La Guma, 'Why Must We Move?' in Andre Odendaal and Roger Field (eds.), *Liberation Chabalala: The World of Alex La Guma* (UWC, Bellville: Mayibuye Books, 1993), pp. 118–20.

38 Personal recollections conveyed to the author at function for ex-Claremont cricketers at Sahara Park Newlands, 2 January 2009.

39 Keith Miller and R. S. Whitington, *Catch! An Account of Two Cricket Tours* (London: Latimer House, 1951), pp. 74–75.

40 P. Bills, 'Old School Ties: A Lifetime Dedicated to Bishops', *Sunday Independent*, 9 November 2008.

41 *Cape Times*, 18 September 1968.

42 Oborne, *Basil D'Oliveira*, chs. 9–11, esp. pp. 147, 152.

43 Quoted in P. Briggs, *Lives in Cricket: John Shepherd, the Loyal Cavalier* (Cardiff: The Association of Cricket Statisticians and Historians, 2009), p. 65.

16

ROB STEEN

Writing the modern game

Like its subject, cricket writing might be divided, however simply, into two ages: imperial and post-imperial; the first dominated by English publishers and pens for the best part of three centuries, the second by an internationalism that removed England as the centre of attention. Was it mere coincidence that 1963, the year that saw Frank Worrell's West Indies team confirm the end of Test cricket's historic Anglo–Australian duopoly by trouncing England on their own pitches (two years later they would win a series against Australia for the first time), also saw the publication of *Beyond a Boundary* by C. L. R. James, the first internationally acclaimed cricket book by a non-Caucasian?

To James, familiarity with life beyond the boundary was essential to understanding what went on inside it, making him the first modern cricket writer. 'The first to see beyond the two-dimensional were Sir Neville Cardus and Raymond Robertson-Glasgow', attested the latest admirable editor of *Wisden*, Scyld Berry, whose own blue-sky thinking and dedication to the cause for *The Observer* and *The Sunday Telegraph* have been a blessing for close on four decades (his 1982 book *Cricket Wallah*,[1] furthermore, was remarkably prescient in anticipating India's ascent). 'They perceived the human side, the character, of a cricketer – Cardus as a subjective impressionist, Robertson-Glasgow from objective experience … Neither, though, went beyond the field of play to see a place where the cricketer was born and brought up, where he went to school or what community he represented. The first to do this, in my reading of the game, was C.L.R. James.'[2]

Mike Marqusee, a fellow Marxist, is James's spiritual heir. A native New Yorker, he came to England to study in the early 1970s and stayed, growing to love the game and producing, in addition to iconoclastic and profound studies of Bob Dylan, Muhammad Ali and the Labour Party, two of the most challenging and vital cricket books of our time, *Anyone But England: Cricket and the National Malaise* and *War Minus the Shooting*: the former the finest book on cricket's role in society since *Beyond a Boundary*, the latter a travelogue revolving around the 1996 World Cup and the author's burgeoning affection for South Asia, which saw him delve deep into the game's inexorable shift towards India. Nobody has better captured the pleasures, contradictions and complex issues that continue to swirl about the game's modern heartbeat and financial stronghold. We shall return to him.

The imperial age was marked by nostalgia, poetic licence and an almost supine reverence, for tradition, Lord's, MCC and authority in general. Only with the utmost reluctance was it consigned to history. Indeed, averred Stephen Moss in the 2000 *Wisden*,[3] 'a hundred years ago most of the elements of 20th-century cricket writing were in place: the pastoralism; the belief in the rootedness and essential Englishness of the game; the obsession with figures; the co-opting of famous players in commercial enterprises ... and the defence of past against present.' At the dawn of a new millennium, nonetheless, Moss still felt the need to clamour for muscularity and global perspectives:

> The rosy-eyed romantics should declare and let the revisionists into bat. Subvert the stereotypes of cricketing parsons and public schools, hymn the joys of global cricket, let writing play its part in re-energising the game for a new age, a generation less devoted to a dreamy past ... we want our prose in black and white, not purple. Its anglocentricity is absurd for a game where the balance of power now lies on the Indian subcontinent and in Australia. The commemoration of the past is dangerous for a sport which must quickly find a role for the future. Cricket writing, like cricket as a whole, must remake itself ... Wit, vision, a close reading of the game, a sense of its languor and lunacies, rather than unremitting reverence, should henceforth dictate the play, dominate the field.[4]

Laudable as such sentiments were, it was odd that Moss – who listed the writers he admired, Englishmen all – should exhibit so little awareness of those already doing his bidding within and beyond his own shores; even stranger that he should ignore one of cricket writing's comparatively new functions – to explain the game's geopolitical conundrums and economic intricacies. Fortunately, the advent of the World Wide Web and, more specifically, the emergence and development of Cricinfo as one of the globe's most popular sports websites, has enabled followers to access an unprecedented amount of writing, and hence a wider range of voices.

That it is now possible to read an edition of *The Hindustan Times* and *The New Zealand Herald* without having to leave one's laptop has broadened perspectives. Granted a global stage, the diverse talents of the Indians Rahul Bhattacharya, Pradeep Magazine, Sharda Ugra and Gulu Ezekiel, Vaneisa Baksh (West Indies), Richard Boock (New Zealand), Telford Vice (South Africa) and Osman Samiuddin (Pakistan) have surfaced and flourished, augmenting our knowledge and appreciation, breaking down insularity and challenging received wisdoms. Reverence, moreover, is refreshingly unrife. The result is more erudite and balanced writing. Aficionados, whether their source is the press, books, magazines such as *The Wisden Cricketer* and *All Out Cricket* or the all-seeing Cricinfo, with its correspondents in every port, are almost certainly better-informed than those who follow any other sport. Welcome to cricket writing in the post-imperial age.

Rising above information's noisy hum

From 1999 until 2003, I had the privilege of editing *The New Ball*, a conglomeration of themed essays promoted as 'the cricketing *Granta*'. The fifth volume, a celebration-cum-dissection of cricket writing, was subtitled *The Write Stuff.*[5] Twenty-one selectors nominated their favourite passage and outlined the rationale, including Richie Benaud, Ted Dexter and a clutch of prominent journalists from England, Australia, India, New Zealand and Sri Lanka. The intention was twofold: to bring current sensibilities to bear on past masters while offering a primer to those familiar with contemporary practitioners but less well-versed in those rich traditions.

For one writer, distance and experience had diminished youthful enchantment. Kevin Mitchell, then chief sports writer of *The Observer*, nominated an interview with Wilfred Rhodes, conducted by Cardus in 1950 when the great Yorkshire all-rounder was in his seventy-second summer. Cardus remains the game's most celebrated chronicler but it is difficult not to suspect that this is partly because his quotable prose and classical references dignified the profession, elevating cricket writing, its exponents believed, above all other forms of sports writing. 'This is the best and worst of Cardus, which so often went hand in hand', wrote Mitchell. 'Our Neville was no infallible tape-recorder of history, though – more a notorious embroiderer of distant, uncheckable events, especially those that lent substance and colour to his own troubled youth.' Mitchell cites the passage where, discussing the 1902 Ashes Test at Old Trafford, Cardus claims to have been there himself, to watch his hero Archie MacLaren, the England captain. He recounts seeing the infuriated MacLaren throw his bat in the dressing-room after being caught, and even quotes his verbal outburst. 'Admirable forensic skills', as Mitchell put it, 'for a 13-year-old schoolboy.'[6]

Then again, noted Mitchell, Cardus 'lived in more detached times, not one like ours, so humming with information we can hardly hear ourselves dream'. That humming has changed cricket writing in ways that would have been unimaginable even twenty-five years ago. Satellite television, and latterly the Internet, have made experts of us all. Could Cardus have got away with his modus operandi now? One doubts it. The loss of lyricism at the expense of accuracy, though, seems a reasonable trade. Fortunately, although the focus, led by the tabloids and emulating trends in football, is increasingly on news, personalities and quotes, the modernisation of cricket writing has not spelled the end of the match report as an art form. While fewer newspapers now carry extended descriptive reports that focus on the play – in good part because of the global obsession with football and the tendency of modern editors to fill their pages accordingly, but also because the action has already been extensively covered by television and the Internet by the time they are published – the slack has to an extent been picked up by websites, where space is far less of a constraint. In addition to the likes of the online incarnations of *The Times* and *The Guardian*, Cricinfo and the newly founded Test Match Extra are filling the breach, although the onus is likely to fall increasingly on the stand-alone websites as newspapers struggle for their future. Furthermore, while international coverage is more extensive than ever – editors often send three or more reporters to cover a Test match – only a supreme optimist would predict a revival in interest for domestic fare beyond the all-star Indian Premier League.

The closest to a modern Cardus is Frank Keating. Another *Guardian* man prone to sublime flights of fancy, Keating's inimitable style, part-colloquial hipster, part-folksy romantic, enlivened by his own adjectival nouns yet grounded in reality, could buoy even the most depressed crests:

> Cardus saw WG Grace only once, but it was enough for him to tell how 'he played cricket with the whole man of him in full action, body, soul, heart, and wits.' And so say us who saw Botham in his pomp of 1985. On the cricket fields, we would not forget him if we could (and could not forget him if we would), as morning after morning the summer's sun rose for him and he went forth and trod fresh grass – and the expectant, eager cry was sent about the land: Botham's In![7]

When that voluptuously vowelled actor Peter Ustinov read extracts from the paper in a television advert for *The Guardian* in the mid-1980s, Keating, quite properly, was the honoured sports writer. The best cricket writing, the best writing, merits recital, Keating's melodic prose above all.

Foot soldier

The writer most responsible for bridging past and present, for continuity, is David Foot, a gentle, genial West Countryman who has spent sixty years examining the humanity of this sporting life, painting vivid and insightful portraits of the giants and the garrulous, the humble, the unconfident and the disturbed alike, most memorably in his books and his summer work for *The Guardian*. That generosity of spirit, questing mind and perceptiveness, untainted by age and underpinned by an appreciation of how the demands on the professional cricketer have mounted over the course of his journalistic career, have infused biographies of tragic West Country icons such as Walter Hammond and the suicidal Harold Gimblett, together with collections of essays such as *Fragments of Idolatory*. Foot's county reports, his bread-and-butter, lose nothing by comparison. Compressing the myriad aspects of a day's play into 400 words can be trying at best, but the artistry always shines through. Never in his immaculately crafted musings does one derive a sense of snobbery or nostalgic longing, both surpassingly rare traits. If you didn't know the following extract was written in 1993, you could just as easily guess at 1953:

> If Caddick, sweet of action with the purring smoothness of a Rolls-Royce, was the ultimate match-winner, there were unlikelier heroes, such as Van Troost for his batting. He went in last when Somerset batted a second time and was top scorer. He spurned caution or the niceties of the game. The flying Dutchman generally thought of as the county's fastest bowler, really belongs to the halls when he goes to the wicket. He backs to square-leg and still, with that phenomenal stretch of his, manages somehow to reach the ball. He hit two sixes off Martin and, seemingly with blows from the base of his bat, reached 35 before succumbing to a catch at long-off.[8]

Witness, too, an interview with Gloucestershire and Pakistan's Zaheer Abbas. Foot's compassionate humanity, sense of proportion, temperate tone and elegant, recitable prose are all on parade:

> Zaheer leaves Richards and Botham to corner the pages of *Wisden* with the more dynamic flourish. He goes into cricket almost by stealth. 'Where do you bowl to him?' asks his good friend [Indian Test spinner Dilip] Doshi, to no one in particular. 'What are you complaining about – you've just taken five Test wickets,' says Zed. Doshi grins and returns to his PG Wodehouse. Far away in Pakistan Zaheer is, at the age of 35, demonstrating once more the receding art of pure batsmanship. 'See you back in England,' he waves. I edge uneasily past the armed police – one of whom stops me taking some innocuous holiday cine film as if I were a fugitive from a le Carre novel – and I know indisputably in my heart that the bat is mightier than the gun.[9]

I once asked Foot what motivated him. 'I've been told I have a suicide complex', he giggled gingerly, almost guiltily:

> Most of my books have either been about people who committed suicide or been on the point of killing themselves, which may suggest a slightly warped personality. I hope not, but ... I'm writing about someone I'm desperately

interested in, someone with a complicated life. I'm fairly complicated myself. If there was a war, even though I'm a pacifist, I'd be one of the first to sign on. I wouldn't have the courage to be a conscientious objector. I'd like to think I am [compassionate]. I think that's the nicest compliment anyone can pay me. And that perhaps comes from my background ... We might have had the wireless on but nobody ever spoke at our dinner table. I never learned the art of conversation. Which is probably why I write.[10]

Even in the summer of 2009, at the age of eighty, nothing, outwardly at least, had altered. If the palette was now dominated by the shades and hues of well-tended memories, the following passage from a *Guardian* column underlines the timeless appeal of that felicitous way with syllable and verb, that innate soulfulness:

Archie was often known as 'The Bishop', even if his ecclesiastical stature fell short of David Sheppard's. Teasing fellow amateurs were apt to change Wickham to 'Snickham', a snide description of his batting frailty. But no one could take too many conversational liberties when it came to his keeping. His stance, in distinctive grey flannels with a black cummerbund, was comic (if not acutely painful) as his legs seemed to stretch all the way from point to the square-leg umpire. But he must still have been nimble, not conceding a bye when Hampshire scored 672 for seven.[11]

In another *Guardian* column, Foot availed readers of his least enjoyable cricketing experiences, among them Hammond's comeback for Gloucestershire in 1951, strictly, cruelly, at the cash-strapped club's request:

His stay at the crease, following the warmest of romantic welcomes as he strolled to the wicket, was brief and cruelly misplaced. He kept playing and missing; the coordination had gone. Up in the stands, the members and his once doting fans fidgeted. The Somerset slow bowler Horace Hazell, who had always idolised Hammond, swore that he tried to encourage him with half-volleys ... England's great batsman and captain had made a serious mistake in agreeing to play. When mercifully he was out, the big crowd, still palpably affectionate, was silent and only wished he had left them with merely his wondrous memories.[12]

Foot's 'saddest' experience was conveyed in three concise sentences, the compassion undimmed, the economy of expression still a model for aspiring journalists and fictioneers alike:

I found myself talking to a blind man for whom a companion was giving a running commentary. 'How I love cricket and desperately wish I could see the play.' He was George Shearing, the great jazz pianist who liked to be taken to a Gloucestershire match during summer visits to this country.[13]

Wit and wisdom

In the final third of the twentieth century, Alan Gibson (*Times*) and Doug Ibbotson (*Daily Telegraph*) elevated their reports above the norm with their penchant for wry observation. Humour, though, was in short supply until the early 1980s, when Matthew Engel was appointed chief cricket correspondent of *The Guardian*. His spare, conversational style, light on adjectives and full of waspish irreverence, transformed the landscape.

> There is a graffito on the back of the players' tea-room at Hastings: Victoria 1066. Since the cricket ground is the only place in town not full of French students, this must have been put there by one of William's soldiers and could well constitute the longest-running gloat in history. The shortest-running gloat might have come from Northamptonshire after their victory here on Sunday.[14]

Engel, warranted Alastair McLellan, 'was the first to write about the game in a language and style that made it seem part of the late twentieth century'.[15] In his approach to the divisive South African debate of the 1980s, moreover, 'he played a major role in challenging the partial and divisive view of cricket's place in the world'. Engel, most assuredly, was not one of those who only cricket knew. Eager to cover the so-called 'rebel' tours where others refused to set foot in South Africa while apartheid was in force, he was 'unusual', he admitted to McLellan, 'in that although I was opposed to the South African regime, I was riveted by its efforts to survive. This came down to the ambivalence that I have always had between being a sports writer and a political writer. The story was made for me. I was fascinated by it. I am always fascinated whenever sport moves into the real world. That's what really interests me.'[16]

In 1986, when *The Independent* was first being staffed, Engel was offered the post of chief cricket correspondent; he turned it down to write about politics and ultimately edit *Wisden* with passion and innovation, having had quite enough of the endless tour cycle. In his stead, Martin Johnson soon won a cult following that spread far and wide. Aided by the fact that the butt of his jokes and barbs were the England team of the Ian Botham era, a side one could depend on for soap opera rather than victories, Johnson made breakfasts snap and crackle. In 2009, his touch showed no sign of fading:

> The [Oval's] groundsman would have been a strong contender for England's man of the series, had there not been so much competition from the umpires, and Ricky Ponting, having already received two fat lips during a fielding mishap, did well not to draw more blood from biting through his tongue when

stoically declining to point the finger at the officials. There is now a case for teams preparing a Justin Langer-style dossier before a Test series. 'Billy Bowden. Don't bother appealing to the first ball of a game, as he'll still be fast asleep. Or gazing at himself in a vanity mirror.' 'Rudi Koertzen. Don't just appeal for lbw if you hit the pad, ask for bowled, stumped, caught, hit wicket, handled ball, and obstructing the field as well. He'll definitely give it out, but not for the right reason.'[17]

Blind eyes and clear vision

Cricket writing's least admirable chapter remains its acquiescent response to apartheid, which can be interpreted as a key moment in the transition from the imperial era to the post-imperial. To maintain the pretence that sport could transcend political considerations, and thus ensure South Africa remained within the cosy, unquestioning fraternity of white sporting nations, why look further than Table Mountain and the *braai*? In Charles Fortune's account of the 1956–57 MCC tour of South Africa, the word 'apartheid' is conspicuous by its absence. He mentions 'Indian youths in the non-European stand' in Johannesburg, writes sniffily of the inelegant 'Zulu hoick'. Eventually, he talks to 'a solitary African'.[18] The only way one could tell that the 'African' might be coloured is from the word 'sah' with which Fortune peppers his heavily patronised quotes. Only then is one afforded the vaguest hint that South Africa was torn apart by racial divisions.

Reporting a demonstration against South Africa's 1960 tour of England, undertaken shortly after the Sharpeville massacre, the Wiltshire-born Fortune described protesters as 'no more than the cats-paws of certain churchmen who seized on the visit of the cricketers as an opportunity to gain for themselves some public notice'.[19] Later a long-serving secretary of the South African Cricket Association, the media centre at The Wanderers was named in his honour. 'Fortune was a conservative', declared his obituary in the 1995 *Wisden Cricketers' Almanack*, 'and appeared to take South Africa's exclusion from world cricket as something of a personal affront.'

A decade later, R. S. Whitington dedicated his book about Australia's 1966–67 tour of South Africa to 'the lonely land'. An Australian who had recently resided there, not until Chapter 7 does he begin to address the cause of the country's isolation. Even then, perhaps understandably, he takes at face value Prime Minister John Vorster's announcement, in April 1967, 'that South African sportsmen could compete against non-white sportsmen abroad and that non-white sportsmen could be included in international teams making visits to South Africa', thus seemingly clearing the way for Basil D'Oliveira to tour South Africa with England two winters hence.

Whitington called it 'a triumph for quietly-conducted, well-reasoned argument and negotiation'.[20]

Some, however few, were less easily or wilfully deluded. On his first visit to South Africa in 1948–49, John Arlott stopped outside the Nationalist campaign headquarters on the night the general election was won by the party that would impose apartheid. His companion expressed his dismay, whereupon Afrikaner party supporters covered his car in spit.[21] Asked to state his race upon arrival in that benighted land, Arlott famously wrote 'human'. One day he asked a black taxi driver to take him to a township: the poverty left a lasting impression. In 1960 it was Arlott to whom D'Oliveira wrote in search of employment in England, Arlott who befriended him and recommended him to Middleton Cricket Club.

Eight years later, during the so-called 'D'Oliveira Affair', Arlott was livid at the all-rounder's original exclusion from the MCC party to tour South Africa that winter: to him, it was motivated entirely by politics. That anger, expertly controlled in his comments for *The Guardian* and even more effective for their smouldering passion, roused MCC members to revolt as well as guiding public opinion. A few weeks earlier he had told the BBC he had no intention of commentating on South Africa's scheduled 1970 tour of England. He explained his reasoning in *The Guardian*, inspiring the young Peter Hain, the mainspring behind the resoundingly effective 'Stop the Seventy Tour' campaign. According to his son Timothy, Arlott had not wanted his friends 'to wonder what side he was on':

> Apartheid is detestable to me, and I would always oppose it ... a successful tour would offer comfort and confirmation to a completely evil regime ... Commentary on any game depends, in my professional belief, on the ingredient of pleasure; it can only be satisfactorily broadcast in terms of shared enjoyment. This series cannot, in my mind, be enjoyable.[22]

James was similarly unencumbered by wilful naivety, likewise Engel and Keating. Marqusee, the inspiration for a new wave of worldly, uncompromised cricket writing, has emulated their refusal to divorce sport from politics:

> Much as we might like the game to become, once again, merely a game, any human activity as complex as cricket will always carry meanings and invite interpretation. Our aim should be to ensure that those meanings and interpretations are not a burden on but an extrapolation of the game's democratic essence. We cannot return to a pristine cricket which never existed. Instead, we should see in the game's inclusive premises, its autochthonous open-endedness, a rich realm of human possibility – a realm in which even England can find a place.[23]

The value of the outsider's perspective was no less palpable in his description of the 1996 World Cup final between Australia and Sri Lanka in Lahore:

> For this day only, the Pakistani fans had metamorphosed into Sri Lanka fans. Many said this was because the Sri Lankans had vanquished the Indians in the semi-final, and thus exacted revenge for Pakistan's defeat at India's hands in the quarter-final. But there was more to it than that. The Australian refusal to play in Colombo at the outset of the Cup had offended Pakistanis almost as much as Sri Lankans and had aggravated the lingering resentment in Pakistan over the bribery allegations made against Salim Malik by Shane Warne and other Australian players. Subcontinental solidarity had been fractured by recent events in the World Cup, but here, at the tournament's end, it made a welcome return.[24]

Beyond Lord's

Australia's considerable contribution to cricket's written heritage has continued apace, spearheaded by Gideon Haigh, who combines literary eloquence and a reporter's eye with a historian's thirst for depth and context, bringing the present into sharper focus and the past to life, burying many a myth. No contemporary matches his breadth. His biographies of Warwick Armstrong and Jack Iverson (the latter stemming from an essay he wrote for the first volume of *The New Ball*) were resoundingly happy marriages of assiduous research, psychological burrowing and masterly storytelling. Primarily a business journalist, his understanding of global economics and boardroom chicanery, a decidedly unusual trait among cricket writers but increasingly vital in an age of franchises and blockbusting broadcasting deals, has been especially valuable, most notably in his journalism.

Born in London to a Yorkshire-reared father and an Australian mother, Haigh has spent most of his life in Victoria, reporting with flair and distinction for the Melbourne *Age* and other Australian publications while carving a vaunted reputation further afield with his columns in *The Guardian*, *The Times* and Cricinfo. His dissections of Iverson and Armstrong are worthy additions to the retro-modern biographical canon headed by Foot (Hammond and Gimblett), Arlott (Fred Trueman) and Charles Williams (Don Bradman), yet, like Foot, he is far from a nostalgist. Weightier and more invaluable still is his analysis of the Packer Revolution, *The Cricket War*, for which he interviewed scores of participants nearly two decades after that fractiously critical episode and found the lucid, unemotional tone that had eluded the often histrionic contemporary accounts. Even more important is *The Summer Game – Australia in Test Cricket 1949–71*, where primary research, social history and a novelist's flair combine to capture the straitened times that made Packer's intervention both desirable and necessary. The emphasis of the book, he avowed, is on 'people and period rather than games or scores ... there is as much attention devoted to areas previously glossed over: how cricketers lived and worked in a semi-amateur economy, how the game was run, how tours were organized, and generally the place of cricket in Australia'.[25] It succeeds on every level.

That the game's most respected contemporary historians are both Anglo-Australians seems fitting. To date the only writer to win the Cricket Society's Book of the Year award three times, David Frith, who entitled his autobiography *Caught England, Bowled Australia*, was born in London, moved to Sydney then returned to England in his late twenties, editing *The Cricketer* before founding *Wisden Cricket Monthly* in 1979. A prolific author, he has brought his formidable research and narrative skills to bear on matters ranging from fast bowling (*The Fast Men* was the first book devoted to the subject) to slow (*The Slow Men*), cricketing suicides (*Silence of the Heart*) to Bodyline (*Bodyline Autopsy* has now superseded Jack Fingleton's *Cricket Crisis* as the latest final word on that well-trodden terrain).[26] Nobody has done more to contextualise the immediate post-imperial age.

Over the past decade, as publishers on the subcontinent have sought to capitalise on the national obsession and mirror the subcontinent's emergence as the epicentre of the game, Indian writers have expanded their audience, from historians and essayists such as Mukul Kesavan and Ramachandra Guha to the precocious journalist Rahul Bhattacharya, who was just twenty-seven when voted Cricket Writer of the Year in the 2006 Indian Sports Journalism Awards, having previously written the acclaimed *Pundits From Pakistan*, a vibrant diary of India's 2003–04 tour. Witness his atmospheric depiction of the Karachi crowd:

> The noise in the crowd arranged itself into properly deafening rhythms that were then never to cease. The slow-fast bursts of hand on hand, of feet on floor, of rolled-up paper on railing, of 33,000 pairs of lungs ... Ganguly would remark that his players could not hear each other.[27]

Bhattacharya and his peers seek to capture this post-imperial landscape. No longer, they consistently remind us, is this a game run by England and Australia for Englishmen and Australians and filtered through their eyes. No longer are *The Cricketer*, *The Times* or *The Daily Telegraph* the first port of call for cricket obsessives; that distinction now lies squarely with Cricinfo, an Indian website. Founded in 1992 by Dr Simon King, a research scientist and MCC member who had relocated to Cornell University in upstate New York,[28] its original selling-point, ball-by-ball coverage of international matches, was soon supplemented by more considered reports, contemporary interviews and historical features. Now run from India, edited by the estimable and judicious Sambit Bal and recently bought by the American sports channel ESPN, Cricinfo offers unprecedented global coverage of a game whose leading lights are no longer Englishmen and Australians but homegrown icons – Sachin Tendulkar, M. S. Dhoni and Yuvraj Singh. As such, India seems destined to be the launching-pad for tomorrow's most prominent observers.

The changing face of newsprint

Newspapers remain the one constant. Read a discursive day's report in *The Daily Telegraph* or *The Sydney Morning Herald* and it will not differ markedly from those of half a century, even a century ago. There is a greater informality of language, yes, and fewer references to classical music and poetry (albeit not to Shakespeare), but to read the magisterial E. W. Swanton in the *Telegraph* during the 1950s was not an altogether dissimilar experience to reading the endlessly fair-minded Christopher Martin-Jenkins in the 1990s. Both were better-informed, closer to the seats of power, than their rivals; both issued pronouncements and proposals that influenced decision-makers. Their recommendation could win selectorial approval for one player, hasten the dropping of another, set in train a revision of regulations. What *has* changed is the nature of reporting and the backgrounds of the leading correspondents.

The proliferation of tours and formats, allied to the increasing welter of newsworthy stories and column inches, has led to a division of duties, for the sake of health and sanity. Burn-out is not unknown. As was reflected in the rapid turnover of Australian correspondents at the outset of the twenty-first century, and the decision by *The Times* to bill Richard Hobson as 'One-Day Cricket Correspondent' in the mid-2000s. Television has erected another obstacle. With even overseas matches being beamed live to their desk, editors have become accustomed to second-guessing writers who once reported without fear of contradiction. Yet with racism, match-fixing, ball-tampering, on-field behaviour and administrative greed and incompetence perpetually jostling for attentions, runs and wickets have often been also-rans. Happily, match reports have benefited, evolving from bland scorecard recitations into colourful vignettes of people, time and place. And it was assuredly a sign of these globalised times when, one night in London's City Road in the spring of 1999, an over-excited sub-editor succeeded in persuading *The Independent* to relegate a story about the England captain's back trouble in favour of Brian Lara's majestic 153 not out against Australia in Barbados to secure an enthrallingly improbable one-wicket win for the

West Indies. The greatest innings of modern times took precedence over the national interest, and justly so.

No issue proved more hotly contentious than Hansie Cronje's association with gamblers. The pain of white South Africans, betrayed by their national captain, was summed up with barely suppressed fury by Luke Alfred:

> In his handwritten confession ... Cronje wrote that after weeks of soul-searching he was finally able to look at himself in the mirror. But given all the evasions, the manifest inaccuracies, the lies direct and by omission, Cronje's economy of truth was beginning to look a little tattered ... If he was able to live with himself again after his confession ... how easy was it to live with himself in the first place?[29]

The prevalence, from the mid-1980s, of former players among the chief correspondents of the English national papers, none of whom have ever had any formal journalistic training, led to a greater reliance, amid an era of often bitter circulation wars, on other reporters when it came to press conferences, off-the-field news and interviews. Igniting the omnipresent clamour for exclusive stories, those circulation wars have helped change the course of the game, not least in the summer of 1988. That was when the publication of a story in a new mid-market newspaper, *Today*, led to the sacking of the England captain, Mike Gatting. A liaison with a barmaid, chronicled with predictable luridness, was cited as the cause, though many suspected Gatting's employers, the Test and County Cricket Board, of being in cahoots with the paper. Gatting, after all, had hardly had an unblemished track record on tour, and the Board had regretted not sacking him after his shameful chest-prodding dispute with a Pakistani umpire the previous winter.

Long gone, though, are the days when reporters turned a blind eye to players' off-duty proclivities. And when cricket writers were deemed insufficiently disinterested to 'dish the dirt', general news reporters were enlisted, as on England's Caribbean tour of 1986, when a former Miss World boasted in *The News of the World* of having broken a bed while in the enthusiastic company of Ian Botham. All of which served to aggravate the growing mistrust between players and writers, one now echoed in the frostiness between active players and the ex-professionals, such as Michael Atherton, Nasser Hussain and Botham himself, who mix insight with unfettered criticism in the commentary box.

The invasion of the press box by ex-internationals is a peculiarly English development (albeit not uniquely so: Richie Benaud and Jack Fingleton were both journalists before they played for Australia, while Bill O'Reilly also regaled the press box for many years). Nor is this reflected in other sports: the opportunity Oxford and Cambridge University offer to combine a world-class education with first-class cricket experience – for all that the latter is increasingly ill-warranted – is a singular boon, often leading, historically, to the England captaincy. Elsewhere, today's leading correspondents are, almost without exception, trained journalists. Indeed, in Australia, India and the Caribbean, the game's ingrained sexism has been splendidly overturned by the likes of Chloe Saltau, Sharda Ugra, Neeru Bhatia and Vaneisa Baksh. The perennial promise of the Oxbridge passport to career advancement, on the other hand, has seldom been better encapsulated than by the laptops lugged around the globe by Michael Atherton, Steve James, Vic Marks, Derek Pringle, Peter Roebuck and Mike Selvey. These erstwhile professionals have their critics – albeit drawn primarily from the ranks of embittered reporters confined to the donkey-work – but each has carved a niche for himself, and not solely by dint of technical expertise. As of May 2010, indeed, the sagacious but always lively Selvey, appointed by *The Guardian* in September 1987, was the sport's second-longest-serving correspondent in the national press.

Of these purported interlopers, only Atherton, who led England in more than fifty Tests, won worldwide renown as a player. He could well leave the deepest and most lasting impression. Succeeding Martin-Jenkins at *The Times*, an unenviable act to follow, he soon forged a reputation as a judicious judge while shedding his stoicism as an opening batsman to unfurl a fearless array of bravura strokes. Take his analysis of the dilemma facing Kevin Pietersen on England's tour of South Africa in early 2010:

> It is almost as if, now, unlike before, Pietersen wants to get on with things quietly and anonymously. But once you have embraced the cult of celebrity, it is not so easy to retreat. But how far does quiet anonymity suit his game? It was a game that, previously, was based on self-glorification, the 'look at me aren't I brilliant?' attitude that culminated in the kind of wondrous strokeplay that, this observer at least, had rarely seen. Pietersen is not Ian Bell, nor should he try to be. Somehow over the next five days, the Brylcreem Boy has got to find his inner skunk.[30]

The next day he turned his eye to the lamentable lack of a single black player in the South African Test XI:

> Another cricket club opened their doors yesterday, to more pomp and ceremony, in the heart of Johannesburg … But here in Gauteng, the home of the most desperate townships, cricket and rugby are just bystanders to football. Mind you, to stand on the Oval in Alexandra and look down into the slum below is to wonder that any kind of sport is played there at all. Sunshine and space are key ingredients for any sport and while there is plenty of the former, there is none of the latter.[31]

Not that the roll of honour stops there. The affectionately witty Tanya Aldred; the trenchant South African Neil Manthorp; Huw Richards of the *International Herald Tribune* and Sambit Bal, internationalists of the first order; Ed Smith, a searching, inventive iconoclast; the durable Trinidadian Tony Cozier; Christian Ryan, the young Australian whose wide-ranging 2009 biography of Kim Hughes is essential reading; David Hopps, the latest in the roll-call of distinguished Yorkshire addicts; academics such as Hilary Beckles, Richard Cashman, Boria Majumdar, Ric Sissons and Jack Williams: these and many more are prolonging a long and noble line. Better yet, they have branched out and chilled out. At last, cricket has a multinational, multi-octave, multifaceted and distinctly *modern* voice, less constrained by reverence, formality, tradition and nostalgia, more willing to analyse the game's global and political dimensions, embrace its often dizzying pace of change, locate its funny bone and plot its future. Progress by any other name. Stephen Moss should be satisfied.

NOTES

1 Scyld Berry, *Cricket Wallah: With England in India 1981–2* (London: Hodder and Stoughton, 1982).
2 Rob Steen (ed.), *The New Ball Volume 5 – The Write Stuff* (London: Sports Books Direct, 2001), p. 15.
3 Stephen Moss, 'A Century of Cricket Writing', *Wisden Cricketers' Almanack 2000* (London: John Wisden, 2000), p. 30.
4 Ibid., p. 31.
5 Steen, *The New Ball Volume 5 – The Write Stuff*, p. 63.
6 Ibid.
7 Frank Keating, *High, Wide and Handsome* (London: Collins Willow, 1986), p. 209.
8 David Foot, 'Caddick's Nine Wickets Demolishes Lancashire', *Guardian*, 15 May 1993.
9 David Foot, 'Zaheer Abbas' in Matthew Engel (ed.), *The Guardian Book of Cricket* (London: Pavilion Books, 1986), p. 233.
10 Rob Steen, 'The Writer's Tale' in *This Sporting Life – Cricket* (Devon: David & Charles, 1999), p. 105.
11 David Foot, 'Somerset Summers of Dog Collars and Cricket Whites', *Guardian*, 15 May 2009.
12 David Foot, 'Wally Hammond's Sad Reprise Was One of Cricket's Saddest Judgments', *Guardian*, 24 June 2009.
13 Ibid.
14 Matthew Engel, *Sportswriter's Eye* (London: Macdonald Queen Anne Press, 1989), p. 80.
15 Alastair McLellan, 'The Uneasy Figurehead' in Alistair McLellan (ed.), *Nothing Sacred – The New Cricket Culture* (London: Two Heads Publishing, 1996), p. 166.
16 Ibid., p. 175.

17 Martin Johnson, 'Official: Australia's Aura is Over', *Daily Telegraph*, 2 September 2009.
18 Charles Fortune, *The MCC Tour of South Africa 1956–57* (London: Harrap, 1957), p. 247.
19 John Nauright, *Sport, Cultures, and Identities in South Africa* (Leicester University Press, 1997), p. 133.
20 R. S. Whitington, *Simpson's Safari* (London: Heinemann, 1967), p. 133.
21 Timothy Arlott, *John Arlott – A Memoir* (London: Andre Deutsch, 1994), p. 71.
22 Ibid., pp. 166–67.
23 Mike Marqusee, *Anyone But England* (London: Aurum, 2005), pp. 282–83.
24 Mike Marqusee, *War Minus the Shooting* (London: Mandarin, 1996), p. 2.
25 Gideon Haigh, *The Summer Game – Australia in Test Cricket 1949–71* (Melbourne: The Text Publishing Company, 1997), p. xi.
26 David Frith, *The Fast Men: A 200-Year Cavalcade of Speed Bowlers* (London: Corgi, 1977); *The Slow Men* (London: Allen & Unwin, 1984); *Bodyline Autopsy* (London: Aurum, 2002); *Silence of the Heart: Cricket Suicides* (Edinburgh: Mainstream, 2001).
27 Rahul Bhattacharya, *Pundits From Pakistan* (New Delhi: Picador, 2005), p. 64.
28 Alastair McLellan, 'The Cricinfo Story', *The New Ball Volume 6* (London: Sports Books Direct, 2001), p. 150.
29 Luke Alfred, *Lifting the Covers – The Inside Story of South African Cricket* (Claremont, South Africa: Spearhead, 2001), p. 176.
30 Michael Atherton, 'Time for Pietersen to Get in Touch With His Swaggering Former Self', *The Times*, 13 January 2010.
31 Michael Atherton, 'Ntini's Absence Raises Awkward Questions', *The Times*, 14 January 2010.

17

STEPHEN WAGG AND JON GEMMELL

Cricket and international politics

The first agreed rules of modern cricket were laid down in the 1720s. This makes it, effectively, the only modern sport to be established in a pre-nationalist age. For much of its history cricket has been seen as the quirky and defining game both of the English and of the British Empire. While historians divide over whether cricket was an element in some civilising mission on the part of the imperial power or whether it was simply adopted by colonial people, it is clear that the inhabitants of contemporary India, Australia, Barbados, Bangladesh and elsewhere were playing cricket long before these territories were recognised as nations. As an international sport, cricket's present is defined by its imperial past. Ten nations qualify to play Test cricket. One is England; the other nine are all former British colonies – three of which (Australia, South Africa and New Zealand) were established as semi-autonomous dominions between 1901 and 1910. These countries all had substantial native populations, but exclusively 'white' governments. Formally constituted international cricket dates from this period: the Imperial Cricket Conference came into being in 1909, with England, South Africa and Australia its only members. Test matches, it was decreed, should be those solely involving the representative elevens of these three countries. (New Zealand, the third cricket-playing dominion, was allowed to compete in Test matches from 1930 onward.) The word 'politics' rarely, if ever, entered the discourse of cricket in these times. This was essentially for two reasons: first, the convention, which was to endure until the early 1980s, that politics – here interpreted broadly to mean affairs of state – and sport should not mix, and second, because both cricket and the empire were, like the monarchy, seen in British ruling circles as being 'above politics' – that's to say, not matters for contention.[1]

Cricket certainly played its part in the emergence to nationhood of former British colonies. The first white Australian tour to England in 1878, where they beat MCC, helped to build a national self-confidence among the colonists. The Federation was still twenty-three years away, wrote Chris Harte, 'but independence of the mind had possibly just occurred'.[2] By 1895, the Australians competed in the 'national' colours of green and gold of the gum tree and wattle, and as early as 1878 had carried bags emblazoned with the 'Australian Eleven' on them. 'It was the teams we sent to England in the 1870s', wrote the novelist David Malouf, 'that first established us, in British eyes, as a single nation, long before we had made the move to official nationhood.'[3] The South Africans, too, wore symbols of nationhood such as the greenish-bronze caps embroidered with the letters 'SA' for their first Test against England in 1889, and the striped green and gold with the Springbok emblem on their first visit to England in 1894 before their amalgam into the Union of South Africa in 1910. The national project in the Caribbean, where cricket fused with politics and a collective identity, has few parallels in sport history. In 1886, a West Indian team (made up of four players from Demerara, three from Barbados and six from Jamaica) made a tour of the United States and Canada. 'It was', according to Richard D. E. Burton, 'only when they saw their cricket team in combat with that of their English colonial masters that Jamaicans, Barbadians, Trinidadians and Guyanese came to see themselves as *West Indians* possessing a common historical, cultural and political identity.'[4] For much of the twentieth century the West Indies cricket team was a flagship for West Indian nationalism[5] and the nationalist movement powered the campaign to have a black cricketer appointed as its captain – a campaign that gained momentum after West Indies beat England for the first time in England (at Lord's in 1950). After a successful series in Australia in 1961, the Trinidadian C. L. R. James commented that 'clearing their way with bat and ball, West Indians ... made a public entry into the comity of nations'.[6]

The first major intrusion of 'politics' upon the peaceable transaction of international cricket was the fabled 'Bodyline' tour of Australia by England in the winter of 1932–33. England's bowlers had been instructed to use 'leg-theory' (aiming at the batter's body) in order to inhibit the Australian batters, especially the prolific Don Bradman. This strategy was framed by MCC officials, including tour manager Pelham Warner, and carried out by England captain Douglas Jardine. Australian crowds, players and administrators were incensed at the tactic and the Australian Cricket Board cabled Lord's in protest. The Governor of South Australia, Sir Alexander Hore-Ruthven, J. H. Thomas, the Secretary of State for the Dominions, and the Australian Prime Minister J. A. Lyons all became involved.[7] Enflaming Australian nationalism was the last thing the British government wanted. It had recently negotiated the Ottawa trading agreements, introducing a system of Imperial Preference. The Australian government, who were concerned about possible effects on British conversion loans and already poor agricultural prices, sought to counter those who blamed the 'Mother Country' for Australia's predicament in the global depression. MCC, under pressure from both governments and now fearful that Australia would refuse to tour England in 1934, sought to apportion blame to the ex-miner Harold Larwood rather than Winchester College old-boy Jardine. The angry fast bowler refused to make an apology, and never played for England again.[8] Relations between England and Australia are said to have remained strained until the Second World War.

In the post-war era, the cricket match has been utilised as a means to express political feeling. There have been four major disturbances in the Caribbean, each seemingly triggered off by an umpiring decision but each with a strong political undercurrent: a bottle-throwing riot, for example, followed Britain's suspension of the constitution in British Guiana in 1953. Other incidents occurred in 1960, 1968 and 1978. A Test match between Pakistan and England was cancelled in 1969 when protestors stormed the pitch in protest at Pakistan's military dictatorship. White South African cricketers walked off at Kingsmead in 1971 to protest against their government's stand on apartheid, whilst Andy Flower and Henry Olonga exploited Zimbabwe's hosting of the World Cup in 2003 to condemn a 'lack of democracy' at home.

Cricket provides an ideal platform for political protest considering its longevity of contest compared to other sports, that its most popular form is between nations, and that these nations are all linked through their former membership of the British Empire. Issues of cricket and international politics have arisen in relation to virtually every Test-playing country during the postcolonial period. One of the first and most significant of these occurred in 1968; it concerned England, South Africa and the emergent international politics of 'race'.

The D'Oliveira Affair

In February of 1960, the British Conservative Prime Minister, Harold Macmillan, made a speech to the South African parliament in Cape Town in which he talked of a 'wind of change' blowing across the continent of Africa. The speech was a thinly veiled suggestion to the country's white Afrikaner government that they abandon their policy of state racism known as 'apartheid'. Under apartheid, South Africa's huge black African majority was severely restricted in its capacity to earn, travel outside designated areas or associate with whites. With the United Nations now condemning racism and likely to be swelled in number by newly independent 'Third

World' countries, Macmillan feared that an unreconstructed South Africa would become an international pariah, since undue support by 'the West' for an openly racist regime would persuade former colonies to side with the Soviet Union in the Cold War. The South African government, however, was intransigent and, during the 1960s, sport rapidly became a key weapon in the growing international opposition to apartheid – the threat of boycotts, for example, prevented 'white' South Africa competing in the Olympics of 1964 and 1968. English cricket administrators, their international game rooted in the white dominions and their sympathies reflexively with the planters and mine owners of southern Africa, were slow to appreciate these developments.

In 1960, Basil D'Oliveira, a cricketer born in Cape Town in 1931 and designated as 'coloured' under apartheid classification, migrated to England. He became a British citizen and began to play for England in 1966. He played the final Test of the English summer of 1968 (against Australia) and scored 158, apparently making certain his selection for the forthcoming tour of his homeland, South Africa. A furore broke out in the British press when he was not selected. D'Oliveira was subsequently chosen for the tour when a player originally selected dropped out; the South African government then intervened to cancel the tour.[9] Unperturbed, MCC invited South Africa to tour England in 1970. A pressure group called Stop the Seventy Tour immediately formed and promised to bring disruption to any match the tourists might play. In May 1970, the Home Secretary, James Callaghan, formally requested that MCC call off the tour on the grounds that he could not guarantee public order. Two things are significant about this passage in the game's history. One is that, in international competition, South Africa had indeed become the pariah that Harold Macmillan had foreseen and state racism could no longer be dismissed as part of the 'politics' that must be kept out of sport. The more pragmatic and politically astute among MCC administrators will have realised that to maintain its link with white South Africa would be to jeopardise Test cricket with the West Indies and the Indian subcontinent, where apartheid South Africa was becoming a lightning rod for postcolonial anti-racist politics. The other is that English cricket was beginning to be outdone in international competition and MCC was looking to recruit England players from outside the UK. They now turned the ostracising of apartheid South Africa to their own advantage and D'Oliveira was followed into the England team by a series of white South Africans, notably Tony Greig (debut 1972), Allan Lamb (debut 1982) and Robin Smith (debut 1988).

Politics and partition: cricket on the Asian subcontinent

Between the mid eighteenth century and the mid nineteenth, India was ruled by the East India Company, whose responsibilities were assumed by the British parliament in 1858. The subsequent 'British Raj' lasted until 1947, when independence was granted. India is a vast country and the Raj could not have been sustained by the threat of force alone: the Indian nobility was co-opted and collaborated with the British occupier. This frequently entailed the embracing of elite English culture. Indian princes often sent their sons to English public schools and many relished English sports – especially cricket, a game at which a small number of them represented the 'Mother Country'.

The system that had prolonged princely rule was, according to nationalist leader M. K. Gandhi, 'perhaps the greatest blot on British rule in India'.[10] This ancient aristocracy offered little to the national project, and their influence on both politics and cricket declined following independence. The government of postcolonial India would be founded on the Westminster model of parliamentary democracy, universal suffrage and freedom of speech and of the press. Its politics was dominated by the Congress Party, whose leader, Jawaharlal Nehru, was a secular nationalist and modernist. Nehru also took steps to incorporate the 'Untouchables' and other disadvantaged groups into an inclusive new India.

Pakistan, by contrast to Mother India, is a state defined from its inception by little other than its dominant religion, and has a sparse history of democratic rule – it has been governed for much of its existence by military dictatorship. From the outset Pakistan developed an identity crisis. It was hastily created out of the turmoil of partition and was so unprepared that the government did not even have any headed notepaper.[11] Few politicians had any experience in the affairs of state, and a territorial agreement saw East Bengal separated from the rest of Pakistan by 1,000 miles. Punjabis, Sindhis, Pathans and Balochis were urged to relinquish their historical identities and become Pakistani, ushering the new state into a modern world in which provincial division, feudalism and tribal rule would be surpassed by a diffusion of people into a new project. As with many postcolonial experiments, it failed. Fortunately Pakistan's leader Mohammad Jinnah was a cricketing enthusiast, and a quadrangular tournament in Karachi was launched and the sport promoted from schools upwards. Cricket helped to put Pakistan on the map. Test cricketer Hanif Mohammad commented after their victory against England at the Oval in 1954: 'It was a glorious moment for all of us ... The win gave Pakistan a visible identity. Not many had known about Pakistan until then.'[12]

From its inception, the Pakistani state has had a history of friction with India and the two countries first went to war in 1947, the year of their independence. When partition first took place, however, it was hoped that it would not affect cricket. The tour to Australia in 1947–48 was that of a team selected from an undivided India. However, the violence that accompanied separation ensured that not only would India and Pakistan never compete as a single entity, but that they would become intense rivals, though the friendships established in pre-partition times ensured early support for each other. The Pakistan team toured India in 1952 and the series was played in a spirit of comradeship, as it was when India reciprocated by touring Pakistan in 1955. By 1960, however, when Pakistan's cricketers toured India there were small but perceptible signs of a new politics of cricket in the two nations: in Pakistan, civilian and military politicians became increasingly involved in the administration of the national side. Between 1954 and 1963, Mohammad Ali Bogra, Iskander Mizra (successive Governor Generals of Pakistan) and General Muhammad Ayub Khan acted as president of the BCCP. Thereafter, the BCCP constitution recognised the head of state as its patron. Meanwhile, in India the national team captain, Vijay Merchant, complained that national prestige was now too important a factor in Test cricket: the series was characterised by defensive cricket and all five matches were drawn. Following India's 2–1 victory in the 1952–53 series, two five-Test series were played out without a victory for either side. A 'let's not lose to the enemy' attitude now hampered any real contest and delayed declarations and resisted run chases made for dull cricket.

Zulfikar Ali Bhutto's Pakistan People's Party (PPP) triumphed in the 1970 general election. However, in East Pakistan, 90 per cent of votes were cast for Sheikh Mujibur Rahman's Awami League, which had a socialist programme of nationalisation and was opposed to Pakistan's American alliance. The Pakistani army refused to let Rahman form a government and invaded East Pakistan in 1971. India intervened and East Pakistan seceded from Pakistan to form Bangladesh. Many cricketing facilities were damaged in the war of independence, and the national stadium fell into a state of disrepair. Following the murder of Rahman, in a coup in 1975, the military took control and prioritised cricket in a restoration programme that sought to win popular support for the dictatorship and promote the national identity of Bangladesh. This initiative was supported by an MCC tour in 1976–77, in which the tourists won only one of the four matches to be played on matting, while the other three were drawn. The use of cricket as a channel for national optimism was rewarded by a crowd of 40,000 for the three-day contest in Dacca.

Cricket and conflict on the subcontinent

The last forty years have seen two vital political developments on the Asian subcontinent, both of which have crucially affected cricket: one is the rise of populist politics – usually in the form of appeals to one religious faction or another and attendant calls for 'ethnic cleansing' – and the other is the opening up of economic life to global forces.

In India, the first premiership of Nehru's daughter Indira Gandhi (1966–77) was marked by populist appeals to the peasantry over the heads of the land-owners. Rising unemployment, and slum and sterilisation programmes antagonised India's poor and its Muslim minority. In the 1980s, leading political parties abandoned secularism and began to make open appeals to voters on the basis of ethnic and religious affiliation. However, this strategy encouraged separatist movements – notably in the Punjab, where Sikhs were campaigning for their own state; Gandhi was shot dead by two of her own Sikh guards in 1984.[13] In 1992, amid a mass mobilisation against Muslims, the ancient mosque at Ayodhya in Uttar Pradesh was destroyed by a mob. Subsequent years saw the steady rise of the BJP (Bharatiya Janata Party or 'Indian People's Party'), a Hindu nationalist and openly anti-Muslim party; it formed India's government between 1998 and 2004. In 2002, in the province of Gujarat, nearly 800 Muslims died in rioting after a train carrying Hindus was stopped and burned, apparently by Muslim attackers.

India began opening up to the world economy during the premiership of Rajiv Gandhi, but this process was accelerated during the 1990s in the wake of the Gulf War of 1991, which raised both oil prices and government debt. Loans from the World Bank and the International Monetary Fund (IMF) arrived in return for cuts in public spending. A period of economic growth followed, India's western and southern states became very prosperous and the western cities of Bangalore (the heart of the Indian computer industry) and Mumbai (site of the Bollywood film studios) came to typify what Barbara and Thomas Metcalf have described as a 'consumer-driven [India] nearly indistinguishable from that of Western Europe or the United States'.[14] Its wealthy middle class is estimated to be around 150 million in number, but India's poor, living on the equivalent of a dollar a day, is twice that.[15] Moreover, India, along with Pakistan, had detonated a nuclear bomb in the late 1990s, giving a feeling of national virility to its ruling elite and globally minded middle class. Stanley Wolpert captures the contradictions of contemporary India thus:

> So the giant wheel of India's fortune and misery rolls on, now reflecting the wealth and wonders of globalised prosperity that bring salesmen from the world's strongest and richest nations to New Delhi, Mumbai, Kolkata and Bangalore

offering their most modern consumer goods of peace and deadliest weapons of war to a billion heirs of Mahatma Gandhi and Jawaharlal, while leaving the poorest third ... to scavenge for rotting leftover scraps of food, drinking Mother Ganga's waters, green with the ashes of countless generations.[16]

The consolations for that poorest third are chiefly ethnic identity – often entailing an increasingly embattled religious faith – and cricket. For Mihir Bose, cricket provides 'valuable distraction from their appalling poverty and struggle to survive'.[17] (In 2002, Syed Saleem Shahzad wrote similarly of Pakistan: 'In a country as ethnically diverse as Pakistan, it has been said that the two things that bind society together are the Urdu language and cricket.'[18])

Cricket can act as a means through which the animosity between the two nuclear protagonists is played out. Contests were suspended between 1961 and 1978, a period in which the two nations fought two wars with each other, and in the 1990s, when Pakistan was accused of sponsoring cross-border terrorism in Kashmir. Relations were resumed in 2004 due to a process initiated by the countries' governments rather than the respective cricket boards.

'As globalisation strides forward', commented Mike Marqusee, 'the search for national identity becomes ever more desperate and ever more dominated by hostility to perceived national enemies, both within and without the country's borders.'[19] Whilst the BJP-influenced Indian regime permitted football and table-tennis contests, they banned cricket matches against Pakistan. 'We see cricket not as just a game', said the Sports Minister, 'but as a symbol of the nation's sentiments.'[20] When a Pakistan tour of India was finally permitted in 1999, it was accompanied by fervent and hostile nationalist threats from the Indian far right, who opposed all links to Pakistan because of the conflict over Kashmir. Pitches were dug up, the Indian Cricket Board's offices were attacked and further violence threatened. The far-right Hindu nationalist party Shiv Sena, now part of the ruling coalition in New Delhi, opposed the tour and called for public vigilance to ensure that all Indian Muslims were supporting India. 'It is the duty of Indian Muslims', argued their leader Bal Thackeray, 'to prove they are not Pakistanis. I want to see them with tears in their eyes every time India loses to Pakistan.'[21] After more disruption at Eden Gardens during the Kolkata (formerly Calcutta) Test (capacity 100,000) the ground was cleared and the players finished the game in front of an empty house.

New growth areas: commercialism and terror

The combined effects on cricket culture of the growing prosperity of a swathe of Indian society and the increased mayhem on the subcontinent wrought in the name of religion have been considerable. The growth of the Indian economy and its business elite became the basis for a challenge to English hegemony in international cricket administration. The International Cricket Conference (renamed in 1965 as successor organisation to the Imperial Cricket Conference) was reconstituted in 1989 as the International Cricket Council, and in 1994 established a separate commercial arm based in Monaco. In 2005, it moved its main offices from Lord's in north London, the historic centre of the game's governance, to Dubai in the United Arab Emirates, a non-Test-playing country. By then powerful figures from Indian commerce had begun to wield greater influence within the ICC, evidenced notably by the election of the Calcutta construction magnate Jagmohan Dalmiya to the presidency in 1996. This growing hegemony was strengthened, in the opinion of many cricket people, by the awarding of Test-playing status to Bangladesh, a presumed voting ally for India, in 2000. In the 2006 Spirit of Cricket lecture at Lord's, former New Zealand Test player Martin Crowe claimed that Bangladesh (and Zimbabwe) were 'being kept on the international stage for political reasons'. He also referred angrily to 'the way the Asian subcontinent has taken a stranglehold on world cricket'.[22]

India's grip on world cricket's purse strings has been strengthened by the development of the sport for Indian television, and recently the rise of the IPL, both of which are dealt with elsewhere in this volume. Several national cricket boards have raised concerns with the IPL about possible conflicts over player development and availability, though most have succumbed to the lure of the rupee, most notably Sri Lanka, who in return for a loan from the BCCI called off their tour of England for May 2009 because it clashed with the IPL.

During this same period Pakistan has descended further into religious–political chaos. Despite its initial opposition to General Pervez Musharraf's regime, the United States supported the military dictatorship largely to bulwark its purported 'War on Terror'. This war was waged chiefly against the Muslim Taliban in Afghanistan, a group that had received US funding during the Cold War and Pakistani political support and military training thereafter. Since most Muslim terror groups operated from inside Pakistan, the country was now apparently the central locus both of the problem and of the attempt to combat it. Formally, cricket had remained in the hands of the government: Musharraf, like previous military rulers, chaired the Pakistani Cricket Board. But a series of attacks made Pakistan unviable for top-class cricket. Notably, in May 2002, a car bomb was detonated in front of the Karachi hotel where the New Zealand team were staying, killing thirteen people. New Zealand called off the tour within hours of the attack. Recourse to neutral venues was increased. Pakistan now played a home series against

Australia partly in Sri Lanka and partly in Sharjah, after Australia's refusal to tour over security concerns. In 2008, a spate of suicide bombings and a terror attack on Mumbai, which killed 170 people, deepened the crisis and, in March 2009, a bus carrying the Sri Lankan cricket team was fired on in Lahore. Seven people died and a number of players were wounded. The attack in India resulted in the second IPL tournament being relocated to South Africa. Since the early 2000s, Pakistan cricketers have therefore played most of their international cricket on foreign soil (Sharjah, Colombo, Dubai, Toronto, England) and will not play at home in the foreseeable future.

Cricket, the postcolonial and the politics of boycott: the case of Zimbabwe

Southern Rhodesia, as Zimbabwe was then called, became a self-governing colony within the British Empire in 1923. The white British settlers who governed this colony had been attracted by the mineral deposits (it is, for example, the world's largest producer of platinum) and the farmland, where the main crops have been tobacco, maize and soya. The white Rhodesian government declared unilateral independence from Britain in 1965 and proclaimed itself a republic in 1970. A prolonged guerrilla war fought by the two principal political factions of the black majority – the Zimbabwe African People's Union (ZAPU) and the Zimbabwe African National Union (ZANU) – resulted in independence in 1980. After much strife ZAPU and ZANU merged in 1988 and the country has been governed since independence by Robert Mugabe, former leader of ZANU and once feared by the British government to be a Marxist. Since the early 1990s, Zimbabwe has seen increased political unrest provoked by government repression, massive inflation and the compulsory redistribution of arable land to black Zimbabweans.

Cricket has been played in Zimbabwe since the 1890s. While it has remained predominantly a white game, it grew in strength after independence, and Zimbabwe was granted Test status in 1992; the country's first black player, Henry Olonga, made his debut three years later. In 2004, a dispute roughly parallel to the political wrangle over land broke out over political intimidation and selection of the national cricket team. The chief executive of the now overtly politicised Zimbabwe Cricket Union demanded more black players. National captain Heath Streak and a number of other white players in the national side resigned.

With Streak's resignation, increased talk of human rights abuses by Mugabe's regime and England due to tour Zimbabwe in 2004, a press campaign for a cricket boycott of Zimbabwe was mounted in England. The New

Zealand government let it be known that a Zimbabwean team, due there the following year, would not be welcome. In the British *Daily Telegraph*, Donald Trelford summarised a report by the ECB as saying 'that Robert Mugabe's regime is so far beyond the pale in terms of torture, oppression and denial of the rule of law – a view shared by the Commonwealth, incidentally, to which nearly all cricket-playing countries belong – that for England to go there would be seen as condoning or endorsing evil'.[23] Zimbabwe remained an issue in the cricket world: England captain South Africa-born Andrew Strauss, for example, told a large audience at Lord's in June of 2008 that, should Robert Mugabe remain in power, several England players would not be prepared to play against Zimbabwe the following year.[24] However, Mugabe remains head of state in Zimbabwe and commander of the country's armed forces, notwithstanding a power-sharing agreement in 2008 with his principal political opponents, the Movement for Democratic Change (MDC), and there has been no boycott.

The controversy demonstrated a number of postcolonial realities, many of them identified by Mike Marqusee, doyen of writers on the politics of cricket: 'the hypocrisies on all sides', he wrote, 'defied enumeration'.[25] It was now the English cricket authorities, along with the Conservative Party and the right-wing press, all former champions of the belief that politics should not intrude upon sport, who were propounding the opposite view. Moreover, having been willing to sustain friendly relations with a white national cricket board that practised racial discrimination, they now proposed to suspend relations with a black cricket board for apparently doing the same thing.

A similar position was adopted by the African National Congress, whose supporters, in the days of apartheid, had called for 'no normal sport in an abnormal society'. Now, as the government of South Africa, Zimbabwe's main trading partner, they declined to intervene. They appeared happy to support Mugabe's contention that Zimbabwe's problem was simply with the outmoded colonial arrogance of the British. But, in the postcolonial world, Zimbabwe was beholden not to Britain, but to institutions such as the IMF and the World Bank who, for all countries, had made often drastic cuts in public spending the condition of any loan. Mugabe had made the necessary cuts (helping to worsen the poverty in Zimbabwe, of which so many were now complaining) and the call of the MDC, the Zimbabwean trade-union movement and human-rights organisations for wider sanctions against Mugabe had had no response. Indeed, part of the ECB's case for refusing a boycott was that 300 British companies still traded with Zimbabwe and British Airways flew regular flights to the capital, Harare.[26]

The political realities of life in the global economy were further driven home in Dubai and London. At the ICC, the 'Asian bloc' voted against expelling Zimbabwe (although Zimbabwe did agree to secede temporarily from Test cricket in 2004) and the ECB were reminded of their legal–financial liabilities were they to default on any fixture. This enabled the 'New' Labour government to take a moral stance on the issue while stressing that it had no powers to intervene.[27]

Some saw this as political hypocrisy – calling for action in the full knowledge that it would not be taken. Others wondered why there was no talk of boycotting Pakistan, governed throughout the hue and cry over Mugabe by a military dictatorship. In Pakistan itself, Test cricketer turned politician Imran Khan took the argument of double standards further and suggested a boycott of England:

> … how can it be that England is obsessing over the morality of playing cricket in Zimbabwe at precisely the same time that it – along with the United States – is leading the world to the brink of a grossly unjust and potentially catastrophic war against Iraq? Doesn't Mr Blair's acute sensitivity to the plight of the Zimbabwean people look just a little ironic next to his apparent readiness to vaporise thousands of Iraqis? A little rich, even?[28]

Cricket and globalisation: the improbable case of China

The People's Republic of China was established in 1949 under the rule of the Communist Party. Between the late 1960s and the late 1970s party chairman Mao Zedong promoted the Great Proletarian Cultural Revolution, a peasant-based anti-elitist movement aimed at undermining China's emergent class of managers and mandarins. Following Mao's death in 1976, China embraced capitalism, while maintaining Communist Party rule. As the world's only command capitalist economy with an un-unionised workforce subject to government instruction, China became a magnet for foreign capital and, by the turn of the twenty-first century, it was a leading economic power. Like India, China has a huge population (around 1.3 billion people), a thriving market for consumer goods such as mobile phones, and a growing middle class with significant disposable income. Unlike India, but like most countries outside the old British Empire, it has no cricket tradition to speak of: cricket in China had hitherto been largely confined to expatriates. What China has in common with all societies administered by a communist party is a strong, government-sponsored sport culture and a policy to pursue success in international sports competitions. A clear consummation of this policy was seen at the summer Olympic Games of 2008, staged in the Chinese capital Beijing, at which Chinese competitors won fifty-one gold medals, the most of any nation.

China had received regular visits from representatives of the ACC, anxious to promote the game in the region, but, until 2003, the Chinese authorities had shown no more than polite interest. They now embraced it, however, joining the ACC in 2004, becoming an affiliate member of the ICC a year later and devising a five-year plan for cricket development. This plan is not, as might have been expected, for specialist academies, but for a full-scale integration of cricket into the curriculum of Chinese schools – 150 in the first instance – across nine cities: Beijing, Shanghai, Shenyang, Dalian, Guangzhou, Shenzhen, Chongqing, Tianjin and Jinan.[29] The Chinese Cricket Association's goal is to have 15,000 players by 2009, 60,000 by 2012 and 150,000 by 2020. It is believed that China hope to have a team good enough to do well in cricket's World Cup, and perhaps even to gain Test-playing status, by 2020, whilst the prospect of challenging India at Test level provides the ultimate motivation.

A number of factors lie behind this move. In an improbable invocation of Victorian values, government spokespeople have extolled the character-building virtues of cricket, which in China has been given the name 'shen shi yun dong' ('the noble game'). It is also stressed that cricket relies more on skill and strategy than on strength, making it more suitable to the average Chinese physique than, say, rugby. It is also seen as a game offering equal opportunities to males and females. But there is, of course, more to it than that. The Chinese government seeks markets and regional prestige. This helps to explain its huge investment in the Caribbean for the 2007 World Cup. Of the eight venues constructed or refurbished for the tournament, China assisted in the construction of five, providing more than 1,000 workers and more than $140 million. Chinese aid also paid for roads, schools, hospitals and other infrastructure improvements in recent years, earning the allegiance of many nations in the process.[30]

As well as overseas markets and influence China will have an eye on the communications revolution evolving in neighbouring India. As Ian McCubbin, a lawyer specialising in Chinese–Australian affairs and advisor to the China Central TV network, said recently: 'I don't think the success of cricket in China depends on having hundreds of thousands of people playing it in the park on a Saturday afternoon. I think it depends on promoting it as a television product. Look at India, and the commercialisation of cricket there. There is no reason why that can't happen in China. It's a growing economy, it's a changing economy, but it's also an economy that is becoming an avid consumer of western culture.'[31] This view was affirmed in the business magazine *Forbes*:

An estimated 100 million Chinese watched the basketball competition at the Athens Olympics, so there is a latent market to be tapped. China would be an attractive market for the ICC's official sponsors, LG Electronics, Pepsico, Hutchison, HeroHonda, India Oil and Cable & Wireless. The ACC already has HSBC, Standard Chartered and Indian Oil sponsoring its regional tournaments. Other potential sponsors include companies like General Motors, which already spends millions of dollars sponsoring golf in China.[32]

Conclusion

Cricket emerged from myriad forms of bat and ball games played out when the demands of agricultural life allowed. It became codified and institutionalised in England and exploited as a means to promote a certain way of life with the notion of authority, power and knowing one's place at its heart. Thus, cricket was always political, and, through its unravelling via the British Empire, it was always international. Because it has been so central to the nationalist project, contemporary cricket has been subsumed by politics, especially in the developing world, where sport has provided the level playing field that economic and military might could not. This means that in Pakistan, Sri Lanka, Zimbabwe and India governments are formally involved in the running of cricket and regularly intervene. In South Africa, the African National Congress has demanded the selection at Test level of more black cricketers, while failing, as its critics might argue, to effect the radical social changes they promised before taking office. In the Caribbean, individual governments of countries such as Trinidad and Tobago are currently pressing individual Boards on the possibility of playing international cricket independently of the West Indies – a move that many feel would be at the cost of collective strength. The governments of Australia, Britain and New Zealand meanwhile continue to provide guidelines as to whom their respective teams should play. But, pitted against this system of institutional politics lies the might of mammon, especially in the case of the IPL and the potential influence of China (and possibly the USA). In the era of globalised networks the future of cricket will be determined by numerous conflicting interests, where the primary interest lies, in many cases, not in the aesthetics and longevity of the sport itself, nor, of course, in the nation-state.

NOTES

1 Mike Marqusee, *Anyone But England* (London: Aurum Press, 2005), pp. 74–75.
2 Chris Harte, *A History of Australian Cricket* (London: Andre Deutsch, 1993), p. 105.
3 Richard Williams, 'We Hate You England, We Do', *Guardian*, 28 October 2003.

4 Richard D. E. Burton, 'Cricket, Carnival and Street Culture in the Caribbean' in Hilary McD. Beckles and Brian Stoddart (eds.), *Liberation Cricket: West Indies Cricket Culture* (Manchester University Press, 1995), p. 89.

5 See Hilary McD. Beckles, *The Development of West Indies Cricket Volume 1: The Age of Nationalism* (London: Pluto Press, 1999).

6 C. L. R. James, *Beyond a Boundary* (London: Serpents Tail, 1994), p. 261.

7 Laurence Le Quesne, *The Bodyline Controversy* (London: Secker and Warburg, 1983), pp. 67–71.

8 See Duncan Hamilton, *Harold Larwood* (London: Quercus, 2009).

9 See Peter Oborne, *Basil D'Oliveira: Cricket and Controversy* (London: Sphere, 2005); Jon Gemmell, *The Politics of South African Cricket* (London: Routledge, 2004), pp. 146–54.

10 Charles and Sharada Dwivedi, *Lives of the Indian Princes* (London: Century Publishing, 1984), p. 18.

11 Scyld Berry, *A Cricket Odyssey: England on Tour, 1987–88* (London: Pavilion Books, 1988), p. 87.

12 Gideon Haigh, 'The Making of Epics', *CricInfo*, 2 October 2004, www.cricinfo. com/magazine/content/story/142119.html (accessed 31 March 2010).

13 Barbara Metcalf and Thomas Metcalf, *A Concise History of Modern India* (Cambridge University Press, 2006), pp. 254–60.

14 Ibid., p. 297.

15 Ibid., p. 286.

16 Stanley Wolpert, *A New History of India* (Oxford University Press, 2009), p. 497.

17 Mihir Bose, *A Maidan View: The Magic of Indian Cricket* (London: George Allen and Unwin, 1986), p. 41.

18 Syed Saleem Shahzad, 'It's Just Not Cricket Anymore in Pakistan', *Online Asian Times*, 29 June 2002, www.atimes.com/ind-pak/DF29Df03.html (accessed 13 March 2010).

19 Mike Marqusee, *War Minus the Shooting: A Journey Through South Asia During Cricket's World Cup* (London: Heinemann, 1996), p. 268.

20 Quoted in Ramachandra Guha, *A Corner of a Foreign Field: The Indian History of a British Sport* (London: Picador, 2002), p. 431.

21 David Hopps, 'The Game Neither Side Dare Lose', *Guardian*, 7 June 1999.

22 Martin Crowe, '2006 Cowdrey Lecture', www.lords.org/laws-and-spirit/spirit/ mcc-spirit-of-cricket-cowdrey-lecture/2006-cowdrey-lecture-full-text,1197,AR. html (accessed 21 March 2010).

23 Donald Trelford, 'ICC Will Have to Accept Anti-Mugabe Sentiment', *Daily Telegraph*, 16 February 2004, www.telegraph.co.uk/sport/cricket/2373198/ ICC-will-have-to-accept-anti-Mugabe-sentiment.html (accessed 14 March 2010).

24 'Strauss Hints Players Might Boycott Zimbabwe Matches', www.cricinfo.com/ england/content/story/354344.html, posted 11 June 2008 (accessed 14 March 2010).

25 Marqusee, *Anyone But England*, pp. 341–43.

26 Paul Kelso, 'Cricket Defies Call for Zimbabwe Boycott', *Guardian*, 15 January 2003, www.guardian.co.uk/uk/2003/jan/15/politics.cricket (accessed 28 March 2010).

27 'Blair Calls for Zimbabwe Cricket Tour Boycott', *Guardian*, 30 December 2002, www.guardian.co.uk/uk/2002/dec/30/politics.cricket (accessed 15 March 2010).

28 'Who's the Real Villain?', *Guardian*, 24 January 2003, www.guardian.co.uk/sport/2003/jan/24/cricket.iraq (accessed 15 March 2010).

29 http://en.wikipedia.org/wiki/China_national_cricket_team (accessed 16 March 2010).

30 Daniel Erikson and Paul Wander, 'China: Cricket "Champion"', American Dialogue, www.thedialogue.org/page.cfm?pageID=32&pubID=274 (accessed 21 March 2010).

31 'Australia Pushes China for Cricket', undated, http://stg.cricketnext.com/print/33446-13.html (accessed 16 March 2010).

32 Paul Maidment, 'China's Cracking Cricket', 10 March 2005, www.forbes.com/2005/09/30/china-india-cricket_cx_pm_1003chinacricket.html (accessed 16 March 2010).

FURTHER READING

Allen, D. R., *Arlott: The Authorised Biography*. London: HarperCollins 1994.
    ed., *Cricket on the Air: A Selection from Fifty Years of Radio Broadcasts*. London: BBC, 1985.
Allen, D. R. and David and Hubert Doggart, eds., *'A Breathless Hush …': The M.C.C. Anthology of Cricket Verse*. London: Methuen, 2004.
Allitt, P., 'English Cricket and Literature.' *The South Atlantic Quarterly* 95, 2 (1996): 385–435.
Appadurai, A., 'Playing with Modernity: The Decolonization of Indian Cricket.' In *Consuming Modernity: Public Culture in a South Asian World*, ed. C. A. Breckenridge, 23–48. Minneapolis: University of Minnesota Press, 1995.
Arlott, J., *Concerning Cricket: Studies of the Play and Players*. London: Longmans Green, 1949.
    Cricket: A Reader's Guide. Cambridge University Press, 1950.
    ed., *From Hambledon to Lord's: The Classics of Cricket*. London: Christopher Johnson, 1948.
    Jack Hobbs: Profile of 'The Master'. London: John Murray, 1981.
    ed., *My Favourite Cricket Stories*. London: Lutterworth Press, 1974.
    The Essential Arlott on Cricket, ed. D. Rayvern Allen. 1989. London: Fontana, 1991.
Bale, J., *Anti-Sport Sentiments in Literature: Batting for the Opposition*. Abingdon: Routledge, 2008.
    Landscapes of Modern Sport. Leicester University Press, 1994.
Bateman, A., *Cricket, Literature and Culture: Symbolising the Nation, Destabilising Empire*. Farnham: Ashgate, 2009.
Baucom, I., '"Put a Little English on it": CLR James and England's Field of Play.' In *Out of Place: Englishness, Empire and the Location of Identity*, 135–63. Princeton University Press, 1999.
Beckles, H., ed., *An Area of Conquest: Popular Democracy and West Indies Cricket Supremacy*. Jamaica: Ian Randle, 1994.
    ed., *A Spirit of Dominance: Cricket and Nationalism in the West Indies*. Jamaica: Canoe Press, 1998.
    The Development of West Indies Cricket, Volume 1: The Age of Nationalism. London: Pluto Press, 1998.
    The Development of West Indies Cricket, Volume 2: The Age of Globalization. London: Pluto Press, 1998.

Beckles, H. and B. Stoddart, eds., *Liberation Cricket: West Indies Cricket Culture.* Manchester University Press, 1995.

Berry, S., *A Cricket Odyssey: England on Tour, 1987–88.* London: Pavilion Books, 1988.

    Cricket Wallah: With England in India 1981–2. London: Hodder & Stoughton, 1982.

Birbalsingh, F., *The Rise of West Indian Cricket: From Colony to Nation.* St John's, Antigua: Hansib, 1996.

Birbalsingh, F. and C. Shiwcharan, *Indo-Westindian Cricket.* London: Hansib, 1988.

Birley, D., *A Social History of English Cricket.* London: Aurum, 1999.

    The Willow Wand: Some Cricket Myths Explored. 1979. London: Aurum, 2000.

Blunden, E., *Cricket Country.* 1944. London: Pavilion Books, 1985.

Bose, M., *A History of Indian Cricket.* London: Andre Deutsch, 2002.

    The Magic of Indian Cricket: Cricket and Society in India. Abingdon: Routledge, 2006.

Bradman, D., *Farewell to Cricket.* 1950. London: Pavilion Books, 1988.

    The Art of Cricket. 1958. Watsons Bay: Imprint Books, 1998.

Brearley, M., *The Art of Captaincy.* London: Hodder & Stoughton, 1985.

Bright-Holmes, J., ed., *Lord's and Commons: Cricket in Novels and Stories.* London: Andre Deutsch, 1988.

    ed., *The Joy of Cricket.* London: Secker & Warburg, 1984.

Brookes, C., *English Cricket: The Game and its Players through the Ages.* Newton Abbot: Reader's Union, 1978.

    His Own Man: The Life of Neville Cardus. London: Methuen, 1985.

Brown, S. and I. McDonald, eds., *The Bowling was Superfine: West Indian Writing and West Indian Cricket.* Leeds: Peepal Tree Press, 2010.

Cardus, N., *Australian Summer.* London: Jonathan Cape, 1937.

    Autobiography. London: Collins, 1947.

    Cricket. London: Longmans, 1930.

    Days in the Sun: A Cricketer's Book. London: Grant Richards, 1924.

    English Cricket. 1945. London: Prion, 1997.

    Good Days. London: Jonathan Cape, 1934.

    Second Innings. London: Collins, 1950.

    The Playfair Cardus. London: The Dickens Press, 1963.

Cashman, R., *"Ave a Go Yer Mug!": Australian Cricket Crowds from Larrikin to Ocker.* Sydney: Collins, 1984.

    Patrons, Players and the Crowd: The Phenomenon of Indian Cricket. New Delhi: Orient Longman, 1980.

Cashman, R., W. Franks, J. Maxwell, B. Stoddart, A. Weaver and R. Webster, eds., *The Oxford Companion to Australian Cricket.* Melbourne: Oxford University Press, 1996.

Constantine, L., *Cricket and I.* London: Philip Allan, 1933.

Cronin, M. and R. Holt, 'The Imperial Game in Crisis: English Cricket and Decolonisation.' In *British Culture & The End of Empire*, ed. Stuart Ward, 111–27. Manchester University Press, 2001.

Daniels, R., *Conversations with Cardus.* London: Victor Gollancz, 1976.

Davie, M. and S. Davie, eds., *The Faber Book of Cricket*. London: Faber & Faber, 1987.

De Selincourt, H., *The Cricket Match*. 1924. Oxford University Press, 1987.

The Game of the Season. 1931. Oxford University Press, 1982.

Dhondy, F., *C.L.R. James: Cricket, the Caribbean and World Revolution*. London: Weidenfeld & Nicolson, 2001.

Diawara, M., 'Englishness and Blackness: Cricket as Discourse on Colonialism.' *Callalloo* 13, 4 (Fall 1990): 830–44.

Dobbs, B., *Edwardians at Play: Sport 1890–1914*. London: Pelham Books, 1973.

Engel, M., *Sportswriter's Eye*. London: Macdonald Queen Press, 1989.

ed., *The Guardian Book of Cricket*. Harmondsworth: Penguin, 1986.

Farred, G., ed., *Rethinking C.L.R. James*. Oxford: Blackwell, 1996.

'"Victorian with the Rebel Seed": C.L.R. James, Postcolonial Intellectual.' *Social Text* 38 (1995): 21–38.

Fingleton, J., *Brightly Fades the Don*. London: Collins, 1949.

Cricket Crisis. London: Cassell, 1947.

Foot, D., *Fragments of Idolatory*. Bath: Fairfield Books, 2001.

Wally Hammond: The Reasons Why. London: Robson Books, 1998.

Frewin, L., ed., *The Poetry of Cricket – An Anthology*. London: Macdonald, 1964.

Frith, D., *Bodyline Autopsy*. 2002. London: Aurum, 2003.

Frith on Cricket. Ilkley: Great Northern Books, 2010.

Pageant of Cricket. London: Macmillan, 1987.

Silence of the Heart: Cricket Suicides. Edinburgh: Mainstream, 2001.

The Fast Men: A 200-Year Cavalcade of Speed Bowlers. London: Corgi, 1977.

The Golden Age of Cricket 1890–1914. Guildford: Lutterworth Press, 1978.

The Slow Men. London: Allen & Unwin, 1984.

Fry, C. B., *Life Worth Living: Some Phases of an Englishman*. 1939. London: Pavilion Books, 1986.

Gemmell, J., *The Politics of South African Cricket*. London: Routledge, 2004.

Gikandi, S., *Maps of Englishness: Writing Identity in the Culture of Colonialism*. New York: Columbia University Press, 1996.

Giulianotti, R., ed., *Sport and Modern Social Theorists*. Basingstoke: Palgrave Macmillan, 2004.

Green, B., *A History of Cricket*. London: Barrie & Jenkins, 1988.

ed., *The Cricket Addict's Archive*. London: Hamish Hamilton, 1977.

ed., *The Wisden Papers of Neville Cardus*. London: Stanley Paul, 1989.

Guha, R., *A Corner of a Foreign Field: The Indian History of a British Sport*. London: Picador, 2002.

'Cricket and Politics in Colonial India.' *Past and Present* 161 (1998): 155–90.

'Cricket, Caste, Community, Colonialism: The Politics of a Great Game.' *The International Journal of the History of Sport* 14, 1 (April 1997): 174–83.

ed., *The Picador Book of Cricket*. London: Picador, 2001.

Haigh, G., *Silent Revolutions: Writings on Cricket*. London: Aurum, 2007.

The Big Ship: Warwick Armstrong and the Making of Modern Cricket. London: Aurum, 2003.

The Cricket War: The Inside Story of Kerry Packer's World Series Cricket. 1993. Melbourne University Press, 2007.

The Green and Golden Age: Writings on Modern Cricket. London: Aurum, 2008.

The Summer Game: Cricket and Australia in the 50s and 60s. Sydney: ABC Books, 2006.

Haigh, G. and D. Frith, *Inside Story: Unlocking Australian Cricket's Archives.* Sydney: News Customs Publishing, 2007.

Hamilton, D., *Harold Larwood.* London: Quercus, 2009.

Harte, C., *A History of Australian Cricket.* London: Andre Deutsch, 1993.

Henry, P. and P. Buhle, eds., *C.L.R. James's Caribbean.* London: Macmillan, 1992.

Hill, J., 'Reading the Stars: Towards a Post-Modern Approach to Sports History.' *Sports Historian* 14 (May 1994): 45–55.

Sport and the Literary Imagination: Essays in History, Literature and Sport. Oxford: Peter Lang, 2006.

Sport, Leisure & Culture in Twentieth-Century Britain. Basingstoke: Palgrave, 2002.

Holt, R., 'Cricket and Englishness: The Batsman as Hero.' *Journal of the History of Sport* 13, 1 (1996): 48–70.

Sport and the British: A Modern History. Oxford: Clarendon Press, 1989.

Hornung, E. W., *Raffles: The Amateur Cracksman.* 1899. Harmondsworth: Penguin, 2003.

Hughes, T., *Tom Brown's Schooldays.* 1857. Oxford University Press, 1989.

Hughson, J., D. Inglis and M. Free, *The Uses of Sport: A Critical Study.* Abingdon: Routledge, 2005.

Hutchins, B., *Don Bradman: Challenging the Myth.* Port Melbourne: Cambridge University Press, 2002.

James, C. L. R., *A Majestic Innings: Writings on Cricket.* London: Aurum, 2006.

Beyond a Boundary. 1963. Various editions.

Cricket, ed. A. Grimshaw. London: Alison & Busby, 1986.

The C.L.R. James Reader, ed. A. Grimshaw. Oxford: Blackwell, 1992.

Jardine, D., *In Quest of the Ashes.* 1933. London: Methuen, 2005.

Kesavan, M., *Men in White: A Book of Cricket.* New Delhi: Penguin, 2007.

Kilburn, J. M., *In Search of Cricket.* 1937. London: Pavilion Books, 1990.

King, G., *The Hansie Cronje Story: An Authorised Biography.* Oxford: Monarch, 2007.

Lara, B., *Beating the Field: An Autobiography.* London: Partridge, 1995.

Macdonell, A. G., *England, Their England.* 1933. London: Picador, 1983.

Magazine, P., *Not Quite Cricket: The Explosive Story of How Bookmakers Influence the Game Today.* Harmondsworth: Penguin, 2000.

Majumdar, B., *Cricket in Colonial India, 1780–1947.* Abingdon: Routledge, 2008.

Lost Histories of Indian Cricket: Battles Off the Pitch. Abingdon: Routledge, 2006.

The Illustrated History of Indian Cricket. Stroud: Stadia, 2006.

Malcolm, D., J. Gemmell and N. Mehta, eds., *Cricket: International and Interdisciplinary Approaches.* Abingdon: Routledge, 2009.

Mangan, J. A., *Athleticism in the Victorian and Edwardian Public School.* 1981. London: Frank Cass, 2000.

The Games Ethic and Imperialism: Aspects of the Diffusion of an Idea. 1986. London: Frank Cass, 1998.

Mangan, J. A. and B. Majumdar, eds., *Cricketing Cultures in Conflict: World Cup 2003*. London: Routledge, 2004.

Manley, M., *A History of West Indies Cricket*. 1988. London: Pan Books, 1990.

Marqusee, M., *Anyone But England: Cricket and the National Malaise*. 1994. London: Aurum, 2005.

War Minus the Shooting: A Journey Through South Asia During Cricket's World Cup. London: Heinemann, 1996.

Martin-Jenkins, C., *Ball by Ball: The Story of Cricket Broadcasting*. London: Grafton, 1990.

McDevitt, P. F., *'May the Best Man Win': Sport, Masculinity, and Nationalism in Great Britain and the Empire, 1880–1935*. Basingstoke: Palgrave Macmillan, 2004.

McLellan, A., ed., *Nothing Sacred: The New Cricket Culture*. London: Two Heads Publishing, 1996.

Meyer, M., ed., *Summer Days: Writers on Cricket*. Oxford University Press, 1983.

Midwinter, E., *From Meadowland to Multinational: A Review of Cricket's Social History*. London: Cricket Lore, 2000.

Quill on Willow: Cricket in Literature. Chichester: Aeneas Press, 2001.

WG Grace: His Life and Times. London: Allen & Unwin, 1981.

Mitford, M. R., *Our Village*. 1824–1832. London: Bracken Books, 1992.

Mullins, P. and P. Derriman, eds., *Bat & Pad: Writings on Australian Cricket 1804–1984*. Oxford University Press, 1984.

Mulvaney, J. and R. Harcourt, *Cricket Walkabout: The Australian Aboriginal Cricketers on Tour 1867–68*. London: Macmillan, 1988.

Nandy, A., *The Tao of Cricket: On Games of Destiny and the Destiny of Games*. New York: Viking, 1989.

Nyren, J., *The Cricketers of My Time: The Original Version*, ed. Ashley Mote. London: Robson Books, 1998.

Oborne, P., *Basil D'Oliveira: Cricket and Controversy*. London: Sphere, 2005.

Odendaal, A., *The Story of an African Game*. Claremont, South Africa: davidphilip, 2003.

Pointon, M., '"A Latter-Day Siegfried": Ian Botham at the National Portrait Gallery, 1986.' *New Formations* 21 (Winter 1993): 131–45.

Pollard, J., *Australian Cricket: The Game and its Players*. Sydney: Hodder & Stoughton, 1982.

Rae, S., *W.G. Grace: A Life*. London: Faber & Faber, 1998.

Ranjitsinhji, K. S., *The Jubilee Book of Cricket*. Edinburgh: William Blackwood, 1897.

With Stoddart's Team in Australia. 1898. London: Constable, 1985.

Renton, D., *C.L.R. James: Cricket's Philosopher King*. London: Haus Books, 2007.

Richards, V., *Hitting Across the Line: An Autobiography*. London: Headline, 1991.

Robertson-Glasgow, R. C., *The Cricket Writings of R.C. Robertson-Glasgow*. 1966. London: Pavilion Library, 1985.

Ross, A., ed., *The Penguin Cricketer's Companion*. Harmondsworth: Penguin, 1981.

Ryan, C., *Golden Boy: Kim Hughes and the Bad Old Days of Australian Cricket*. London: Orion, 2009.

Ryan, G., *The Making of New Zealand Cricket 1832–1914*. London: Frank Cass, 2004.

Sandiford, K. A. P., *Cricket and the Victorians*. Aldershot: Scolar Press, 1994.

Scott, J., *Caught in Court: A Selection of Cases with Cricketing Connections*. London: Andre Deutsch, 1989.

Searle, C., *Pitch of Life: Writings on Cricket*. Manchester: Parrs Wood Press, 2001.

Simon, R. and A. Smart, *The Art of Cricket*. London: Secker & Warburg, 1983.

Simons, J., 'The "Englishness" of English Cricket'. *Journal of Popular Culture* 29, 4 (1996): 41–50.

'The Golden Age of Cricket.' In *Readings in Popular Culture: Trivial Pursuits?*, ed. G. Day, 151–63. London: Macmillan, 1990.

Sissons, R., *The Players: A Social History of the Professional Cricketer*. Sydney: Pluto Press, 1988.

Sissons, R. and B. Stoddart, *Cricket and Empire: The 1932–33 Bodyline Tour of Australia*. London: George Allen & Unwin, 1984.

Stoddart, B. and K. A. P. Sandiford, eds., *The Imperial Game: Cricket, Culture and Society*. Manchester University Press, 1998.

Swanton, E. W., J. Woodcock, G. Plumptre and A. S. R. Winslaw, eds., *World Of Cricket: The Game from A–Z*. 1966. London: Collins, 1980.

Underdown, D., *Start of Play: Cricket and Culture in Eighteenth-Century England*. London: Allen Lane, 2000.

Wagg, S., ed., *Following On: Cricket and National Identity in the Post-Colonial Age*. London: Routledge, 2005.

Whannel, G., *Fields in Vision: Television Sport and Cultural Transformation*. London: Routledge, 1992.

Wilde, S., *Caught: The Full Story of Cricket's Match-Fixing Scandal*. London: Aurum, 2001.

Williams, J., *Cricket and Broadcasting*. Manchester University Press, 2010.

Cricket and England: A Cultural and Social History of the Inter-War Years. London: Frank Cass, 1999.

Cricket and Race. Oxford: Berg, 2001.

Williams, M., ed., *Double Century: 200 Years of Cricket in* The Times. London: Guild Publishing, 1985.

Wodehouse, P. G., *Wodehouse at the Wicket*, ed. M. Hedgecock. London: Random House, 1997.

INDEX